CLUES
I COM 00 0068399 V

JUL 2000
JUN 2004
JUL 09
JUL X X 2015

The Ironies of Progress

Henry Adams and the American Dream

WILLIAM WASSERSTROM

SOUTHERN ILLINOIS UNIVERSITY PRESS
Carbondale and Edwardsville

Permission to quote from the following sources is gratefully acknowledged:

New Directions Publishing Corporation. William Carlos Williams, "Poem," "The Rose," "Classical Scene," from William Carlos Williams, *Collected Earlier Poems of William Carlos Williams*. Copyright 1938 by New Directions Publishing Corporation. William Carlos Williams, "Choral: The Pink Church," from William Carlos Williams, *Late Poems of William Carlos Williams*. Copyright 1949 by William Carlos Williams.
University of California Press. Kenneth Burke, "Creation Myth," in *Collected Poems, 1915–1967*, published by the University of California Press, 1968.

Printed in the United States of America
Edited by H. L. Kirk
Designed by Dan Gunter
Production supervised by Kathleen Giencke

87 86 85 84 4 3 2 1

Library of Congress Cataloging in Publication Data

Wasserstrom, William.
The ironies of progress.

Bibliography: p.
Includes index.
1. Adams, Henry, 1838–1918—Criticism and interpretation.
2. American literature—History and criticism. 3. United States—Civilization. I Title.
PS1004.A4Z95 1984 818'.409 83-16990
ISBN 0-8093-1155-0

For Rose

and

Andy, Eric, Jan, Jim, Leslie, Rob, Sue

If we think that history progresses, or that we are bound to progress, then we commit the same mistake as those who believe that history has a meaning that can be discovered in it. . . . For to progress is to move towards an end which exists for us human beings. "History" cannot do that; only we, the human individuals, can do it; we can do it by defending and strengthening those democratic institutions upon which freedom, and with it progress, depends. And we shall do it much better as we become more fully aware of the fact that progress rests with us, with our watchfulness. . . .

—Karl R. Popper, *The Open Society and Its Enemies,* 1945.

There are some enterprises in which a careful disorderliness is the true method.

—Herman Melville, "The Honor and Glory of Whaling,"
Moby Dick, 1851

Suddenly and mysteriously the "Tall Ships" became the prime symbol of whatever it was Americans yearned for, and doted on, in 1976. What they sought was confirmation of a national myth, the myth of America as the land of youth, always seeking renewal, a new greening, the eternal Peter Pan among nations. . . . On the eve of the national celebration . . . America lost a war. It was a shattering blow to two pillars of the myth, not an abandonment of it, but the defense divided Americans ideologically between adherents of the two pillars. On the right were those so dedicated to the tenet of invincibility that they were prepared to incur any burden of guilt . . . to carry their point. On the left were those so dedicated to the myth of innocence . . . they were ready to paralyze the government. . . . Many were caught between left and right but the primary concerns of both were mythic.

—C. Vann Woodward, *New York Times,* December 29, 1976.

Contents

Preface

IF EVER A BOOK DERIVED FROM a distinct occasion, from traceable influences and confluences, in the instance of this text, in my own instance, the place, date, time, and event are indisputable, exact. At Oxford University in May, 1968, during a week long symposium of advanced students and extramural teachers of American literature which I'd been invited to address, there and then this work was begun. Though the set subject that week was vanguard movements and modernist trends in American writing, conversation radiated far beyond the usual concerns of literary talk. During that season of uprising, England was quiet; Oxford—stirred by the politics but not the passions of Paris or Berlin, of Berkeley or Harvard or Columbia—was grave and people were grim. And no one in that company was prepared to abandon the matter of crisis in order to concentrate solely on problems of the kind usually contained within the scope of literary study.

Perhaps because avant-garde writing always quickens thought, the liveliest group of participants decided that upheaval on the streets in the United States seemed, strikingly, to match disorder, chaos on the page. No less astounding, they felt, was a connection till then unappreciated—that the strongest and most characteristic ties binding the lives of writers to the life of literature in America were unfamiliar in Great Britain, not in the least characteristic of writers there.

No single demonstration bore these points home. But in that seminar, in British criticism then current, in the new universities and new interdisciplinary curricula of American studies, suddenly it was clear that the pressures of history—more pronounced that month than at any other time anyone could recall—had detached American writers from a common literary heritage and replaced this with a language and culture that were, from a British perspective, unquestionably foreign. It was this process of detachment I set out to understand, to portray. And though my earliest intentions continued to support my final intention I found myself groping toward and lingering in the shade of Henry Brooks Adams, first of those "latter day Puritan Jeremiah[s]" to present himself as the "American symbol" incarnate. Transmitting and transmuting primordial forms and radical motifs of national doctrine, Adams invented a persona at once commanding and dextrous enough to stand in eponym for the only nation in history, Gary Wills says in *Inventing America* (1978), to be "founded on a creed." As set down by Jefferson for the Declaration of Independence, Wills adds (quoting Chesterton), the American creed is the more stunning, the Declaration itself all the more phenomenal for constituting "perhaps the only piece of practical politics that is also theoretical politics and also great literature." As transposed by Adams, however, the American credo foments heresy of the most fearful and portentous kind: an ambivalence of principle in the era of Revolution; a duplicity of dominion in the Age of Progress; the riddle of void in epochs that follow. Crudely displayed, here forthwith is the tripos on which in my fancy Adams sits perched:

American Errand (or Dream)—Social Progress—Social Chaos
Providence—Destiny—Doom
Organicism—Vitalism—Technologism
Mechanical (or Natural) Law—Dynamic Law—Thermodynamic Law
Energy—Power—Entropy

This distinctive pattern, these abiding strains in politics and art, this "repertory of ideas," in Lévi Strauss's phrase, are invariably recorded in those dreams, acts, myths which in *Tristes Tropiques* (1955) are said to compose "the ensemble of a people's customs." Disposed according to its own "particular style," an American repertory of the sort I've assembled offers a way of systematizing events and attitudes both recent and remote. Particularly, it advances my larger ambition, to compose a history of ideas on founding, flourishing, and failing within a society whose writers, adopting a visionary idea of vocation, seem habitually to associate their personal fates in life and in letters with the fate of civilization on this continent. "It is an exaggeration, of course, to suggest that we can interpret the whole of American history in the person of Henry Adams, but it is no very shocking exaggeration," Henry Steele Commager wrote forty-five years ago (reprinted in *Critical Essays on Henry Adams,* 1981), "to insist that to the student of American history the contemplation of Adams is the beginning of wisdom. For whether we confine ourselves to the mere outward aspects of Adams's career or embrace the history of the entire family which he recapitulated, or penetrate to his own intellectual and psychological reactions to his generation, we will find that Adams illuminates, better than any of his contemporaries, the course of American history." I reproduce Commager's remarks at length. For I have followed a similar pursuit, taken a similar course in order to isolate and identify those states of mind, multilayered as well as sequential, by means of which this people—grown wary of all programs and pieties of deliverance—arrive at that condition Henry Adams can be said to personify.

Probing the triptych of subjects to which my ensemble alludes, I have sought to negotiate a passage amid trios of interlocking themes in American literary and cultural history from the eighteenth century to the present day. It is then the *ironies* not the *ironists* of progress I have sought out and set down. If nonetheless the whole affair looks florid and sounds dense, if my means seem presumptuous and my arias too loud, consider the medallion John Hay commissioned as a gift for "Henricus Adams Porcupinus Angelicus," his disputatious and inspired friend. Showing Adams in profile, face joined to "the body of a porcupine and the wings of an angel," this trimorphic figure of Augustus Saint-Gaudens's art fixed forever the character of a man who concentrates in his own person those triplets of ideology, those tercets of myth which mold the arts of imagination, the imagination of society and the imagination of disaster in the United States.

I am delighted to thank formally those who provided opportunity to offer, as lectures, segments of this work in progress: Seymour Fisher, Department of Psychiatry, Upstate Medical Center, Syracuse, N.Y.; Lester Friedman, Northeast Modern Language Association; A. Robert Lee, University of Kent in Canterbury (England); John Lydenberg, Hobart and William Smith Colleges, Geneva, N.Y.; National Alliance for the Prevention and Treatment of Child Abuse and Maltreatment, Inc.; Ruth Prigozy, Hofstra University, Hempstead, N.Y.; Robert Seidenberg, Psychoanalytic Society of Western New York; Whitney Museum of American Art, New York City; Sergio Perosa and Rosella M. Zorzi, Associazione Italiana di Studi Nord Americani, Venice (Italy). I am grateful too to those editors in whose journals various sections of this work, in earlier forms, have appeared.

The Ironies of Progress

I

Strangeness of Proportion in America

The whole point of being American is that we are unique. This, however, is exactly what the French think about themselves. We Americans look upon our differences from the rest of the world as progressive and normative—the leading edge of a development in liberty, where others must follow. The French see themselves as exclusive, a fixed civilization, a unity, always apart from the rest—but also exemplary. We and the French will always feel a tension between us. Our rivalry has nothing to do with politics. It is a moral rivalry.

William Pfaff, *The New Yorker*, January 24, 1977

ANYONE WHO WRITES AT LENGTH about the point of being American, about the synoptic designs of art and letters and politics in the United States, cannot avoid starting as a prophet and ending as a bore. It's indeed the oldest curse of American studies, this habit of grab and lunge for the absolute truth, a will to synthesis which so often produces works of sterile invention and infertile labor. How tempting it is therefore to abstain from the wearisome task of self-examination and self-specification, of weighing, measuring, tallying which traits of race, which faults of geography, of continental drift and divide, which causes of climate or statistics of income impose a definable stamp on the American people, on temperament in America. Early on, it was axiomatic that an independent, isolated, and original people set down in a brave new world must cultivate a proper curiosity of self-regard. But in more recent times, the American custom of self-appraisal was perceived not as a sign of health but as a symptom of disorder, a defect not a triumph of character. Today, however, defect or no our quest is all the more urgent and it would be unpardonable if literary intellectuals in America were to abandon their studies, their tally of symptoms.

For today it's power that afflicts and baffles us, power that defies measure, power which must itself be accommodated to or discharged from or contained within any American design. In politics power generates force and force exerts compulsion, spurs tenacity of trespass against a "natural prey," says Bernard Bailyn in *The Ideological Origins of the American Revolution* (1967), against a "necessary victim," against "liberty, or law, or right."[1] Because American governments today possess an immense temptation to and capacity for and distaste of trespass, public officials constantly reassert both our faith in and our repudiation of force as an instrument of policy. Their ambivalence of mood is in any event matched by our muddle as a people. For no doctrine or motto, no dogma or axiom explains why, however resourcefully our leaders labor to impose an American style of order and progress on the world at large, however energetically they increase the rate of speed at which under our national auspices people in general are supposed to come together, the quicker and more inexplicably things come apart. It is this paradox of pressure that requires the most vigilant study. And it is vigilance in studying questions of American styles of order and chaos, a renewed vigil that returns us once again to literature, to the arts, to those classic figures and historic texts in which the indelible stamp is clearest seen.

Reviewing this old business of pinning down and classifying the American experience in literature, observing that the stamp is done in a sort of Mayan, a code whose glyphs we can't crack, we begin with ways less new than little valued, the contrast between British and American language, British and American style. A contrast between British and American repertoires of ideas in art and myth is the more appropriate today in that literary power, as Stephen Spender said at the Cheltenham Festival in Great Britain in 1967, has been transferred from the Mother Country to this place. Less than a half-dozen years later, reviewing for the *New York Times* the latest *Supplement to the Oxford English Dictionary* (1972), George Steiner circled back to the point of Spender's observation. Granting that British writing today is marred by a parsimony of invention, maintaining that "literature is only the surface" of things and language the center, Steiner selected those clues of language which demonstrate a radical divergence both of literary and social style. Because "today the dynamics of English are centrifugal" and "are most evident in America,"[2] British readers must learn to listen not just to American accents but to accommodate their ears to hear an inner voice, a "cadence," as Hugh Kenner says in *The Pound Era* (1971). For cadence it is that enables us to "tell which sentence is British, which American," and "know accordingly what scope of feeling to accord the words, and do this so well we do not know we do it," do not even know "how much of what we suppose a dictionary can sort out (it cannot) is controlled by our sense of the voices cadence imitates."[3]

Inner voice and inner ear united by cadence: these commonest of terms connote the subtlest of functions, the function of literary style in supplying means with which to measure the pressure that governments struggle to exorcise or control. "Their prose at its best grows fiercer," we're told in an *Observer* review (March 29, 1981) of the *Oxford American Dictionary*, "and ours more elegant." There's the scope of speech and spirit in America from colony to culture: uncontained, incontinent. Indeed, the one characteristic thing native American writers do, have always done—the last task on earth which could charm adoptive writers such as Vladimir Nabokov, say, or Wystan Auden—is to charge multitudes with the duty of moving mountains. American writers cannot resist leaping for the sublime. That this is an authentic American note, incidentally, Auden himself noticed. American writers, he said, feel that the whole burden of mankind rests on their shoulders, feel an excruciating sense of duty nobody in Europe feels about Europe. If the French see themselves as a fixed civilization, finished, intact, apart, then the English think of themselves as members of classes. What one person can't or won't do, another of the same class inevitably will do. In America, however, people generally think Well, everything finally falls on me, on the single self at last. It is this sense of burden, let it be said, which supports the American belief that literature is itself a sublime calling. Habitually absorbed by a Platonic idea of America, the American writer responds to this most burdensome idea by assuming a lacerating sense of obligation to his countrymen—even, indeed, at those times when he is out of sympathy with them, when they are hard at work subverting the American Idea. What's tiresome about America, Robert Lowell insists, is the monotony of the sublime. But too, he's quick to say, what's best cannot be separated from what is "worst and most dangerous and inhuman about us": all gets "swept up into this ideal."[4] Lowell's words, intended to refer to the pursuit of literary careers, very obviously characterize the vocation of politics, too, the presidential styles of Lyndon Johnson and Richard Nixon who behaved in office as if the presidency were itself a sublime calling. Dangerous men, they endangered us all.

Although American life and thought are in some degree ennobled and stigmatized by reason of the sublime, Common Readers everywhere can hardly be expected to adopt American ideals or immerse themselves in an American landscape before they read American books. They can of course cultivate and train both voice and ear. And if they choose, they can also acquire enough history to perceive an aureole, a vision at once mean and miraculous, in which the Idea of the self is fused with the Idea of the nation and the Idea of a national literature. No like aureole appears in West Germany or the Soviet Union today, where the life of literature is thought to have direct bearing on the political life of society. No similar conviction occurs even among those writers who abandon a large measure of private life for the performance of public roles and who therefore take very seriously the value of poetry and fiction as a last resort of conscience. Literature, said Solzhenitsyn in his Nobel Prize address, is "the one great heart that beats for the concerns and misfortunes of our world." But this is not quite the American Idea. For what he and others approve is a view of the artist's task which is in the widest degree Continental. And although it is applied to global matters, it takes its inspiration from those great Europeans of the last generation, Joyce and Mann, exemplars of whole legions of writers-in-exile who reformulated for the contemporary world a Romantic version of artists as monitors of their race.

The artist in America, often an expatriate, nearly always a troglodyte but rarely an exile, has traditionally opted for a parallel but separate idea of calling. Impossible as it is to know precisely when the chief strains of an Americanist doctrine acquired definable form, William Ellery Channing's historic essay, "The Importance and Means of a National Literature" (1830), is nonetheless often taken as a point of departure. Applying to letters the cadence of American sermon and tract, the hortatory note of solemn duty, Channing also reproduced the gist of Thomas Paine's remarks in the noted *Letter to Abbé Reynal* (1782), remarks with which Paine hoped to persuade a transatlantic audience that Americans "are now really another people." In "style and manner of thinking" metamorphosed by "a revolution more extraordinary than the political revolution of this country," we Americans "see with other eyes; we hear with other ears; and think with other thoughts, than those we formerly used." The great advantage gained by revolution, Channing urged, reward as yet not publicized, is that "man is the great subject of literature" in the New World: "by which we mean, human beings conscious of their nature," unobscured by the artifice of social class, undisguised by rank.

Like Toqueville at approximately the same time, Channing proclaimed the blessings of a "new freedom" of the human mind to "explore new paths and reap new harvests."[5] Unlike Channing, Tocqueville discerned which path led to a bounty of harvest almost beyond reckoning. For he beheld a "magnificent image" permeating the American scene, ineluctable sign of a wilderness nation, a people whose attention was fixed "on their march across the American wilds." Agreeing that the great subject of literature in the United States would be an inquiry into the human mind itself, what excited him about this subject was its concentration in the lives of people who invaded waste places, who dried swamps and turned the course of rivers. "To scrutinize the hidden depths in the immaterial nature of man"—this was to be the chief source of inspiration for the "poet of democracy."[6] Whoever would understand human nature in all its wildness and variety, even so tame a literary man as Washington Irving agreed, must "plunge into the forest, must explore the glen, must stem the torrent, and dare the precipice." When Auden, British expatriate turned American citizen, in self-parody rejected this American gambit—"Oh dear! the insects, and the *snakes* and the poison ivy"—surely he intended to disclose his true color no matter what color his official papers bore (Auden's emphasis). "It is not then to the written but the spoken language," as Tocqueville perceived, that "attention must be paid." Only in this way will we "detect the modifications which the idiom of an aristocratic people may undergo when it becomes the language of democracy."

Whichever way we turn, therefore, back to Channing or forward to Lowell, still further back to *The Federalist Papers* and still farther forward to, say, Thomas Pynchon, we discover a common set of traits supplying timbre to an inner voice. Arising from the revolutionary idea of "another people," our genius is said to be manifest in an exploration of the wildness and variety of human nature, itself revealed by way of an immersion in the disorder of civilization in America. As a result our language has enlarged its range beyond Tocqueville's or anyone's prophecy. Although the British tongue is of course remarkably adaptive, quick to respond to personal caprice and public whim, English speech stresses what Steiner calls "accentual propriety." In contrast, American speech maintains no unbreachable links between accent and social class. Despite Noah Webster's effort in 1828 to furnish a standard "which we shall not be ashamed to bequeath to *three hundred millions* of people, who are destined to occupy" these vast territories, we possess a strumpet's not a mother's tongue, ready to embrace whatever grossness or indelicacy seems fit for the play of its passions. Far below improprieties of accent, then, Steiner finds a deep dissonance of discourse, an "articulate energy" which discloses "the pressure of language on the imagination." WASP pioneer and urban Jew, black militant and white junkie and academic metatype—all our best writers exhibit the force of this pressure, this dissonance, this energy. Combining the act of self-revelation with the conquest of an exemplary American conceit, successive generations of poets and novelists and critics have made an icon of the Brooklyn Bridge, have explored our virgin lands, examined our virgin loins and even, a few years ago, wondered if orgiastic sex or hallucinogenic drugs or possibly a religious fix would penetrate to the very center of private and public peculiarity. Even the most immediate concerns of social protest, Alfred Kazin observed of Norman Mailer's *The Armies of the Night* (1968), inevitably adorn the myth of creative life in America.[7] Examining the motives which led to the steps of the Pentagon in October, 1967, Mailer discovered himself to be made in the image of those nineteenth-century American writers who strained to establish an "organic" connection between the self and the world by means of the Word.

Although virtually all our books draw on "articulate energy," by no means is the genius of American literature evident in the language deployed by all our writers. Nor do our writers uniformly advance the cause of ideology. Mailer does, of course, especially in moments of duress on those occasions when the need of self-validation is most acute. In a news conference following his testimony at the trial of Jack Henry Abbott (January 19, 1982) "Mailer, who won his first Pulitzer [Prize] in 1969 for *The Armies of the Night*, said he would take the same course again. 'Democracy involves taking risks,' he said, and to fail to take those risks would be 'fascistic.'" Whether or not this one remark quite captures the point of being American, it does banish any trace of minor motive or narrow intent. Removed to the loftiest realm of ideology, Mailer even on that grim occasion presumed it to be his duty boldly to embody the American Idea.

Thus once again it turns out to be the quality of hurt, in Chester Himes's phrase, which flavors our lives, our arts, not the "distinctive humanities" F. R. Leavis favored. Leavis, whose fame rested on the brilliance of his powers of discrimination, is noted for distinguishing a fusion of motives and modes and morals within *The Great Tradition* (1948). Dismissing the very notion of a divergence in ideology, Leavis linked England and America in a transatlantic alliance of letters. The sort of argument Walter Allen was to develop in *Tradition and Dream* (1964) left him cold. A distinctive mark of imagination in Britain, Allen observed, was its involvement with pattern, source of inclinations and customs at once strengthening and suffocating at large and in small. But in America literature springs from a passion to explore "what it means to be American." Disdaining distinctions of this sort, disregarding English classes and American quests, discarding the American writer's half-tiresome and half-sublime zeal to investigate his own inimitable self in order to locate there the wellspring of collective life—this investigation in Leavis's view led nowhere.

What was worth applauding, celebration of the mind's sanities, he discovered in those texts which exhibit D. H. Lawrence's sort of faith in "life and growth amid all this mass of destruction and disintegration." Without question, indeed, key big Anglo-American books do compose an oeuvre resolute to withstand the horrors of irrationalism and to exalt the blessings of humaneness. But the case for convergence hangs on a thread, on a supposed set of principles conserving the continuity of civilized order both in the United Kingdom and the United States. And this reliance, as Richard Chase said in his famous response to Leavis, *The American Novel and Its Tradition* (1957), this faith in Tory imagination is unjustified by politics, undocumented by art in America: "The fact is that many of the best American novels achieved their very being, their very energy and their form, from the perception and acceptance not of unities but of radical disunities." For when we are responsible readers of American texts, sensitive to American genius at the top of its bent, immersed in works having more in common with one another than with British counterparts, we find that what vivifies and excites the American imagination, Chase said, is "contradiction," a "broken circuit . . . traceable to certain historical facts." Beyond the briefest mention of "doctrines of Puritanism," however, reinforced by "frontier conditions" and by "the very institutions of democracy as these evolved in the eighteenth and nineteenth centuries," Chase supplies just the barest trace of historical fact.[8] Drawing on certain varieties of national experience unaccounted for in Chase's splendid book, I propose to identify the leading causes of polarity, of contraposition, of imbalance in society and letters.

The subject cannot be rendered in broad strokes of allusion, however thick. So grand a theme, a distrust of symmetry in American language and literature and culture, implicates very large questions of national style. For if indeed it is a fact of history that "the American imagination" is less interested in "reconciliation than in alienation" as Chase contends, then surely we inhabit a society that from the start welcomed the risk not only of disorder but of disintegration too. A relish of risk, therefore, constitutes the very soul of style in the United States from the moment of disaffiliation in 1776 until the present. The trouble is, of course, that talk about common traits of style, analysis of "shared consistencies in the handling of scope and structure" in the plastic arts, the arts of literature, the designs of government, and the pursuits of science—talk of this kind, however lucid, too often fails to distinguish a mosaic, a fretwork of ideas, and instead annihilates pattern.[9] In this enterprise, then, eager to take up whatever help is at hand, I grasp some clues available in Wylie Sypher's breezy and adventurous book *Four Stages of Renaissance Style* (1955). Though little admired by historians of art, Sypher does in fact convincingly isolate signal and interpenetrating motifs of design in speech and dress and literature, in architecture and governance during periods of history—Renaissance, mannerist, baroque, late-baroque—which preoccupy us now.

Despite his habit of blurring genres in literature, of eliding types and times, Sypher does unmistakably disclose a consistent European taste for combinations of symmetry in all modes of imagination during the era of the late baroque. Inadvertently opposing European ideas to the American Idea, Sypher discovers a "basic premise of late-baroque style" in the last of "Sir Isaac Newton's three laws of motion." Unquestioned in the late seventeenth and eighteenth centuries, Newton's Third Law it was ("the mutual actions of two bodies upon each other are equal and directly opposite") that imposed order in the Old World. And as we shall see, it was the Third Law that *The Federalist Papers* undertook to repeal.

Although Sypher does not himself refer to that unsurpassed stylist of late baroque, Edmund Burke, unchallenged arbiter of British thought in this epoch, Burke's *Reflections on the Revolution in France* (1780) exhibits an incontestable union of Newtonian science and British ideology. Justifying counterpoise not oscillation in politics, Burke's treatise is unrivaled for the assurance and persuasiveness with which it advocates the case for stasis in government. At a most portentous and pivotal moment in the history of political philosophy, Burke invokes the dogma of equipoise in order to condemn the common folk of Great Britain for presuming to claim the right to cashier their kings. The "cosmic order of masses in motion according to law," the principle of order itself taken to be "the final good" in eighteenth century philosophy—order as a provision of Newtonian and natural law, E. A. Burtt insists in *Metaphysical Foundations of Modern Science* (1954), was beyond impeachment. "Man exists to know and applaud it: God exists to tend and preserve it." God, Burtt remarks as if with Edmund Burke in mind, "now the chief mechanic of the universe, has become the cosmic conservative" Who has charged the British aristocracy with the duty of maintaining the status quo. "The day of novelty is all in the past."[10] Much like Henry Adams in the next century, whose brief against America rested on the Second Law of Thermodynamics, on an increase of motion as perfect proof of disorder, Burke argued against revolution by invoking a social theory derived from a science imbued with Newton's Third Law.

Captivated by metaphysics of this order, Burke contended that the British system of government flatly barred revolution. The deposition of a sovereign for misconduct was unthinkable in a nation in which parliament withheld power from the crown and reserved for itself central civil authority. Because the king does not obey men and because men obey the law embodied in him, to speak of discharging a king is to talk of an act unjustified by natural philosophy and unsanctioned by natural law. Insofar as Britons inherit their laws and their possessions from their forebears, they do in fact possess a pedigree of liberties, "an entailed inheritance" which includes an inheritable crown, an inheritable peerage, a house of commons and a people confirmed in privilege, franchise, liberty. This idea of inheritance furnishes Great Britain sure procedures of conservation, of transmission: men receive and transmit their government quite as they receive and transmit their property and their lives. Had the revolutionaries in France profited by the British example, they might have accomplished a redistribution and transfer of authority based on a similar recognition of harmony. But choosing to act as if 1789 was the year when liberty was first born, in caprice they dissolved an ancient partnership. And even if, as revolutionaries maintain, a civil state is based not on inheritance but on a contract, no matter. That contract links the dead, the living, and the unborn; connects the visible and invisible world; guarantees eternal not ephemeral forms; and therefore cannot be dissolved. It is not a civil pact but a holy bond which in Britain is sanctified by an established religion grounded in God's power to hold all physical and moral natures in their appointed spheres.

"Late-baroque minds," Sypher says, write "exact equations."[11] And Burke's very exact equation, which has little to recommend it save "long observation and much impartiality," leads to the conceit which closes his book and simultaneously illustrates the shape and character of British sensibility from Shakespeare's time until the present instant. In that "'most fine, most honoured, most renowned' golden unity of the Elizabethan world," the law governing the acquisition, exercise, and transfer of power had "all the prestige and sanction of divine prescription," was a "natural" law like other "natural laws, instituted by God for the ordering of events." It was an Elizabethan horror of asymmetry, therefore, which in part led Shakespeare to focus on a phobic dread of illegitimate sovereignty. Horror was intensified by a general belief that "the mode of transfer implies a model of the universe." And it was that shaky Elizabethan mode and model, that dialectic of chaos and order which most troubled William Shakespeare, for it offered no assurance that society would steer its course safely between rebellion and misrule.[12] Edmund Burke, then, at a long remove from that post-Elizabethan age of rebellion and chaos and misrule through which British society had barely managed to steer—Burke cultivated a state of aplomb unimaginable a hundred years earlier. And it was in this hard-earned state of mind that he viewed parvenu nations of revolt. Mindful of Shakespeare's dilemma and faithful to Newton's God, this specialist in colonial and foreign affairs invoked baroque doctrine and thereby certified his opinion, the judgment of a man who "when the equipoise of the vessel in which he sails, may be endangered by overloading it on one side, is desirous of carrying the small weight of his reason to that [side] which may preserve its equipoise."

Thus Burke received from Shakespeare even as Leavis inherited from Burke an old and unquestioned faith in the consolation of symmetry, a "just equilibrium" in eighteenth-century discourse, which transmits and renews its flavor in each generation, including our own. Providing the British with what must surely be a final cause of condescension, in an interview for the *New York Times* (1972) Peter Walker, former Tory Minister for the Environment (unaware of possessing a baroque imagination) explained that problems of ecology and pollution that stymie us don't faze them but are surmounted because of "traditional British sense of obedience, propriety and order." Lest this seem too self-indulgent a choice on my part, too idiosyncratic a remark, I cede to Steiner a last word of commentary on the *OED*. That dictionary, he says, "like England itself," is superbly suited to play a "formidably important role in making visible a new equipoise" between Great Britain ("genuine civilization") and the United States ("the energies of colloquial change").[13] It's therefore not at all infelicitous though perhaps just a touch too neat to suppose that the three great ages of modern history are beheld in the glint given by classic words: symmetry and its proved proprieties; energy and its untested incitements; progress and its untold discontents.

Two hundred years ago, responding to an onrush of change, the people who met in Philadelphia, determined to regain momentum dissipated by the effort to run an inert Confederation, had come to a climax of faith in the practice of Newtonian politics. The legendary decade that ended in 1787, phenomenal in the usual ways of watershed in the life of cultures and the growth of nations, is astonishing for its confluence of ideas on the problem of finding a proper fit between the character of men and the nature of government. Each of its surpassing events—Declaration, Revolution, Constitution—exhibits an utterly concentrated will to exchange the rule of exact equations for a program and theory of government which would bring society and personality into formal, less mechanical order. To unravel the swarm of causes underlying dispute in those stupefying times, dispute resolved by those sublime principles which constitute the American Idea, we require an archeology of knowledge. For an American archeology we must have an anthropology too, if out of disintegrated moments of the past, out of major museum pieces of history as well as unrelated shards of document we are to discern the American Idea in a poetry which, like the nation itself, stems from deeper and juster views of the self than are found elsewhere. Poetry, which Thoreau defined as "a piece of very private history which lets us into the secret of a man's life"—the innermost and secret subject of our poetry according to a contemporary master of the art, John Berryman, is this, that out of the private history of the disordered self a writer's imagination undertakes "the construction of a world."[14]

In speaking about complexities of dispute between home country and colonies from 1688 to 1776, from the moment of zenith in British constitutional practice to the period of nadir under George III, treating these matters of international colonial affairs, I do not plan to claim space in a crowded field. Fortunately the angle I've adopted is augmented by sights seen from other point of vantage. At the beginning of the eighteenth century, it is commonly said, a reformed British government had contrived to establish and maintain inside Parliament a balance of competing interests. Because their system was grounded in the historical process and justified by scientific principle, English and colonial Whigs first assured one another, it was foolproof, perfect, adaptable, and exportable anywhere. In the course of time, however, British government was nearly undone by corruption up and down its lines of authority. Observing foulness of maneuver emanating from ordinary people under prompting by the crown, American Whigs at first stood steadfast. Eventually, prompted by "disaffected Englishmen" and "the scattered writings of European intellectuals," New World Whigs decided that their mission was to purge English custom and politics of contamination. Transposing the act of purgation into a program and a politics, they were convinced that an "uncorrupted English constitution" was the best imaginable "model of what a constitution should be." And not until they had come a long distance into the century did they reluctantly begin to reject the Old World habit of conceiving human society in "rational, mechanistic terms." Rather late than early, drawing on New World experience, they began to equate the social order with the life process, began to speak of society not as fixed but fluid, as "organic and developmental."[15]

Before that time, however, before Whig politicians were metamorphosed into Founding Fathers, they perceived their world and its functioning in much the fashion represented by a device which was again to become popular in the 1960s, the self-regulating orrery. American museums today, which display that mechanism for deploying the planets and correlating the motions of bodies in our solar system, must now house the Ur-gadget of our time, hula balls, a perfect toy for "up and coming executives with jangled nerves" in our epoch. A "fascinating study of Newton's Third Law of Motion," the advertisement reads. "For every reaction there's an equal and opposite reaction. Plastic frame with five suspended steel balls." You don't win and you can't lose: pure play.[16] What's remarkable about hula balls is less their physics than their sociology. Inspired by a nostalgia of history common during the Vietnam era, this device returned us to the period preceding adoption of the Constitution, restored us to that first age of jangled nerves in the United States, the 1780s, when Newton's Third Law did literally preside over the Articles of Confederation. Those Articles, that baker's dozen of governments arranged in no-win can't-lose Newtonian order, this disposition of thirteen unstable states had been in fact an invention of American Whigs. Charmed by a fashionable science of symmetry and captivated by British social theory, they had sought to restore British government in the New World to its finest hour of baroque balance, the equipoise of 1688. Having convened a national congress, they chose to immobilize it by insisting that it could take no action without unanimous consent. And because the "concurrence of thirteen distinct sovereign wills" was the rarest of occurrences during this unmanageable regime, national union under the Articles turned out to be a static show, the exercise of kinetic energy in affairs of state.

Having gone more than half the distance but not the whole way from monarchic to republican rule, in 1787 they met to amend the Articles; that is, to enliven a ruinously inert but superbly symmetrical compact. "The great counterbalancing power centers of British society and government—the monarchy (symbol of unity and authority), the nobility (honorable defenders of stability), and the commons (vigorous, liberty-loving people of the realm)—simply didn't exist in the same relationship in America."[17] And delegates who had begun their work by addressing one another in the discourse of British parliamentary politics ended by drafting a Constitution which dispensed with the politics of equipoise and dispelled forever any lingering trust in symmetry. I repeat and rephrase this familiar and beautiful old story in order to recall those eighty-five essays written by Madison, Jay, Hamilton in New York from October, 1787, until August, 1788, papers which set the scene for a quite new enterprise in the life of nations. "We're a nation founded on a Constitution," Robert Lowell remarked, and "that makes us rather different from the usual country that's founded on a history, a culture. We were founded on a Declaration, on a Constitution, on Principles."[18] Good enough. What's miraculous, however, is not the creed only, the Constitution alone, but the audacity of its principles. For there was no warrant to be found in the sphere of inherited wisdom which justified a republican union based not on baroque principles of equilibrium, of action and reaction, but instead supported by "proportions" just a touch off. The magnificence of the Constitution, of that ensemble of ideas which stylizes cadence and validates conduct in America, is found in its élan, its venturesomeness and risk. It invented a post-baroque ideology of an asymmetrical but steady state: a fabric of government, said Madison, for which there is "no model on the face of the globe."

James Madison, whose duty it was to justify this fancy and minimize its risk, knew precisely how bold the whole project was. And because he was certain that the structure would withstand stress, that its shape was not discreditable merely because it fell outside the canon of neoclassic taste, he chose as his central figure of speech the image of an edifice, a house, a habitation, an architecture strong and versatile though irregular. But before he resorted to metaphor he spoke plainly about radical things. My countrymen, he said, do not permit yourselves to be turned against the Constitution solely because its general scheme is unprecedented among nations. "Hearken not to the voice which petulantly tells us that the form of government recommended for your adoption is a novelty in the political world; that it has never yet had a place in the theories of the wildest projectors; that it rashly attempts what is impossible to accomplish. . . . Is it not the glory of the people in America, that, whilst they have paid a decent regard to the opinions of former times and other nations, they have not suffered a blind veneration for antiquity . . . to overrule the suggestions of their own good sense, the knowledge of their own situation, and the lessons of their own experience." Happily, for the whole human race, they pursued a new and more noble cause.

Its nobility as a cause, everyone understood, rested on trust in the common man. Unblinded by veneration for authority, they devised principles of order unanticipated here or elsewhere, a pattern of society which divorced the process and organism of government from the mechanics of social class. For as Henry Adams noted in his study of the administrations of Jefferson and Madison, the Founders dared to entrust this untried set of principles to an entirely new figure of man, unexampled, risen in a New World. "Stripped for the hardest work, every muscle firm and elastic, every ounce of brain ready for use, and not a trace of superfluous flesh on his nervous and supple body, the American stood in the world a new order of man." Indeed, Adams believed America itself stood the world upside down. In contrast to a peasantry which spoke only in dialect and which rooted itself in fixed places of residence, in contrast to a continent where barriers of birth paralyzed "half the populace" and turned it into a "mass of inert matter"—reversing an Old World system in which the lowest orders of society were the least animated, "the American stimulant increased in energy" as it reached "the most ignorant class." Picturesque Europeans surely were. But "compared with this lithe young figure, Europe was actually in deprepitude." In America, where the climate was trying and labor was scarce, where slow, easy, comfortable, old ways "must be exchanged for quick and energetic action"—America in 1800, an abode of sinewy democrats, was at a farthest imaginable remove from a politics of equipoise and stasis.[19]

In Europe, we discover Adams saying, "the conservative habit of mind was fortified behind power." In America, where the "balance between conservative and liberal forces was close," the principle of power had been supplanted by the principle of energy, an amalgam of "unity and energy" in government, Madison had said. For as Madison had remarked in a letter to Philip Mazzei (1788), the real danger to America and to liberty lies in the "defect of *energy & stability* in the present establishment of the United States" (Madison's emphasis). Given the inherent problem, self-government; given too imperfect and refractory human nature, Madison reassured his audience, it was not in the least surprising that the new Constitution should deviate from earlier models of social analysis and political theory, models based on notions about "artificial structure and regular symmetry" which no one had ever managed to support with fact. To the apparently unanswerable charge of heresy, the accusation that the Constitution did not promote a purely federal form of government, a confederacy of sovereign states, but instead offered a strong central union, Madison said that the Confederation had been a "lifeless mass."

It was in the most eloquent paper in the lot, Number 37, that Madison's mind crystallized around images which in my view present unequivocal first signs of transition of Whigs into Founders. Remarking that the Confederation had been at fault for a failure to combine "requisite stability and energy in government with the inviolable attention due to liberty and to the republican form," Madison insisted that American theory must not be hamstrung by a rigidly held dogma of connection between human government and so-called natural law. If the most "sagacious and laborious naturalists have never yet succeeded in tracing with certainty the line which separates . . . vegetable life from . . . unorganized matter," how much more uncertain and evasive was an "exact science of government. . . ." Far better to rely on "the genius of republican liberty," on an American genius for inventing uncommon means to mingle "together in their due proportions" those agencies of government which best unite the principle of energy and the principle of stability. Though cavalier in its neglect of science, America might freshen the causes of law and liberty. Energy, essential for the "prompt and salutary execution of the laws," requires a concentration of power. And stability—necessary for that "repose and confidence in the minds of the people, which are among the chief blessings of civil society"—is assured when a blessed people confers power on representatives neither disproportionately many nor few in number, for a period of time neither disproportionately short nor long.

The problem then, easily put, was to establish institutions guaranteed to ratify these ends. No matter how simply put, as the North Carolina delegation wrote its governor, the problem itself might be compared to an effort to cross a vast plain without a "single straight or eligible road that has been trodden by the feet of nations." During that hot spring and summer in 1787 "the Committee of the Whole," the Convention itself, heard Hamilton represent New York by saying that he still thought that the British government was the best in the world and that he "doubted much whether anything short of it could do in America," heard George Mason and Edmund Randolph, representing Virginia, forecast that this shaky compilation of compromises would probably lead to a "monarchy or a tyrannical aristocracy."[20] But despite months of deep cleavage and general distrust, the Founders floundered toward harmony and in the end made a Constitution which, Madison insisted, though irregular was trim. What man would refuse to quit a "shattered and tottering habitation," the Articles of Confederation, for a far more "commodious building" merely because the new house "had not a porch to it or because some of the rooms might be a little longer or smaller, or the ceiling a little higher or lower than his fancy would have planned them"?

With this imagery, this conceit, this symbol American imagination comes to life, its instant of origin coinciding with the end of any hope of ordinary political reform, of Whiggish purgation. In place of baroque illusions of perfect balance, the Federalists framed the question of interdependence and independence according to principles which registered their disavowal of Augustan dreams of symmetry. Which is to say that the Constitution, neither consummately federal nor unambiguously national, in its asymmetry nicely manifested the bent of human physiology and character evolved under novel conditions of culture in the New World. A document which went against the grain of many of Madison's colleagues he contended was written in an American grain. And in this unique attainment of American imagination, Hamilton by way of an unorthodox monarchism, Madison by way of eccentric republicanism—realizing that no society could, despite Newton, devise a perfectly articulated and regulated system which ran itself—in composing *The Federalist Papers*, these two men, allies and adversaries, gave new life and new style to the arts of literature and government. Balancing risks and risking imbalance, the Founders anticipated a key doctrine of modern social science, the recognition that "living systems all show symmetry" which, "making for stability, makes a living system viable, gives it integration." Simultaneously, however, if a living system is to flourish, we're told in an essay on "Symmetry in Physics and Information Theory" (1970), a "small asymmetry" is needed. Because complete symmetry is static, "a little instability" must be allowed.[21]

When native American eighteenth-century statesmen in Philadelphia and New York agreed to experiment with asymmetry, therefore, they released quite new dynamics of culture. What their experiment involved, what Madison's conceit implies was an appreciation of the fact of discord in society, of disorder, or discontinuity—of disjunction, Gordon S. Wood remarks, between the interests of a sovereign and the interest of a populace. Instead of perfect equipoise there was conflict, mitigable but irremediable conflict between "the passions of the rulers, whether one or a few, and the united interests of a people." During the final years of that century, therefore, theorists of republican order, recognizing the unalterable fact of antithesis in the body politic, shaped "one of the most coherent and powerful ideologies the Western world had yet seen." In radical dissent from conventional British wisdom founding theorists of American society sought to moderate, to modulate, to temper but not to eliminate a natural tension between self-interest and public interest, between "power and liberty, tyranny and licentiousness." Beginning in 1787, Americans accepted the burden of operating a government and maintaining a civilization, spread far and stretched thin, in which people were "both equal and unequal at the same time." No wonder then that the divided self is the American type par excellence, the American holotype in art.

Fifty years ago Claude Lévi-Straus, approaching the farthest reaches of isolation in Brazil, recognized two modes of social organization which led him to construct a solid keystone of theory in *Tristes Tropiques*, that famed and fanciful study of societies in general, from the most distant to the nearest at hand. One he called "binary and symmetrical" and the other, rarer, "ternary and asymmetrical."[22] Good European that he is, Belgian and French, he has always preferred the former. Provided with clues of this kind, I find irresistible the analogy linking those pre-Columbian peoples with North American colonials who fashioned a document recording in infinitesimal but inadequate detail a social model, "ternary and asymmetrical," which was supposed to ease the American passage from an unnatural toward a more natural, a more civil state. Advertising their system as an experiment whose success required the alert attention of a whole citizenry—reversing the old equation linking the health of the body politic with the repression of vitality in the life of the body—the Founders assigned to a mettlesome but divided people, both the periwigged and the leather-aproned man, the sublime burden of tending a society whose charter authorized, legalized, engendered yet held in check the rule of imbalance and irregularity in the affairs of men.

"There is in fact," Adrienne Koch observes in *Madison's "Advice to my Country"* (1966), a "split personality" within *The Federalist Papers* apparent in Hamilton's rejection of and Madison's insistence on a transfer of power from a single sovereign to a whole people whose will, uncontrolled in itself, could control everything.[23] The prospect was fearful. Still, facing the specter of chaos Madison and his colleagues prepared the way for a historic transfiguration of style. The old style had led Palladio to build his baroque masterpiece outside Vicenza in Italy, the Villa Rotunda, in which a metaphysics of symmetry rises from cones and cubes, arcs and squares in perfect disposition. Widely imitated until "the people in America" had been metamorphosed into an American people, Palladio's monument is precisely the sort of dwelling Madison hoped to dismantle.

There is no beauty, said our proto-Romantic poet Poe, which does not show some strangeness in proportion. That phrase, strangeness in proportion, which Poe imported from Lord Bacon, we have not known how to understand except as a clue to pathology, as a foretaste of frenzy. Yet it is nothing other than strangeness of proportion which Madison bequeathed to us as a cardinal principle of the American Idea in politics and art. Invoking the irregular beauty of man's divided self as a supreme justification of this "more perfect Union," Poe harmonized the ideology of a nation with the idea of a national literature. Importing Bacon's mot, Poe caught that romance of spirit which was to animate this "people of paradox" during its first fifty years of postrevolutionary history, from the Federal period into the industrial age.

II

The Aboriginal Demon

Irving, Cooper, Hawthorne

Two hundred years ago today, the industrial revolution became assured of a prime mover, an economical steam engine. . . . The assurance came from a business arrangement . . . on June 1, 1776, a 25-year partnership between the Scottish inventor James Watt and the English industrialist Matthew Bolton. . . . This crucial event, which some scholars think provided a material guarantee of the increased liberty sought in the political revolutions . . . of the United States and France—has gone almost unnoticed. . . . Mediated through the writings of John Locke the same investigations of air pressure and gravitational attraction that influenced the 18th century "physiocratic" ideas . . . were eventually embodied in an American Constitution that sought to create a balance between competing forces in society.

Victor K. McElheny, *New York Times*, June 1, 1975

ALTHOUGH POE'S WORD CONVEYED a cardinal tenet of ideology underlying the great tradition of vitalism in American thought, there were of course competing programs. Transplanted Britons of the Enlightenment, Tory to the bitter end, continued to speak a European rhetoric exalting the "grandiose symmetry" of a divine universe whose perfection all men were supposed to adore. Others dispensed with adoration and awe in favor of what's been called a doctrine of "biformity," still another term intended to describe a system which incorporated Hamilton's design for an exquisitely balanced state empowered to impose unquestioned rule, within Madison's blueprint, Madison's mode of sponsoring the play of human energy no matter how volatile.[1] Embodying a "strangely ambiguous idea of history," the American system was equipped for dialectic but not for synthesis. And no one in 1800, not even Jefferson, could be sure of anticipating the exact moment in the oscillation of government, the precise pressure point when "tilt might be expected and progress cease to be progress."[2]

A strange ambiguous cultural style of tilt therefore not only controlled the operation of government but also provided the sole safeguard of progress in society at that turn of century. As the risk of tilt was chaos so too the danger of biformity was disequilibrium—risks and dangers permanently acute in a "country boiling with odd revolutionary notions about law, language, loyalty oaths, land holding, representative government and the disestablishment of religion."[3] In smallest measure tame but in greatest part wild, in 1800 it was this people that undertook to conduct affairs according to the contradictory rule of an untested Constitution. More slave than free, less civil than savage, from that time forward the American people have sought to preserve a society and maintain a culture in which adhesiveness not cohesion provides a principal motive for community.

In literature the consequences have been both phenomenal and fatal. Confronted by disjunction in affairs of state a particular sort of American writer has especially relished, we know, the obligation of risk imposed by democracy in the United States. From Poe to Scott Fitzgerald, Fitzgerald to Norman Mailer and others, our literature harbors writers of distempered spirit who have plunged into the heart of private disorder so as to elevate personal disarray to the plane of national myth. I mention Fitzgerald, incidentally, because he perhaps best embodies the contemporary style of strangeness in American proportion. It is he indeed who connects our era with Poe's. In a historic statement not unlike Poe's in drift, like Poe's too in being usually cited as a point of conclusion rather than a point of departure, Fitzgerald said that the "test of a first-rate intelligence is the ability to hold two opposed ideas in mind and still retain the ability to function." Magnified to encompass American ideology, his utterance offers a first-rate test of government in the United States too. Fitzgerald's remark is in fact flawless: overtly self-revealing, it is of unchallenged accuracy in catching the spirit of a civilization in which awry is aright, in which athwart and askew are American.

Treating Fitzgerald's old maxim as a fresh gloss on culture in the United States, let's return to selected and illustrative texts of the last century, fiction written between 1800 and 1850, the work of writers persuaded that there was no American order in synthesis. Choosing tales that record the movement of our people from a bucolic to a technological state, we revisit key texts by writers thought to share little more than nationality in common: Irving, Cooper, Hawthorne. What we find indeed is a literature based on ratios of balance to tilt, of power to energy, of Providence to progress. Drawing parallels between the psychology, the physiology of growth in individual persons and in society as a whole, each in his turn probes the limits of irregularity both within the frame of society and within the human frame. Raising—but not resolving—these arresting questions by way of the figure and fate of a child, they exploited the theme D. H. Lawrence pronounced distinctively American because it sanctified process not completeness. Associating process with reversal, reversal with metamorphosis, metamorphosis with a return to origins, in classic American literature the condition of childhood is the national condition par excellence because it discloses a civilization in act of reversing and thus renewing itself. The genius of civilization in the United States is that "it starts old, old, wrinkled and writhing in an old skin" but ends with a "gradual sloughing off of the old skin towards a new youth."[4]

He was actually referring to Cooper's fiction. But for all Lawrence's preoccupation with Natty Bumppo, despite a total neglect of Rip Van Winkle, it's Irving's mini-epic to which observation of this sort seems especially apt. "I always think there is, way down in most American men, a weird little imprisoned man-gnome with a grey beard, and a child's quickness, which knows, knows so finally, imprisoned inside the man-mountain while the man-mountain goes on so lively and so cheer-o! without knowing a thing. Till the little sprite ceases to live, and then the man-mountain begins to collapse."[5] Though Lawrence himself didn't notice the connection, it's in "Rip Van Winkle" that a mountain man falls in with a plot to rescue the sprite within. In executing this plan, in pursuing an adventure which ends in the release of a man-gnome from a mountain prison, Rip finds himself engaged in a rite of growth which Irving almost surely must have realized would propel his hero, his people, the new republic itself toward a new stage in the life process of the organism. If the sprite had not just slept but had died, Irving can be legitimately thought to say goodbye to manhood and mankind. Farewell America.

Irving's tale is indeed another of those American fictions, supposedly written as light entertainment and long treated as kid stuff, which repay the closest attention. Following the lead of Lawrence's *Studies*, Philip Young's persuasive essay "Fallen from Time: The Mythic Rip Van Winkle" restores to the simple frame of Irving's plot an unexpected accretion of detail drawn from ancient legends, stories of Barbarossa and Charlemagne, and in this remarkable way helps to account for the long and flourishing life of this modest-seeming but "wonderfully rich tale." In a reading which joins Teutonic myth with American lore Young presents Rip as a man who evades the prime of life, loses himself in a dark wood, and emerges to find himself delivered into safe and complacent old age. By means of that magical sleep whose result is at once mythopoeic and run-of-the-mill, he goes "from childhood to second childhood with next to nothing in between." More to the point, however, is Irving's correlation of unendurable domestic life with an alien national scene. Having dodged his duty and eluded his Dame, Rip has escaped manly function both at the hearth and on the streets in a time when heroic men of affairs led a whole race of rebels in earth-shattering revolt. An artful dodger indeed, Rip employs a guile so playful, a playfulness so purposive that play itself cancels mere cunning and confirms his power to perform a political as well as mythic role. "Once he had ended his self-transforming sleep he rises a man set apart, incarnate figure of a realm both older and younger than his fellows," a personage of the play sphere, seat and source of humaneness, of eternally childlike spirit. Which is to say that Rip, in having been set wrong for colonial American culture is somehow set right.

Relieving Irving's very elaborate tale of any tie to a routine world, Young underscores a will to truancy common to most men of middle years and made charming in Rip. Guided by this will Rip falls out of a troubled world into a state of "timeless infancy" and becomes in the end a man who has "peered toward the dawn of civilization, witnessed the ancient mysteries and stared at his essential nature." In this changed state, a traveler whose journey had led him to uncover a "hidden childishness" in himself and others, Rip returns a figure "both Gerontian and child." Somehow appointed to inform his countrymen about the ends and beginnings of things, Young says, Rip assumes in old age a vocation heroic enough to change the course of history. In the usual way of travelers in the occult, however, he cannot find words with which to tell his tale: he is at a loss for language to reveal, in a society of get-up-and-go, the secret of that other timeless place. Speechless or not, in Young's mind Rip is "meek, blessed and pure in heart" and if we "mock him for what he has missed"—twenty years of adult male life—"we do it tenderly because it is something in ourselves we mock" too, our own disfigured lives and lost directions.[6]

A resourceful reading, Young's. But in the end its tenor does not quite catch the timbre of Irving's tone. Nor does Young's final word account for Rip's bearing on history or ideology in the United States. A proper accounting must in truth contrive to distinguish, as Young does not, among childhood and childishness else there's no justification for Rip's annointment, for his transformation from a demeaned to an elevated man. Meekness and purity of heart are saintly Christian virtues indeed. But Rip's excursion takes him back earlier than the Christian era to an archaic order of being which is blessed for reasons set down not in the New Testament but in Johan Huizinga's much-admired little book *Homo Ludens* (1944). Contending that civilization is rooted in the "primaeval soil" of play, Huizinga insisted that a main test of a culture is the degree to which its institutions promote and do not thwart the "play-element" in human nature. Derived from the oldest and most primitive layers of the mind itself, play is a civilizing force which brings the unconscious life of dreams—so Jean Piaget's studies have confirmed—and the conscious life of the self into a state of concord. It is the exclusive function of the "play-spirit" in a word, which preserves men and women from the condition of alienation to which a workaday and barbarous world would otherwise condemn them.[7]

Right or wrong, Huizinga's theories, speculations, proofs are anticipated and documented in Irving's prophetic story. Precisely because the play-spirit was absent from the New World during the days preceding and following Revolution, Irving incontestably observes in "Rip Van Winkle," America risked becoming the least congenial society on earth. By no reckoning benign, it is a place in which not Rip but Dame Van Winkle, acerbic though she may be, is most at home. A woman of intemperate heat, she's governed by a pioneer busyness of ambition, given to paroxysms of passion so fierce that she herself is a cause of disorder. More a bitch mom than termagent wife, she rules a roost from which Rip prefers to be excluded. About town and at the tavern, his paternal and husbandly duties suspended, he's a quick and genial and responsible friend. At home he's sly and craven. Like his dog whose tail outside the house swells, erects, plumes, sways but inside their home droops, banished between his legs, Rip lives in a phallic rhythm of tumescence and detumescence which has little to do with lust. Irving's point is not that he's a loutish boy of advanced years. Rather we are invited to understand that Rip cannot be perceived in his true nature until he's removed from this habitat and set in another landscape. Not until he's recognized as the closest modern counterpart to those tiny males with old faces, Dutch dwarves playing games in a remote amphitheater within those mountains Philip Young equates with Valhalla but Irving, referring to Indian lore, calls the abode of the squaw spirit, Mother of the Catskills—only then can Rip be judged at true value.

There's his proper sphere, she's his true mate, these are his fit companions. Meeting these ancient children whose sole nourishment is a kind of home brew, distilled spirit of legend and region, Rip engages to drink their potion and join their games. A game, Young observes, is always the most important element of those stories from which Irving drew mythic detail. "And the fact that the game in these stories is always bowling," which "makes the sound of thunder, gives the whole show away: we are dealing ultimately with the gods" of thunder and lightning, with power. Young believes that Irving introduced a variant locale of Odin's retreat, transported the abode of the godly dead to upstate New York, so as to accommodate a group of ancient and uprooted and transplanted creatures who impersonate a disguised Thor. But Valhalla is elsewhere. And the sound of distant thunder carries a resonance of force worldlier in kind. In this arena (a playground is always a consecrated and "forbidden spot," Huizinga notes, "isolated, hedged round, hallowed, within which special rules obtain; a temporary world within the ordinary world, dedicated to the performance of an act apart")[8] Rip arrives bearing credentials Young describes not quite accurately enough. "Well into middle age, and saddled with a wife who had completely lost her desirability, he laid down his gun and entered the mountains." Given Irving's symbolism of sex, this is tempting surmise. In fact, however, Irving's legend enables his hero to exchange a real woman of the most outrageous virulence of will for the Squaw Spirit of the Catskills. It's not Odin and Thor, not thunder and lightning that bewitch Rip but the thunder and lightning of war that bedevil Mother Country and upstart Colony. In contrast, in antithesis to battle it's the play of eternally childlike gods, the energy of pure play which, providentially, Rip is chosen to share, to preserve, to convey. Having been introduced to this eternal fellowship of players, having been initiated into their rites and appointed their companion, their emissary, he nods through two decades of tumultuous worldly time under the patronage of Manitou of the Mountain. In this sacred spot, a place that fused "old time charm" and "aboriginal mystery," Henry James said in *The American Scene* (1906), Rip slept through Revolution.

On awakening from his twenty years' sleep, missing Wolf and finding his gun a rusted ruin, its stock worm-eaten and its lock fallen apart, Rip utters true and clairvoyant words: "they've changed my gun and everything is changed." And on returning to the village, discovering that the politics of rebellion have indeed exchanged Union Jack for Stars and Stripes—both the ensign above the old tavern and the new flag in the new capital city—he finds himself a privileged person, unique among men of his generation both for what he'd gained and lost, for the glorious adventure he'd found and the glorious revolution he'd missed. In a country at boiling point, the will to liberty, property, and power must be counterbalanced by principles of conduct and culture which Irving was the first of our writers to associate with childhood and the play sphere. Relieved of matrimony, unsullied by the politics of rebellion, untainted by vices foreign to the spirit of games, reborn an ancient sage, a sagelike child, Rip Van Winkle survives as the one man in America who is utterly unblemished by crimes committed in that rage for new order, that act of usurpation which led this tribe of brotherly colonials to cast down their father-king and install one of their own number in the deposed ruler's place. Which is to say that Rip alone is relieved of murder and spared of guilt of the precise kind Freud was to investigate in *Totem and Taboo* and Fenimore Cooper was to introduce into *The Prairie*. And an old German story, borrowed for the express and original end of monumentalizing the American adventure, reminds us that this bawling, brawling, illegitimate brat of a nation could flourish only if it struck a balance between natural force and unnatural passion, between energy and power. Seeing in Rip's son a carbon copy of Rip, we are in some degree reassured. Natural children of Henry Hudson and the Squaw Spirit, born of European myth and Manitou mischief, possibly the bloodline Van Winkle will succeed in mitigating from generation the penalties to be paid, as Freud said about civilization in general, by a society which was now "based on complicity in the common crime."

Within a decade after the appearance of Irving's story in *The Sketchbook* (1820) Cooper was to recast for *The Prairie* (1827), on a scale spacious to accommodate the birth, growth, and destiny of the new society, his treatment of similar motifs. Although Irving developed the lightest touch possible and Cooper worked with the heaviest of hands, though Irving settled on a frolicsomeness of art and Cooper was, as Lawrence said, haunted by the "shadow of violence and dark cruelty," nevertheless both Irving and Cooper sought to shape fiction which matched the human frame to the American scene, the American scheme.

Unlike Irving, however, Cooper is a bard, a teller of tales on Continental scale, a writer nearly as acute as the Indians and the frontiersmen whom he prized, as quick to infer a thing in the thicket from the lightest quiver of a twig. *The Prairie*, his own favorite in the Leatherstocking series, the novel in which his gifts were most fully displayed and never surpassed, is also the only one of his romances which is both programmatic and symbolistic but neither a tract nor an allegory. Written out of chronology, number three in a sequence of five, it portrays the death of its hero, Natty Bumppo, avatar of the American Titan in our golden age, who is dispatched from the American scene not because he's old but because he's displaced, doomed not by reason of age but by force of destiny. That this is not just a personal but a national fate furthermore is confirmed by the arrival at the edge of wilderness not of others of his kind, trappers and scouts, but of first settlers, husbandmen not hunters. Without question, therefore, individual persons given to his sort of holy harmony with Mother Nature, his sort of virginal intactness, must yield their ground to clusters and communities of people used to obey worse laws, more arbitrary ties of compact. Which is to say that a perfect childlikeness of spirit is indeed the least likely cause of adhesion in the life of an emerging nation.

Cooper at his worst, as Mark Twain knew, was an artificer without cunning. But in *The Prairie*, at his best, he summoned out of his unconscious imagination a psychology of motive consistent with the sociology of settlements. Instead of natural law in its purest form, the law of Creation, Ishmael Bush and his band are ruled by unnatural law, by passion of impurest kind, by power, by the power of passion—by that rivalry of passion and power with which Freud, nearly a century after Cooper, was to account for the appearance of human society at its earliest moments of development. For it was indeed a miracle of intuition which led Cooper to represent the origins of culture in the United States by way of an oedipal drama which anticipates the entire scheme of psychoanalytic social theory introduced first in *Totem and Taboo* (1913), next in "Psycho-Analysis and Religious Origins" (1919), again in *Group Psychology and the Analysis of the Ego* (1921), and finally in that vexing little book *Moses and Monotheism* (1939). In each of these extraordinary works Freud postulated exactly those events Cooper, a century earlier, had imagined, had dramatized, had proposed in order to account for the most primitive causes underlying the creation of society in the dimmest dawn of time both in the life of this people and the history of our race.

Given this confluence of motive, given the fact too that both Cooper and Freud, like Cooper and Irving, shared certain intellectual traditions and held in common certain aims, their colleagueship seems odd only at first gasp. Freud's essays did not after all involve theory or therapy alone but did in fact return in time, time immemorial, to those days when men lived dangerous but more or less untrammeled lives which at some moment in prehistory they renounced for safer and tamer, more inhibiting though better regulated systems of law. Freud is after all, we're now accustomed to say, a modern exemplar of all those natural philosophers of Enlightenment under whose auspices Cooper came to maturity. He would have had no difficulty, therefore, in understanding either Freud's vocabulary or his metapsychology, his account of the ways union developed among primitive men as a "sort of contract" based on "renunciation of instinctual gratification." Cooper, who admired the frontiersman's freedom but recognized its cost and foresaw its inhibition by all the unremitting forces of civilization, like Freud claimed that anarchic freedom, however inspiriting, provided little protection against the forces of destruction which in fantasy and in fact men saw threatening them everywhere. Most strikingly too, both men, saddened by the high price mankind pays for the comforts of ordered life, participate in a tradition of thought which claims that the discontents of civilization occur because institutions defile and distort human nature.

On a still deeper level of communion each would have respected the other's reliance on a unique theory of evolution, the phylogenetic. Freud required this theory, the principle of "phylogenetic inheritance," in order to explain the recurrence of certain phenomena within man's unconscious life. For he held to the view, against the opinion of colleagues, that the "mental residue" of primeval times is a "heritage which, with each new generation, needs only to be reawakened." Then men recall ancient crimes and feel anew a sense of guilt. Cooper borrowed from eighteenth-century cyclists of history and of culture, theorists who are, as David Riesman remarks, like Freud in that their thought is "phylogenic and teleological"—from Condorcet and Turgot, Cooper borrowed some early versions of this principle and applied it to the American frontier. According to this view of social evolution all human societies pass through a series of fixed states "from that of the hunter in the forest through the patriarchal stage of migratory pastoral tribes," Henry Nash Smith says, "and so on through ever more complex and stable forms of organization." According to Cooper's view in *The Prairie*, therefore, social conditions at the frontier resembled a situation "as near barbarity" as that under which men lived in the prehistoric past. Because America in the course of its development must pass through all the classic stages of culture, much as ontogeny was thought to recapitulate phylogeny, then surely "the march of civilization" was located without question at "those distant and ever-receding borders which mark the skirts and announce the approach of the nation."

In order to portray the migratory patriarchal phase of evolution, the period of transition from wilderness man to settled society, Cooper introduced the tribe of Ishmael Bush. And it is at this point of intersection that a casual interplay of intelligence, of sensibility, a coincidence of history notable because two men of irreconcilably varied times and places see eye to eye—at this point interplay turns schematic. Freud drew on information available in modern biological and biblical, archeological, and anthropological studies in order to bolster his hypothesis of a tribal horde controlled by an archetypal father and ruled by a patriarchal code. So too did Cooper, in inventing the Bush family and moving it westward to that remote frontier where society in incipient form is clearest visible, find his theme. Originally he had intended it to take shape around the Old Trapper, an epic hero whose ideal proportions of being are usually treated as the principal subject of this novel. But in contemplating the frontier—that place where, he remarked a year later (1828) in an essay on American literature, a writer could find "subjects to be treated with the freedom that the imagination absolutely requires'—and allowing his imagination breathing space beyond its usual limit, he undertook to explore what Henry Bamford Parkes has called "the embryonic beginnings, in patriarchal form, of organized law and order."[9] That is to say, Bush and his clan serve as the center of interest in a fiction designed less to lament Natty Bumppo's death than to define the American condition of alliance and misalliance with nature.

Bush's character and circumstance are therefore crucial both in support of Freud's thesis and in discharge of Cooper's epic function. Presented as a figure of legend, Bush is a man of vast and "prodigious power" who marched at some "distance in front of the whole," followed by a "group of youths very similarly attired and bearing sufficient resemblance to each other, and to their leader, to distinguish them as the children of one family."[10] Thus Cooper introduces the primal horde. In his mind as in Freud's a self-contained and self-supporting unit, it is composed of seven sons and an uncounted number of daughters, Ishmael's wife Esther, his brother-in-law Abiram, his wife's orphaned niece Ellen. "Including both sexes and every age, the number of the party exceeded twenty." There are two outsiders recruited to flesh out various segments of Cooper's program: Dr. Bat, a scientist whose natural intelligence has been corrupted by cyclopedic but inept learning, and Inez, a lady of Creole New Orleans whose marriage to Duncan Uncas Middleton unites aristocratic refinement with natural nobility, a renewal of vitality among the upper classes which bodes well for the long term of democracy in America.

These persons perform certain obvious tasks within a formal plot which is crammed with detail intended to embellish Cooper's theme. Inez's abduction by Bush and his brother-in-law, for example, expresses their lawlessness, their disavowal of the usual rules of civility and property, even of paternity—the only rules men establish in a region where crimes are unpunished by public authority. And although the abduction is unquestionably a prototype of the chase conventional in all Westerns, a device to allow Cooper to show off his buffalo, his Indians and the rest, Inez's kidnapping does double duty in that it clarifies the drift of far-reaching events enacted within the inter life of the tribe itself. For it was in "a weak moment," we learn, urged on by Abiram White that the Patriarch had carried off this young lady and introduced her into his "peaceable and well-governed family." Henceforth peace and good government are gone. For despite the fact that his ostensible aim was merely to receive high ransom for her return, the actual consequence of his act is to precipitate a smoldering clash between generations, a rebellion of sons against the father. Ishmael, "grave in exterior, saturnine by temperament, formidable in his physical means, and dangerous from his lawless obstinacy," wields what Cooper calls a peculiar "species of patriarchal power" which is threatened when his eldest son Asa revolts.

The revolt starts slow and is provoked by a trivial event. It is initiated when Ellen disobeys Ishmael's order to stay far from the secret place in which Inez is hidden. Shamed by his secret and dastardly deed, unwilling to allow others in his family to discover his guilt, Ishmael has hidden her in a wagon "covered with a top of cloth so tightly drawn as to conceal its contents with the nicest care." The others are told that the wagon holds a dangerous beast brought out by Abiram into the wilderness to serve as a decoy should they be forced to use that device. When Ellen disregards the standing order to stay clear of Inez's hiding place, Ishmael commands her not to open the flap. But she is less docile than Ishmael's own children and she disobeys. He fires his rifle; she shrieks and disappears inside. It is this act which precipitates the quarrels that follow, between son and uncle, between uncle and father, between sons and father.

For the first time in their lives, Ishmael's sons are outraged by a display of their father's autocratic rule. They "manifested, in an unequivocal manner, the temper with which they witnessed the desperate measure. Angry, fierce glances were interchanged, and a murmur of disapprobation was uttered by the whole in common." Their response is extraordinary, Cooper says, and cannot be attributed to sudden gallantry. It is at this point, then, that Cooper introduces the Freudian matter. Asa, the eldest son, speaks for the others:

> "What has Ellen done, Father," said Asa, with a degree of spirit which was the more striking from being unusual. . . .
>
> "Mischief . . . boy; mischief! take you heed that the disorder don't spread."

Keep your place, Asa, Ishmael answers, and control your brothers. But Asa, enraged, forgets his first purpose, to defend Ellen, and seems to want to provoke a battle, man to man. Ishmael senses his mood and reminds him, "I am your father, and your better." "I know it well; and what sort of father?" Ishmael again warns that disobedience will bring severe punishment. But Asa is ready to provoke a crisis in the rule of the tribe because at this critical moment in his own life he is no longer willing to remain inside the "web of authority within which Ishmael had been able to envelop his children." Ellen is indeed forgotten. And we realize that the scene is composed less to portray a debate on the propriety of firing bullets at young women than to represent the psychology and sociology of rebellion, during the patriarchal stage of civilization, within the tribal horde. In the final exchange between the two men, therefore, we see how far behind they have left its original cause. "I'll stay no longer," Asa says, "to be hectored like a child in petticoats." You keep me down "as though I had not life and wants of my own." And there we have Asa's main grievance: he is ready to risk his father's wrath in contention over the only nubile woman available in their private world.

Asa's assertion of sexual needs no less valid than his father's is symbolized in the very next occurrence, when Inez materializes and stands at some distance from the assembled company. Seeing her, Asa turns to his uncle and remarks, "This then is the beast." He had known Abiram to be a slave trader, "a dealer in black flesh," but not till now had he realized that "you drove the trade into white families" too. Abiram answers, "Look to your own family"—that Ishmael and his sons are not renowned for their honesty. And Asa in accumulated fury hits Abiram a "back-handed but violent blow on the mouth that caused him to totter." It is a fateful act, directed against a surrogate but in fact meant for the father himself, as everyone but Abiram is aware. And because Ellen's disobedience and Asa's blow are traceable to Inez's presence, we realize that this genteel lady of high station and Roman Catholic breeding is, in quite another sense than the irony reports, indeed a "ravenous, dangerous beast."

Inez is a fragile woman of iron virtue but her "sylph-like form," which Cooper calls the "beau ideal of female loveliness," is lush. "Long, flowing and circling tresses of hair, still blacker and more shining than her robe, fell at times about her shoulders, completely enveloping the whole of her delicate bust in ringlets." Seeing this vision, all the men are stirred. The young Pawnee chief "riveted his eyes on Inez" and immediately his head is turned. "He had the air of one who maintained a warm struggle . . . in the recesses of his own thoughts." Even his sense of direction is lost. Although he is absolutely at home on the prairie, his return to his village is delayed when, setting off, he rode for a moment in circles, as if uncertain of his course. Middleton, a gentleman, is no less moved but is better at disguising his passion. Indeed, no violence is done to the text if we read it as a kind of teaser in which this young man chases his lady all over the prairie in order to get her back where she belongs: in bed. For Ishmael and Abiram had kidnapped Inez as she returned home from her prayers, during the short time between her wedding and its consummation. She had disappeared while Middleton—"the lover, the husband, the bridegroom"—impatiently waited.

Asa's accusation is wrong: Neither Abiram nor Ishmael had planned to sell her into sexual bondage. But his error is consistent with his mood and his mood is provoked by the odor of passion Inez exudes. She is a genteel female of Cooper's sort and simultaneously a woman of peculiar erotic power. She is therefore ideally suited to play the role Cooper reserved for her, to take her place at the center of a plot encircled by crimes of passion.

When Cooper removed Inez from the darkness of her prison-tent and, at a critical moment in the argument between Ishmael and Asa, placed her high on a windy hill, dress fluttering "like gossamer around her form," in the image we recognize his way of exposing to the light of day what it is that animates Asa's rebellion. The young man is ready to enjoy the perquisites of adult manhood. And these are unavailable so long as Ellen Wade, who provokes the crisis, and Inez, who symbolizes its meaning, are held within his father's heavy hand. In the instant before he hits Abiram, Asa has two choices. He can somehow overmaster his father and put himself in the older man's place or he can leave. Before Inez's appearance, he had threatened to leave and, with deadly playfulness, his father had replied, "the world is wide, my gallant boy. . . . Go." When he strikes the blow, however, we understand that he has undertaken to follow the first course. We realize, too, that Cooper has conceived what Freud later was to call the "crime of liberation," that this version of the Oedipal drama must now be enacted, ritualistically, to its inexorable close.

The classic story is "told in a very condensed way," Freud said, "as if what in reality took centuries to achieve" had happened just once. Its substance is given succinctly in *Moses and Monotheism*, where Freud maintained that "all primeval men, including, therefore, our ancestors," underwent the fate which Cooper's fiction unfolds. The parallel is not merely striking; it is extraordinary. "The strong male was the master and father of the whole horde, unlimited in his power, which he used brutally. All the females were his property, the wives and daughers of his own horde as well as perhaps also those stolen from other hordes. The fate of the sons was a hard one; if they excited the father's jealousy they were killed or castrated or driven out." There is an echo of the "expulsion of the eldest son," Freud observed, "in many myths and fairy-tales."[11] Its echo in *The Prairie* is quiet, however, because Cooper decided on one of the alternate choices. When Asa refuses his father's invitation to leave and instead commits an act which threatens the Patriarch's rule, he is exposed, vulnerable. And his hopes for survival are modest indeed.

It is the uncle, Abiram, who kills Asa, revenging himself for the hateful insult. Cooper's readers long have accepted this as a valid motive because Abiram is a demonstrably vicious man. But they have accepted it on less persuasive grounds too. Cooper, a notoriously careless writer, customarily sacrificed the world of fact in favor of the larger universe of fancy. Comprehending the essence of an idea or an experience, he was impatient or neglectful when he set out to describe its surface. In this instance, Asa's death at Abiram's hand is true to the spirit of the whole situation but inappropriate, unbelievable when presented as a result of the mere insult alone.

The necessary reasons for murder transpire once we realize that Abiram has a dual role even in the explicit plot. He serves as Ishmael's evil genius, a tempter whose "voice is like a raven in my ears," and simultaneously as the instrument of Ishmael's will. Murdering Asa, he accomplishes Ishmael's design: it is Abiram's gun that shoots but it is Ishmael who calls the shot. This is not Cooper's figure of speech, but one evoked by Ishmael's ruminations in the scene where Asa's body is discovered and buried. Ishmael tries to dissociate himself from the crime, but he shares the murderer's guilt if only because he feels relieved to learn that his eldest son is dead. Asa had not followed his father's commands to keep the disorder from spreading; on the contrary, "the spirit of insubordination, which emanated from the unfortunate Asa, had spread among his juniors" and had threatened the father's rule. Freud would have said that it threatened the father's life—one of the sons sooner or later would have murdered Ishmael. That Cooper shared this opinion too is indicated by Ishmael's recollection of his own past, of the time when "in the wantonness of his youth and vigor" he had "cast off his own aged and failing parents, to enter into the world unshackled and free." The fear of being similarly cast off, of being sacrificed to a rivalry of sex in the sons, crosses Ishmael's mind but is immediately replaced by a more comforting thought. With Asa's death, "the danger had abated, for a time at least," until the time when another son grew rebellious. And he is pleased, thinking that although his "authority was not restored with all its former influence," it nevertheless maintained "its ascendancy a little longer."

In order to underscore Ishmael's sense of his own danger, of temporary reprieve, Cooper diverts our attention to the private thoughts of the mother and the remaining sons. And we learn that the latter "had glimmerings of terrible distrust as to the manner in which their elder brother had met his death." These glimmerings are the more remarkable, Cooper observes, because the young men are dull. Even their mother, a most loyal wife, suspects her husband, as Ishmael later remarks. Neither mother nor sons have as yet any reason to accuse Ishmael, not the least clue confirming his guilt or innocence. Nevertheless, each of the sons fears for his life. Their thick minds grow suddenly supple, prescient, and they wonder if Ishmael is ready to "imitate the example of Abraham without the justification of the sacred authority which commanded the holy man to attempt the revolting office." Invoking the biblical story, Cooper causes the figures of Abiram–Abraham and Ishmael to merge and become one. The horde of restless sons, recognizing in this person an absolute ruler who killed their brother though he had no sanction higher than that dictated by his own nature and by his tribal rank, know that he is ready to deal with each of them in a similar way.

And the main result of this awareness, Cooper notes, is to strengthen "the authority of Ishmael" for a while longer. His reign has been extended because he, the man whose own youthful rebellion had succeeded, has overridden the challenge of his eldest son and kept disorder down. Primal justice has triumphed and a primitive culture, having contained revolution and withstood anarchy, has survived. And a story with which Cooper hoped to symbolize primeval experience in the growth of the nation came somehow to comprehend what Freud was later to call the template of man's racial experience at an early and convulsive moment of social development.

But we have not even yet fully described all the ways in which Cooper anticipated and applied these intricate ideas. Freud contended that the desire to kill a tribal leader is itself the source of the idea of original sin. And this idea, in turn, distinguishes Hebrew from Christian organization. "Paul, a Roman Jew from Tarsus, seized upon this feeling of guilt and correctly traced it back to its primeval source," to a crime "against God that could be expiated only through death." This is Ishmael's opinion too when, later in the novel, he does finally recognize an authority higher than his own. "Abiram White," he says, at the moment when Abiram's crime is discovered, "you have slain my first born and according to the laws of God and man you must die." The Patriarch, no longer a kind of Hebrew nomad chieftain, instead speaks as a Christian who has received God's Word and knows what he must do in order to gain salvation. In the period preceding that moment in which he pronounced sentence, he had searched the Bible to find those "rules of conduct which have been received among all Christian nations as the direct mandates of the Creator." Asa's murder, a crime committed without God's sanction, had abrogated God's law. Originally the crime had pleased Ishmael, but now he regards it as the work of "the devil incarnate," inflicted as a "terrible retribution from Heaven." In the idiom and form of the novel the event does indeed carry the whole weight of original sin. And if Ishmael is to be purged of guilt, he himself must suffer and must somehow die.

Cooper solves this problem not only by causing Ishmael to sentence Abiram, the actual criminal, to death but also by intimating that both men share one soul and a common fate. Abiram stumbles as he moves toward his "last agony," and appears to totter "beneath a load of . . . guilt." Ishmael, though implacable, is also moved, for he feels as if he "had been suddenly and violently separated from a recent confederate forever." We realize that his unaccustomed emotion does not represent a sudden affection for his brother-in-law. Rather, Ishmael feels that he is about to be rid of nothing less than his own concupiscence, malice, envy. This is why, in the next instant, Abiram's death cry "seemed to have been uttered at the very portals of [Ishmael's] . . . ears." Suddenly, feeling his own blood gush "from every pore in his body," he is amazed to hear "a sort of echo burst . . . from his own lips." Having offered in sacrifice that part of himself, as we may say, which is culpable, Ishmael assumes his own share of guilt, participates in Abiram's agony, achieves expiation and is reborn.

In these transmutations of plot we recognize a transformation of its religious tone. What Freud would have called the Mosaic order has been replaced by "the new religion founded by Paul," based in the twin principles of "original sin and salvation through sacrificial death." In the action of Cooper's novel, transformation occurs when the remaining members of the family depart from the primitive West and return to "the confines of society," where their "train was blended among a thousand others" and where their descendants renounce forever the "lawless and semi-barbarous lives" of predecessors, founders of the ancestral line. Everything this tribe has done, therefore, what each of its members has learned about himself and others, about Indians both treacherous and trustworthy, about the Trapper and his dog, the prairie itself, about property and honor and passion and love—all this informs the body and its members and will underlie the politics of government in this society throughout its entire history. In a masterstroke of imagination, Cooper portrayed conflict between father and sons as a paradigm of contradiction, mitigable to modest degree, but set deep within the nature of the beast hence irremediable, to be contained by a flexible and compassionate system of law, divinely blessed. For not only is the march of civilization ceaseless but too its momentum, its progress, advances by means of a dialectic between natural law and natural lawlessness, between what Freud called the sublimation of instinct and the instinct of destruction. And if a childlikeness of manhood is perceived as a sign of grace while a barely repressed brute appetite for power is taken as a sign of sin, then the American republic in Cooper's view derives its vitality from institutions which emanate from the "organic" life of a people and operate according to an eternal dialectic of blessedness and damnation.

How unfortunate it is that Freud's distaste for American life barred him from the study of American letters, of Cooper's novel where his own speculation would have been supported by testimony he was ever delighted to receive, by that found in the arts. The more self-indulgent, too, this prejudice, this neglect, for it denied him attestation got nowhere else despite lifelong and comprehensive research. The only idea, incidentally, which Cooper did not anticipate and exploit, Freud's Lamarckian notion that each of us inherits and retains a memory trace of the primal event, is the one suggestion which remains unconvincing still. Its absence from Cooper's imagination implies that it is one of the least reliable contrivances of Freud's prodigious mind. Cooper's opinion on this matter is the more creditable and the more amazing when we remark finally how completely his work incorporates every other element in Freud's argument, even some suggestions that Freud attributed to Otto Rank concerning the origins of art and the nature of myth. These emerge, the two men agreed, when someone, moved by the aspiration to replace a tribal father, chooses to invent a story in which this temptation, aspiration, and accomplishment are described as having actually occurred though in fact nothing may have happened. In the "exigency of his longing," Freud says, he is "moved to free himself from the group and take over the Father's part. He who did this was the first epic poet." He "invented the heroic myth."[12]

When we recall how precisely Cooper's own life, his replacement of his father as Lord Temporal over thousands of acres of Cooperstown,New York, accords with purposes implicit in his fiction, we realize how persuasively and comprehensively Cooper's motives in life and art justify and document Freud's views. Concerning Freud too Erich Fromm has demonstrated how the events of a career exhibit personal rivalry with no less a personage than the greatest of Western culture heroes, Moses himself. Freud did indeed see himself as a spokesman of new and ineffable and revealed wisdom, a creator of the last word in man's understanding of himself and of the world, a kind of lawgiver.[13] Arriving at this last twist of argument, therefore, we must observe paired tendencies of character in Freud and Cooper, traits which disclose in each a passion for primacy, the volition to assume a heroic and prophetic role. Unlike Freud, however, Cooper identified the origins of human society with the first stage of American civilization and synchronized the principle of conflict within the self with a principle of contradiction in society. Recasting the mold of culture to fit the aberrant nature of man, Cooper became our first epic poet, inventor of the heroic myth of America. Conceived in crime, American history is enshrined in art which rehearses and re-creates the memory of affliction and the recollection of remedy.

Within a fairly short period of time, before midcentury, writing in America encountered a new and extraordinary source of affliction, a scourge for which even now there is no known remedy: machines. As William Blake had been perhaps the first man of letters to appreciate, society in America was in principle hostile to the very thought of shackling people to machinery and therefore was unlikely to harbor so ignoble, so debauched a use of energy as was already habitual in worse places. Although native American writers were soon to lament how blinding was the allure of technology, they continued to behold that Blakean image of organic energy which had elated earlier generations. Early on Blake had proclaimed that energy in its most debased forms had ensnared the soul of motive in Great Britain at the start of its age of dominion; in contrast, a transcendent vision of energy inspired the life of society, the life of the mind, and the life of imagination in the United States. Indeed, he chose the United States of North America as his adoptive homeland because it was here, he supposed, that his famed dictum ("Energy is the only life, and is from the body; and Reason is the bound or outward circumference of Energy") was unofficial law of the land. Unofficial, it must instantly be said, because official opinion two hundred years ago tended to oscillate between Burke and Blake, between the *Philosophical Enquiry into the Origins of Our Ideas of the Sublime and Beautiful* (1757) and the poem *America* 1793). "I know of nothing sublime," said the celebrated Edmund," which is not some modification of power." Blake, who had read Burke's treatise when he was young, who at middle age said he felt the same "Contempt & Abhorrence then that I do now"—in *America* Blake opposed the spirit of English Toryism, Urizen, with his Eros, "red Orc," son-god and progenitor of American revolution. In copulation with the "shadowy daughter of Urthona" Orc begets out of the mother country a new nation disposed to embody vital living force rather than political and technological power.

The one great achievement of the baroque artist is the "imaginative use of power." And in Blake's myth, central source of organicist imagery in Romantic thought, the sole great attainment of Urizen is to exercise power over events in the new age, an epoch blighted by imperial wars and beset by tyrants. Reserving praise for those great men of American constitution who preferred to place their faith in risky living systems rather than controlled mechanical ones, Blake caused Urizen to incarnate a peculiarly English kind of law-and-order despotism suited to the dawning age of industry and empire. In that Blake's villain was blamed for "checking all movement and renewal or forcing energy into perverse and wasteful forms," Urizen may very well have been cast in the image of an authentic British national hero, James Watt. As if consecrated to play the role of "Albion's Guardian" in Blake's epic, this admirable Scotsman applying heat to machines enabled Britain to place itself first among nations inspired by progress and obsessed with power. A celebrated figure, by Blake alone upbraided, Watt found himself enshrined at the highest altar of fame. "Here I sell what all men crave: power!" Watt's colleague Bolton said of his machine shop, of their steam engine.[14]

Given later horrors and disenchantments it does surely require a wrench of memory to recall this nineteenth-century British view of Watt as the most eminent pioneer of a race of technologists that would harness power to work and thereby exalt the life of earth. Because a man of this unprecedented kind, Carlyle said, "with blackened fingers, with grim brow, was searching out in his workshop the 'Fire-Secret,'" England henceforth was "not only to have had her Shakespeares, Bacons, Sidneys but to have her Watts, Arkwrights, Brindleys" too.[15] In *Chartism* (1839), usually approved for containing the "greater part of what is best in Carlyle's social thinking," Carlyle foresaw which aptitudes and appetites would entice men to action in the new industrial era. Because "in all senses we worship and follow after Power," Carlyle said, it was the solemn duty of intellectuals to instruct "the classes with power to equip themselves for the right exercise of power."

Adoring the great orchestral sound of that resonant word, more than two generations of men and women of letters in England joined Carlyle in undertaking to adapt British character to the machine age and to mold this new British culture of power toward humane ends.[16] And though American writers were soon to assume a similar vocation, before 1850 that role went unfilled in the United States, that function unwanted. During decades when English technocrats developed Promethean uses for the "Fire-Secret," Americans of utopian impulse established enclaves, communes, phalanxes (by the mid-fifties these exceeded eighty in number and ran from New England to the Mississippi River) in which they strove to inspire body and soul with energies radiated both by solar and divine light.[17] In contrast to an English ideology of power which required that "men, women and children [be] yoked together with iron and steam," said an American observer in 1832—"animal machine chained fast to iron machine"—American ideologues refused to entrust vital life and organic society to the "spinning-jenny and the steam engine."*

This is not at all to say that inventors here lacked following or that utopian zealots were unshakably rural. It is indeed to say, however, that the merger of technology with its auxiliary idea, progress, did not until mid-century rule the central contrivances of culture in the United States. Despite a huge effort of propaganda by enthusiasts of industry, Henry Adams remarked, not before the 1840s did machines become an unexceptionable means of felicity in the public mind.[18] Before that time a society of seafarers

*Not far from "Woedolor Mountain," descend "Black Notch" into a hollow "called Devil's Dungeon," there discover "Blood River" leading to a "large whitewashed building" set against "the sullen background of mountain-side firs": a paper mill. "I stood spellbound," Melville wrote in "The Tartarus of Maids" (1855). Passing in procession "along the wheeling cylinders, I seemed to see, glued to the pallid incipience of the pulp, the yet more pallid faces of all the pallid girls I had eyed that heavy day," their agony "outlined on the imperfect paper, like the print of the tormented face on the handkerchief of Saint Veronica."

and settlers, uncertain which routes to follow into the future, preferred to plant its first factories, like its early prisons, in a bucolic setting. In pursuit of a "balance of art and nature," Leo Marx has said, they envisioned a culture of the "middle landscape" in which the balm of green fields might blanch the stain of smoke and smooth the abrasion of brick. "What a place for engineering!"—thus does Elting Morison evoke that perfect innocence of joy felt by pioneer American technologists who believed Nature on this continent to be "an amicus curiae, a force to conquer which offered the terms on which conquest was possible. The result was an interchange that worked to the advantage of both parties." For the better part of a hundred years indeed, this sort of symbiosis stirred fevers of technocracy not unlike more traditional fervors of faith—as in the instance of John B. Jervis, who drew on belief well entrenched in the history of ideas in America, the tribal tradition of covenant. "The railway," Jervis said, "combining works of art with those of nature," would in fact "improve the scenery" by preventing the erosion of earth and preserving the health of trees. Not to worry: engineering in the United States would unfailingly enrich the lot of man without scarring the beauty of earth. Lyrical indeed, utilitarian too, this "imaginative fusion of spirit and geography, morality and landscape," this symmetry of "New England beliefs and New England scenery," as Larzar Ziff remarks in another connection, is an "unsolicited gift from the Puritans." In America "bad roads meant bad morals." Or rephrased to conform perfectabilitarian with thermodynamic belief, the American Errand was guided by those "god-fearing, high-minded, open-hearted" pioneer technocrats, "Nature's Noblemen," self-taught engineers who assumed responsibility for the manner in which American energy in 1860 was "released to do work." "A canal passing through Rome, New York," in Morison's account of "the westward course of empire," a furnace built in Londonderry, Pennsylvania, rails laid in the Berkshires "drew boys off the surrounding farms. Thus energy locked up for a century or more in the enclosing cycle of growing and harvesting small crops was discharged into the expanding economy. In the form of physical and intellectual power applied to building and making things," this new source of vitalism "acted with explosive force upon the whole society."[19]

Toward midcentury, therefore, a native race of technologists engaged to deploy machines which would exploit the resources of this unviolated land in a principled American way. Beneficiaries of that Puritan gift they may well have been. But it was the master builders of British empire they envied and imitated. For what these American counterparts aimed to achieve here was a style of being not unlike *The Age of Equipoise*, as W. L. Burn called it, a society in which symmetries of industrial, social, economic, and political power were taken as confirmation of the Lord's blessing on Victoria's rule. "The high tide of Victorianism," says Gertrude Himmelfarb in echo of Burn, was indeed "'The Age of Equipoise' insofar as any age can warrant so sanguine a title."[20] In contrast America, already embattled North and South, East and West, was demonstrably the less sanguine the tighter it attached itself to those means of production which turned the shafts and wheels of Victoria's England. And as local captains of industry ever more boldly invoked alien principles of order and adopted foreign myths of invention—the invention of the idea of invention being, as the philosopher Whitehead was to say, the high-water mark of industrial imagination in the nineteenth century—in 1844 Nathaniel Hawthorne composed "The Artist of the Beautiful," ridiculing those technicians who sought to force benign organic American energies into malign, mechanical forms.

Traditionally, this tale has not invited concentrated thought by either the specialist scholar or the seasonal critic. Given its close ties, its general resemblance to other texts more openly driven by a malevolence of machines, inattention so flagrant is uncommonly hard to explain. Its absence from standard lists of Hawthorne's tales and sketches treating the parabolic literature of technology is to my mind a lapse of taxonomy which must be got right. A quite formidable list, usually it runs from "The Procession of Life" (unexceptional but for the narrator's horror of a "manufactury where the demon of machinery annihilates the soul") through such minor pieces as "The Old Apple Dealer" ("he and the steam fiend are each other's antipodes"), "Earth's Holocaust," and "The New Adam and Eve," and ends with a celebrated story, "The Celestial Railroad" and a major novel, *The House of the Seven Gables*. Granted that Hawthorne's mind was beset by a variety of ideas about engines; granted too that his well-established "hostility to progress" never rivaled Melville's and that on occasion he is found admiring certain new technologies of mass production. But as his American notebook entry for July 31, 1838, attests, an item that comes straight out of nightmare, the brute impersonal force of machines simply appalled him: "A steam engine in a factory to be supposed to possess a malignant spirit; it catches one man's arm and pulls it off; seizes another by the coat-tails, almost grapples him bodily;—catches a girl by the hair, and scalps her;—and finally draws a man, and crushes him to death."

It is indeed this sort of notation—all the more frightful in that it stands stark without consolations or evasions of his usual kind, without the benefits of distance or the mediations of irony—that compels us to recognize the seriousness of duties reserved for Owen Warland in his cautionary tale. For it's nothing less than a demonic ghost in the machine, sheer malignancy of spirit, that manifested itself in the "long shriek, harsh, above all other harshness," inescapable "whistle of the locomotive" conceived as the pulse and power of the steam engine invading the land. Noise so discordant, he remarked on July 27, 1844—one month following publication of "The Artist of the Beautiful"—that "the space of a mile cannot mollify it into harmony," this "startling shriek" provided him with a definitive conceit for the whole "noisy world" of modern times, an era ruled by a tumultuous will to conquest of nature. With "all unquietness" itself assaulting his ears, therefore, early on he set Warland a task fantastical in character but "rational" in purpose—to invent a device enabling "all the harsh dissonances of life [to] be rendered tuneful."

It must be said, then, that we do Nathaniel Hawthorne no service by treating this story as just another meditation on the idea of beauty common among poets of Romantic sensibility everywhere. A view widely held, it is perhaps most persuasively argued by Millicent Bell who portrays Warland as still another member of the "great nineteenth-century company of real and fictional beautiful souls who live misunderstood by the coarser spirits of the world and seek an early grave."[21] Because her book, *Hawthorne's View of the Artist* (1962) long had this field pretty much to itself, readers have come to treat Warland as an ordinary pathetic figure in one of Hawthorne's standard problematic parables. To my mind, however, the fiction centers on an epic contest between twin forces of culture in America at a turning point of history. "Personify the Century," Hawthorne exhorted himself in 1845, "talk of its present middle-age—of its youth, and its adventures—of its prospects." To this end above all, Hawthorne conjured up a Prospero, a man of genius engaged in a culminating work of self-realization, not a Lycidus, not a lost soul. Only such a one could justify the writer's resort to mythopoeism, to the creative principle itself, as proper means to preserve this post-Puritan people from vice in the new mechanical age, from cupidity. From sin.

So ambitious an enterprise warrants graver commentary than is offered by Bell and others who are perplexed by Hawthorne's choice of a "mechanical butterfly" as an emblem of the creative process. The thing's too trifling. How can a mere "scientific toy" appropriately divulge the drift of Hawthorne's theme—unless its aim is irony? Well: manifold uses of irony there are without question, but none are turned against either Owen or his butterfly, a gorgeous device indeed in that it enables both the artist and magus to poke about those mysterious powers of nature which unite the process of creation in art with the process of invention in science. It was of course Hawthorne's conviction, furthermore, that no artist could ascend to the Absolute, that sublime realm of truth and beauty, unless his own creative force flowed in confluence with the powers of Creation. And though Owen's experiments do surely begin in necromancy, their completion—the materialization of a butterfly which to the naked eye appears to possess properties indistinguishable from insect life itself—this triumph is not the fruition of mechanical skill merely but of organic imagination in its purest state and most original kind. Indeed "The Artist of the Beautiful" is exemplary on this count above all, that it records perhaps a first union in American letters of Puritan precept and organicist creed. For it's not the method of magic or manufacture Owen must master, some Chthonian might he must summon so as to commute base matter into treasure of the most commanding value and use. Mere transmutation is bootless labor. Rather it's a private metamorphosis, a conversion of body and spirit he must himself undergo so that he can recapitulate in his own person, his own organism, that procession of changes which brings the actual living thing, God's perfect butterfly, itself to life.

The trajectory of the tale is therefore overarching, its tone lofty and its address grand, despite Owen's tininess of scale. Indeed size itself is Hawthorne's oxymoron. Endowing this man of "diminutive frame" with a genius for the minuscule, Hawthorne thrust him into an age given over to the worship of giantism in men and gigantism in machines. Born into an epoch in which sheer magnitude is far likelier to be monstrous than momentous, Owen Warland is the sovereign figure of invention within a microsphere which he commands by virtue of the dexterity and "marvelous smallness and delicate power of his fingers."[22] He alone carries the germ of an irrepressible energy, infinitesimal indeed but vital enough to prevail against the juggernaut of industry. Foreseeing that Owen might nonetheless fall outside the ken of readers who mistook modesty of size for meanness of endowment, Hawthorne warned his audience not to confuse the sense of beauty with a "sense of prettiness." Nor must they dismiss Owen's mastery of tiny things as endowment less elevated than painting or sculpture. For Hawthorne ventured to trust the fate of American civilization to the restorative powers of this childlike virtuoso of art and science because he rested his case on another axiom of Romantic thought. "The beautiful idea has no relation to size, and may be as perfectly developed in a space too minute for any but microscopic investigation as within the ample verge that is measured by the arc of a rainbow."

By nature and birth out of touch with his fellows and out of tune with his world, bounded in a nutshell Owen dreams of infinite space.* His patron and employer, Peter Hovenden, mistaking the drift of Owen's

*"The drop is a small ocean," Emerson had said two years earlier in "The Poet."

dreams, sets simple tasks and assigns more profitable work. "I know what it is to work in gold," says that master watchmaker, "but give me the worker in iron," give me "main strength for my money." It's Danforth whom Hovenden has in mind, the blacksmith, Owen's schoolmate and opposite number. And too in this hitherto unattended way, long before R. H. Tawney equated Protestants and capitalists, Hawthorne portrayed our classic Yankee zeal for profits not as a gain but as a loss of punctilio. A writer accustomed to refer to "his puritans as 'men of iron,'" in this instance he did not intend his figure of speech to connote praise for Calvinist rigors of worship. On the contrary: in "The Artist of the Beautiful" Hawthorne inserts Warland into an age of iron where a steady and matter-of-fact people "hold the opinion that time is not to be trifled with, whether considered as a medium of advancement and prosperity in this world" or as a "preparation for the next." In this scrupulous and economical way, therefore, Hawthorne invites us to see Owen through the eyes of compatriots who viewed him as a sort of technocrat of salvation. On one day or the next, out of his workshop would materialize a fabled thing, perhaps even the "perpetual motion," they say, animated by eternal force itself. It is as we shall see a view nearer damnation than deliverance.

Unquestionably guided by a higher will, implacable to reconcile the concerns of matter and spirit, Owen in truth couldn't have cared less about an invention that would merely serve uses "as are now effected by steam and water power." An artisan who is appalled by the perfidiousness of technology itself, a boy who'd been horrified by the awful "size and terrible energy of a steam engine," he disdains to be "honored by the paternity of a new kind of cotton engine."* In this respect he is, as we know, an uncommon man of the American 1830s and 1840s. For if he'd been an ordinary clever fellow, maker and mender of the clocks, he'd have sought to make "the visibility of progress," as Hawthorne observed, "plain for all to see." Indeed, those readers today who complain of Hawthorne for having wasted his time on a story about work of low order, about pedestrian labor, tend to forget how highly esteemed clockmakers were in New England 150 years ago. Neither prosaic nor low, as Lewis Mumford remarked in that section of *Technics and Civilization* (1934) devoted to a historical account of clocks, Warland's occupation involved work of unquestioned cachet. Tracing to monasteries in the Middle Ages the earliest widespread use of mechanical methods to measure passage of time, Mumford argues that it was the rhythm of bells tuned to the dial and hands of a clock which synchronized

*In "Ethan Brand" Lawyer Giles's "entire hand [was] torn away by the devilish grip of a steam engine."

the actions of men, accustomed them to the "regular, collective beat and rhythm of the machine" and first initiated mankind into the uses of technology. Once this synchrony had spread beyond the monastic wall, Mumford adds as if reporting the exact functions Owen's townsfolk expected him to perform, its beat "brought a new regularity into the lives of the workman and the merchant." It is therefore the "clock not the steam-engine" that in Mumford's view serves as the prototypical machine of the industrial age, a "new kind of power machine, in which the source of power and the transmission were of such a nature as to ensure the even flow of energy throughout the works and to make possible regular production and a standardized product."[23]

Mumford anticipated by thirty years the very claims which were to catapult Marshall McLuhan (who preferred Gutenberg's press to Mumford's clocks and substituted movable type for gears and wheels) to fame as a sage of the 1960s. One man's escapement is another man's printing press in this long-lived inquiry into the origins of technology, an inquiry to which "The Artist of the Beautiful" adds its forgotten fleck of fact. In juxtaposing blacksmith and watchmaker, Hawthorne realized too that a man in a smithy could have hammered out "thousands of suits of armor or thousands of iron cannon" without reaching the level of prestige reserved for watchmakers in the late-Newtonian age. In furnishing the power that kept the planets spinning like clockwork, Newton's mainspring had provided theoretic sanction as well as reliable instrumentation for a machine that mimed the integration of heavenly bodies. And in deriving elements of technology from configurations of motion made available by Newton's account of gravitation, watchmakers had invented a type of movement, the eighteenth-century chronometer, which at long last guaranteed precision of measurement on earth. As an amalgam of natural law and mechanical principle, therefore, clockwork movement was an astounding feat of science and engineering. No less historic was its allure as an emblem, an amalgam of sacred and profane realms of being in America. Indeed, little violence is done to Melville's improbable work, *Pierre* (1852), if Plinlimmon's pamphlet "Chronometricals and Horologicals" is treated as an account of Owen's condition, of Owen's vocation and artistry. In a tradition first "outlined by John Cotton and John Winthrop," Sacvan Bercovitch contends, Melville proposed to prove that "God's truth" and "man's truth" by their very contradiction are "made to correspond." Two hundred years after our original immigrants undertook to contravene what Melville called the "watchmaker's brains of this earth," an ancient medieval capacity to segment diurnal time merged with a well-established handicraft of watchmaking. And in those early times of the Age of Progress, New England horologicals—first of our native craftsmen to do so—converted a Puritan dream of redemption into a Yankee industry devoted to the mass production of interchangeable parts. "The American System," it was generally called.[24]

Although the instrument itself symbolized a new style of work, the cost of efficiency came high. Quite as progress drew in its train a heavy load of stress, so too were clocks ever more frequently seen as a pervasive cause of American nervousness. Until those infernal instruments had come into general use, it was said, procrastination had meant little. But by 1881, when everyone decided to translate time into money, punctuality had become a far crueler thief of "nervous force" than dally or delay.[25] A bad diagnosis, this distinctive detail of social history coincides with other details of fable and fact which enrich a story whose hero finally refuses to exercise his gifts to harmful effect, personal and national, refuses to work at "the perfection of clocks and the invention of watches." At first, however, Owen cannot bring himself to affront his townsfolk, cannot overtly disavow the values of a whole people, apparent in the intimidating and towering person of the village smith. His presumptive ally, Danforth, stands ready to play Bolton to his Watt. And one day unhinged by this friend's curiosity, by his unwelcome presence during an experiment on a system for fastening musical devices to the machinery of a watch (so that the harsh dissonance of life "might be rendered tuneful"), unnerved, Owen makes a mess of the job and goes into a funk. "He spent the next few sluggish weeks with his head so continually in his hands that the townspeople had scarcely an opportunity to see his countenance." And though Hawthorne chooses merely to evoke an undefined blacksmithy magic emanating from Danforth's person, Owen's depression is unmistakably a variant form of disorder described not long ago in an anthropological account of "The Blacksmith Taboo" in history. Like the "blacksmith complex," Warland's syndrome is bound up with a secret fantasy in which the smith is perceived to be at once "impure" and peculiarly masterful. Impure because of "contact with iron (a loathesome and repulsive element) or with fire," he is also masterful because he commands a fearful and hereditary power of forging "murderous weapons." What he commands indeed is nothing less than a technique which, "likened to lightning," transmits a spark from tool to man, from man to metal and metal back to man.[26]

Drawn inside Danforth's orbit Owen remains in a state of stupefaction until, rousing himself at last, he emerges and displays a countenance on which a "cold dull nameless change was perceptible." First of a series, this alteration manifests itself in a decision to suspend experiments of the kind interrupted by the blacksmith's loathsome presence. Instead he will devote himself exclusively to Danforthian interests, humdrum work of this time, of this place. Determined to resist temptation to engage in weird enterprises, queer inventions, he applies himself "to business with dogged industry." So industriously does he engage in the business of business that he's soon awarded with custodianship of the church steeple. "He succeeded so admirably in this matter of public interest" (Hawthorne's comment has the sound of Mumford's thesis) that "the merchants gruffly acknowledged his merits on 'Change.'" As in *The Scarlet Letter*, however, where Hawthorne observes that a man may talk openly and "still keep the inmost Me beyond its veil," so too in "The Artist of the Beautiful" he permits Owen, despite lower depths of agitation, to pretend that he's in full and open accord with the life of commerce he serves unstinting well. Simultaneously we are informed that this donkey work of the clocktower is not in Owen's style and won't last.

Suddenly an "innate tendency of his soul surfaces." Although the populace in general is delighted with his superintendency, with the soundness and regularity of affairs conducted under the shadow of the steeple or within audible range of the "iron accents of the church clock," he resigns the office. And in another dramatic shift of temper he wanders "like a child" chasing butterflies through wood and field. His wanderings, we soon learn, are not just aimless gambols of unfettered soul but include concentrated study. By day he roams observing botanical and zoological wonders of God's creation. And at night he sweats to invent a counterpart of those marvels, a replica which would coalesce nature and culture, body and spirit, earth and sky. Absorbed by this problem, by the "slow process of re-creating the one idea to which all his intellectual activity referred itself," he is interrupted one night by Annie Hovenden, his employer's daughter, whom he adores. When in sheer blunder of physical energy she puts a rough hand to his cunning machine, undoes "the toil of months and the thoughts of a lifetime" and displays a temperament far closer to Danforth's than his, her gross touch impels him to take another step in self-transformation, a step consistent with disillusion in love.

All during his period of apprenticeship Annie had served first as his mainspring and then as his muse. But because she too is infected by the temper of the times, he cannot in her name continue to conduct experiments and must supersede her claim on his devotion and transcend her hold on his art. Unable to dissolve in his mind's eye a vision of Annie Hovenden as the "visible shape" of the "spiritual power that he worshipped," he finds himself at an impasse of choice which he drenches in drink. Under a cloud of grief he "looked at the world through the golden haze of wine," a haze dispelled one day when the sight of a butterfly recalls him to himself, reminds him of his calling, and restores him to his bench. It is a short-lived restoration. And it ends when he hears of Annie's engagement to marry Danforth, ends when he drops and shatters still another "little system of machinery that had, anew, cost him months of thought and toil." Crushed by irrevocable proof that human love is irreconcilable with transcendent duty he falls once again into a condition of dysfunction, a state both more traumatic and ominous than heretofore. "It was as if the spirit had gone out of him, leaving the body to flourish in a sort of vegetable existence." Plump as an infant, he chatters about the occult. In his raving he confesses that from the outset he'd hoped to discover which proportions of matter and spirit would imbue his artifact with the semblance of life—that is, discover how to "spiritualize machinery."

Outgrowing babble and girth he decides to forgo once and for all the work of invention. "Now that I have acquired a little common sense, it makes me laugh to think" of all those schemes to merge a "new species of life and motion" with an "idea of Beauty which Nature has never taken pains to realize." But of course the laugh is on him. Somehow this man of the most uncommon sense imaginable in Hawthorne's world has groped his way through a maze of dissolutions and reconstitutions and arrived at the verge of mastery, plump with Art and Beauty. "Perhaps the torpid slumber was broken by convulsive pain," Hawthorne says, disclosing without equivocation at last what is on his mind, revealing the process which has brought Owen to term. Perhaps a birth pang awakened him. Maybe too it was another butterfly roused him, Hawthorne says, referring one final time to this "creature of the sunshine" that always had "a mysterious mission for the artist." Whatever the cause, lepidopteral or magical or mystical, Owen's keen again, ripe, overripe indeed and fearful that he may have waited too long, that he'll burst and die before the thing's done. That is to say, he intuits the final step of metamorphosis through which he must pass and frets lest that stage arrive too early and abort his labor.

But he does have time enough to fashion his masterpiece, "Nature's ideal butterfly," as a wedding gift for "the man of iron" and his bride, Danforth and Annie. Miraculously it flutters to the touch. "Is it alive?" "Alive. Yes, Annie; it may well be said to possess life, for it has absorbed my own being into itself," the "sensibility, the soul of an Artist of the Beautiful!" Hawthorne at *bel canto* on a favorite theme, conjunction of "ethereal" and "earthly" states of being in history, in society, in the life of creation. Not unlike Blake in advancing a notion of sacramental art in which the work of human imagination realizes work of God's invention, he was also like Emerson in cultivating an "imperial self." Insofar as he too sought to convert "earthly to spiritual gold," Hawthorne shared with Emerson and others an "exorbitant role" among writers who attempted to define national consciousness by removing "the task of self-validation within." Unlike his Concord neighbors, however, he did not undertake to gobble up the world, as Quentin Anderson observes, and restore it "as the Word."[27] Instead Hawthorne proposed a no less radical but rather more original venture. Justifiying the idea of vocation adopted by those American artists who in Anderson's view were convinced that their "fate was wholly bound up in the fate of the polity," crystallizing organic ideas of growth in national culture, Owen Warland in his own person duplicates, recapitulates, the process which brings the actual insect, the living thing, the real butterfly itself to life.

Treating mimicry as the sole method of attaining sublime art, correlating Owen's behavior with those flawlessly calibrated steps of metamorphosis, that unalterable sequence of stages which mark the development of a butterfly—imitating the Creator Who doesn't mint His marvel in a flash—Hawthorne conducts his hero through a series of organic changes no less marvelous than those which convey the lepidopteran from egg to larva to pupa to nymph, from imago back to fertilized egg.* The energy of transformation (whose gross external signs are exhibited first in Owen's state of funk, then in a spurt of diligence, next in a decline into torpor followed by a recrudescence of a zest which culminates in his finished thing), the consummate energy of creation, contained within the germ of lepidopteral art, fecundates the work of Owen's genius too. A man so monomaniacal that he "would turn the sun out of its orbit and derange the course of Time" if derangement of the solar system were needed to expose national disarray, Owen is anointed to reprove but not redeem a people reduced by blacksmith fire.

Forebodings of Ahab. Foreshadowings, too, in 1844 of Vladimir Nabokov's announcement in 1944 that mimesis is the ultimate attainment of style in the arts. Hawthorne's art does not of course relieve the Great Vladimir, Russian refractionist of American styles in fiction, of his laurels as our foremost entomologist of letters. Perfecting a literary theory which justified a lifetime of practice along lines which Hawthorne's intuition sought and found just once, Nabokov detected in the "cycle of insect metamorphosis" a "controlling metaphor for the process" of creation. "As

*Probably, too—unprovably perhaps—this process of organic change adumbrates the classic course of stages which constitutes the Puritan route to salvation: vocation with its piercing pain, contrition, justification, sanctification. "It might be fancied," Hawthorne notes, that the bright butterfly was indeed a "spirit commissioned to recall him to the pure ideal life."

in the scaling of insects the wonderful color effect may be due not to the pigment of the scales but to their position and refractive power," Nabokov said in his study of Gogol, so too in literature the most vivid effects are produced by almost intangible particles of recreated life."[28] And because Nabokov believed in unbreachable links between "butterflies and the central problems of nature," often "a moth or butterfly" will appear at "the end of a Nabokov novel when a cycle is complete."[29]

Coincidentally, in fortuitous concord with Nabokov's studies (which don't, so far as I know, include "The Artist of the Beautiful") Hawthorne's fiction condenses and consummates its meaning in an object craftily made to mimic resemblance and mirror mime. Rehearsing the cycle of Owen's hieratic career, this fantastical engine of auspice and augury is so pigmented as to increase or diminish in intensity within the ambience of those to whom it is drawn. Ostensibly a belated gift to the bride and groom, Annie and Danforth, in truth it's designed as reprobation of a post-Puritan people willing to squander virtue in the worship of force. Possessing refractive capacity identical to that of a live insect, color draining to dullness "in an atmosphere of doubt and mockery" but freshening to full radiance in an aura of humility and trust, Owen's masterwork confronts Baby Danforth. And in this climactic scene, converting a modest rite of benefaction into a ritual of divination, Hawthorne reminds his readers that the whole future of their society is concentrated in the hands of an infant prodigy whose own nature—crude spirit at odds with rude matter—personifies the state of national sensibility in this fearful time.

Exploiting this trope, the story presses its point home. Released from a jeweled case into the Danforth's house, place of forge and factory, Owen's flitting fragile profitless thing had dimmed on approach to Annie. Near the blacksmith, her husband, it had lost luster but retained the power of flight. On arriving in the space around her father, Peter Hovenden, it had grown pallid, almost powerless either to glitter ro fly. Finally tempted to alight on the child, "it alternately sparkled and grew dim" in puzzlement of refraction caused by an alternating flow of hospitality and hostility emanating from this American mutant, humanoid assuredly but unclassified still. Gauging the child's crosscurrents of character to represent fields of force both blessed and accursed, the butterfly tries to return to Warland but is stopped. "Thou has gone forth out of thy master's heart. There is no return to thee." Pronouncing this sentence, irreversible passage from heart to hand, from the hand of the maker to the hand of the taker, Owen knows that its final resting place must be the prehensile fist of this "little personage who had come so mysteriously out of the infinite, but with something so sturdy and real in his composition that he seemed moulded out of the densest substance which earth could supply." Both seraphic and fiendish in accord with Puritan discourse, at once naive and knowing, Baby Danforth is infected with his mother's milk by a contagion of greed. Indeed it's the grasping old watchmaker himself, Grandfather Hovenden, who is compressed into this "baby shape." No wonder that their darling "knows more of the mystery than we do," his mother says in unconscious parody of Romantic cliché. Spoken both in pride and self-burlesque, her vain words do indeed allude to a mystery which the reader understands must ever elude the likes of Annie Hovenden Danforth.

For what is in fact bespoken is nothing less than Hawthorne's hypertrophic sense of evil—on which, incidentally, Henry James's famed pronouncements are in nearly equal degree miraculously keen and curiously blunt. Although there's not a trace of cause to think that it was Owen Warland's situation James had in mind, the choicest part of James's conjecture can be legitimately read as a gloss of "The Artist of the Beautiful." In commentary just pointed enough to pierce the surface but not penetrate the heart of this particular text, James speaks of the "almost exclusively *imported* character of sin in Hawthorne's mind" (James's emphasis). It seems "to exist there merely for an artistic or literary purpose," he says, to be "played with," used "as a pigment." Maintaining that what pleased Hawthorne "in such subjects was their picturesequeness, their rich duskiness of colour, their chiaroscuro," James confessed himself charmed by the "brightness" of an irony not at all bitter or cynical or melancholy or even in the end "what I should call tragical."

Fair enough. That there's more than a jot of condescension, more than a touch of aspersion in James's tone is incontrovertible if we replace the word *tragical* with a word more consistent with James's gist: *serious*. Only a mind as playful as Hawthorne's (James implies) could survive, in connection with its "natural heritage," attachment so snug. "Looking into his soul," facing "the Puritan conscience," Hawthorne etablished and endured a relation which, "intellectual merely," was neither moral nor theological. One wonders why James persevered in behalf of this thought. Surely not to reinforce claims made in his name by Millicent Bell, in whose book on James and Edith Wharton we are told that "James's answer" to "The Artist of the Beautiful" is to be found in *The Ambassadors*. Counterbalancing Warland, "an artist who fashions his ideal only at the price of renouncing life," James positions Strether. A man of the sidelines, an observer, he discovers that "he, the contemplator" lived after all "as keenly as any of the others."[30]

Surely there's little cause or justification to entangle Warland and Strether in a forced alliance, a faked conflict of interest. For however arguable are the uses of Puritan conscience in "The Artist of the Beautiful," there's no mistaking the morality or history, theology or sociology implicit in the scene to which we return, that portentous scene in which Owen's butterfly approaches its nemesis, the Danforth child. "While it still hovered in the air, the little child of strength, with his grandsire's sharp and shrewd expression in his face, made a snatch at the marvelous insect and compressed it in his hand." Because he grabs, clenches, crushes the thing Hawthorne presents as a lodestone of national character, Owen's prodigious work betokens a tilt toward perdition in a society enthralled by power at the start of our materialist age.

As for its creator, he "looked placidly on what seemed the ruin of his life's labor, and which was no ruin." And there following Owen's gaze we discern the cast and color emitted by this pertinaciously Christian tale. Himself first of a long line of artists in America who bear witness to a delinquency of trust, a malefaction of duty in upholding the Idea of Errand, Owen is out of sync with a culture which is itself out of phase with its God. In that gesture of self-denial which ends the story, in tune with his genius and in touch with a Higher Will, Owen mutely condemns the sin, avarice, which fuels the energies and engines of progress. If as a people we inherit from our first forebears any prize worth possessing, it's the reputation earned, the example set not by willfulness but by self-sacrifice. Not an infernal and barbaric and brutal worship of power must animate the American people in the Age of Industry but the power of piety and love must possess them, veneration for the work of Providence. And if it happens that history, on arriving at modern times, manifests this work as a gift of technology, then that divine creative gift—itself given by God's grace—must be freely bestowed else it cannot advance and enlarge the life of civilization, humankind taken whole, and will instead enrich just the private hoards of shrewd and acquisitive Yankee businessmen, industrialists in embryo who sire oligarchs in utero. Should this occur, should the Danforths' man-gnome obliterate not just Owen's object but the play impulse too, source of Owen's genius, should Baby Danforth grow up with the country and take charge of its affairs, then Nature's organic plan of progress, the metamorphic cycle, must fail not prevail.

In stories of the smallest as well as the widest scope, therefore, writers of the first and second American generations selected for very close scrutiny a single and central and national event: dilemma of Revolution, conquest of wilderness, disaffection of technology. Supported by a species of "social Freudianism" in which "the childhood years of a nation's history" are thought to be "crucial for the formation of its character," writers associated the ordinary act of growing up with the extraordinary fact of American origins.[31] Correlating the origins and evolution of civilized order with the life cycle of this people, both Cooper and Irving exhibit a national will to penetrate the pith of personality in search of means to measure arcs of oscillation, dynamism to demonism, which enlivened the self and endangered the republic. At an early state of post colonial art they aligned the constitution of man with the Constitution of society in the New World.

And then, at still another moment of crisis in the history of national development, responding to the most solemn claims of citizenship and of conscience, Hawthorne too bore witness to a collision of energies of the most compromising kind. Memorializing this dilemma, a conflict of affinities in the American mind, he wed a theology of "The Beautiful" to an embryogenesis of art in the United States. Adopting the genre he most favored, romance, he set the scene for the form of drama he most prized, a theater of irony not tragedy. And in a rhetoric more wintry than derisive he deplored but didn't damn the judgment of a people who chafed for Urizen's rule and were therefore slated for drudgery as victims of "technology and complex machinery" according to the cycle Blake construed. Like the far more histrionic Henry Adams, a satirist who in later years would arrive at Hawthorne's theater and share its platform, he scoffed at all forms of apostasy, heresy in all its works and ways. Above all it was the apostasy of progress he censured. What Hawthorne was disposed to renounce, however, Adams was determined to despise. What Hawthorne perceived as a delinquescence of spirit Adams, a half-century nearer our time, regarded as a defilement of ancestral writ, of holy law. Insinuating the science of thermodynamics into the myth of mission, Adams contended that progress expedited the cause of chaos everywhere. Transfixed by the Idea of Entropy (a "net increase in the disorder of the universe"),[32] inventing a vast new apparatus of myth, Adams spent the best years of his life proving that this Danforthian society was fated to rush the rate of decay throughout the world. What Hawthorne's fiction foreshadowed, therefore, in Adams's distempered mind came to seem foreordained: a view of history in which "All begins with A," said D. H. Lawrence, spraying Hawthorne with venomous words. "Adulteress. Alpha. Abel. Adam. A. America."

Without venom but pervaded by what Melville called "this black conceit," it was no "blue-eyed darling of a Nathaniel" who testified to the debasement of American men of iron, Puritan and post-Puritan alike.[33] Abandoned by Providence, they abased themselves at the altar of Progress and thereby forswore, probably forever, the duty to install and preserve organic civilization on God's lovely earth.

III

Abandoned in Providence

Harriet Beecher Stowe, Howells, Henry James

A 15-year-old girl with a rich father, a mother from a wealthy family and a cattle rancher uncle worth $7 million is costing Rhode Island $59 a day as a ward of the state. . . .

The girl lived with her natural parents for her first two years. After the parents were divorced in 1959, the mother was given custody of the girl, took her to Texas and remarried in 1960.

In 1965, her stepfather adopted her. When that marriage broke up in 1969, the girl was placed in the custody of her mother's parents in Connecticut.

Assorted troubles ensued and since that time the girl has lived in eight places, with varying people, for periods ranging from a week to a year.

Just before becoming a ward of the state last July, the girl lived in Rhode Island with her natural father and his second wife. They eventually brought her to a hospital in Providence.

—"A Ward of the State Has Rich Family," *New York Times*, February 24, 1973

THAT AMERICAN WRITERS HAVE often been drawn to the figure of the child, Tony Tanner remarks, "is scarcely a new observation."[1] That Baby Danforth's will to power augurs ill for future generations is rarely deemed to be more than a small twist of plot in a minor tale; nugatory. That Hawthorne's parable raises hard questions bearing on an antinomy of character and purpose in American culture at an axial moment in its history is usually unrecognized. But in introducing an idea of dynasty, a family which pairs naivete and cunning, diabolic energy and epic force, and then placing the Hovenden–Danforth household within the shadow of that church steeple, Hawthorne prepared the way of a subject which has turned out to be perhaps the most poignant and grave in our literature.

Melodramatic though my epigraph may be, the matter it calls attention to, a disreputable condition of family and child and dwelling, first moved to the forefront of literature during the period of Civil War. It may be the unavoidable lot of children everywhere to be indulged and neglected, pampered rather than truly loved. But in fiction written during those decades which preceded and followed war, an interregnum of Providence and a consolidation of the forces of progress, writers were drawn to children whose genealogy is in doubt or whose lineage is cloudy. Not just in the pop art of sentimental novels but in far more appreciable fare as well, fiction is preoccupied with young people whose connection to real or surrogate parents is based not on natural bonds but on diverse sorts of unnatural bondage.

What a morass of contradiction! Victorian America, reputed to be a high holy time of rectitude and righteousness turns out to be the original age of the fractured home. This is not to say that the institution of the family in those decades suffered trauma beyond repair. It's rather to note that the sudden crush of waifs and wards and foundlings, though perhaps new in American letters a century ago, was by no means unprecedented in our national history of hearth and home. Seizing on two causes of perturbation which predate the colonial era, a frailty of framework both in the composition of families and the articulation of houses, writers exploited a recurring anxiety to specially fearful effect. Documenting an era in which the United States was perceived to be less a fostering than a festering state, pariahs both black and white, outcasts, bastards, orphans turn up as victims for sacrifice. And an intermingled hope and despair of the American experiment, along with a well-entrenched habit of ascribing disasters of national order to irregularities of national origin, conspire to form a typology of the betrayed child.

"Insofar as legitimacy is a psychological phenomenon," Milton Kammen observes in *People of Paradox* (1972), "a particular set of institutions" are presumed to be "appropriate for a certain society." But no such match of home and homeland authenticate the behavior and goals of a people who constantly encroached on Indian lands, whose Constitution had no sanction either in divine or civil law, whose righteous fervor of self-justification clashed with a perfervid guilt of reprobation in all spheres of social policy. Why such large eighteenth-century questions of "social legitimacy" should have also affected the conduct of life at "the most literal levels, such as marriage and the family," is perhaps explained by an unusual fact of American social history. Among a people already nervous about an exceedingly high number of "clandestine and common law marriages," just the mere belief "in rising illegitimacy caused social and psychological repercussions" enough to unsettle a society in troubled quest for bona fides.[2] Abashed by the epigram which said that the most visible effects of religious revival were literary and erotic, this novice nation was represented in a burst of books about bastards both literal and figurative.

It also found itself very early on portrayed in novels in which a disquiet of family is centered is inextricable from a style of architecture which has habitually represented the American dilemma in its starkest form. Beginning with those first struggling outposts "isolated at the very edge of the Atlantic world" and later, in the course of development, set down at one or another edge of place, this "immigrant society, marked by fragile family life, a shortage of women, and a high death rate," invented an American species of homestead jerry-built for the short term. It was of course true, as Cooper noted in *Home As Found* (1838), that "the materials, the climate, the uses of America" did not provide for harmonies and symmetries in the Palladian mode.[3] But this hardly explains why, throughout Maryland and Virginia, Madison's sort of abode failed to displace lodgings of the most "primitive and temporary kind." Containing "no more than four rooms, two up and two down—built not on a permanent foundation but on wooden posts driven at intervals into the ground," the house "usually rotted away in twenty or thirty years." Precisely because this was typical construction "even for people who could afford better," we're told by the Director of the Institute of Early American History and Culture, the trope of a "tottering habitation" must in fact mirror a state of mind that is somehow not accounted for by simple economic hardship.[4]

However improbable, the fact is that a mirror of sorts and an accounting are to be found near the end of the century in Henry Adams's meditations on the flying buttress, found in that famed last paragraph of *Mont-Saint-Michel and Chartres* (1904). For on trailing this much-traveled man in his ascent up that Norman redoubt, we're startled to realize that his pilgrimage there included an approach to America too. In order to understand what this "mass of encrusted architecture" meant to its builders in the Middle Ages, Adams insists that we observe how closely the Norman shore "facing us, recalls the coast of New England. The relation between the granite of the one coast and that of the other may be fanciful, but the relation between the people who live on each is as hard and practical a fact as the granite itself." Implicating both the medieval and the American adventure in a symbolism of stone, veiling his vision in a figure of speech that unites granite of coast and granite of culture, he fixed his eye on the overarching shape of a flying buttress. Certain that its function was not intended to solve complicated problems of architecture, Adams wondered what other kinds of need were answered by this fabled device of medieval art. "The equilibrium is visibly delicate beyond the line of safety," he says, almost as if he held in view an American not a French artifact. "Danger lurks in every stone." Concluding a book plainly intended to advance ideas that go beyond a passion for churches, musing on danger and meditating on need, he claimed to resolve his dilemma by following the buttress in its "leap downwards," a plunge in which he saw a "visible effort to throw off a visible strain" of faith. And though the cathedral itself monumentalized the rapture of human aspiration "flung to the sky," nonetheless the buttress in its downward arc buried in the earth "as its last secret" the "pathos of its self-distrust and anguish of doubt."[5]

Deciding that strain was a fundamental feature of structure in France four centuries before his time, Adams succeeded in clarifying the nature of stress in his own society before, during, and after his own lifetime. And a book in which the cathedral in Normandy and the cathedral in Chartres are treated as seats of Family—a book which teasingly pretends that an American reader and writer cannot any longer stand in the historic relationship of "son and father but only of uncle and niece" (since "nephews no longer read at all")—Adams once again contrived to equate his own spiritual life with the moral life of his nation. Not by means of chitchat about Uncle Henry and a phalanx of nieces is this accomplished. But by means of what R. P. Blackmur calls a rehearsal of "spiritual autobiography," a tune-up for *The Education of Henry Adams*, did Adams prepare to instruct multitudes of American readers and writers in self-distrust and anguish of doubt. "You can make out of it whatever else pleases your youth and confidence," he concluded *Mont-Saint-Michel and Chartres*: "To me this is all."

Without question therefore Adams's symbol of the flying buttress must be set alongside similar images of structure with which generations of writers have portrayed American states of equilibrium as similarly delicate and invariably perilous. Beginning with the text in which Madison bid his countrymen to erect a home that would contain the idea of experiment, would domesticate risk and accommodate peril and disarm distrust of the American Idea, danger has lurked in every stick and stone. From *Uncle Tom's Cabin* to George Washington Cable's Belles Demoiselles Plantation; from Hawthorne's legendary house ("emblem of aristocratic pomp and democratic institutions") in Salem to James's manor house, Bly, in Essex; from the house of Usher to the professor's house in Willa Cather's novel; from Pap's shack and the Phelps's farmhouse in *Huck Finn* all the way down to

Faulkner's Yoknapatawpha, a landscape of Sutpen, Compson, and Burden: for two hundred years the misfeasance of a people torn between glory of faith in and distrust of their power to fulfill the aims of Providence or control the energies of progress has been presented as a misprision of family.[6] In contrast to the English novel, which usually "revolves about great houses and conjures with the perquisites of a settled order,"[7] American novels concentrate the pressure of large events on disorganized groups of ordinary people whose vulnerability to ruin is the real property of lives set down in shelters built askew, oriented wrong for wind and weather. Even our skyscrapers, always going up and coming down, the English see as exhibiting our "science of invention" both to fair ends and foul, see as forming our landscape of adventure. There's a "terrible truth in this American fable," says a fabulist of high interest, Edward Dahlberg, "every discoverer we have had has been a wild homesteader among the seers of the world. Melville, Thoreau, Parkman, Prescott, and [William Carlos] Williams are all river and sea and plateau geniuses, ranging a continent for a house and all of them outdoors."[8]

The structure of stress it is that our buildings enshrine, the unsettled state of a society at once sympathetic to human need and hostile. Most strikingly too, as I'm now prepared to argue, this paradox of hospitality surfaces as a formal element of composition in those novels in which a mismanagement or mystification of plot itself serves to substantiate a text. No wonder, then, that Melville's notion of "careful disorderliness" has turned out to be the method best suited to write a quintessentially American book.

Let us consider two writers seldom read in concert, Harriet Beecher Stowe and William Dean Howells. In turning to Stowe, however, we must avoid most of the usual reasons given for studying *Uncle Tom's Cabin* and instead reach deep inside this unparalleled tale for nuance of disclosure it is not conventionally thought to possess. It's indisputable that this motherless, religiose daughter of Lyman Beecher, following forty years' subservience both to her father and her husband, in a shriek of horror did indeed write her own emancipation proclamation. But it is unarguable too that a distraught woman whose crisis of middle age coincided with American crisis at midcentury did somehow contrive to manifest distemper not in her private life alone but in society as well. And it's a writer of the most consequential kind who had daring enough to allow an anonymous character, the sodden alcoholic slave Prue, a figure without serious bearing on Stowe's private life (a sphere biographers ransack for clues to her messianic art and evangelic Christianity), to voice the writer's own despair, to pronounce an abandonment of hope in America.

If therefore Harriet Beecher Stowe cannot be dismissed as an "unremarkable purveyor of Sunday-school fiction," neither is she to be taken at her word. Recorder of God's dictation, she believed herself to be chosen by the Lord to express His outrage with the United States of America, to convey a Jehovan threat of justice in a society befouled by usurpation and misuse of power. And if she is unkindly judged by those who say that this sloppy sprawl and sport of a book written with a "ready command of broadly conceived melodrama, humor and pathos" barely receives passing marks, she's ill served by advocates who award her high grades for having woven a dense fabric of family, Northern and Southern, informal and formal, found at home or on the road, housed in comfort or at hazard in establishments running from ramshackle to Palladian.[9] In spite of dogged work on both sides, the one that unites architecture and action and the one that stifles the thought of a controlling image of any kind whatever, neither side masters the novel. Given so closed a circle of persons and places, so homely an emblem and demotic a theme, who would not welcome an argument which proved unwaveringly the case for equivalence between subject and symbol? But *Uncle Tom's Cabin*, a work both extraterrestrial and subterranean, a book whose angles and seams and joints don't marry, nevertheless holds together. And because what holds it holds us, Stowe cannot be faulted but must be applauded for a fiction which proposes but fails to merge home and family, which coordinates but fails to fuse derangements of marriage with the disarray of a people callous to the rule of decency governing right order in any Christian state. With God's help surely she could have devised a plot less slack. Even without His help she could have managed to write, and later did manage to write, suitably capacious and considerably better-crafted work. It is after all a truism that the most solvable of problems in nineteenth-century fiction was how to tell a tight tale. Scribblers to formula, moralists all, allegorists beyond count, didacts to the end, popular writers were immunized against bad form by a common code.

Crudeness of composition, then, a distinctive trait of Stowe's art, is exaggerated in writing which treats one or another variation of her general theme. Misgovernment is her special subject. And misgovernment in America she presents as abuse of family by heads of household and of state. Selecting two New England brothers who serve to condense the range but not dilute the gall of conflict, she presents both as equally "upright, energetic, noble-minded," of "iron will." Whereas one brother had "settled down in New England to rule over rocks and stones, and to force an existence out of Nature," the other had "settled in Louisiana to rule over men and women, and force an existence out of them." The Northern brother had shared in the truest benefits of nineteenth-century Anglo-Saxon vitality, the mechanization of force. But the one in the South, in frightful Dixie transmogrification of Yankee will, had developed a cursed scheme which treated slaves themselves as interchangeable parts.[10] "They're all labor-saving machines themselves, every one of 'em," says George Harris's owner.

No wonder at all that direst instability threatened a civilization which transformed the dominant trait of American virtue—energy—into unregenerate vice. Political ruin must await an improvident people that degraded the management of national affairs by relying on a dehumanized economy, a barbarism of mass production. If government in America so waywardly abandons God's trust, then governors North and South dispel any last shred of a claim to legitimacy. Identifying the dangers that follow from a violation of the twin mandates of Providence and progress, staged in domiciles twisted in the beam or afloat or asway, *Uncle Tom's Cabin* just barely hangs together. There is in truth no right way it can hang, no way it can hang right—mismanagement of plot being in fact unavoidable whenever convolution of form, that most intractable trait of our literature, is at stake in a story. Its fable doesn't boil down to or translate into a moral—subvert the family, pervert the polis—but instead exhibits a Hawthornian revulsion from but not repudiation of countrymen who permitted their common estate to fall into a condition of dilapidation nearly surpassing the imagination of repair.

For it's not at all the thrill of Gothic which lures our writers to cement vipers of spirit and flesh in a dank masonry fundamentally flawed. And although English novels which feature houses tend to spy out perversity, what few disclosures of that sort are offered in American books implicate national traits far more unsettling than private intimacy no matter how lurid. Race or no race, therefore, *Uncle Tom's Cabin* is a primer, a primary text in a long history of books irremediably off-center but central—like *The Rise of Silas Lapham*, in which Howells revealed himself to be the very soul of contrariety both as a man of letters and a man of his time. Indeed, precisely because Howells is himself denied a fixed place in the history of American writing he acquires special value as an agonist, an arresting case study of resolve and irresolution in the era of progress. And *Lapham*, foremost among nineteenth-century fictions which fail to survive modern times, is the exemplary work of a writer whose very seepage of reputation is best construed as a manifestation of a certain kind of merit. Having tantalized many generations of critics who tried to explain why it is scarred by visible flaws of construction, *Lapham* is defended today by a determined battery of scholars who persist in trying to prove that Howells, in developing much of the action around Silas's Beacon Street house, triumphantly fused the symbol of a dwelling to the history of its family. A main result of their barrage of books is not the rescue of Howells but the obliteration of *Lapham*. The one novel in American literature impaled on two opposing points of view, it has been alternately condemned and celebrated by Howell's most devoted adherent, Edwin A. Cady, who in 1948 admired Howells's extraordinary range as an editor, critic, and novelist but confessed that no one of his fictions was first-rate. "Even in *The Rise of Silas Lapham* where parallel plots are more firmly joined" than in *A Modern Instance*—Howells's first effort to make a major novel—"one sometimes has the feeling of watching two simultaneous tennis matches on neighboring courts." These gradually merge as "Silas's business problems and the Lapham-Corey romance gradually blend. Defensible if sometimes dizzying as that is, what shall we do with the hiatus devoted to the building of Silas's house?"

By 1958, after two volumes of biography which brought to an end eight years of study, Cady decided that the structure of *Lapham* presents problems only to the rude not the keen mind. The origins of our modern age, 1870s and 1880s, coincide with the time Howells himself came to maturity. Eager to record the effects on democratic society of an unequal distribution of wealth and opportunity, in *Lapham* he recreated the process whereby decent people, the privileged classes, permitted the control of culture to pass to indecent people, the barbarians of business. Among the many aims of this novel is a portrayal of the ways each of the Laphams resists one or another kind of blandishment. Irene rebels against the cliché of innocent genteel American girlhood; Mrs. Lapham purges herself of cheap ambition; Silas of course in the end refuses to pay the cost of fortune; and Penelope rejects the attractions of a purity so exacting it would immobilize not enliven her virtue. Observing these acts of decency, we know that our civilization will continue to flourish even among men reared to cherish the gospel of cash, among women intimidated by the cult of conscience. "*The Rise of Silas Lapham* is the testament of a realist who wishes his readers to see directly the moral confusion into which the new times have fallen." Observing too that this "drama of the moral imagination" is performed in a succession of homes (the Lapham farmhouse in Vermont, the house on Nankeen Square, the house on Beacon Street, the Corey house), Cady decided that the novel, properly read, was itself a great edifice erected on plots broad enough to accommodate all Howells's projects and people.[11] Devised according to a tongue and groove of the imagination, *Lapham* is built to the scale of the culture it is supposed to symbolize. Big and roomy.

Surely the novel is made to stand so. Clearly Howells planned to achieve this kind of confluence and effect. For Silas himself says that his first wrong act of business, the Rogers affair, is best conceived as the first brick in a row of bricks which tumble one after another. "It wasn't in the nature of things that they could be stopped till the last brick went." But no one has managed to say precisely how Howells's art itself manifests the design of national life in the Gilded Age. Instead, having contracted to show why *Lapham* is a sturdy novel, scholars industriously modify the novelist's plans a little. Refurbished here and there, in their hands, *Lapham* becomes a palatial book written by a prince of a man. Monumental in the life of its creator, it must be restored, they believe, to a capital place in the life of letters. I exaggerate a little. But I must underline the fact that nobody has contrived to show how each of its components—the scene of drunkenness, the coincidences of love and discontinuities of time, the hokey business of Zerilla—merge in faultless or even formidable unison.

Despite decades of sustained and zealous work Howells's standing remains low. For all his skill, *Lapham* is indisputably diffuse—though not, as H. L. Mencken said of Howells's writing in general, hollow. Even in his heyday, when his personal brand of plainness of speech and murkiness of motive both pleased and perplexed his immense public, the strain shows. For deep down he was unconvinced by the system of ideas to which presumably he'd given his official assent. Struggling to prove that his countrymen were heirs to an American constitution vital and stable enough to survive any threat of bankruptcy, he believed neither in the future of American illusions nor in the power of ordinary people to reclaim government from the control of plutocrats. Nor did he put much stock in alliances between old family and new money. The public person, the man who'd come from an Ohio boyhood to the first presidency of the American Academy of Arts and Letters, had started as a printer's devil, autodidact of languages and literature, and ended with offers of professorships at Johns Hopkins and Harvard and Yale. From *My Year in a Log Cabin* to *The Rise of Silas Lapham*, this Horatio Alger of American letters had fashioned a career solider than any one of his plots. And although the career itself was no illusion, what principles of social or political or moral or historic or ideologic order did it embody?

This question, rooted deep in his own life, he hoped to resolve in his work. The more closely we study the rise of William Dean Howells, the more obvious it is that the man, unlike the character Silas, could not decide where to live or what to live for. I introduce the echo of *Walden* because I suspect that Howells, despite the year in the log cabin, throughout his life was obsessed by Thoreau's questions. We know that he was plagued by episodes of personal stress, of distress seeing the sorrows of friends and countrymen whose virtue should have been rewarded but was instead punished. Knowing that Howells was periodically distraught because he could neither accept Thoreau's admonitions nor assent to Alger's creed, we are led back to *Lapham*. There, no single house, no cluster of homes symbolizes the drama as a whole. What is symbolized is the dislocation of a homely Midwestern boy who had made an elegant Eastern marriage to Eleanor Mead—herself, coincidentally, the sister of William Rutherford Mead, leading partner in the architectural firm McKim, Mead and White, famed for having established the fashion of grandeur along Fifth Avenue and elsewhere in New York City. In 1877, seven years before *Lapham* appeared, Howells's brother-in-law built him a house outside Boston, in Belmont, about which Henry James's father said he had never seen a place that "took my fancy more captive."

In Howells's own fancy it was merely another in a succession of dwelling places in which he never felt thoroughly at home. Like Mark Twain always an outsider, Howells lived in almost permanent discomfort everywhere. But it wasn't in fact Mark Twain whom he chose to model himself on. Rather it was the great outsider himself, Thoreau, whom Howells on his first Eastern visit had come to see and to "revere," whose example Howells could not bring himself to follow. Although it was Thoreau's views on the abolitionist John Brown that Howells had originally prized, what stayed with him, what he hoped to register in his own work was the elder man's clear vision of "the falsity and folly of society." Deriving from this vision a permanent lesson both in morals and mathematics, applying this lesson to Silas's house, Howells computed its costs of construction according to Thoreau's arithmetic. For the cost of anything, it was said in *Walden*—a computation less famed in Howells's day than in our own time—is "the amount of what I will call life which is required to be exchanged for it, immediately or in the long run." Although Howells permitted Silas to decide that the cost of his mansion demanded life in amounts he was unprepared to pay, Howells himself was unable to resist doing precisely what Thoreau condemned. Unable either to renounce or remodel the breakaway house of capitalist culture, he was as a result incapable of composing a literary work tight from subcellar to attic. "When I consider how our houses are built and paid for," said Thoreau, unremitting in contempt, "I wonder that the floor does not give way under the visitor."

When we consider how Howells's houses were built and paid for, there's small cause to wonder why *Lapham* cannot merge those two opposed lines of action Thoreau selected for praise and blame. Because most men undertake to erect "for this world a family mansion and for the next a family tomb," the "best works of art are the expression of man's struggle to free himself" from a debased joy in monuments. But the chief effect of American writing in this epoch of getting on, of boom and crash, is "merely to make this low state comfortable." Howells in his own person, good and decent man that he was, settled uncomfortably into a low state of high luxury of the sort to which New York became accustomed in the heyday of Beaux-Arts, the period from 1885 to 1910 when McKim, Mead and White designed and built the Metropolitan and Harmonie clubs on East 60th Street, the University Club on West 54th Street, the Racquet and Tennis Club on Park Avenue and above all the Henry Villard Houses on Madison. It was furthermore a legacy transmitted from uncle through father to son, from William Rutherford Mead through William Dean to John Mead Howells, who in 1927 designed the Panhellenic Hotel, "one of the city's most forward-looking skyscrapers of its time."[12] Hard and authentic though Howells's personal struggle was, therefore, he reserved for imaginary figures like Silas a triumph rather than a failure of self-emancipation. Although he was himself satisfied to hold out for socialism, in Silas's behalf he orchestrated a crash of fortune. A fire which consumed the townhouse freed Silas, money gone and place wiped out, to rise from the ashes cleansed of rubble, detritus of the Gilded Age, inheritor of Thoreau's estate preserved even in industrial society.

Howells imagined, I think, that he had learned from Thoreau how to make a pure American work of high art. But Thoreau's myth, manifest in that ugly one-man cabin—Thoreau's simplicity was not Howells's style. Given the rapture of that adoring audience which "hung on every issue of the splendid and fortunate magazine," *Century*, in which *Lapham* was first serialized, we can be certain its effect was both to discredit and to consecrate a national delight in mansions and monuments. Indeed, it must be said in appreciation of William Dean Howells that for all his talk about conscience and honor and purity, impurity constitutes the very soul of his art. Long ago in a semi-psychoanalytic essay on his women characters I sought to show that with one exception—Margaret Vance in *A Hazard of New Fortunes*—all are portrayed not as *jeunes filles* without blemish but as tainted angels.[13] What I did not then recognize was the degree of harmony between Howells's imagination and American life, between biloquism and American doubletalk. Cabins and castles, cabins built of scrap timber and scrounged stone, castles in Carrara marble designed by Stanford White: Howells's landscape, inhabited by saints and sinners, cheek by jowl, not only encloses the American scene in his own day but strikingly anticipates a leading school of social theory today.

One of its most famed theorists, the architect Robert Venturi, is a builder whose work is intentionally made to appear both at one and at odds with the American scene. "Ordinary and extraordinary at the same time," his noted beach house in New Jersey is said to be. "Like the landscape and not like the landscape, ugly and beautiful," it specifies a tension between opposites inherent in culture and, as Venturi maintained in *Complexity and Contradiction in Architecture* (1966), addresses radical questions which antedate modern times but which are pronounced in the disagreeable environments of our day.[14] Elevating disorder into a principle of composition, cementing irony into structure, Venturi, his wife Denise Scott, and associate Steven Izenour in a lavishly made essay called *Learning from Las Vegas* (1972) advance a "counter-revolutionary" view of design derived from the shape of urban sprawl. If the Venturis were to design a Holiday Inn "whatever emotions Holiday Inns are supposed to stir would be stirred." But because their work expresses an Americanist ideology of "messy vitality" rather than "obvious unity," their Inn would "turn things upside down or sideways." In execution of a principle which another designer in a similar vein, John Wines, calls "de-architecture," this style of construction undertakes to "embrace a series of conflicting issues" in the form of "questions not answers," aims in truth to erect an architecture which embodies social and structural "tentativeness and instability."[15] Unsurpassed in Nevada, borrowed for and adapted to California and Texas, American taste is fluorescent in a strip which looks like chaos but is in fact itself a comment on the look of chaos.

Architecturally à la mode perhaps, Venturi's twist of mind would be merely chic if an imperfect unity of urban and architectural forms had not been foreshadowed in *The Federalist Papers* and prefigured by discontinuities of plot, disjunction of pattern, disruption of person in classic American books. Consider, in this connection, the contrasting example of Edith Wharton. Her "addiction" both to houses and "the arrangement of rooms within houses," R. W. B. Lewis observes, to "the make-up of properly designed gardens," provided a chief source of "metaphor in her fiction" as well as the theme of two notable essays in social history, *The Decoration of Houses* (1897) and *Italian Villas and Their Gardens* (1903). Nonfiction studies of palaces and settings, of public places and municipal sites in the Old World, both books display Wharton's delight in formal European clusters of enclosure in contrast to her discomfort on contemplating the democratic vista of "unbound space." Like many others who transplanted themselves abroad at that turn of century she found herself blooming there and withering here. At home everywhere in Europe, in London and Paris and Florence, but lost amid her proper haunts, Old New York and Old Newport and Lenox, in 1903 she confessed herself to be quite "out of sympathy with everything" in the United States: streets, sounds, voices, the whole "wild dishevelled backwards look of everything" American.[16]

What Wharton saw as the look of dishevelment was but an aspect of "Dynamic Symmetry," said a disciple of the pioneer designer Louis Sullivan, Claude Bragdon, describing his railroad terminal in Rochester, New York, begun six years later.[17]

What folly it is in advocacy of *The Rise of Silas Lapham* to insist that a full inventory of its bits and pieces must finally prove it to be faultlessly made. Written as if to comply with a major motif of analysis in current architectural talk (post-modern buildings should pull together different kinds of meaning and establish a "discourse between different and opposed" tastes, purposes, images), Howells's novel is subsumed under Charles Jencks's influential theory, "Radical Eclecticism," of design today. A building should be both "contextual and dialectic," Jencks argues in *The Language of Post-Modern Architecture* (1977), so that it can be "read on at least two distinct levels" as "telling parallel stories which may or may not be inconsistent" but which "work together in deepest combination." Had Jencks wanted literary testimony there's no document that could have served his purposes better than *The Rise of Silas Lapham*. For in housing a drama of collapse and continuity in the age of expansion, Howells's fiction bears witness to the rise of alienation, of an Adamsesque anguish and doubt, in the land of opportunity. And though Howells in *Lapham* didn't in the least aspire to write a fiction which conformed either to Jencks's theory or Randall Jarrell's definition—a novel is "a prose work of some length that has something wrong with it"—invariably his best work goes wrong exactly the right way. In this work, therefore, where weakness of structure is decidedly a cause of strength, he achieved a triumph of misalignment. As a result the final effect of his disjointed tale, not its aim but its attainment, is to assay and appreciate the high cost of junk.

Although Howells's decay of reputation is ordinarily not seen as a sign of merit, we do in fact learn from *Lapham* a lesson similar to Jencks's and Venturi's. As a result we're better equipped to appraise the uses of misconstruction in the endings of two books by writers who flank Howells, Stowe and Mark Twain. Those ill-made final scenes of *Huck Finn*, historic examples of labored art, of platform comedy that fakes an upbeat climax to a story which runs downhill when everyone gathers downriver at the Phelps farm, this convulsion of narrative does not exhibit a special case of personality, Sam Clemens at odds with himself. Rather it illustrates a general rule of household art in the later nineteenth century. It's not just Tom Sawyer's high jinks of rescue which degrade Jim, demean Huck, and embarrass us all. And it's surely not just the flop of parody, of burlesque with which Mark Twain hoped to defuse the ferocity of a people who in 1882 and 1883, the year before his book appeared, conducted or assisted at 248 lynchings.[18]

Neither does the joke which opens his romance (the "Notice" which threatens persecution, banishment, and execution to anyone who attempts to find a motive or moral or plot) nor the solemnity of Tom's mischief which closes it, the bitter playfulness of a respectable boy with a place in the world and a character to lose—nothing justifies the hysteric invention which shapes the end of the story.

Nor is it Mark Twain's want of dexterity that mars the finale of this book. Rather his failure was preordained once he chose to ally his plan for an ending with the creed which underlay Tom's fancy. Having stolen a manumitted slave out of slavery, having been fortuitously caught in the act and proved beyond cavil that Jim's not just legally free but is "white inside," Tom had expected to confirm the inevitable victory of American optimism, of human enlightenment, in resolving the issue of slavery at last. The certainty of betterment, so Mark Twain professed to affirm, was invincible at the Phelps farm, seat of American civility. Bedrock. What is resolved, however, is Jim's fate alone. For, as Mark Twain knew, at bottom it's the institution of slavery and the Idea of Progress that were at odds. As if gripped by forces outside any writer's control, therefore, once he turned his characters homeward he found himself unable to avoid perils both technical, the shredding of a plot, and ideological, a covert uncertainty of belief in the energies of enlightenment, in the American notion that the world will be redeemed when a formula for progress was assured. Although Tom's antic formula does—barely—work down on the farm, *Huck Finn* envisions no ampler scale of salvation. Indeed, in its final stages this epic story draws on Mark Twain's own anguish of distrust of those home folks who compel Huck and Jim to spend a major portion of their time hiding in corners which provide the merest semblance of refuge.

Refusing Aunt Sally's offer and uttering the famed words that close the book, Huck doesn't at all refer to the trivial matter of clean hands at table, as Mark Twain's fooling is supposed to suggest. What the words insinuate the tone belies and we end knowing that not all the waters in the Mississippi River can wash American hands clean. Aunt Sally's proposal, adoption of Huck and provision of a place in Tom's world, wouldn't legitimize him but would in fact subject him to the legal force of illegitimate law. In a society where inversion of justice controls the rule of law and a reversal of morals molds human conduct, oxymoron is true vernacular speech. The precise form of disclosure Hawthorne favored, oxymoron was indeed the mother tongue of this old "Youth" (Mrs. Clemens' pet name for her husband) whose portrayal of American character hinged on the behavior of a pair of opposites, Tom and Huck, the one madcap for rules and regulations and the other an outcast ruled by criminal virtue. Impersonating each other, exchanging names in the zany game that closes the story, each boy in his own being embodies contradiction. "Notice" or no, then, Mark Twain notified the world that he had a "lessen up his slave," as Berryman says in the *Dream Songs*, a moral in tow. For when the figure of concord is manic in energy and the figure of discord is restrained by vows sterner than any magistrature, surely there's crisis at hand and no assurance that this people of paradox, attempting to hold in mind two opposed ideas, would retain wit enough and skill enough to pull through.

"There's no doubt that our system is a difficult one to train children under," St. Clair says in *Uncle Tom's Cabin*. And though it's a "too-free scope of the passions" under a hot sun in a slave state he's alluding to, it's no mere misadventure of lust but the "betrayal of good faith and the taking away of trust and love" we find uppermost in Stowe's mind. "If ever I was conscious of an attack of the Devil trying to separate me from the love of Christ," she said, it was in the days after hearing word of her son's death by drowning. Satanism of social force, then, not mere "baffled mother love" as Leslie Fiedler insisted, is evoked by those multitudinous "scenes of separated families" which run through the novel. In these scenes it was Stowe's intent, Fiedler argued, to manipulate her "bourgeois readers" into condemning slavery not on humanitarian or constitutional grounds but on a parochial ground he particularly despises, as an "offense against the sacred family and the suffering mother."[19]

In fact, however, there's evidence to spare in support of a rhetoric which maneuvers readers into a position intrinsically political. Because the cohesiveness of family depends upon the adhesiveness of society rather than the other way round, a system that pulls people apart must tear itself to pieces. Treating slavery as an abomination so evil its measure cannot properly be taken in a work of fiction, Stowe rises to the occasion by unmasking the family itself as a creature of state, a Satanic agent of defilement. And though she herself hoped against hope that a house divided might withstand collapse her audience, reading this demented story about deformed families and lopsided houses, knew that the structure would be scrapped not salvaged. Even though she struggled to convince her readers that their union, during these last moments before a "final convulsion"—not Civil War, Apocalypse—might reconstruct and stabilize itself anew, neither she nor anyone else believed that a place so far out of kilter, a place denied God's buttress, the despoiled American tabernacle would continue to stand.[20]

Within our nineteenth-century canon of letters, *Uncle Tom's Cabin* is in a class apart, a category of one. But the text that most audaciously introduces disequilibrium into the very soul of family is of course *The Turn of the Screw* (1898), a tale in which danger does literally and incontrovertibly lurk in every stone. And because it is an especially complex ghost story; that is, a fiction in which structure itself is a subject of consuming interest, no inquiry into the art of Henry James's narrative can fail to take into account his brother William's zeal to authenticate experience of this kind. For Henry's unique achievement is in having discovered, by way of William's researches, a way of flummoxing a plot which would avoid evident defects in his brother's position and yet preserve certain aims both men held in common. In that the "totality of truth," William wrote in an essay called "What Psychical Research Has Accomplished" (1896), will elude human comprehension so long as "the scientific-academic mind and the feminine-hysterical mind shy from each other's facts," the goal of The Society for Psychical Research is to being "science and the occult together in England and America." By far the largest number of facts to be assembled by science in confirmation of mystical experience concern "seven hundred cases of apparition" in which the appearance of ghosts coincided "with some calamity happening to the person who appeared." According to the best explanation available, William continued, anticipating Henry's habit of conjunction, "the mind of the person undergoing the calamity was at that moment able to impress the mind of the percipient with an hallucination."[21]

Unlike William, as others before me have established beyond dispute, Henry was no advocate of the "laboratory" as a source of "credentials" for "attested" ghosts. On the contrary, he said in his Preface to "The Aspern Papers," his chief task was to decide "between having my apparitions correct" (by which he meant conform to requirements set down by para-psychologists) and having *The Turn of the Screw* produce the "designed horror." Convinced that neither of his ghosts, Peter Quint and Miss Jessel, should be qualified to stand as a "modern 'psychic case' washed clean of queerness" but must be regarded as thoroughly "abnormal agents," Henry was determined to deny them credentials William would have been quick to confer. Only by departing "altogether from the rules" of The Society for Psychical Research could Henry fortify the action of his gruesome tale with "hovering prowling blighting presences" that expressed his "subject directly and intensely" and at the same time succeeded in rousing the "old sacred terror."

I revisit these scenes of crime, Henry's imaginary house in Essex and William's historic laboratory in Massachusetts, not because there's crying need of still another volunteer to unearth a missing link or clue which will put an end to mystery at last. Nor indeed am I driven to recapitulate good work of investigation, hard work of good criticism by others, notably Robert W. Stallman's *The House That James Built* (1961), Martha Banta's *Henry James and the Occult* (1972), and Richard A. Hock's *Henry James and*

Pragmatistic Thought (1974). I mention this trio for the obvious reason that each has written a work of considerable merit on a subject that adjoins my own. Setting Stallman aside (his essay treats at length a contrast of house and garden in *The Portrait of a Lady*), we find that neither of the other two nor any others I know of recognize in James's Grand Guignol a compound of elements invincibly Jamesian and undeniably American in kind: convulsion of family, disorder of dwelling, subornation of children.

Given the place reserved for "haunted children" in American books, James's tale is unusual only insofar as it anneals a British setting to American themes and in this way adds that fillip of mystery Hawthorne said was missing in New England: "picturesque and gloomy wrong." Given too James's disgust with an unrelieved vulgarity of texture and tone in the United States, by 1895 when he recorded first intimations of his "excursion into chaos," an American house was simply out of the question. It was indeed only a few years later, on revisiting the United States for the first time in two decades, that he confirmed at first hand what he'd long suspected, that the best place to observe the domestic life of Americans was not at home but in hotels. There "blissfully exempt from any principle or possibility of disaccord with itself," might not the "hotel spirit just *be* the American spirit most seeking and finding itself?" (James's emphasis). The detailed way in which these prophetic words set the subject and method of "The Jolly Corner" (1907) we shall very soon be in a position to assess. For it was not until he'd defined the role of hotels in America during the Gilded Age (as a "synonym for civilization") that he was himself properly positioned to take up the case of Spencer Brydon in that story. Meantime, traveling about a society in which houses provided no "achieved protection, no constituted mystery of retreat, no saving complexity," in *The American Scene* (1907) our "brooding analyst" was appalled to find that "the silvered ghostliness" of "great white boxes" possessed "only the look of having cost as much as they knew how." Wandering about the Waldorf-Astoria, a "caravansary" that offered in "untempered monotony" a brocade of walk, talk, dine, dance, drink, James affected to find a "social order in positively stable equilibrium."[22] Recalling how contemptible in his view was the "French passion for completeness, for symmetry," for "squeezing things into a formula that mutilates them," we know beyond the shadow of doubt that he couldn't have conceived of insult more odious.

Supplementing more traditional reasons to justify an English setting, let us therefore now add this, that an American abode couldn't have sustained James's explorations of mystery, complexity, irresponsibility, disaccord, antithesis, instability—the dynamics of equilibrium, in a word—composite subject of *The Turn of the Screw*. That his "sinister romance" was nonetheless both an English masque and an American stunt is I think indisputable. In form an anecdote, "amplified and highly emphasized and returning upon itself," it incorporates the risk of chaos by way of a "villainy of motive in the evoked predatory creatures": evoked, let it be said, by both the author and his heroine. And that motive, the most damnable James could ascribe to predaceous adults hired to care for abandoned children, is villainy so foul that Bly reeks "with the air of evil." Though deliberately undefined, motive in *The Turn of the Screw* is unequivocally just a viler form of "the scent of selfishness" which pervades the salons of *What Maisie Knew* (1897). Gentility of scent in the drawing room is of course sheer stink in the schoolroom. And though a nursery was the one Victorian place on earth from which even the least breath of contamination was supposed to be banished, it's precisely there that a noxious air rises not only from the "bad dead," Quint and Jessel, but too from the Governess herself. A woman preternaturally keen of nose in her own right, as Oscar Cargill was early to stress, she is shown to exude a reek of self-interest so high that in the end it asphixiates her charge, Miles, helpless victim of blight.[23]

As a central conceit of James's imagination, aroma thus turns moral experience, decay of spirit, into incontestable physical fact. Varied to include the faculty of sight too, this metaphor recurs in the preamble to *The Turn of the Screw* where it confirms ghostly presence in a child's nightmare (invariable evidence of calamity, William said) by making it visible to the mother who comes to console him. No question then that James's idea of insufferable torment is based on a child's intuition of the fate that must befall him when trapped among predatory adults who pretend to a concern for his welfare. On switching the seat of intuition from a precociously advanced child to a tardily mature woman, on bringing apparitions to life before the eyes of a postpubertal but prenubile Christian gentlewoman ruled by the will to believe and thus armed against sin, James chooses to exchange the host but not to discredit either the fact or the mode of perception.

In fact all he's really done is raise the ante by doubling the danger so that it includes both child and adult—much as he was to do in "The Jolly Corner," a story in which the "silvered ghostliness" and the "hotel spirit" of *The American Scene* meet in Brydon's ancestral home near Washington Square. Having returned from three decades of sojourn in Europe, revisiting his empty old house, Brydon stalks a ghastly apparition of the man he'd probably have become had he stayed in New York City and (like Henry's Grandfather William upstate) gone triumphantly about the business of land, of buildings and rent. On being seen "twice over" by Alice Staverton, Brydon's sisterly friend, maternal fiancée-to-be, this ghost of his American self yields ground before the force of Alice's consolation. Whether or not ghosts win or lose in James's fiction, therefore, the "bad dead" never tire of their poisonous work, swindling victims of the power to love. And in each instance Henry James chooses to house "science and the occult" not in William's laboratory of "viridical" research but in a whited sepulcher of Anglo-American mind.

The Governess, then, at once sibylline and hysterical, is Henry's most famous medium of entrée into the arcane, the uncanny. That ominous word whose root meaning in German, Freud noted in his 1919 essay, encloses the word for home—*unheimlich*—teases out into the light of day all that should remain hidden and secret. But though Freud's paper "The Uncanny" has been repeatedly mined for use in these connections, it's less to Freud himself than to William we cleave once again, to *The Will to Believe*. For it was there, in "Is Life Worth Living?" (1895), William argued that the truly unbearable thing about the uncanny, a "sinister nightmare view of life" which compels us to hold "two things together which cannot possibly agree," is its power to cancel all "religious effect on the mind." In contrast, he said in "The Moral Philosopher and the Moral Life" (1891), every sort of "energy and endurance, of courage and capacity for handling life's evils" are "set free in those who have religious faith."

Unlike William or Henry Senior, both of whom "believed in believing," no directly religious "experience ever stirred in me," Henry Junior remarked in the memoir of his father.[24] As if in blatant disavowal of a family belief in belief, Henry rooted in religious faith his Governess's incapacity to cope with life's evils. Unlike William, quite literally terrified by the peculiar "poisonousness" inherent in *unheimlichkeit*, it was precisely because "beauty and hideousness, love and cruelty, life and death keep house together in indissoluble partnership" that Henry became a convert to the uncanny. A writer who believed that the unbreakable law of narrative was the law of antithesis, as he wrote in the Preface to *Roderick Hudson*, Henry James held that the truly marvelous thing about *unheimlichkeit* was its power to express the demonic effects of religious belief on a dangerously suggestible mind. Transposing William and anticipating Freud, he "deceives us into thinking that he is giving the sober truth and then after all oversteps the bounds of possibility." Primitives, neurotics, and children, Freud added, those who believe in the magical omnipotence of thought, imagine that the human will can transcend the limits of possibility and attain whatever it sets itself to achieve or conquer.[25]

So it is that this neurotic young woman, the Governess, wills herself to conquer those "prowling servile spirits," those abnormal agents who fill Bly. As in *Uncle Tom's Cabin*, where families are presented as witting servants of defilement, *The Turn of the Screw* is peopled with parental figures who forfeit trust in the exercise of parietal duty, beginning with the warden, the Master in London, a shirker of office. Stylizing material shared with American writers both before and after his time, James follows the odor of wickedness from this center of virtue to those great halls in which grand personages perfect the play of licentiousness in the world at large. Here's the stink not of some unspecified blight but of calculable vice, the unchecked pursuit of self-interest, and it saturates the Governess's senses. For this great drifting ship of which the Governess has sole charge, this hegemony of immaculate women and inconcupiscent men who serve as models, instructors, protectors, arbiters of decorum to the young: this nest is foul. Having "pitied the poor chicks," their uncle had sent them to Essex, the "proper place being for them of course the country." But the country is a mess. Ostensibly a place in which everything seems "pretty well fixed," as Isabel Archer too at first believed, "all settled beforehand," this "small ripe country" which Isabel at first thought as sweet as "the taste of an October pear," in fact is rotten. In that it's Quint and Jessel on whom James pins the task of guiding the Governess toward the heart of the matter—an anarchy of morals adroitly masked by a grandeur of manners disguising a corruption of power in Great Britain—the issue of their palpability is sheer red herring. The main enterprise of *The Turn of the Screw* is to connect mess in the nursery with ruin in Whitehall, to link depravity of will in Essex with dereliction of duty in London. Because Bly is a breeding ground of worldlings, a disarray of morals in this preserve of trusted menials and trusting children must irremediably manifest disarray in the domain of masters. And a society whose rigid hierarchy of social class masks an increase of favor for the privileged and a decrease of concern for the ill-favored and powerless—Great Britain in the late nineteenth century was prepared at any cost to preserve its equipoise.[26]

In this fashion James's theme sustains the Governess's intuition. And whether or not scholars will ever agree on means to validate her "proofs," at each turn of the screw a child's nightmare is uncannily, inexplicably visible to an attendant adult who shares some miserable knowledge of grief. What the Governess observes, only she and Flora, she and Miles together can perceive, whatever Flora or Miles may see or may deny seeing. According to specific rules of James's devising, we're given no stupefying knot to unravel in the Governess's failure to convince Mrs. Grose of the actuality of Miss Jessel's ghost. Though not the slightest shimmer of a spirit is apparent to the housekeeper's eyes, there's no doubt about Miss Jessel's actual infamy. Mrs. Grose had known about that long since. Indeed she herself had lodged a formal protest with the Uncle, her employer, though in protesting she had risked her job. A housekeeper in service doesn't go over the head of the one in charge. But Mrs. Grose hadn't been able to resist interceding in protest against Miss Jessel's encouragement of Quint's presumption. Observing him behaving as if he were Miles's tutor, "and a very grand one" at that, she had made a "frank overture to Miss Jessel" about "the incongruity of so close an alliance" between "man" and boy. Miss Jessel however had "with a most strange manner, required her to mind her business, and the good woman had, on this directly approached little Miles. What she had said to him, since I pressed, was that *she* liked to see young gentlemen not forget their station." Like Quint who had pushed himself above the constraints of place, Miss Jessel, in subordinating herself to a valet, had indeed forsworn her rank. Choosing to pretend that she was responsible "only for the little lady," Flora, Miss Jessel in "abasement" had allowed Quint the fullest possible freedom to tutor Miles in the tools of his own specialized trade, the craft of deceit, pretense, conspiracy, concealment.

The irony, lost on Mrs. Grose but not on the Governess, is that Jessel and Quint by example and precept provide Flora and Miles with tuition perfectly suited to train them for the life of Society. Unworldly our heroine may be, she's nevertheless keen enough, literary enough to understand that Jessel's intent (to corrupt Flora utterly, James says) is to finish an education interrupted by death. Despite the fact that Mrs. Grose cannot comprehend how the Governess discovered that Jessel was disreputable, she's even fiercer than the Governess in condemning a "lady" for having undermined the codes on which respectable society must depend. "Little bundles of impulses needing control," as children were then thought to be, a highly schooled impulse of duplicity turns out to be the form of damage wreaked by Jessel and Quint, whose skillful conduct of a forbidden affair offers the children a textbook example of deception.[27] And this has been their assignment to master, imitate, practice.

The whole matter can be epitomized so. Quint and Jessel in violation of their office have proselytized these pliable children, initiated them in rites necessary for the undetected play of illegitimate passion. Overriding those codes and customs on which traditional society is rooted, subverting the family—that rigidly "hierarchical unit" according to Burn's study of Victorian England, a strict system of seniority and subordination in role and function which linked wife and husband, servants and employers, children and parents—from which equipoise was said to radiate, Quint and Jessel undermine the vast architecture of imperial Britain at its base. Though irregular ardor is not itself calamitous, its effect on these orphans is catastrophic. Steeped in a voluptuous sense of the charms of passion but untutored in the need for its licit regulation in human affairs, these quick, volatile, precious, precocious, and vulnerable children have been turned fiendish. Skilled in artifice, they've become brilliant at the most devilish uses of art in love: to cheat, deceive, betray. Not only have they been ill-taught, therefore, but too they've been utterly defrauded of knowledge about all the other emotions of love, particularly the chief one, a disinterested concern for the well-being of other persons. At Bly, therefore, cornerstone in the structure of society, these innocent and unformed children have not been prepared to conduct useful and honorable lives. Instead they've been deformed by demons whose pedagogy has coached them to regard other people as fair game, as instruments and creatures of private need, want, will. It is in a word the lewdest and basest uses of power they've mastered. And it is their dishonor, wickedness learned within the family circle, which confers on this sinister romance, as James said, the stuff of tragedy.

If the melodramatic tale itself offers to our eye too flimsy a platform to mount big ideas on—declassé lust, craft, and class in a country seat—remember that the principle of moral action Prince Amerigo offers to Maggie Verver in *The Golden Bowl* is "doing the best for one's self one can" but always "without injury to others." And though no one in *The Turn of the Screw* is conventionally self-serving, each is prepared to inflict prodigious injury to helpless children whose best interests are attended by none. Miss Jessel, said to "want" Flora for herself at whatever cost to Flora, does in fact cause havoc indistinguishable from that done by the children's guardian, their uncle by remote control, who wants them isolated far from him, wants himself insulated from their need whatever the cost to them. Uncannily intuiting evil in its basest form, absolute egoism, the Governess finds herself conjuring up real ghosts whenever the nightmarish force of selfishness threatens to engulf the social, spiritual, and sexual lives of her precious pupils. A visionary endowed with transcendent powers of perception she is also, alas, a naif whose narrow vocabulary of Christian belief, faith in the power of self-sacrifice, in the omnipotence of pure love, twists the screw its final turn.

Breaking the rule of employment, disobeying the Master, she dares to write informing him what he's done, what particular pollution—egoism in all its guises—he's been the cause of. The fitness of that term pollution, incidentally, is underscored by a useful work of ethnography, Mary Douglas's *Purity and Danger* (1966), which offers as much information on evil as has ever been found outside the tale itself. Because witchcraft, she says, is always ascribed to anomalous figures who are placed outside the bounds of legitimate society, bewitchment in the primitive world is customarily traced to "malevolent persons in interstitial positions, anti-social, disapproved, working to harm the innocent." In the demonology of social life, furthermore, pollution is "a type of danger which is not likely to occur except where the lines of structure, cosmic or social, are clearly defined."

By every standard of taxonomy, psychical or psychological or ethnological, Quint and Jessel belong to a class of polluting demons who have "crossed some line which should not have been crossed," Douglas observes, and thereby "unleashed danger for someone."[28] In James's story of "general uncanniness and horror and pain," danger is unleashed for everyone. And our pure-spirited young woman is unhesitatingly sure that she'll purge the house of witchcraft once she's restored lines and limits, once she's redrawn boundaries of garden and schoolroom and nursery. Despairing of any hope for Flora, she decides to interpose herself between boy and man, to bind Miles to herself with a love so exclusive as to allow no space for Quint, a love so boundless that it must obliterate bondage itself, enslavement to self, nihilistic egoism, the worst pollution of Christian spirit she can imagine: pride. Flora is so far gone in pride, she decides, so seductive a temptress, that all she requires is the passage of years until she can qualify for entry into the great world where her will must have its way.[29]

Granted the Governess is right about Flora and Miles, in James's mind she's dead wrong about righteousness. And by proclaiming that Evil is against nature, that the conquest of vice requires only another small turn of the screw of ordinary virtue, she sets herself a course which must end in catastrophe. For it's a nineteenth-century gospel of the crudest kind she preaches to poor Miles, a higher athletics of spiritual endeavor. God's grace flows toward those who work a little harder to be a shade better. All that's needed, she thinks, poor parson's provincial little girl that she is, what's wanted to bring Miles around, is a tiny extra effort of manly will. On her own part too, an extra dose of womanly tact and effort and patience and faith, a dollop of pure goodness will carry the day. And she imagines herself leading the forces of light into battle against the powers of darkness which will be routed only if she can convince her disciple to exhale and thereby expel the Devil's name.

Before the story ends Miles says two names. First, as if in preparation for the ambiguities of salvation which his utterance conveys, James allows the Governess to extract from Miles a confession of crimes committed at school in the spirit of Quint's tuition. Miles does confess that he'd been sent down for deceiving people, especially those who trusted him. In confessing this much, participating in the work of redemption, he reconfirms her belief in homely vicarage virtue as the means to restore Bly to an unblemished state as well as to purge the poisons of a polluted world. When therefore she exhorts Miles to repeat the evil words he'd spoken at school she's certain that naming names he'll be released from the grasp of the demiurge. No longer possessed he'll be sublimely good, her angelic child once more.

She persists, tempts him to divulge the terrible words he'd used to deceive friends at school. When under pressure he blurts "Peter Quint—you devil," in these four historic words he frames an answer to all the questions posed by this "strange encounter," as James called it, the whole ghost-story side of life that invades and ends his novel. Although all final solutions are withheld, Miles's last words plainly say that the horrible devil whose villainy destroyed him, whose Satanism it was that led him to betray schoolmates as if in rehearsal of powers needed to conduct an accomplished English life—Peter Quint is the beastly name I now in contrition offer up to you, most saintly woman. Simultaneously, of course, he equates his tormentors, valet and Governess: you succubus, we're supposed also to hear him say, you and Quint are the devils who dispossess me of myself.

James himself naturally doesn't say one thing or the other, doesn't resolve the antithesis. Instead he insisted that "those questions *may* perhaps then, by the very nature of the case, be unanswerable" (James's emphasis). In any event the "supernatural" is in his view always shown to best effect when it's exhibited as an "impression strongly made" and "intensely received."[30] And in an encounter so intensely received that its force cannot be withstood, insisting that Miles identify the ghost of Quint at the window—gone when the boy turns around—the Governess believes that disappearance is due to the magical effect of Miles's words, of speech so sacred and potent that it draws the line barring that demon from this manor house forever. Purged of Quint Miles may indeed be. But in saying the words she forces him to speak he's instantly repossessed by the new devil, our heroine, whose terrible trust in a purely generous love now consumes him. Entirely possessed, Miles's own life is utterly spent.

After long hard years of work on this story is it true that "we don't really know or feel what Quint and Jessel are doing to Miles and Flora?"[31] On the contrary we know quite accurately what the poison is. We even know the ways it is administered and spread, how virulent are its symptoms, at which levels of toxicity the infection menaces mankind. We also know that the Governess's remedy includes two American tendencies of belief, Puritan and Romantic. Every child begins the world anew, Thoreau said in *Walden*. And the Governess so mistakes the lesson implicit in Thoreau's comment that she converts a complex mystique of mission into a smarmy preachment of uplift. "Unless ye become even as one of these," she thinks belief boils down to, Christian civilization is in peril. On this score no less provincially American than English in outlook, she may well personify a Puritan savior predestined to fail at her errand. Virtually indistinguishable from others in a line of women required to face James's recurring attacks on New England and its tradition, she embodies its naivetes of faith in nostrums of salvation. Bly, too, exempt from the "hotel spirit" and supplied with "functions, forms, the whole element of custom and perpetuity" which alone stirred James's fancy, is at bottom still another of those dishonored houses commonly found in overtly American books. A haven under siege, a fortress guarded by genteel females of an innocence so unassailable as to warrant the trust of children shielded from taint, Bly turns out to be a last resort of sanctuary and a field of battle—a structure solid enough to support James's denunciation of British hypocrisies and American cant.[32] In Miles's conversion, which the Governess fatuously thinks must begin the world afresh, James prefigures an end to everything the world holds dear.

Repudiating both the English ideology of equipoise—a condition of stasis perfectly maintained by an establishment in which each social class is accorded a due allotment of power—and an American will to believe in the perfectibility of man, James conjured up a model of civil and moral life less parochial than either, more humane by far. Convinced that children possessed an inherent "keenness of vision" which was at any moment stronger than their faculty of composed thought, he preempted a range of ideas made more or less coherent today by social psychologists who say that the special gift of children derives from an "imagination in close touch with the unconscious" and so on. It is a subject on which James was himself all the more ingenious because he decided that the state of childhood held a key that would unriddle whole mazes of motive all but invisible in other kinds of human attachment. What James had in mind bears no resemblance to, say, Dickens's view of children as homunculi harnessed at birth to an immense machinery of empire. Nor on the American side does James rely on the sort of stereotype which led Sherwood Anderson a few years later to say that a man "if he is any good never gets over being a boy." Moved to present children as blameless and helpless objects of adult violence, inspired to apply a modernist psychology of childhood to the study of history and culture, he invested this typology with a power of penetration unparalleled in life and letters.

From a child's struggle to endure with "all intensity, perplexity and felicity" an unbearable encounter which must nevertheless be borne, James adduced nothing more modest than a general rule of art, of society. "No themes are so human as those that reflect for us, out of the confusion of life, the close connection of bliss and bale, of the things that help with the things that hurt."[33] To my mind James's words circumscribe the irreducible core and seminal source of imagination in the United States. An unpolluted impurity of sexual and moral and political and social energy—this is the American element in Henry James's Anglo-American alloy, James's program for the survival of individual persons and whole societies. When he causes the Governess to impose her version of unalloyed bliss on children who are taught that life in the world is just an "extension of the garden and park at Bly," he compels this misguided young woman to pursue a plan of conquest so superbly symmetrical and mutilating that European styles of stasis, of hierarchy, of equipoise are discredited forever. Neither the European Idea, fit only for a nation of dynasts, nor the American Idea, not quite right even for a nation of democrats, could in isolation support the social and spiritual life of a race of orphans, humanity in general, constrained to live in a condition of permanent disaccord.

Only when James's art is seen to bear a Madisonian hallmark, as I'm concerned to observe about *The Golden Bowl* next chapter, can it be fairly said to interpose the full force of our "American Romance tradition" within "the Great Tradition of the British nineteenth century." At a pivotal moment of that fabulous novel the principle of alloy recurs in a mode of imagery, a discourse of equilibrium, commonly used by most prominent men of ideas in that generation. It was, we recall, the equilibrist metaphor to which Henry Adams had referred when, sensing danger, fearing chaos, he confessed anguish and doubt. Others, William James above all, eager to specify those aspects of American genius which sustained the energies of progress, seized on the concept *vital equilibrium* as a way of authenticating the promise of industrial democracy in the United States.

Among the manifold uses of equilibrium in American thought in the end it records an irreversible decline of interest in the Idea of Providence. Dispensing with guilt about convenants broken and betrayed, between parent and children, between founders and successors, between national constitution and national society, it defines an ascending curve of trust in science and technology. Associating alloy and equilibrium in letters and government, Henry James's oeuvre culminates in a masterpiece of domestic art, unsurpassed setting in which to register that alternating current of bliss and bale, that antithesis of self-interestedness and selflessness which generates the energies of individual persons, molds the culture of nations and animates the motion of history.

IV

Hydraulics and Heroics

William James, Stephen Crane

If George Balanchine were a novelist or a playwright or a movie director instead of a choreographer, his studies of women would be among the most discussed and most influential achievements of our time. . . . He is unique, too, in going beyond the limits of what women have conventionally expressed on the stage. In "Diamonds" . . . Suzanne Farrell [displays mastery] . . . of continual off-center balances . . . that reveal new and sweeter harmonies of proportion . . . Farrell's style is based on risk: she is almost always off balance and always secure. . . . Unlike [other distinguished ballerinas] who perfect held balances, Farrell perfects the act of balance/imbalance as a constant feature of dancing. It is not equilibrium as stasis, it is equilibrium as continuity that she excels in.

Arlene Croce, "Dancing," *The New Yorker*, February 24, 1975

BLIND FAITH IN AN EQUILIBRIUM OF STASIS. This is the flaw of temperament, the European fault of social and moral intelligence which sets off the Governess, separates her along with other nineteenth-century European women from their American counterparts in James's fiction and elsewhere. And *The Turn of the Screw*, taken less as an entertainment than as a cautionary tale, a story of detection inquiring into the sort of Victorian household chartered by the Establishment to train recruits—as a side effect of narrative, *The Turn of the Screw* bares the root causes of psychic and social instability in an Old World. There unsettled mind is not quietened but is indeed crazed by a claustrophobia of culture inevitable, so James thought, in that closed society. In contrast, persons of distinctively New World origin, women bred to combine stamina with delicacy of spirit, stubbornness and flexibility, reared to disavow perfectly held balances in favor of riskier angles of poise, James's exemplary women conduct their lives along lines of equilibrium more flowing than European, less stiff by far, principles which parallel the mode and style and history of a society shaped at hazard and given to gamble.

It is however in his masterwork, that fatidic text anticipating which myth of order would shape American high style during the industrial age, in *The Golden Bowl* James devised a program which discredited statis and glorified movement without forswearing form. In descent as well as dissent from a Swedenborgian father, Henry James Senior, both William and Henry James endorsed a creed of "vital equilibrium," an American ideology which presupposed the existence of cultivation of a self galvanized by the dynamics of tension. I mention the Swedenborgian motif in connection with *The Golden Bowl* to call attention to its effect on Maggie's sensibility at the outset. For it is Swedenborg's shade and Henry Senior's spirit which haunt Maggie's mind early on. And it is her bedeviled mind which must be exorcised if the very idea of family, of domestic life, is to recoup its power, is to revitalize high culture in the Age of Progress. Recalling Swedenborg's sovereignty over the James family, observing too the doctrine advanced in his *Treatise Concerning Heaven and Hell and the Wonderful Things Therein* (1758), we must assume that it's on this authority Maggie initially entrusts herself to a static and perfect equilibrium in marriage, in society. Characterized in that Newtonian *Treatise* as consisting "in the equality of an action and reaction between two opposite powers, producing Rest," conceived as "necessary to the existence and subsistence of all things," equilibrium it is which justified Maggie's faith in a "beautiful symmetry," as she first conceives it, of licit marriages held in a perfect state of rest, hers to Amerigo and Adam's to Charlotte. And James, who set himself the task of redefining the dynamics of character necessary to promote movement yet maintain continuity—in the final scenes of this portentous story James permits Maggie to produce a maximum bearable measure of asymmetry, of unrest, without introducing the least degree of disequilibrium.

Finding herself bound hand and foot by illicit "marriages," her husband's to her stepmother, her own to Adam, raptly beloved father, marriages whose exquisite symmetry she herself, a self-evident case of arrested growth, has inadvertently fostered, Maggie reacts with virtuoso finesse. Jamesian ancestor in literature of Balanchine's heroine of dance, Maggie Verver performs a ballet in which she manages to tilt everyone off balance yet hold each member of her company secure within configurations that cause everyone to change places, sexual and spatial, at once. The miraculous thing too about the conceit which unites figures of ballet in our time with figures of fiction in James's imagination is that the conceit itself controls the action of *The Golden Bowl* during its last moments. At her sublime instant of danger Maggie is portrayed *en point* unsupported by either her father or her husband. "On vertiginous point and in the very glare of Adam's observation," James says, "she balanced for thirty seconds, she almost rocked: she might have been for the time," that half-minute, herself "the very form of the equilibrium they were, in their different ways, equally trying to save." Assuming that pose, the "*act* of balance/imbalance" as Croce says of Farrell, "perched up," Maggie feels "the dizziness drop." Holding "herself hard," knowing that "the thing was to be done, once and for all, by her acting, now, where she stood," she spins herself away from Adam, releases him to his wife, ships both off to America and restores herself to her husband, the Prince, by whom she can be properly partnered at last.[1] James's prima ballerina, she alone excels in those off-center balances which display sweeter harmonies of sex and self, more daring dynamics of proportion, self to society, than the world has ever known.

The Golden Bowl for all its artifice is clearer-sighted and cleaner written than works of similar drift written by blunter-speaking men, Melville surely, William James himself perhaps. Because a warmth of affection between the brothers did not include a compatibility of taste in art or ideas, William, who insisted on a literary style which mirrored human hurly-burly in simple strong talk, whose only dogma of composition was "to say a thing in one sentence as straight and explicit as it can be made, and then to drop it forever"—William was taxed beyond bearing by the circumambience of the Master.[2] How "far apart and to what different ends we have had to work out (very naturally and properly!) our respective intellectual lives," Henry wrote to William in 1905, is apparent in the latter's failure to admire *The Golden Bowl*, recently published. I'm always sorry to hear you're reading one of my novels, he said, "and always hope you won't—you seem to me so constitutionally unable to 'enjoy' it, and so condemned to look at it from a point of view so remotely alien to mine . . . that all the intentions that have been its main reason for being . . . appear never to have reached you at all."[3] Not until late in their lives did the brothers agree to a stand-off. Henry might unselectively applaud William's science but William was not required to appreciate Henry's art.

Wasteful, their arms-length fraternity, in that Henry's intentions and William's tend to coalesce round the equilibrist metaphor. Indeed, a similar vocabulary recurs not alone in their late texts and last testaments but too invades all categories and subclasses of vitalist thought and discourse during the final period of the nineteenth century and the first years of the twentieth. "As a nodal concept probing physico-chemical phenomena," we're told in Cynthia Russett's monograph, *The Concept of Equilibrium in American Social Thought* (1966), the term itself equilibrium charts a "nineteenth century shift of interest from physics to living things," from organic forms to organic culture.[4] Derived, as it turns out, from Clausius's thermodynamics, the subject of equilibrist theory is worth considerably more than a word or two. According to Russett's account, the term has a history and momentum of usage all its own. Transmitted from Claude Bernard's *Introduction to the Study of Medicine* (1865) and from Vilfredo Pareto's essay in applied mathematics, the idea of equilibrism taken either literally or metaphorically made its way into Willard Gibbs's work in the new field of physical chemistry, "On the Equilibrium of Heterogeneous Substances" (1878), as well as into Lester Ward's studies in the new field of social science, *Dynamic Sociology* (1873). "The great difference between living and non-living matter is this," Ward held, the former is in a "state of movable or partial equilibrium, whereas the latter tends always to a condition of rest or statical equilibrium." In order to explain the process of change Ward invoked rules that controlled living matter rather than non-living matter. And in justification of his preference for "organic" models rather than mechanical laws Ward conjured up a theory of "dynamic action." It was, he said, the conversion of a "partial equilibrium into a moving equilibrium" which underlay dynamic social process particularly in the United States. Indeed, Russett observes, as a result of this effort to attach the "notion of equilibrium to a peculiarly American faith" Ward acquired elevated rank among early native practitioners of social science. Rather more to the point, Ernest Becker insisted in *The Structure of Evil* (1968)—itself dedicated "to the Memory of Saint-Simon, Comte, Fourier, Lester Ward, Dewey—this "Darwin of the Social Sciences" reasserted by means of sociology the historic role and epic mission of progress: "to foster genius." At the core of Ward's new science of man, Becker said, "*the preservation of genius and the maximimization of the talents of genius*" unequivocally defined the fundamental aims both of science and society in the age of industry (Becker's emphasis). It was therefore in celebration of the genius of this nation that Ward sought to demonstrate why organic technological democratic civilization in the United States, seat and center of "dynamic action," of "a moving equilibrium," alone among social systems possessed "the direct means to Progress."[5]

Although I must now anticipate a little, it's useful to know that equilibrist theory did indeed, nearer to our time, manage to attach itself to a myth of culture less improvisational and more formidable than Ward's.

Drawing on L. J. Henderson's noted work *Blood* (1928), invoking Bernard's notion of a milieu interior, Walter B. Cannon in *The Wisdom of the Body* (1932) undertook to locate the environment of progress inside the human organism itself and in this way associate advances in the social order with the life process of the self. Proposing a rule of equivalence between simple and collective organisms, between principles of physiology and practical politics, Cannon claimed to discern a general law of social stability and social harmony in bodily rhythm and order and function, in constancy of "blood volume, lung capacity, blood pressure and cardiac power." Homeostasis, he called this steady state. If men somehow were able to achieve a condition of homeostasis within and without, he prophesied, if mankind could fashion an organic society modeled on principles of physiological order, then at last humanity might liberate "the highest activities of the nervous system for adventure and achievement."[6]

Although Cannon's creed, which linked life science to social science by way of the equilibrist metaphor, cannot be said to have inspired the work of an entire generation of sociologists, it did in fact tend to justify the labors of those who were intoxicated by the prospect of coordinating technological dogma with organic doctrine. Duplicating the "rise of the mechanical model in an era of physical science," we're told in a comprehensive study of *Sociology and Modern Systems Theory* (1967), "the organic model," though "literally ancient history," assumed renewed authority during the modern era because of major "advances in biology."[7] Of unquestioned authority indeed, its sway was exercised by so-called functionalists of American social thought, theorists who ostensibly disavowed ideologies but did in effect underpin conservative principle in politics. According to functionalist precept, progress occurs when a "sociocultural system" maintains a "steady state" even as it adapts, modifies structure in response to stress. That so anti-Federalist and nonrepublican a view should have become a prevailing motif in social science does surely dramatize the vagaries of organicism in any history of the American Idea of Progress.

Directions taken by Cannon's successors, therefore, led along routes not traveled by Cannon's most eminent predecessor in organicist thought, William James, who with Ward stood at the van of vitalism in its heyday. Furthermore, it was James who held steadfast against that nonpareil of influence, that renouncer and denouncer of progress in their Saturnian time: Henry Adams. James, who allied a dynamic sociology with a dynamic physiology and a dynamic psychology of equilibrium and in this fashion set the stage for Cannon's utopian biology—William James alone took Adams seriously enough to resist virtually with his last breath Adams's dispraise of this country, of technological civilization in general, of the human race as a whole. James and Adams, high priest and anti-Christ of progress, together provide us with signs and symbols, images and emblems which mold and embellish and encompass leading ideas from the Progressive Era to our own day, ideas which apply theories of energy and entropy to the American dream of order.

Although Adams's influence is of course widely known, James's is as yet barely acknowledged. The more ironic neglect, in that despite obvious unlikeness of styles and subjects it is in James's views on mind, in Crane's on character and Stein's on language we find family and generational resemblances both intimate and extensive. Each sought to invade those "deeper and deeper strata of combustible material which is discontinuously arranged," James argued in his famed presidential address to the American Philosophical Association, "The Energies of Men" (1907), but is "ready for use by anyone who probes so deep."[8] Extraordinarily popular as a lecture, James's paper served as the bellwether essay in a celebrated book, *On Vital Reserves* (1911), which surveyed a field that had been opened, astonishingly, by Crane in *The Red Badge of Courage* (1895). Somewhat less astonishingly, experimental work by James's former student at Radcliffe, Gertrude Stein, involved effort (at nearly the same moment as James's address to the Society) to isolate those modes of speech and composition which might uncork the latent power of combustible words. As early as 1907 indeed, Stein had crystallized the gist of James's lecture, had solved the problem of access. Her solution, her soundings occur in a tell-tale phrase "rub her coke," to which we turn in chapter 7. And although both James and Stein seem to have missed seeing in Crane's fiction a confirmation of their common interests, all three probed deepest mind itself for energy necessary to achieve great ends: the transfiguration of art, the salvation of society, the transformation of the self, and the assurance of progress.

In James's instance too a personal bias was reinforced when Freud, avatar of the dominant mode of inquiry in James's field of interest, during a legendary visit to the United States in 1909, gave the most persuasive possible evidence in support of his American colleague's search for a reservoir of instinctual energy. Admiring Freud and treasuring his books, James was enchanted to discover that Freud's map of an unconscious mind schematized his own homegrown variety of vitalist thought, a linsey-woolsey chiliasm derived both from his father's mind and from like-minded men of his father's generation. Remarkable, this arabesque of thought, of social history. Remarkable too to find Freud, who considered James the only man of genius he was to meet in America, discovering in James an ally whose predisposition of sympathy was due less to the latter's understanding of depth psychology than to the residual effects of Henry Senior's vitalist ideas on his son's seismic sensibility.

Inherent in this transmission, this flow of doctrine is a synchronism of views uniting Henry Senior to a man he especially admired, the Christian socialist utopist pre-Freudian sexualist John Humphrey Noyes. Founder of the Oneida Community in Central New York, Noyes it is, or rather it is the evangelic presence of Noyes whom Henry Junior introduced into the novel which bore tangentially on evangelism and social reform, reform and sex: *The Bostonians* (1886). On these and like subjects, which all members of the James family classified under the heading "Father's Ideas," William had brooded two years earlier as he'd gone about the job of editing Henry Senior's papers, *The Literary Remains of the Late Henry James* (1884). And it was in these *Remains*, devoted in good part to the task of reconciling Fourier and Swedenborg—itself a persistent passion of certain American reformers from the day of Transcendentalism well into the Age of Progress—in "Socialism and Civilization" Henry Senior set down arguments to prove that human society was well-suited to foster the "spontaneous and divine life in man" on earth, here not hereafter.

Himself a noted exponent of what Noyes, in his lovely book, *History of American Socialisms* (1870), called "Revivalism and Socialism," the elder James could well have incarnated that generation in which divinity had seemed to be near at hand in America. For he was at one with the Revivalists who, Noyes remarked, "had for their great idea the regeneration of the soul," and with the Socialists whose great idea "was the regeneration of society, which is the soul's environment." Like Henry Senior insisting on the indivisibility of salvation and progress, Noyes undertook to establish the right environment for the union of soul and body. Perfectionism, he called this "vital society." Perfectabilitarian without doubt, in his view a society is vital to the degree that it succeeds in uniting the dual principles of generation and regeneration.

Both exalted and down-to-earth, in "communication with the source of life," with the life of spirit and the life of sex, vital society is indeed doubly blessed. Only when the "amative" rather than the "propogative" effect of "the sexual relation" is paramount in human affairs, Noyes insisted, can "vital organization" of men and women in fact occur. Once the amative relation governs the behavior of all, once holiness is the condition of each, then the Perfectionist society—in which work becomes "sport, as it would have been in the Eden state"—can be said to achieve its end.[9] Said another way, in Henry Senior's parlance, the millenium is reached when mankind becomes "the very play-thing of God."[10]

Two generations of visionaries in America—chiliasts, millennarians, engineers, inventors, Perfectionists—thus prepared William James for Freud's materialization in the New World and equipped James to lecture his countrymen on the uses of Viennese psychology for American social philosophy, on a fusion of flammable instinct with vital equilibrium. What a marvelous prospect! When overbred men and women, iridescent with instinct, articulate lessons inherent both in native dogma and foreign science then surely the American Age of Progress will be buoyed high and propelled far. Progress was assured too by a system of ideas which solved the oldest dilemma in democratic culture: Why, even in an egalitarian society, is there an immense range of performance and a disparity of talent for "physical work, intellectual work, spiritual work?" The answer is found, said this exemplar of the equilibrist generation, in the concept "effeciency equilibrium." It is this phenomenon rather than inequity of endowment which determined the diversity of life in a given society. Contending that anyone who cannot "energize" himself effectively, who falls below "his normal maximum," must inevitably fail "by just so much to profit by his change in life," James's analysis joined two thoughts which were exquisitely apt to express the American diktat of Progress. "First, that few men live at their maximum energy, and second, that anyone may be in vital equilibrium" whatever his birth, whatever his station, whatever his function. For it is neither genetic fate nor social circumstance which established fixed and universal "rates of energizing" but rather a power of will to tap remote sources, resources, reserves of vital life. Vitality of will determines one's condition. And because, finally, the same power which animated individual men sustained society, it followed that a nation run by men whose "efficiency equilibrium" occurred at a pretty low level of force was incontestably "inferior to a nation run by a higher pressure."[11] So much, I guess his audience was supposed to infer or assume, for Southern peoples, for sluggards of color.

Devising means of improving one's level, proposing some conventional as well as certain exotic modes of plunging through the doors of perception (alcohol, hallucinogenic drugs, yoga, autohypnosis, religious conversion), James concluded that Americans must engineer a proper apparatus of access and exploitation. The machinery he preferred, a sort of pump, he visualized as somehow plunged into a great pool, a North Slope of the self from which at will endlessly it would draw up a fossil fuel of character and action. In 1910 writing a half-serious account of this notion in a letter to Henry Adams, James asked Adams to imagine the "hydraulic ram" as a symbol of this "machine of human life." Placed in a brook, set down in a flow of water which in James's mind corresponded to the flow of "cosmic energy," the ram will always raise just "so many kilogrammeters" of liquid. It's not a function of hydraulics to appraise the "*value* of this work as history," not a question of technical equipment or training but of "the uses to which the water is put in the house which the ram serves." Laughing at the student in James's course whose examination paper referred to the ram as a hydraulic goat, at this moment in their history of colleagueship the two old friends could in fact share little more than a run-of-the-mine academic joke. Indeed James, who took very seriously his metaphor, his analogy, his mechanics of progress, was impelled—not long before his death—to rebuke Adams for frivolity of mind in preferring static to vital equilibrium and in elevating entropy to higher standing than energy as a principle of thermodynamics and history. To the very end he retained an optimism, a family faith in an Eden state afloat on "vast quantities of energy [which] may well be stored up, which may be tapped" and which may well increase the pressure to raise the ante of performance among men and nations during endless vistas of future time.

Although James was the chief spokesman of standard wisdom on these matters, dissent less grim than Adams's was not uncommon. George Santayana, for example, in *Character and Opinion in the United States* (1924) cautioned optimists of James's stripe that any reliance on the unconscious self was risky indeed. "At times a tyrant, parasitical, wasteful, and voluptuous," at times even "fanatical and mad," the "inner man" was by no means a trustworthy guardian or ally of culture.[12] James did of course acknowledge the force of this sort of opinion but serenely dismissed dissent from his mind. Surely cut-throat cannibals of Africa were of a different order of being from general officers in the American army, however martial. What Santayana stressed and James misconstrued Stephen Crane had earlier found a figure for and made a fiction of, Henry Fleming in *The Red Badge of Courage*. An incomparable and unconquerable novella, subject to usual as well as unusual methods of critical attack, it has yielded little that isn't easily granted but resisted surrender to the very end. Because criticism invariably loses its grip on Crane even as it strains to tighten its hold I must concede at the outset that both the man and his book are unfathomable. It's indeed the only conclusion on which everyone agrees, the one unmistakable opinion on Crane evident in any forced or quick-order march through biography and comment. "Once in a while a piece of writing comes along that one wants to call a miraculous emanation," Richard Chase said of *The Red Badge*. Lacking a real center, Chase decided, its meaning emerges from, issues out of a continuing American obsession: a "certain mysticism of death."[13] At the other end of opinion an eminent and lifelong student of Crane, Robert Stallman, argues an ingenious though unconvincing case for allegory. And Larzer Ziff in his turn stresses a union of antinomies, a failed fusion of concreteness and evanescence, failed because this dreamlike story never manages to "realize a life apart from the dreamer."[14] In a similar vein John Berryman's semipsychoanalytic essay turns up dreamwork which has less bearing on Crane's mind and art than on Berryman's "Dream Songs." There are riches to spare in Berryman's book but the treasure, Crane himself, is missing.

Crane evades everyone, therefore, men of genius like Berryman as well as Eric Solomon, an old friend who in *Stephen Crane in England* (1964) said that he had spent "ten years in planning a study" but "ended by deciding that there was no such animal," although he had known Crane for eleven years.[15] Even among those who knew him longest or studied him hardest Crane moves incognito, a writer given to spasms of self-disclosure which at once bare and bury the secret springs of his art. T. S. Eliot's famed remark about the roots of Henry James's strength touches the source of Crane's mastery too. That same baffling escape from ideas which Eliot prized in James turns up in Stephen Crane as an art of camouflage. In his instance, however, its effects are exaggerated by those readers who insist on using the very tags (realism, symbolism, naturalism) which camouflage flight. Labeling of this kind must be after all the least useful way to contain or trap an escape artist who, according to still another well-informed old friend, Corwin K. Linson, disguised his story as "a boy's book about a boy trying to do a man's work."[16] For if we adopt views of this sort, if we take up Linson's literalist version—that *The Red Badge* was written in eulogy to thousands of real boys fourteen and fifteen years old who forced their way into the Civil War and were killed—then what are we to make of Crane's letter to Nellie Crouse in 1896 saying that the subject which really fascinated him bore not on those "majestic forces" the world pits "against man's true success" but on another source of power "more strong than chains," on "man's own colossal impulses"?[17]

I propose to take Stephen Crane at his word, to take his clue at face value. Henry Fleming, then, who like Crane discovered that "the fight was not going to be with the world but with myself"—Fleming finds himself ill equipped to do a man's job of work at war not because he is peculiarly callow but because he is, as a typical young man of his generation, peculiarly disabled. Precisely because war releases those energies and powers which genteel American society was determined to fetter, the action of Crane's plot in its entirety as well as Fleming's process of self-discovery from first to last anticipate William James's thesis to its final nuance. Only when we bring to bear James's hydraulics on Henry Fleming's heroics do we acquire a sure gloss to Crane's text, a gloss all the more valuable for its use of a technical vocabulary distinct from but parallel to Crane's. A Progressivist discourse flavoring both kinds of language, the language of technology on which James depends and the language of organism to which Crane resorts—an American discourse of dynamism it is that defines those principles governing the inner life in times of war, in times of peace. Without strain of argument, therefore, we can alternate Crane's and James's modes of speech. Either way the story comes out right, as if Crane's performance justified James's science, James's speculation.

Let us then right off waive the claim imposed by received opinion. It's not social Darwinism which underlies the ruling fashion of thought in *The Red Badge*, not *On the Origin of Species* Crane evokes with words like "wolfish," "tempestuous," "awesome," "barbaric." These words identify Santayana's "inner man," the self unchained, conjured into being so as to justify Henry's response to actual soldierly need once he's overcome the tin-horn glamor of derring-do. A "typical" American boy-man of "great energy," Fleming—much like Johnnie in "His Majestic Lie"—is "ready to accomplish a colossal thing for the basic reason that he was ignorant of its magnitude."[18] Similarly, Henry at the outset is sure that modern warfare must be a piece of cake because battle today cannot compare with Homeric struggles of earlier epochs when men were more brutish and more brave. Henry's delusion, incidentally, was widely held in Crane's time. First appearing in literature during the nineties, it lasted far longer in the United States than elsewhere because small wars, quick invasions, easy incursions satisfied the imperial tastes of a people under anaesthesia during the Age of Confidence. A most durable time, that age, in that it outlasted even F. Scott Fitzgerald whose Amory Blaine in *This Side of Paradise* (1920) twenty-five years after Crane, a war and a half nearer our era, visits a Union cemetery, mourns his own depredations of vigor, repeats Fleming's thought in crisper speech. "Grown up to find all gods dead, all wars fought."[19] Updated by a generation, Blaine's remark echoes a complaint which it had been Crane's aim to dispel by assigning to Fleming the function of revealing how malevolent are the tempests which lurk just below the skin of gentlemanly manners. Having grown up in the Progressive era, having been reared to believe in emergent evolution, having been enclosed inside a chrysalis of mind which held that humanity had got "better, or more timid," Henry manages to battle his way out because in battle he finds reserves of venom. Sulfurous, pitiless, weaned at last from his mother, temporarily disconnected from a society in which all the right people agreed that "secular and religious education had effaced the throat-grappling instinct, or else firm finance held in check the passions," in the end he is vulcanized into an efficient figure of formidable force. Because he is far less timid he is unquestionably more hale.

Let us in fact now consider Mother Fleming. It is she, genteel culture incarnate, who enables us to gauge the distance Henry travels during those two days of war, those twenty-four episodes which seem to advance so short a step beyond a yarn of adventure that any inference based on an unsustained scene or a flashed image or an undefined portrait must appear out of scale, a cleverness of criticism rather than an illumination of text. And Henry's mother, who says so little and disappears so fast that she is usually overlooked, is dispensed with for the very good reason that at first glance she appears to represent nothing much. What she does say however, once his enlistment is an accomplished fact, serves as a code, shorthand for the very kind of indoctrination Crane's own family had dispatched him to Syracuse to acquire. There an aimless boy with a passion for baseball would be transformed into the kind of muscular Methodist gentleman cherished by his family and exemplified in his exalted grandfather, the Bishop. Mrs. Fleming's advice to Henry therefore cannot but have been Mother Crane's too. And it was no more useful in instructing Fleming how to behave on a battlefield than New Jersey and Syracuse Methodism were to be useful in preparing Crane for maneuver around the New York slums.

Always be careful, Henry is told, and choose your mates among wholesome folk. "There's lots of bad men in the army, Henry. The army makes 'em wild and they like nothing better than the job of leading off a younger feller like you. Jest think as if I was a-watching yeh. If yer keep that in yer mind allus, I guess yer'll come out about right." Along with this farewell address intended to shield him less from the dangers of soldiering than from the wages of sin, she includes eight pairs of socks, all his best shirts (so that her boy can be just as warm and comfortable as anyone in the whole army) and a "cup of blackberry jam." Finally as if in afterthought she warns him "to take good care of yerself in this here fighting business." And though of course no one lone young man can "lick the hull rebel army" he mustn't shirk danger and duty on her account. "If so be a time comes when yeh have to be kilt or do a mean thing, why, Henry, don't think of anything 'cept what's right, because there's many a woman has to bear up 'ginst sech things these times, and the Lord'll take keer of us all." So off you go, Henry. Watch out, be good. Better to die than break the rules. And if you're killed, rest assured that a gold star American mother will receive her due from the Lord.

Crane renders the speech straight. Presenting Mother Fleming, his tone offers only the tiniest clue how we're supposed to regard this woman, her speech, the scene itself. Henry squirms a little and reflects that her remarks had "not been quite what he had expected" in that he had hoped for Spartan commandment. But a scene which sets a tonal key for the story from start to finish, whose tone is irony—this scene has gone unnoticed or unappreciated by a couple of generations of scholars who have persevered in the search for subtler tips on the ties between tone and meaning in *The Red Badge*. Perhaps the reason for disregard is that the episode is casual enough to be taken as a grace note of this realistic plot or mistaken for faulty management of tale by an erratic prodigy. But it is in fact no more casual, still less an afterthought, than a similar scene invented by another prodigy of vastly different time and place, Pushkin, who treated virtually the same material in nearly identical ways. In *The Captain's Daughter*, parental advice—watch over your reputation while you are young and your clothes when they are new—equips and sends Pyotr, aged seventeen, off to an army whose duty is to put down civil rebellion, a peasant's revolt. Hardly out of earshot of his father's voice Pyotr meets a stranger barely clad against a blizzard, gives him a new hareskin coat, and thereby earns the friendship of Pugachov himself, the rebel peasant whose favor is at first the ruin of Pyotr's reputation but whose patronage in the end enhances his honor and saves his life.

In both stories the writers are so skillful at hiding ideas inside events that we are captivated by a triumph of artlessness. Like Pushkin who speeds his hero off to a war for which he is by education undone, Crane sends Henry out well-provided for citizenship in a static and immobile and devitalized society but utterly ill-equipped to survive conditions of worst conceivable volatility and disorder. If he is in fact to endure at all he must contravene every Sunday-school rule he's ever been taught. The gist of his mother's words, be a good boy even if they kill you for it, words which Crane implies every mother's son hears in farewell, turns out to be as bootless in war as his extra socks. And instantly as the men move off toward their first day's engagement, all "shed their knapsacks . . . extricated themselves from thick shirts. Presently few carried anything but their necessary clothing, blankets, haversacks, canteens and arms and ammunition." Like Mom's blackberry jam, all that junk too is soon discarded. You can now eat and shoot, said "the tall soldier" to Fleming. "That's all you want to do." Although Henry does indeed rid himself of jam and socks, does next day heave away gun and power too, not until he's stripped down to terror alone is he ripe for frenzy. Only then is he in Crane's view ready for war, ready to share in the work of bestialized men who have somehow recovered old savage ways, who have recovered instinct. And instinct alone can sustain them because instinct alone is immune to all the canonical agents of repression in genteel America.

This theme is so well masked that Crane's readers continue to speak of Henry as a victim of blind rage who eventually learns to live with the shame of flight from the battlefront, who finally manages to control fear of death but who fails to fulfill his heart's fancy of heroism. In this view Henry's pride of battle, his behavior on the second day is unwarranted, as if Crane's own testimony were so fuzzy that the reader must be receiving a scrambled signal. But even if Crane's words were not in fact straightforward, the weight of his meaning would still be equivalent to that of an already known quantity, James's in "The Energies of Men." Surely it's clear that a variant of James's theory found its way into a story which presents us with a soldier boy who, denied the energies and deprived of the powers of men, mistakes a lull in the fight for the end of an action, repeats his mother's remark, reminds himself that he hadn't "come here to fight the hull damn' rebel army." And bolts. As yet he has no access to that "explosible material" which will enable him to meet fire with fire and which, win or lose, will furnish him with surer, solider proportions of character rooted in profounder sources of being than are commonly acquired in a culture based on a virtual eradication of instinct.

At this moment unstable in the extreme, distraught, Henry is also annoyed by those of his comrades who remained in their places at the front, those who had stood firm. For he cannot make out their reasons for staying, their "lack of sense in holding a position, when intelligent deliberation"—that most advanced attainment of civility—"would have convinced them that it was impossible" ground to hold. Why did those men suspend their God-given powers of reason to face annihilation? Although "he knew it could be proved that they were fools," his superior knowledge offers no balm of guilt. Nor do his proofs provide solace when he trips over annihilation itself, the abstract idea manifest in the corpse in the chapel. Tempted to touch this body teeming with vermin, with "black ants swarming greedily upon the gray face and venturing horribly near to the eyes," an instant later he is propelled by this apparition into still more frenzied flight. In torment he hears from a distance the "tremendous clangor of sounds" as if "worlds were being rended." Suddenly it is revealed to him that war is not the work of temperate mind but of intemperate will and distempered spirit: no act, no thought, no one can make sense of battle. Appalled, "his mind flew in all directions," and in panic he takes off again, this time running toward instead of away from the front.

By afternoon on this first day under fire Henry has come a long way from home. And when before long he overcomes panic, gets himself turned round again, and joins the line of wounded and tattered men and thereby finds himself compelled to witness Jim Conklin's death—forced to perceive there's no recourse from war and no recompense for death—he arrives at the verge of resolution. In the time between forenoon and evening he has seen putrefaction in the flesh, watched a brave man in torture uncomplainingly die. It is almost time for him to put aside infantile thoughts and childish fears, to exchange fantasies about death and duty and valor and love in favor of wilier wisdom. Boy that he is nonetheless he's quick-witted enough to see that life and death happen in this wild world according to principles which no exercise of disciplined mind can fathom, no power on earth can control. Even though young Fleming is hardly the first fledgling hero in nineteenth-century literature required to master this Dostoevskian lesson, nevertheless America in Crane's day remained a bastion of conscious intelligence, a stronghold of determined will, an empire of applied science. And it is a mark of Crane's genius that he discredited these fixed ideas of national belief without resorting to European fashion, without proposing caprice as a cosmic law.

What he proposed instead, indifference, is inherent in one of the most perplexing scenes in literature, the scene which ends "The red Sun was pasted in the sky like a wafer." Words that indirectly comment on the frightful death of Jim Conklin, these also direct attention to those natural laws which war alone discloses even to Henry's baffled mind. His ideas fogged, his passions pettifogged by those checks on thought and behavior which govern the life of society back home, he is horrified to learn that out here the fundamental law is abandon. It's a ferine world Crane reminds us of and introduces Henry to when, observing that Conklin's body "looked as if it had been chewed by wolves," he turns toward the fighting, shakes his fist, and seems "about to deliver a phillipic": "Hell—" And straightaway saying that the sun is pasted in the sky (like a "fierce" wafer, according to the London Folio Society Text) Crane ends the Conklin scene and sets the stage for the climactic event of the first day, Henry's encounter with "the tattered man." Like Conklin mortally wounded, the tattered man is inexplicably more concerned for the welfare of a missing friend than he is fearful in his own behalf. Himself beyond help, this most ordinary man is brave, selfless to epic degree no matter who brings what standard of judgment to bear on honor in any war anywhere at any time.

Passing through a triad of scenes which picture a raw recruit under pressure to become an able-bodied man, Henry begins to discriminate between the ferocity of soldiers in combat and the wantonness of extinction on earth, between a simplemindedness of love in the ordinary domestic life of the age and a simplicity of love on the line. Dispelling at last Henry's naive habit of calibrating duty and heroism and devotion along some sublime or transcendent scale, ending this first day of war, Crane's wafer accents meaning in a motif that runs through the three episodes, corpse and Conklin and tattered man. Intended to relieve our novice soldier of shibboleth, these episodes leave an apprentice adult free to experience the exhilaration of "blaze and blood and danger."

Although Crane's art never again contrived so faultless a fusion of act and emblem, its meaning would be forever opaque had he not expressed the same meaning sans emblem elsewhere. What is symbolized in *The Red Badge* is asserted unadorned by figure of speech in "The Open Boat" and is said so unequivocally that there's scarcely tangle left to untie. At the moment when "the correspondent," Crane's persona in this story, wonders why if he's not going to be saved but is to be drowned after all, why has he been allowed to come within reach of sand and trees—at that moment he recalls a poem about a soldier of the Foreign Legion dying in Algiers. By way of the correspondent's association, connecting the experience of shipwreck with the wreckage of war, Crane discloses a central obsession of his life and art. It is neither the inexplicable cruelty of the sea he's concerned with in "The Open Boat" nor the sheer hostility of earth which preoccupies him in *The Red Badge of Courage*. What the actual experience of shipwreck and the imagined experience of war brought home to a tubercular young man soon to die far from home in England was the loneliness of oblivion. "When it occurs to a man that nature does not regard him as important, and that she feels she would not maim the universe by disposing of him, he at first wishes to throw bricks at the temple, and he hates deeply the fact that there are no bricks and no temples." Like Henry's undelivered "phillipic" the correspondent's refusal to reconcile himself to cosmic indifference is addressed to empty space. "But I love myself," he says, hoping that nature will give him a sign. "A high cold star on a winter's night is the word he feels that she says to him." Bleak red sun and high cold star: these natural signs convey a message whose meaning is unmistakable, connote the sinister hospitality of earth and sky, of sea and beach, to men who must reconcile themselves to their fate.

Existence and extinction, sun and star, are not concerns for which the universe, as Crane said in *War Is Kind* (1899), assumes obligation. But *human* concern, *human* obligation, as Henry learns from the implicit example of Jim Conklin and the explicit instance of the tattered man, abandonment and betrayal of friends is another matter entirely, not a matter of indifference at all. And he returns to the line, to his comrades. Allowing them to believe he hadn't fled but had been injured in the first engagement,

Henry perceives that battle had disoriented all its survivors, had subdued the bold and emboldened the timid. Taking stock, he decides that this first day's lesson had unquestionably belied in every conceivable way every last rule he'd spent his life till now straining to master. Amazed, he realized that punishment for bad deeds is not sure and swift but "laggard and blind," that "many obligations of a life were easily avoided." Not only were the "dragons" less hideous than he's been trained to believe but too "they were inaccurate." And because "they did not sting with precision" henceforth he might well "leave much to chance." Lessons taught by generations of the same ladies who were to preach to Fitzgerald's Dick Diver identical versions of our national gospel, of rewards and punishments for service well or improperly done, of speedy retribution as the price of sloth and the cost of sin, their "vague feminine formula" for doing "brave deeds on the field of battle," for fighting like a gentleman, was flatly wrong. And as he prepares for the second day, prepares at dawn to launch himself into war, he plans to replace this muddle of morals with plain fury. Yesterday when his world had buckled he'd "imagined the universe to be against him." Today he knows that the universe is neutral, that his sole adversary is "the army of the foe," an enemy against which now he feels a "wild hate."

Rage, drawn from sources and reserves of energy so deep and archaic and brutish as to be beneath the notice of civilized men, ungovernable rage it is which enables him to fight "not like a kitten chased by boys" but like a wildcat. "By heavens, if I had ten thousand wild cats like you," his lieutenant says, "I could break the back of this war in a week." Only a "barbarian, a beast" that fights like a "pagan who defends his religion" can be a hero; only a man at bay can earn the red badge. For barbarians, beasts, pagans are sustained by a fiat of instinct, volatile stuff summoned up under pressure of intensest stress. Commanded to charge—Crane's account of the second day rounds out the work of paganizing Henry—the regiment turns "vicious, wolf-like." Fleming, who himself "felt the daring spirit of a savage, religion-mad," in an ecstasy of mindlessness, of "wild battle-madness," set himself the task of capturing the Confederate standard. It is a manic "enthusiasm," a lunatic "delirium" which enables him to win this deadly game of capture the flag, a boy's game now played for keeps, and it teaches him that courage in battle is just an external sign and symptom of blood-lust. "The average church-going civilizee," William James was to say in 1903, realizes "absolutely nothing of the deeper currents of human nature, or of the aboriginal capacity for murderous excitement which lies sleeping in his own bosom."[20] James's civilizee in the flesh Henry Fleming, in the grip of aboriginal power, is amazed to find a license to murder exciting enough to ignite his spirit. Above all, he is comforted to discover that rabid passion had not been turned into jelly or jam, that American gentility had merely kept the lid on.

When the charge is over and the flag captured and the brigade withdrawn from the front, Henry subsides. Although Crane refuses to allow him to regress, to revert to his former condition, docile and kittenish, neither is he permitted to remain permanently rabid. On returning from that "land of strange and squalling upheavals" his mind must "cast off its battlefield ways and resume its customary course of thought. Gradually his brain emerged from the clogged clouds, and he was able to more closely comprehend himself and circumstance." But he had undergone a "subtle change" in self-perception which he registers by recognizing the fatuity of his former fantasies about heroes who once battled beyond endurance. As he thinks "back upon the brass and bombast of his earlier gospels," he realizes that he too has at last done a colossal thing, touched "the great death." Thus a palpitating half-grown youth knows finally that battle is not the work of Titans, knows that all men, Mycenaean pagans or New Jersey Methodists, must be in touch with the "black of passion" before they can dive into "the red of blood." Having been forced to extend his reach a very long way down inside himself, having palpated the pump of life and death, he had been immersed in that sphere of being which Conrad, soon to be Crane's friend in England, would call the destructive element, the heart of darkness, and so on. Although an immersion must be quick, cannot be long sustained lest the "civilizee" like Kurtz go native, the result is lasting. No longer the pink and gentle boy he'd been two days earlier, Fleming is now colored red and black, livid, a human not a superhuman or a godly hue.

It turns out, incidentally, that these associations of theme and pigment cut pretty close to the bone of Crane's intention. For we learn from a friend in Syracuse, Frank W. Noxon, that not long after the book was published Crane said he'd been impressed and affected by Goethe's analysis of the influences of color on mind.[21] With this plausible and presumed fact in mind we cannot fail to see a circumambient aura radiating from Crane's climactic image. Slogging through the "trough of brown mud," Fleming visualizes a scene of "tranquil skies, fresh meadows and cool brooks." And as if in coordination with his mood the leaden sky parts to display a "golden ray of sun," parts too on at least one classic problem of interpretation, Charles Walcott's, Richard Chase's, Jean Cazemajou's, which finds foaming fury too airy a principle to sustain Crane's sermon on manliness.[22] Its very flimsiness, they say, attests to the lightness of Crane's interest in the moral he thinks he's supposed to draw and testifies to the heaviness of weight he placed on the insanely grotesque world of battle itself.

But this is criticism of sheerest bafflement. It divorces the writer from the man, segments art and mind, parts Crane from his biography, his biography from his career, the career from culture or history. There's simply no need for bafflement or divorce, as in fact H. G. Wells knew in discerning a "mixture of violence and repose," a tension between "active service and peaceful contemplation" apparent in Crane's "work as well as his personality."[23] A reportorial eye, Wells's, keen for what it sees not blind because of what it fails to see. Piercing Crane's disguise, his view leads us to associate red and black and brown and gold, a chromatics of tension in *The Red Badge*, with the dynamics of energy as prescribed by equilibrist doctrine in Crane's time and nation. And a story treating global loneliness and human homeliness, terror and swashbuckle, conscious constraint and unconscious, uncontrolled volition of appetite—kitten and wildcat—two insane and grotesque days of battle, one day of terror and one day of wrath retire the child and inspirit the man and enable the author to celebrate the didactic functions of war in a society which according to Theodore Roosevelt was imperiled from within not without. Favoring a psychology and politics of combustion which would increase the "efficiency equilibrium" of ordinary men, Crane transforms an inert youth whom Roosevelt in 1899 urging invasion of the Philippines would have called a malingerer and a mollycoddle—Crane metamorphoses Henry into a man of Roosevelt's sort. Endowed with a zest for conquest, both the president and the private soldier are prepared to pursue a course of heroic action necessary to fulfill the destiny of this vanguard nation of the new age.

There finally in the words of our Rough Rider do we hear the last resonance of meaning in Crane's story. Because soldiering required the most effective pump of energy ever devised, as William James was to say in his famed essay on war, Crane imagined that it alone would force men to ram their way to a roused condition of manliness unprovided for by the genteel tradition in American letters and thought. Because war annulled those homespun lessons American boys were supposed to believe about their sex, Crane enlisted himself alongside those who celebrated the life of action as the key to progress and personality in the United States, those who insisted that the ascent of man required descent into the most archaic realms and menacing origins of the self. Behind the smokescreen of powder, therefore, Crane managed to ventilate some fresh thoughts on the ties between the untrammeled self and the Age of Progress, contrived to bootleg into "a boy's book" notice of an immense pool of energy, gigantic reserves of repressed force rising at need from the innermost depths of even the most sedate and principled and banal of youths.

The final word on war, however, is neither Crane's nor Roosevelt's but is William James's in the essay "The Moral Equivalent of War" (1910), provoked by that degrading Spanish adventure. Written shortly after "The Energies of Men" and published in the year of James's death, this landmark essay—invoked by President Carter in his speech on energy in April, 1977—was composed in order to dispel nineties' cant about American destiny. Taking up Crane's theme, James pillories McKinley and Roosevelt and all greater and lesser cultists of a Prussian faith in battle as the expression of "human nature at its highest dynamic," of warfare as an instrument of salvation in an era of "industrialism unlimited and feminism unabashed." Crane the war lover belonged to the party of peace. And he did not himself either acclaim or denounce all those in public life who insisted that this combative and feverish people should pursue, in its own behalf or in behalf of the chosen races, an imperial policy. Nevertheless, in extolling a life of adventure apart from war, he embodied in his person an article of faith central to James's philosophy of moral equivalence: "the martial type of character can be bred without war."

James without reference to Crane, and Crane, denied the benefit of James's theory, meditated on means of access to those measureless reserves of virtue and strength that Crane, in defining courage under fire, called a temporary and sublime absence of selfishness and traced to an atavism of savagery. Unlike Crane, James was revolted by the notion of a common and collective savage mind. And he refused to equate ravening aborigines, "the black warriors in the Congo who pursued Stanley's party" yelling their "cannibal war-cry of 'Meat! Meat!'" with the war cries of a "General Staff of any civilized nation." The grand illusion. But James was undeluded about the benefit got by boys who enlist themselves in the sacred task, the "immemorial human warfare against nature." Achieving dominion over the fish of the sea, the birds of the air, over all things that move on earth, Young Battalions assumed a biblical vocation, a calling twice holy. Required to pay what James called a "blood tax," they are empowered to cultivate, to perpetuate "even in the midst of a pacific civilization" those "manly virtues which the military party is so afraid of seeing disappear." James of course never denied the utility of war as a mechanism—his hydraulic ram—of deliverance. But he did deny that it was fear alone, the fear of being killed in battle, which is "as our military enthusiasts believe and try to make us believe, the only stimulus known for awakening the higher ranges of man's spiritual energy."[24]

Rejecting the very stimulus Crane injected into his novel, James insisted that a declaration of war on nature would accomplish the same end, would rescue that endangered species, manly men, from extinction. First introduced in *The Varieties of Religious Experience* (1902), then sketched broad in "The Energies of Men" and fleshed out in "The Moral Equivalent of

War," his thesis mediates between a Christian socialist "reign of peace" on the one hand and on the other hand those "energies and hardihoods" and heroics glorified by the war party. Unlike the Italian pre-Fascist literary intellectual Marinetti who announced in "The Foundations of Futurism" (1909) that he and his friends scorned feminism, apotheosized war, and honored force—the force that builds bridges, moves locomotives, invents airplanes—unlike authoritarians of Progress at home and abroad, James disdained to idealize violence and power.[25] Tough-minded American men who like Henry Fleming cast off excess gear do not want brown shirts. Instead of an army arrayed for the conquest of nations James proposed to establish phalanxes for peace. He envisioned a planetary peace corps run according to military discipline and trained to battle jungles and deserts, forests and swamps, mosquitoes and snakes, even I suppose Auden's poison ivy. For if James did perhaps sentimentalize the idea of manliness, if he erred in considering sovereignty over nature a God-given right, he never confused power over earth with tyranny over men.

Crane's story, read in conjunction with James's essay, would well be paired with another work on war written four years earlier by yet another ironist of progress, Melville in *Billy Budd*. For it wasn't only the fate of his amniotic hero that fascinated Melville, Baby Budd's "concern for moral and spiritual integrity, enthusiasm, a total revulsion in the face of evil and corruption."[26] No less intriguing was the work of sorting all possible reasons why a retrograde society, the English ship of state, despite its derision of trust and its flirtation with tyranny, did in due course improve the condition of those under its dominion. Was there a dialectic of progress in the very nature of things?—so Melville put the question. If therefore we place James and Crane and Melville on one side of a great divide in intellectual and literary history, on the other side we must situate Henry Adams and as yet uncounted others bound to him in an indenture of drama and poetry and fiction executed from the twenties till now. "All of my friends own and speak of 'The Education of Henry Adams' with such solemnity," Hemingway wrote in 1925, that even he tended to agree it might indeed be required reading.[27] Before that time, however, this dynamic, aberrant and unsettled people, less and less dependent on the promise of Providence and ever more faithful to the cause of progress, was widely perceived to embody a surmise advanced by A. Javary in France many years earlier. "From the beginning of this century," he had written in 1851, "the idea of progress has in effect established itself in such a way that in principle" the one question left open to inquiry concerns "the conditions in which it is realized."[28]

Almost half a century later James and Crane in their separate ways engaged this question. James's avowals of faith in an hydraulics of regeneration, Crane's resort to the power of manly militarism ("It had been necessary for [Henry] to swallow swords that he might have a better throat for grapes") as a means of restoring pagan instinct into a state of dynamic equilibrium with Christian virtue—these variations on vitalist themes defined the terms of inquiry within this most promising nation of the modern world. Until Adams undertook to disabuse his countrymen of the delusion of progress, standard opinion held it to be "the rare fortune of the American people" (said an eminent professor of sociology, Franklin Henry Giddings) that indispensable traits of progress had "left a deep impress" on both "the moral and mental life" of their civilization. "Objectively viewed" as a straightforward series of transformations of energy leading to "an increase of physical power and material resources," the Idea of Progress in the United States fulfilled the "Christian missionary enterprise" of "uniting the classes and races of men in a spiritual humanity."[29] American destiny once more.

Dynamic equilibrists of Lester Ward's sort, "demogenic" Christian evolutionists of Franklin Henry Giddings's kind—toward the end of the nineteenth century a ruling class of intellectuals brought the Idea of Progress to its moment of culmination. Thereafter, as J. B. Bury said of E. von Hartmann's thesis in *Philosophy of the Unconscious*, "Progress means an increase of Misery."[30] Henceforth too it is Adams's account of reasons for an increase of misery which interposed itself, his certitude of chaos, his formulation of a politics of decay and disorder which would acquire authority in our literature. Beginning in 1907, when *The Education of Henry Adams* was privately printed for distribution to friends, Adams has been unofficially a presence or officially present in all those literary texts which either glorify the will to negation or represent the American imagination of disaster in its modernist guise. Within three years after William James published "The Energies of Men" Adams loosed on the world his studies in Entropy Law and the American condition. Discovering in thermodynamic law an ingenious way of baiting the bears—that is, a way of applying the image of equilibrium to a climax of being on earth—Adams launched a series of works which confronted dynamic equilibrists with virtually irrefutable claims. In place of James's amateur geology of renewal he proposed an amateur physics of doom based on "time's arrow," as Sir Arthur Eddington said, on entropy. The measure of randomness in any closed system, of energy unavailable because irreversibly held in a state of static equilibrium, in Adams's view entropy represented the debauch of order in the cosmic and social and psychic scheme of things.

For all Adams's idiosyncrasy of thought, despite his snobbism of mind, he shared with others of his time and circle an ambition to capture the genius of his American era in a work of boldest imagination. Exhibiting in exaggerated degree the taste and learning of a people and a period that sanctified the man of genius, in essays, poems, monographs, letters composed from 1907 until his death in 1918 he contended that the Second Law of Thermodynamics was in fact manifest in his particular person and validated by his own life and career. It was as an exemplary ironist of progress, then, that he presented himself, spokesman for a social class with a genius not for triumph but for failure. And he concluded his career demonstrating that a powerlessness to avoid failure, an alienation from the new national politics of power, represented a process of evolution beyond the control of his crowd but obedient to the mastery of worse folk, Israelites from Crakow and still more debauched, more detestable others.

Having decided that the Age of Progress had peaked, had hit zenith during the period of Theodore Roosevelt's febrile presidency, that progress brought life on earth to boiling point, to the point of self-consuming heat, Adams fancied himself a guest of honor at a ceremony of the doomed whose funeral oration he alone was cool enough to compose and deliver. Because the first Adams had shaped the origin of things in the New World surely this last in a distinguished line, Henry, was fated to explain why America perforce prefigured a collapse of civilization on earth. By reason of an eighteenth-century education and a nineteenth-century breeding, he possessed a grand enough idea of vocation and calling as well as art and science enough—genius enough—to formulate in the language of *The Federalist Papers* a twentieth-century law of degradation and decay. So it was that he interposed himself. And so engrossing were his proclamations of chaos, so seductive his prophecies, so grim the national experience from the mid-twenties until this very moment that major figures and main movements of modernism in America are held captive, confined by shackles forged in Henry Adams's mind.

V

NOTES ON ELECTRICITY

Henry Adams, Eugene O'Neill

Why does this strange doom hang over bourgeois culture, that its progress seems only to hasten its decay?. . . . In art, philosophy, physics, psychology, history, sociology, and biology the "crisis" of bourgeois culture is always due to the same cause. And this is no accident, because that destructive illness was originally the dynamic force . . . but now . . . it is a power for ill. Worn-out engines have become brakes. Outworn truths become illusions. Bourgeois culture is dying of a myth.

Christopher Caudwell, *Studies in a Dying Culture* (1938)

HOWEVER NORMATIVE WAS ADAMS'S CHOLER, however automatic his impulse to transpose private thoughts into national themes, still it must be said that his lugubriousness coincides with leading fashions of thought apparent first in London and Paris and later, during the twenties, in Berlin and Zurich and Vienna and New York. Now too, if we follow Robert Penn Warren's lead, it turns out that the origins of disenchantment occur much earlier in America than elsewhere. "Long before the bad news from France" and from "*fin-de-siècle* London had reached us," Warren says, long before Adams presumed to function as our official bearer of bad tidings in America, the idea of failure, the failure of the American Idea had become less and less fleeting and casual and more and more imperious a thought. Shortly before the Civil War ended, Warren argues, Americans first "patented our own version of alienation." Civil War and Great War, in Warren's view these large events span the years when an "unprecedented energy," an "untameable energy" impelled this astonishing nation to seize and occupy a continent. Incontinent and unchecked, it satisfied a stupefyingly huge array of appetites but was sanctioned by one reason only. The American concept of the free man, the "responsible self," the "self-perfected in selflessness" alone justified seizure and occupation. If this vision of selflessness failed to enliven the "spirit of the nation we have promised to create," then nothing on earth could rationalize those crimes. Following the Civil War, Warren maintains, literary intellectuals recoiled in horror at American irresponsibility, a belated recoil stirred by the crisis behind and the quandary ahead. What appalled them was America's default of promise, not just the specter of default but its flesh and bones. And it was this prescience of horror which constituted the very core of alienation among a widening circle of writers, bearers of bad tidings, who reckoned the price of betrayal, found it insupportable, and foresaw bankruptcy in the long run of American enterprise.[1]

Though Warren does not refer to *Uncle Tom's Cabin* or to Stowe or others less rabid than she but equally keen to forewarn society against following a ruinous course to a dismal end, nonetheless his testimony is twice welcome. Returning attention to that state of mind which antedates Adams's, simultaneously it plants Adams's mind in a proper field. For it was Adams who identified the specter, the ghost in the American machine at *fin de siècle*, Adams who devised an epic system explaining why this apparition must haunt a society which adopted technology as the instrument and end of civilization. Adams alone cannot be held responsible for the pall of dolor which shrouds post-modernist art in America. But it was indeed Henry Adams who first insisted that America itself belied progress, that these States did in fact symbolize the hope and despair of advanced industrial order in the world. Contrasting the sexual splendor of American women and an inattention, an attenuation of love; measuring the abyss separating his friend Cabot Lodge's power of imagination from his literary performance; observing the bearing, the *bêtise* of his social and intellectual inferior, the President of the United States, himself the cause of bedlam in the Progressive Era—wherever Adams turned he chose to see in operation only that contraposition of force which he insisted must signify a betrayal of energy in the most dynamic society the world had known. "Power is poison," he said reflecting on his former friend Theodore Roosevelt, that "stupid, blundering, bolting bull calf." A wild man, Roosevelt made sense only if his conduct was understood to express a last hysteric flare of meteoric vitality, a show of power, a shower of energy before final dispersion. "Power when wielded by abnormal energy is the most serious of facts," Adams sneered, pondering the "effect of unlimited power on Presidents." Deciding that the effect is indeed worth noting "because it represents the same process in society," correlating Roosevelt's style with American sensibility, Adams gauged the force both of man and country by means of a formula which paired the twin and countervailing powers of imperial Russia and industrial America—both embryonic superstates—in a standoff of means and ends of government. Roosevelt, who possessed a kind of immoderate primitive energy which belongs to ultimate matter, was "pure act."[2] And America, characterized as a society which fused pure act to sheer will, must eventually confront Russia, so Adams foresaw, because that "vast continental mass of inert motion, like a glacier," that "ice-cap of *vis inertiae*," moving eastward, must pull Europe into its orbit as if by gravitational force and bar America from the Pacific. The end, in Adams's historical judgment, was not co-existence but co-extinction.

Having read Ernst Mach he knew that "Matter was Motion—Motion was Matter." Knowing too, as he said in his biography of Lodge, that the Will or "what we now call Energy" alone was "perfect," he anticipated Heisenberg's version of a main proposition in modern physical theory: energy is "not only the force which keeps everything in motion" but too like "fire in Heraclitus's philosophy" is the "basic stuff of which the world is made."[3] Coordinating energy and matter, matter and motion, motion and inertia (demonstrated by a mathematics beyond cavil and applied to systemic function without exception); equating mechanical power with will power and applying this equation to the body politic and its members everywhere; then, finally, conflating American energy and Russian inertia, the ideology of progress and the law of entropy, Adams presented the results of computation. America, the very model of a modern materialist society, the place where motion was most violent because fueled by a national myth of energy, American society moved toward oblivion at a gallop of acceleration whose velocity could be clocked by applying the Second Law both to international and domestic affairs. Most especially it pertained to the subject of women.

The Woman Question! What incomparable good fortune it was for Henry Adams to have lived at the very moment when virtually everyone agreed that women embodied polarity and contradiction in America. Beginning with Adams, indeed, writers put the problem of progress as a form of this prodigious Question. And from the 1920s to the present moment, one or another incarnation of womankind in the United States has been required to bear witness as it were either on James's behalf or Adams's—that is, give evidence in support or denial of the proposition which portrays this society as a presentiment and manifestation of disorder in the grand scheme of things. Quite as the question of Woman thus provides both a historically accurate and rhetorically choice way of subsuming the whole subject of damnation and salvation of modern industrial civilization in our era so too do Adams and James present themselves as figures, both literal and fictive, of authority. And though henceforth I shall refer to Henry Adams and William James as if both men were live lobbyists fierce at the task of advancing their interests, claims, ideologies, I'm not truly passionate about proving irrefutable claims of influence. Although as household gods James and Adams really do preside over modern and post-modern times, nevertheless it's not only in the work of their disciples and surrogates—scholars, intellectuals, writers who stretch in apostolic succession back to the first decade of this century—that a continuity of power is found. Gods and their heresiarchs, Edward W. Said remarks in *Orientalism* (1978), give "reality and presence" to a set of ideas that has "a history and a tradition of thought, imagery and vocabulary," hegemony not confined solely to or limited by the names of persons.[4]

After James's death, for example, in the period following the First World War it was Charles Beard, inheriting James's legacy, who in one forum after another honored machinery itself, the technnological era in its entirety, for "engaging human energies in a manner surpassing the lure of war." Ingeniously fusing prewar pacifism with postwar nationalism, Beard amended James just enough to compensate for twenty-five years of elapsed time, time enough to support his contention that the "dynamic character of technology" is indisputably, axiomatically, the "supreme instrument of progress." Endorsing J. B. Bury's noted book *The Idea of Progress* (1932), writing its general introduction Beard invited "historical thinkers" to "trace to their uttermost ramifications the influences of technology upon the warp and woof of civilization, including poetry and art." Not that he solicited still another book on the industrial revolution. What he sought, what he hoped to elicit was evidence that technology, viewed as the "fundamental basis of modern civilization," possessed "something intrinsic" which promised "indefinite operation," limitless growth and perpetual motion. Inviting his colleagues to regard their individual subjects in this new light of understanding, he hoped for proof that the age of industry did in fact confirm sovereign law, did in truth disclose a "dynamic force of inexorable drive" by means of which the "progressive conquest of nature can be effected." Conceding that the "past has been chaos, without order or design," Beard nonetheless found irresistible the "haunting thought that by immense efforts of will and intelligence, employing natural science as the supreme instrumentality of power," humanity would launch itself on a course which leads "above necessity into the kingdom of freedom, subduing material things to humane and rational purposes."[5]

Needless to say I focus on Beard not for want of Jacobites ready to defend machine civilization in that age of innocence but because no other apostle surpassed him in conviction or influence. So certain was he that civilization would be saved by a lock, stock, and barrel of machinery that he put his career and reputation to unswerving service in behalf of the cult of technology, its establishment as official myth and permanent dogma. Although there's no clinching proof of Beard's effect on the warp and woof of poetry and art in that period, it does seem likely that Eugene O'Neill, for example, was driven to write *Dynamo* as if to test the force of Beard's belief: technology "surpasses all religions." Given O'Neill's state of mind at the start of that play in contrast to his turnabout of position at its end, given too the thesis on which it is hinged—a fulcrum of female—there are solid reasons to regard *Dynamo* as a standard source in any modern history of our liaison with machines. And though both James and Adams together did indeed set the scene for O'Neill and Fitzgerald and William Carlos Williams and Gertrude Stein, nonetheless it was Adams—with credentials for clairvoyance authorized by the deaths of two women to whom he stood in the closest possible connection, his wife's and his sister's, the one by suicide and the other by accident—whose gift best illustrates the power of wound and bow. Mourning the loss of accomplished young women whose American type not only he extolled but the world at large acclaimed—nullification so ominous, Adams maintained, augured disintegration not just of American female force but too of the life process in its entirety. It was this particular kind of dying, death without purpose, beyond consolation, Adams delivered and O'Neill accepted as proof of futility, prime fact of life.

Had Henry Adams lived long enough to see *Dynamo* performed, therefore, he couldn't have failed to applaud the sight of James vanquished, himself vindicated in the denouement of O'Neill's unprecedented, unordered piece. Indeed what's most amazing about this manic play is that it pinpoints the time and place and arena, the precise occasion of reversal in the history of an idea. Although O'Neill was himself cursed with a temperament in which despair not hope was endemic, simultaneously he had the good fortune of genius and the great luck to discover in personal torment a gift for portraying the uses of mania in the derangements of any system—individual, social, cosmic. About halfway into this work, his luck held. And he found in technology a principle so equivocal at its very core, so undeniably dual, that deception was assured of patronage even under the most secular of sovereignties: science. Incorporating within a single text the animadversions of both James and Adams, composing a melodrama of self-promotion and self-repudiation, in this convulsive play O'Neill anticipated and enshrined the process whereby a next generation of countrymen in ever-increasing numbers would come to think that decline was constant and irresistible and remorseless.

That rarest of attainments, a work of imagination which provides a complete inventory of features peculiar both to the career of a single writer and to the temper of a whole society at a moment of transformation, of revelation, in the life of the age, fifty years ago *Dynamo* nonplussed virtually everyone. Restored to the repertory, it now acquires the patina of a recovered relic. But in 1929, denounced by its original circle of reviewers, denied any merit at all, it introduced a theater of oscillation which not only recorded O'Neill's seduction by and revulsion from the public philosophy but too confounded trash and tragedy. Yoking vanguard doctrine on sexual pathology to retrograde dogma of religious faith, *Dynamo* raised so ruinous a din of disapprobation that only John Simon today could rival in distemper the tone of comment treating a flawed play which despite its imperfections is in ten different ways extraordinary. Within the disturbed mind of Reuben Light, sexual mania is fixed on energy itself, on technology, on the dynamo conceived as a malign mother-goddess who converts him into a Freudian cripple. And although this is by no means an uncommon state of being among O'Neill's sons, Reuben is unique in that his fate underscores the subversion of American society as a whole, a society perverted by worship of an exterminating angel, energy incarnate in the power plant.

For good and ill, therefore, O'Neill executed a work both phantasmagoric and visionary, hallucinatory and prophetic. Anticipating ill-will and wrong judgment, however, during fall and early winter 1928 he sent long cautionary letters from the South of France, letters which were supposed to provide self-justification and self-exculpation enough to last lifetimes of labor on a "symbolic and factual biography" of the "American (and not only American) soul." In support of this immense theme, O'Neill set down a theory of epic art in drama. And in meditation on what he took to be the peremptory interest of American history as a whole, of modern theater in particular, and of human sensibility in general, he conceived a trilogy of plays led off by *Dynamo* which would portray the "death of the old God" and mankind's helplessness to find new objects of worship.[6]

Why is it then that reviewers who had cheered O'Neill for performing Herculean efforts of literary innovation suddenly in 1929 chose to admonish him for daring to venture beyond the fringe of experiment? O'Neill wrestles with God, it was said, and is thrown in the first round. Surely, his friend George Jean Nathan remarked, this can't be the same writer who "dug deep into the human heart in *The Great God Brown* and who in *Beyond the Horizon* and *Strange Interlude*" showed himself to be a "brilliant interpreter of the hopes and disasters and pitiable bravery of mankind." Surely that other fellow is not the O'Neill of this "amateurish, strident and juvenile concoction."[7] A Greenwich Village atheist, St. John Ervine called him and begged him to renounce "thinking" forever and instead concentrate on "feeling," the sphere of a poet, O'Neill's proper realm, lest science and philosophy exhaust his mind and bankrupt his art. A womb with a view, Noel Coward said—let's hope for the first time—encapsulating the table talk of Benchley, Broun, and Charles Brackett, Algonquin wits. The dynamo must not have been grounded, one of the wits remarked, referring to Reuben's final and berserk act of self-immolation.

Unarguably *Dynamo* is no masterwork. Granting its ebb and flow of skill in the disposition of ideas, granting too that there's a flavor of porridge in its mix, still it's a choice piece documenting the exfoliation of a major writer's career, anticipating an increase of energy and a desuetude of industry in American writing during the last fifty years. For as Lewis Mumford said in another connection, "the ultimate religion of our seemingly rational age," the myth of the machine, is sustained by lunacies which must have catastrophic effect on the act of faith and exercise of reason in the heyday of technology. Perceived in Mumford's way, therefore, *Dynamo* is a seismic work of American modernist art. For it records and crystallizes the ambivalence of a generation of writers, backed by two centuries of faith in dynamism, who entered the second quarter of the twentieth century with a diminished trust in society's power to maintain what their predecessors had spoken of as a condition of dynamic equilibrium between technological society and the state of nature. By the third quarter distrust was the conventional state of mind and disorder the usual state of society, particularly in the work of writers who were, like O'Neill, given to alcohol or drugs or suicide. And by the fourth quarter, when chaos came to seem an irremediable state of being in all spheres of social life, betrayal of trust was recognized as a universal and unalterable principle of behavior in the conduct of private affairs. Masterwork or not, *Dynamo* is a seminal text. In pursuing a private inconsolable quest for relief from the dilemmas of faith, in selecting modernist drama as his vehicle and addressing himself to the principal myth of our era of industry, of power, O'Neill alone among writers for the American stage undertook to experiment with the technique, craft, and mechanism of theatrical production in order to exploit the benefactions and appraise the bereavements of the Age of Progress. "Machines acting in time space, and hardly existing save then in action," Ezra Pound had said in approval of America's contribution to "an aesthetic of machinery"—in his little book *Antheil and the Treatise on Harmony* (1927)—machines "belong chiefly to an art acting in time space."[8]

For all its adventurousness of stagecraft, however, for all its look of anomaly, in eroticizing electrodynamic energy *Dynamo* followed a well-charted course. Despite O'Neill's zest for novelty, for experiment, his play reproduces a subject he had adorned and embroidered and embellished throughout the twenties. Inspired by Strindberg and sanctioned by Nietzsche—as everyone knows—O'Neill's most popular plays portrayed the lives of characters whose names (Eben, Dion, Reuben, Orin) bear a family resemblance because each shares a motive O'Neill derived from the principle of eros, from Dionysus. These intimations O'Neill's contemporaries caught. What they missed is less dazzling but more illuminating. For the play does in fact receive and emit lines of force stemming from mentors less compelling than Nietzsche and more influential than Mumford but no less magisterial than either man: Adams and Lawrence.

Although a couple of reviewers did casually connect *Dynamo* and *The Education of Henry Adams*, their attention lapsed after a glance or two at Adams's key chapter, "The Virgin and the Dynamo." And except for Joseph Wood Krutch, who insisted that O'Neill's play warranted more respect and praise than it got, critics remarked how clever a schoolmaster Adams was and how dull a pupil O'Neill seemed to be. As a result they failed to recognize in Reuben's prayers to the dynamo—a machine which is metamorphosed in his mind into a maternal deity to whom he vows absolute fealty and from whom he solicits a miracle to confirm him as her redeemer—they caught no echo of Adams's "Prayer to the Virgin of Chartres" (1920). A Swinburnian poem noisier and murkier though shorter than O'Neill's Strindbergian drama, Adams's prayer provides a persuasive source of O'Neill's ideology. "Listen, dear lady!" Adams's prayer foreshadows Reuben's devotions, "You shall hear the last / Of the strange prayers humanity has wailed." Although an Adams–O'Neill lineage of ideas cannot be finally proved, Adams's last weird wail, addressed to the dynamo and interpolated within the frame of his poem as a whole, the prayer to the Virgin which it interrupts—Adams's "Prayer to the Dynamo" could stand intact as the ground of Reuben's faith, the rationale of Reuben's last frenzied act of worship. "Mysterious power!" Adams addressed the machine. "Gentle Friend! Despotic Master! Tireless Force!" We "know not whether you are kind" or "cruel in your fiercer mood," but we do know that "prayer to you is thrown away. For you are only force and light; / A shifting current; night and day; / We know this well, and yet we pray, / For prayer is infinite, / like you!" Ending with verses far too grand for Reuben's mode of adolescent speech, Adams's poem mimics prayer and elevates chant to the exact degree of loftiness Reuben aspires to ascend:

> Seize, then the Atom! Rack his joints!
> Tear out of him his secret spring!
> Grind him to nothing!—though he points
> To us, and his life-blood anoints
> Me—the dead Atom-king![9]

Shifting Adams's gender, O'Neill portrays the dynamo as a despotic mistress who, to Reuben's fanatic mind, requires an undeviating purity of allegiance. "O Dynamo, who gives life to things, hear my prayer!" Reuben raves. "Grant me the miracle of your love!"

In outrageous fantasy, coalescing Adams's two prayers, O'Neill causes Reuben to solicit support from a despotic and deceitful queen of force whose reign is pernicious and everlasting. Outrageous surely but perspicuous too, O'Neill was caught up in the passion of Adams's irony, unlike Lewis Mumford. A man of far more stalwart mind, Mumford in 1962 wrote an "Apology to Henry Adams" which treated Adams's arias of obeisance to the Queen of Heaven not as grand opera but as pure piety. So unaccountable were his words of contrition, however, that there's irresistible lure in searching out impulse more Mumfordian than Mariolotristic. In still another attack on "the dehumanized ideology and methodology of our time" Mumford credits Adams with having been "saved" from "sterilization of mind" by a feminoid creed which Adams adopted and proposed as a "counterpoise to chaos." Moved by womanly faith, a woman's faith in her own creativity, in the ramifying processes of life, above all those of sex, love, motherhood, glorying in reverence for "woman's healing love and nurture"—redeemed by this "countervailing form of energy, the energy of erotic love, reproduction and creation"—Adams in Mumford's reincarnation strove to save unborn generations from the blunder of waste in technology.[10]

To construe snobbism as high-mindedness and find a savior in the disbursements of that parched soul—taken literally, Mumford's "Apology" is even less comprehensible than Adams's "Prayer." What Mumford recycled fortunately O'Neill retrieved: attention on the void. Listen Ada, says that closet chaotic, that failed Lucifer, Reuben Light: "Tonight the miracle will happen" establishing "my kingdom on earth," an imperium of primal power manifest in the machine and expressed in sounds which I alone can construe. The song of dynamo, "isn't that the greatest poem of all—the poem of eternal life?" Because a dynamo, "the Great Mother" in her material aspect, is driven by turbines in a rush of river filled by rain fallen from clouds risen with air afloat from the sea, Reuben fancies it must be the sea which "makes her heart beat too!" Furthermore his textbooks say that "the sea is only hydrogen and oxygen and minerals, and they're only atoms and atoms only protons and electrons—even our blood and the sea are only electricity in the end! And the stars! Driving through space, round and round, just like the electrons in the atom! But there must be a center around which all this moves" and that center "must be the Great Mother of Eternal Life, Electricity, and Dynamo is her Divine Image on earth! Her power houses are the new churches." And I Reuben am appointed, by a dead parent returning from "the Great Mother into which she passed when she died," to serve as a "new saviour who will bring happiness and peace to men."

Pretty Ada Fife wants no miracles, no savior. The daughter of an atheist who runs the power plant, she loves her neighbor, the boy next door, this feckless son of an evangelist preacher terrorized by God, and of a sanctimonious, deceitful mother seductively chaste. Familiar stuff of O'Neill's imagination, solemnized by psychoanalysis, by an impasto of Jung and Freud, archetypal pattern and neurotic compulsion, in *Dynamo* it is laid on with an especially heavy hand, relieved only by O'Neill's playfulness in the choice of names. Fife and Light, Light and Fife—life fight, fie flight, fight life—both family names personify themes which develop from Reuben's forfeit of faith in the God of his fathers in favor of faith in power, in energy, in the First Law of Thermodynamics. Devastated by passion and envenomed by guilt Reuben is unhinged by the whole apparatus of circuits and systems, both metaphysical and mechanical. In contrast, Ada and May Fife, her mother, are women of the age attuned to instinct and fecundated by force. Mrs. Fife Reuben first regards as a goddess of the machine robed in vestments of Venus. "You're like her," he tells May, "Dynamo, the Great Mother, big and warm." I love the plant, she sighs. "I love the dynamos . . . I could sit forever and listen to them sing . . . they're always singing about everything in the world." To Reuben's ear that "harsh, throaty metallic purr" seems to emanate from a machine which looks as if "it had breasts . . . but not like a girl . . . not like Ada . . . no, like a woman . . . like her mother . . . or mine . . . a great, dark mother! . . . that's what a dynamo is! That's what life is!" In the end, however, he renounces Fife for Light, life for flight, kills Ada so as to free himself to serve his dead mother "who wants some one man to love her purely." That is to say he rebuffs the inviting figures of Venus and clutches instead this avatar of the Virgin, a tenebrous ghost who returns in a dream to appoint him her messiah.[11]

In this ironic way, old wives' tales of the genteel tradition, restored to a place of priority in the era of mechanical force, led O'Neill to install both Venus and Virgin in a cathedral built by the Light & Power Company. "The new American, like the new European," Adams had acquired a large posthumous fame for saying, "was the servant of the powerhouse, as the European of the twelfth century was the servant of the Church." Like Auden years later, whose essay on "The Natural World of the Dynamo" argues that Adams erred in identifying the power of Venus with the passion of the Virgin, erred again in dissociating both power and passion from energy in its modern and mechanical forms, from machinery—like Auden, O'Neill saw lines of power and passion linking both Virgin and Venus with the dynamo. And Auden in his turn contended that Adams's project, to track down "female energy" wherever it could be found, had turned up nothing because he hadn't known whose trail he followed. It was the Venus-dynamo not the Virgin Adams had worshiped from the first. "Venus is the dynamo in disguise," Auden said, a "symbol for impersonal natural force," for those very "masses, identical relations and recurrent events" whose icon Adams had insisted was absent from this modern materialist world.[12]

Auden, though understandably blank on *Dynamo*, would have found in O'Neill's play a pioneer version of his own thought. In May Fife, a voluptuary of the natural world, "humming to herself, her big body relaxed" but electrically charged, her heart beating to the rhythm and sound of an "unbroken and eternal continuity," in this iconic figure O'Neill embodied the luster of sex, the utility and vitality of earthly love, the productivity of labor. In contrast, Amelia Light, a polluted Venus disguised as the Virgin, an unnatural mother who betrays her son's trust—Mrs. Light is moved by eddies of passion in which O'Neill discerned an Oedipal current, source both of the guilt of lust and the destructiveness of power. Because Reuben was torn between duty in the hydroelectric plant and service to the Church he alternated between love of May and adoration of Mary. Unlike the speaker in Henry Adams's "Prayer" (who confesses that he has "ceased to strive" because he "feels the energy of faith" not in "the future of science, but in you!") Reuben's last words represent a loss of faith in energy and science, in Church and mother, in culture and cosmos.

Although in the thirties O'Neill struggled to recover reasons to believe in some sort of future, continued to transvalue archaic systems of belief and behavior, henceforth his drama disclosed the conviction which was to inspire his last plays: no form of service, no system, no force at all would root out mankind's bottomless depths of mendacity or emancipate man from a thralldom to deceit. Beginning with *Dynamo* O'Neill's imagination tended to invent actions which exhibited an irreversible drift toward disorder and degradation in family affairs, actions which appear to apply the Entropy Law to human relationships much as Adams had applied Kelvin's Second Law of Thermodynamics to the study of American history. Enlisting Freud, whose theory of eros and thanatos he anticipated by a year, O'Neill fortified his own judgment and simultaneously plumbed the mind itself as if to test the validity of Adams's prophecies. The first American writer after Adams to dissent from conventional wisdom on the uses of technology, O'Neill was also among the very first to uphold a position which in recent years has itself become cliché. In the modern age, the principle of negation, nil, a death instinct not a life force governs man's activities more tyranically, more ruthlessly than any other power or agent or agency has ever done.

In *Dynamo*, then, O'Neill followed an unusually labyrinthine route to return to his accustomed place, a cul-de-sac of history from which he can be retrieved by way of Adams's chart, Freud's map, Auden's gloss. In encompassing the gist of Adams's "Dynamic Theory of History" (1904) within the spectacle of this portentous play, in closing on a wild act of worship of the Dynamo-Virgin-Mother-Venus, O'Neill doesn't just exorcise his private demons but manages also to transform Reuben's madness into a fearful vision of diabolism on a grand scale, a debacle of technology and progress and power in the United States. How unaccountable it is therefore that reviewers, critics, colleagues, scholars from 1929 to the present have treated Adams's autobiography as a masterly work of strenuous learning and O'Neill's play as an embarrassment of patchy science. Why anybody could think, O'Neill was later to say, that "I would waste my time on a piffling struggle between pseudo-religion and pseudo-science is more than I can make out"—particularly in that *Dynamo* attributes the cause of Reuben's "psychological mess" to his mother's betrayal. She "really smashes him."[13]

No question that betrayal is O'Neill's theme. No question either that betrayal was on his mind that season, 1928–1929, as he fumed over the terms set by his wife Agnes Boulton, conditions he must meet before she agreed to divorce. Considering how O'Neill did indeed waste his time on a piffling struggle between his wife and his mistress, he virtually invited critics to deride his character, patronize his mind, and dismantle his play. Reviling Agnes Boulton, fretting to marry Carlotta Monterey, he refused for the first time in his career to help cast, stage, rewrite a new work. All New York, knowing the reach of his imagination but skeptical of his grasp, instead of *Dynamo* saw O'Neill himself writ large, saw the maunderings of a distraught drinking man drowning in a turbulence of sex, a surfeit of female. Today it is idle to shield this play against twenties gossip. But *Dynamo* is at once well-favored and ill-served enough to warrant the support of an advocate or two. For not only did it open a vein which was to infuse the high art of O'Neill's last work but too in it he sought to demonstrate the value of a method intended to revolutionize custom, convention, and habit in Broadway theater.

Not in the mechanics of plot is interest to be found, nor should it be sought in the lives of people who were, O'Neill noted, "psychologically simple" because animated by "direct primitive drive." Its authority rested on a complex instrumentation affecting the production as a whole. The most original and venturesome of O'Neill's experiments with a synchrony of sound and sense—experiments he insisted he had introduced in *Emperor Jones*—*Dynamo* doesn't struggle to solve problems conjured out of Wedekind, say, or adapted from Shaw. Not on this occasion does O'Neill plunder "the more radical of the rebel dramatists" whose techniques Robert Brustein accuses him of copying in an effort to "disguise the banality" of his own material during the twenties and thirties. O'Neill's mimicry managed to "fog up already familiar ground," Brustein says in *The Theatre of Revolt* (1964), not to open up uncharted territory. Harsh true words, Brustein's indictment has no bearing at all on O'Neill's conduct in composing *Dynamo*, on his ingenuity of mind in conceiving the uses of sound as a component of structure in a play which combined cadences of human speech and tones of nature in amalgam with the noise of machines.

"This is a machine age," O'Neill wrote in a memo to the designer Lee Simonson. And the circumambient effect of machines on the life of our age can be captured in drama by means of tones, vocal and mechanical, which exploit all the resources of the "instrument (the theatre as a whole) on which one composes." In *Dynamo*, thunder and lightning, water flowing over the dam, the hum of the generator are not "incidental noises but significant dramatic overtones that are an integral part of that composition in the theatre which is the whole play." Because too it has always been his habit to write "by ear for the ear," critics have been accustomed to reproach him for repetitiveness. "Blamed for repetitions, which to me were significant recurrences of theme," he admitted to being a "bug on the subject of sound in the theatre." What he was after, reverberation, resonance, he insisted on despite a failure to overcome that "slipshod, old-fashioned disregard of our modern theatre for what ought to be one of its superior opportunities (contrasted with the medium of the novel for example)" to express "the essential rhythms of our lives today." Having scored the new play to register "overtones of characteristic, impelling and governing mechanical sound and rhythm," he hoped it would provide exactly the right "background for lives" molded by engines. And if at last the Theatre Guild were to set the piece in the sort of environment it required, then audiences could not fail "to be surprised by the added dramatic value," the "*modern* values," his work would take on. "Machines are now a part of life, it is proper that men should feel something about them," Ezra Pound had said, publicizing Antheil's music. "There would be something weak about art if it couldn't deal with this new content."

All this theorizing, O'Neill continued, doesn't have much to do with plays like *Strange Interlude* or *Marco Millions* but has "a hell of a lot to do with *Dynamo*." Where lightning is called for O'Neill did not want the literal flash "but the reproduction of the dramatic effect of lightning on people's faces." Thunder must have a "menacing, brooding quality." And the "queer noise of the generator" must work in counterpoint with the "strained, unnatural effect of the human voice raised" in an effort to dominate the generator's hum. However fluently put, these ideas were ineffable. Whether or not O'Neill in 1929 was capable of articulating first principles and final drafts, he put out for production a text whose force gained momentum by way of a controlled crescendo of noise. All styles of discourse—Reverend Light's archaic formality of speech, Ada's flapper slang, May Fife's ooze and gurgle—O'Neill aspired to unite in cascades of sound, human and inhuman, which finally overpower both the play and its audience. It wasn't therefore just a bigger bag of tricks he drew on or even a tighter bridge of subject and setting. It was the clairaudient art of an age of industry he hoped to invent. And with its invention, a modernist idea of drama and a modern dramatist's mastery of theater would be attuned to major motifs of modernism in art, letters, and social thought.

Although we cannot know if the Guild production came off slipshod or old-fashioned we can be certain that it failed to catch O'Neill's rhythm. In that entire company only Simonson, who had followed "the trail of O'Neill's mind from a powerhouse on the Connecticut River to the play it inspired" and heard the sound of the river below mingle with the whine and whir of the transformers above—Simonson alone seems to have known what was at stake. Seeing "water become fire," he said in his memoir *The Stage Is Set* (1932), he understood for the first time why "primitive people cringed with terror before thunderbolts and erected altars to invisible gods," understood too how to take the "commonplace mechanical shapes of our industrial environment" as symbols of the "forces for good and evil that they released." From *Dynamo* he learned "how the designing of a stage setting could be made into a creative act, whether or not I myself could make it one." Unfortunately the sets he designed for the storm and the power station (a pair of houses in cross-section, transmission lines, a huge mechanical thing) gave exactly the effect O'Neill had warned against, "an old melodrama thunderstorm, and a generator sounding obviously like a vacuum cleaner."[14] Bad luck all round, therefore, that this vaunted alliance between art and technology was bungled in *Dynamo*. Worse luck indeed that the play, in failing to drive toward its finale in a Niagara of power, portrays Reuben Light not as a scapegoat of our age of industry but as a victim of Oedipal caprice. For it does seem likely that designer, director, actors reduced the substance of O'Neill's theme to a diatribe of hatred and self-pity, as Arthur and Barbara Gelb observe, an angry play by an angry man who should never have visited that plant at Stevenson, Connecticut. Reduced so, *Dynamo* appeared to concern nothing more momentous than Reuben's "pathological desire for sexual purity," stuff too base for tragedy, Stark Young said.[15]

Despite the fact that O'Neill abandoned a play which was supposed to score winning points of theory, nevertheless this waif of a work is neither witless on stage nor lifeless on the printed page. For anyone who is concerned to root out the origins of O'Neill's obsession with treachery in its manifold forms, the preeminent theme of his last years, *Dynamo* is unquestionably a central source. Although it is by far a less outlandish labor of mythopoesis than the plays that flank it, it does not on that ground merit reinstatement to a favored place in the annals of theater. The best reason for its elevation, however, is its unexampled value as a palimpsest of ideas chronicling that moment of reversal in a society which fifty years ago still conceived itself to be the heir of long ages of experiment—mainly successful—in devising a habitable world, a civilized order, but suddenly overnight came to perceive itself as a precursor state, forerunner, herald, symbol of the dissolution of order in Western civilization. Unmatched by any other single poem or novel or play *Dynamo* examplifies, quite as Scott and Zelda Fitzgerald are real-life exemplars without rival, the reasons American sensibilities in the late twenties suffered a sea change of spirit, an inversion of mood whose chief features each year grow more pronounced as our century runs its course.

"Pure science is high religion incarnate," Walter Lippmann announced with cozy confidence in *A Preface to Morals*, his sensational study of the "moral difficulties of our anarchical age," a book which was in press that January, in print that May, 1929, and reprinted six times by the end of the year. Maintaining that there was "something new in the modern world," a thing unparalleled in any earlier civilization, "power-driven machinery," Lippmann's *Preface* ended where *Dynamo* had begun. "As we discern the ideals of machine technology," Lippmann closed his famed book, the more comfortably do we adapt to those modes of production which stylize life in the modern world: "we find ourselves in harmony with the age we live in." Less cozily but far more cannily O'Neill's discernment had led to an about-face of belief, a turnabout which reviled the judgment of those reigning minds, Lippmann's, Charles Beard's, H. G. Wells's, whose authority that year crested at a high-water mark of influence as apologists for "machine civilization." Having opened with an endorsement identical to theirs and ended with a dereliction of their idea of harmony, *Dynamo* dramatized reversal in the most persuasive and unexpected way possible—by reversing itself. To what precise degree O'Neill deliberately weighed and instinctively grasped reasons why annulment was in order I waive the opportunity to say. What must not be forsaken, however, is the occasion to praise O'Neill for charting the course followed by two generations of writers who have tested and disputed Lippmann's law. "Mechanical progress has ceased to be casual and accidental and become systematic and cumulative."[16]

Having espoused the ideals of technology and found himself in a state of disharmony inside and out, O'Neill renounced Lippmann's newfangled faith in a high religion of progress. But before I continue to speculate on the roles played by diverse contemporaries in formulating, designing, codifying systems of thought O'Neill could scarcely have avoided knowing, I must confess that there's no proof O'Neill read anything I have mentioned. There's no evidence that O'Neill had near at hand, as he composed *Dynamo*, a copy of *Harper's Magazine* for August, 1928, the issue in which Charles Beard published an article called "Is Our Civilization in Peril?" Whether or not O'Neill availed himself of these materials or associations, he would have had to read virtually nothing which bore on his subject, see nearly no one, if he was to avoid knowing who took what position in this debate. Hard indeed to miss Beard taking up a position antithetical to Adams's, Beard contending that "machine civilization differs from all others in that it is highly dynamic, containing within itself the seeds of constant reconstruction." In confraternity or not, therefore, a singular group of intellectuals in the United States, spanning the fields of history and journalism and literature, insisted that the age of technology contained within itself the key to survival or collapse of civilization. When we find Beard, to whom Lippmann deferred, addressing himself to Adams's subject and O'Neill's theme, we are induced to mark a unison of ideas even if we cannot establish a union of minds. And when we recall that O'Neill's imagination teemed with ideas borrowed from a circumscribed group of mentors we cannot help wondering if this circle has not been too narrowly defined. Knowing the depth of his hunger to master the matter of modernism we are tempted to exclude no writer who was then seriously engaged by the task of deciding if progress would redeem or destroy the world.

In that O'Neill wrote plays as if his life not just his art or reputation hung in the balance it's fair to assume that he knew of the work of those whose names and views and careers I have invoked. Probably too he knew these people themselves pretty well. All those whose names I've mentioned had been assembled by Mabel Dodge—who would before long succeed in enticing D. H. Lawrence to New Mexico—for her salon at 23 Fifth Avenue, beginning in 1912: Lippmann, Lee Simonson, Robert Edmond Jones, and especially John Reed, her lover. So interwoven were these arabesques and intimacies of body and mind that Lippmann, on visiting Reed in hospital in 1916 accompanied by "the tempestuous Louise Bryant," as Ronald Steel writes in *Walter Lippmann and the American Century* (1980), arrived with the woman who was "then Reed's fiancée, later Eugene O'Neill's mistress and ultimately William Bullitt's wife." Most certainly, then, O'Neill drew on common funds of thought. And if it happens that he didn't, no harm is done. For any reasonably responsible treatment of his aims and attainment, his will to penetrate the principle of technology in order to learn whether or not machine civilization justified a continuing faith in some idea of purpose in the universe—no study of O'Neill's imagination should fail to account for his contribution to the literature of dynamism in America. In settling this account, we must place O'Neill's work in its setting, a setting which includes Lawrence's notes on electricity in his marvelous *Studies in Classic American Literature* (1923). By 1929 O'Neill no longer put much stock in anyone's vision of liberation. But it is extraordinary to discover in *Dynamo* the very conceit, the precise configuration of images Lawrence had chosen to justify his own slim hope of redemption in America.

In the vividest possible contrast to Lippmann's kind of easy faith, Lawrence maintained a touchy, quarrelsome, distrustful, discomfited allegiance to a "pristine something" in American experience, slender but sufficient cause for a renewal of hope. Despairing of life in Great Britain, fantasizing about Russia and fiddling about Italy and Australia, he awaited the call to America. "It is not a case of my will," he had told Lady Ottoline Morrell in 1915, but "I shall not go to America until a stronger force pulls me across the sea."[17] By 1922, as we know, transplanted in the American Southwest, at last he found something primordial, "unbroken, unbreakable, and not to be got under by us awful whites with our machines." So he informed Harriet Monroe, founding editor of *Poetry*.[18] He had already of course taken up these matters in book after book, treating the cause of convulsion in the modern world as an expression of its corrupt will to "translate godhead into pure mechanism." In recasting the history of American letters to conform to visions prompted by life in New Mexico Lawrence convinced himself that a "polarized flow" of energy was pronounced in the New World. Consider storms. In life and literature "storms are a sort of violent readjustment in some polarized flow. You have a polarized circuit," he says, taking his cue from Dana's *Two Years Before the Mast*, not to be mistaken for "mechanical machine unison." And when this circuit, this "breath of life," this interchange grows unstable, there are "storms in the air, storms in the water, storms of anger"—storms, in a word, indistinguishable from those unleashed in *Dynamo*. Breaking the circuit of unstable energy, metaphysical and Freudian, O'Neill's thunderstorm ("impelling all those people, effecting their thought and actions") brings the breath of life to Ada and Reuben, establishes a quivering vital unstable erotic equilibrium of Fife and Light. It is short-lived. And before long all circuits are again overloaded, equilibrium is again lost and Reuben, utterly corrupted, worships a "perfect inhuman machine."

The analogue holds first to last. Indeed, there's so sweeping a tide of evidence and so tidy a field of argument that it's hard to resist making claims of indebtedness beyond any borrower's means to repay or any auditor's power to compute. Images intertwine, figures couple in a riot of association whose common element is, strikingly, the sea. For as Reuben observed, mad for absolute truth, it is the sea whose beat we hear in the pulse of a power plant driven by the same water that flows in our blood. And Lawrence, in preparing to correlate landlocked texts and seafaring tales, notes that it was a "great move of imaginative conquest" which led American writers early on to decide that the "earth is too specific, too particular" to support idealizations, mysticisms, symbolisms of an Absolute. As the emblem of a universal, land won't do. But because the "blood of all men is ocean-born," men are drawn to the salt water, the sea, "the greatest material mother of us all," compelled to KNOW her." Almost as if he were ringing changes on Lawrence's note O'Neill, himself a man of sea-wracked imagination, taunts Reuben with a seaborne temptation to hold "his Dynamo-Mother" in his arms. In an act of conquest he cannot resist, Reuben completes a circuit he cannot survive. Electrocuting himself he dies with a "moan that is a mingling of pain and loving consummation." Love the great mother of the sea, Lawrence chants, "the Magna Mater. And see how bitter it is. And see how you must fail to win her to your ideal: forever fail. Absolutely fail." I think now, said Lawrence's wife Frieda in 1953, that "I ought to have handled him better; but how can a poor woman handle a thunderstorm?"[19]

What *Dynamo* leads to finally is a triptych with Lawrence on the left and Adams on the right and O'Neill in the middle, Adams the New England don gone daft on Rome, O'Neill the ex-Papist gone daft for Reason, and Lawrence the expatriate gone native in Taos. It is not therefore a predisposition to gloom which unites them, the glue of alienation which in the late twenties cemented ties among intellectuals, groups, schools whose thought exhibits every tangent and vagary of doctrine. Rather they share a desperation so intense that it spans a continental divide of culture and geography, and even abolishes time. Based on the belief that our age of progress must accelerate the process of depletion and not, as Beard proposed, advance the process of revitalization, their fellowship persists unrecognized into the present. O'Neill's role is unnoticed, too, in large part because of the disappearance of the text, *Dynamo*, which O'Neill decided he would banish from consciousness, purge from the corpus of performable plays. Scholars, theater people in general took him at his word, took as final not his certitude of March, 1929, that *Dynamo* "will come into its own some day" but the despair in July which led him to discard the play itself, the project it was supposed to announce, the experiment in modernist theater it was intended to display. Although O'Neill's other flops retain standing as museum pieces of the twenties and thirties, this one was deaccessioned, as museum people say, first by the defilers and then by the curators of O'Neill's reputation.

However belated, restoration is welcome if it enables us to see, in the radiance of a single light, Adams and O'Neill and Lawrence as triumvirs of a movement which it is today foolhardy to ignore. Associating the force of real women with the generative thrust of a venereal machine, they condemn a people whose passion, bewitched by the spell of industrial devices and mechanical systems, is severed from that subterranean and terrestrial and cosmic flow of energy which validates the spirit of love and vitalizes the whole ball of earth from its center. Unlike Lawrence, however, from whom we part company briefly, O'Neill stands in the van of all those modernist writers who confirm Morse Peckham's thesis in *Man's Rage for Chaos* (1965), itself unthinkable outside this society and period: "After so many centuries of praising order, I think it is time to praise disorder a little, and to give the proper recognition to the men whose task it is to offer disorder, the artists."

Because the matter cannot end with a flourish of Peckhamite praise, we must refer to less global or epic speculation, turn attention away from the great world and its prospects back to *Dynamo*, to some last thoughts on O'Neill and his agitations. Far more telling than his tangle of abilities and disabilities as a playwright, his tone deafness and perfect pitch, his tackiness and grandeur of taste, is his luck in settling on, his wisdom in selecting, his pertinacity in exploring the subject which has harassed American writers from the twenties until the present, the dual question of treachery and fidelity, the uses of fraud in a world of delusions. Not until he wrote *Dynamo* did he begin to take its measure. And not until we gauge the pressure exerted by the idea of betrayal of love, of art, of government, of history, of the American Idea do we begin to account for the intensity with which two generations of our writers have composed books devastated by diverse manifestations of deceit.

Because, too, there's no disputing Brustein's judgment that without O'Neill it's doubtful we could have an American drama at all, there's unconscionable waste in leaving *Dynamo* where George Jean Nathan dumped it. Restored, restaged, recycled it still won't make a hit play. But its family romance identifies the animus underlying those master strokes of theater on which O'Neill's distinction rests. In the four plays that closed out his career, his mind, now sodden with damnation, probed the quagmire of sacred and profane love for new twists of degradation, a new ground of forgiveness. And although the centerpiece of his art. *A Long Day's Journey into Night* (1938–1939), confirms the guess that O'Neill lived through the kind of circumstance recorded in *Dynamo*, the later play discloses that it was not O'Neill but his mother who suffered Reuben's nightmare. That is to say it was O'Neill's real mother, Mary in their actual world, whose situation generated her son's impulse to portray Mary Tyrone's hopelessness, helplessness, faithlessness in his openly autobiographical last play. Realizing that it was her anguish, her ignominy which O'Neill assigned to Reuben Light, we turn the plot of *Dynamo* around so that it duplicates and does not reverse the alignments of O'Neill's family life. And we find ourselves set down in the solid center of the Tyrones' ordeal in O'Neill's masterpiece. Denuded of myth and divorced from ideology, the skeleton of *Dynamo* supports *A Long Day's Journey into Night*.

Indeed it is in the last scene, which Brustein views as among the "most powerful in all dramatic literature," that Mary Tyrone is herself unveiled, revealed stark, disgraced queen of earth, the only Madonna of whom mankind is worthy in a depraved world. Addicted to morphine, she writhes in inexpiable guilt caused by her failure to keep a girlhood vow, a promise to take the veil, become a nun. Haunted by this failure of devotion to the Queen of Heaven Mary Tyrone each day relives her original sin. In like fashion each of the Tyrones during the course of the play rehearses the chronicle of personal and collective defilement which it is at once intolerable to bear and impossible to remedy. Recapitulating the history of his own family, therefore, O'Neill penetrates the hard core of perfidy in our age of modern times. It is, to his mind, the first period in history when a persistence of faith in the Creation must be judged a betrayal of reason and when a disavowal of faith is experienced as a broken covenant, a rupture with the Progenitor, the Creator. Either way, as the Tyrones' fate signifies, breach of trust unavoidably serves as the spring of motive for the conduct of social, sexual, and moral life in a shattered world.

"I went to the shrine and prayed to the Blessed Virgin," Mary Tyrone says near the end of that scene. Recalling her girlhood she remembers her innocent trust in blessedness, remembers a perfect peace "because I knew she heard my prayer and would always love me and see no harm came to me so long as I never lost faith in her." This was of course Reuben's "pipe dream"—as O'Neill characterized the whole principle of self-deception in

The Iceman Cometh—too, the delusion which drew him to the powerhouse, shrine of that blessed "Mother of life" to whom he addressed his prayer: "Never let me go from you again! Please, Mother!" Like Reuben Light Mary Tyrone broke her vow, he with Ada and she with James Tyrone, and thus lost all claim on the Virgin's patronage. In plays written ten years apart, therefore, both mother and son are afflicted by a common ailment, a fear of damnation, and both adopt the classic cure, mortification of flesh. But the appalling thing is that they know what besets them is a dread of abandonment. And they know too there is no mitigation but the numbing of dread.

O'Neill never recovered from the horror of having to typify flawlessness of faith and steadfastness of trust as still additional species of "pipe dream," of surrender to one or another instrument of self-deception, self-betrayal. *The Iceman Cometh* is "about the impossibility of salvation in a world without God," Brustein thinks. Not so. No more than *Dynamo* is about the death of God and mankind's panic search for a successor. What all three plays are about, what the three interconnected plays converge round is mankind's incapacity to abandon hope no matter how hopeless is humanity's addiction to deliverance here or hereafter. For it is the trope of addiction, integrating the biographical fact of alcoholism with a national mythology or disorder and doom which bears his personal signature and records his authentic voice.[20]

Initially in *Dynamo*, a play which misses its mark, O'Neill strained to find a form which would convincingly say that deliverance won't come in the wake of an industrial age, won't arrive in the guise of progress, or electricity or any other guise. The only deliverance is death: not energy, not alcohol, not drugs, not love. "I fell in love with James Tyrone and was so happy for a time," Mary says. And that, we hear O'Neill repeat again and again in his valedictory play, is our sole recompense for eternal lifetimes of woe. Happiness for a time is our reward for faithless love. Faithless love—that's all O'Neill could summon out of himself and bestow on a Judas-people who in anguish retain as if in the form of a racial memory the recollection of pure love, of sanctified love, of virgin love, a mother's love, the Blessed Virgin's love.

O'Neill ended his harrowed life believing that he'd been predestined to bear griefs peculiar to his temperament, exacerbated by his religion and exaggerated in his nation, a society driven to destruction. Although he associated his own fate with a general drift toward debacle, unlike other writers of similar sensibility and drift he was disinclined to make grand sociological or historical sense of his situation.[21] Unmoored, adrift between biology and biography, he settled on sin. And sin, which settled everything, was for him the expedient of choice in that he was freed of any obligation to account for the cultural roots of abandonment and betrayal. How curious, in contrast Lawrence felt, how strange "it should be in America of all places" that a European could "really experience religion, after touching the old Mediterranean and the East," how improbable to receive religious experience from "Red Indians."

Curious or not, its force and flavor are astonishingly intense in a novella, *The Woman Who Rode Away* (1928), composed as if in antidote to the toxic effects of energy and of entropy on imagination in America. An artifact of those few years spent on this continent, a fiction which nearly all English and American critics treat as an anomaly of Anglo-American letters, this cautionary tale distinguishes between the misuses of technological power and the inspired use of American force, between modern defect and aboriginal flawlessness of character in this ancient and newfound land. Perhaps the most schematic of twentieth-century efforts to conceive ways of averting the calamity of progress, Lawrence's story was written as a last word of gratitude to adoptive countrymen, both red and white, who invigorated his art during his short stay of expatriation here.

Borrowing those early tribal rites which alone could release a white American woman from the sorcery of those who preside over advanced society—adopting primitive religious ritual, Lawrence empowers his heroine to unite white and red in a condition of vital equilibrium which equalize landscape and nation, country and culture, nation and state. As if glossing that section of *The Varieties of Religious Experience* in which James refers to diverse modes of religious conversion as changes of equilibrium, Lawrence invents a ceremony of redemption well within the reach of red imagination but far beyond the dreams of white will. And though in this legendary tale Lawrence pretended that the locale is Mexico not the United States, it was the American Southwest he had in mind and Mabel Dodge—American womanhood in quintessence—whose removal from the grandeur of the Villa Curonia in Arcetri, outside Florence, to this savage and fertile land set the scene for his own transformation, his apprehension at last of that "sense of living religion" which came to him here, nowhere else on earth.[22]

VI

Phoenix on Turtle Island

D. H. Lawrence in Henry Adams's America

The Sun God, the symbol of centralized power, became the model of perfection for all human institutions, and the priesthood of science, whose mathematical measurements had first disclosed and utilized this source of cosmic order . . . laid the foundation for . . . the construction of the magamachine. . . . The Sun God had dazzled and blinded them into conceiving scientific reality as a landscape without figures. . . . Not man but the machine became the central figure in this new world picture. Hence the chief end of human existence was to confirm this system by utilizing and controlling the energies derived from the sun, reshaping every part of the environment in conformity to the Sun God's strict commands. In acceptance of this orthodoxy man was to find his salvation.

Lewis Mumford, *The Pentagon of Power*, 1970

The Hopi religio-philosophic system is extremely sophisticated by any standard. Essentially the Hopis view the Earth as a feminine entity of interrelated energy systems which must be maintained in an orderly fashion. If these energy systems are disturbed, the whole will be thrown out of balance and catastrophe will be the result. . . . The Hopis are engaged in the mythic process; we indulge in technico-fantasy.

Jack Loeffler, "The Shaman's Wisdom," *Black Mesa Defense*, 1971

On Hopi and Navajo land, at Black Mesa, the whole issue is evolving at this moment . . . in the form of strip-mining . . . to provide electricity for Los Angeles. The defense of Black Mesa is being sustained by traditional Indians, young Indian militants and longhairs. Black Mesa speaks to us through an ancient web of myth. She is sacred territory. To hear her voice is to give up the European word "America" and accept the new-old name for the continent, "Turtle Island."

Gary Snyder, *New York Times*, 1972

ALTHOUGH *THE WOMAN WHO RODE AWAY*, that underprized and misused and misread short novel, not long ago caused a quarrel between Kate Millett and Norman Mailer, this flash of attention satisfied no valid concern whatever, preserved no vital interest to speak of, performed no legitimate service at all. Caught in crossfire between Millett's *Sexual Politics* and Mailer's *The Prisoner of Sex*, Lawrence's story was hit from both sides, fixed positions of women's lib. What an outrage that a fiction which has survived nearly fifty years without proper attention should suddenly be beset, endangered, by notice of one or another kind—all doctrinaire. In fulfillment of at least one duty of criticism, therefore, to preserve good writing from ill-intentioned reading, and in fidelity not to Millett's clientele nor Mailer's following but to the audience Lawrence in 1922 left England to mobilize, let us in his name convene those survivors whose range of affairs, whose agenda is disclosed in my string of epigraphs.

Let us too, in a by-blow of criticism retrieve or reclaim this tale from advocates and opponents whose praise and blame during two generations have all but erased Lawrence's actual subject. An unexampled display of his Americanized art at its best and worst, anomalous on every count, the story is at once arcane in design and uncomplicated in meaning. Whether or not this contrast between straightforwardedness and convolution, surface and substructure, is a cause of confusion, nonetheless *The Woman Who Rode Away* is one of very few Lawrentian texts which no one seems prepared to take at face value. An inquiry into fault and grace of character among indigenous and immigrant peoples of the Americas in our time, it is also an account of the reasons for the decline of civilization in this age of progress. In arraigning the behavior of those who preside over technological society, it associates—as only Adams had yet done—the idea of disorder in modern society with the invention of machinery and connects the increase of industry with an exhaustion of sex, a desert of women. Despite his British origins, therefore, Lawrence seized on the American mode of computing gain and loss, worth and waste of progress by way not of the energies of men but of the energy of Woman.

"Everything in America goes by will," Lawrence said, a "gripped, iron, benevolent will." And it must be in the end ruinous despite William James's celebrated case for "road-building and tunnel-making" as a moral equivalent for war. It was exactly James's kind of benevolence, of willfulness—*The Will to Believe*—that Lawrence distrusted. Ever canny about native American tics, he despised our national faith in the cash value of good intentions, our reliance on devices to master nature and control events. Unlike James but like Adams, Lawrence considered machinery an unquestioned source of vainglory in American life. And it was this defilement of faith which Lawrence condemned out of hand, this trust in instruments of will and power which encouraged the "charlatan and the witch and the fakir" to summon up energy for "egoistic and mercenary purpose." In illustration of similar traits of character, as we know, Adams had nominated Theodore Roosevelt. But Lawrence, who denounced Americans in general for an incapacity "to trust life unless they can control it," was temperamentally opposed both to James's plan for the dominion of earth and Adams's belief in the likelihood of race suicide. A society that elevated charlatans and fakirs like "Henry Ford and President Wilson," however, was perforce so much "worse, falser and farther gone than England" that it must be "nearer freedom," ripe for transformation.[1] In *The Woman Who Rode Away*, therefore, Lawrence devised a myth of revitalization rooted in a native ground which, as David Cavitch observes in *D. H. Lawrence and the New World* (1969), became "*his* country" (Cavitch's emphasis) once he'd decided to "transfer all my life to America."[2]

Drawn to this land in order to steep himself in the ambience of a place where "the air was newer and the life more monstrous" than elsewhere, Lawrence arrived in New Mexico. Ventilating his mind, dilating his art wide enough to accommodate highs and lows of American scenery and climate, he completed one stunning book of criticism, some stories, notably "The Princess" and "St. Mawr," a novel and a novella, *The Plumed Serpent* and *The Woman Who Rode Away*, one too long and the other too short but both ambitious beyond ordinary aspiration and programmatic beyond decent limit. This radical turn to an unconventional career came in the wake of war when Lawrence found himself quite "unable to write for England any more" but full of hot hope for America.[3] And it is this unprecedented heat of allegiance, signifying a final fling of imagination, which radical feminists today echoing Millett are prepared to discard. In a reading that obscures the solemn pageantry of redemption Lawrence planned for his heroine, for her people, her world, Millett gratuitously misstates the theme of this story: "I was living in this huge Aztec sacrificial altar," says Millett's younger sister Mallary, speaking of her marriage in Kate's film *Three Women* (1971). Boiled down to a "picture of human sacrifice performed upon the woman for the greater glory and potency of the male," Millett's account perverts the reasons why Lawrence conceived a ritual process of initiation which enables his heroine first to absorb, immerse, engross herself in the life of the body and later to burst her bonds of womanhood.[4] And Mailer, in his turn, either missed or misconstrued Lawrence's ethnology, mistook savageries of ritual for fakery of primitivism—perhaps because Lawrence's story does not promote Mailer's cause, the defense of malehood.

In feint, jab, and counterpunch of comment, then, this pair of adversaries misses Lawrence's point. But if their argument in itself is unilluminating it does have the particular merit of displaying precisely how elusive this story is, how unsettled its standing even among those who steep themselves in the uses of Lawrence's art—Julian Moynihan, for example. Customarily clear-minded, in *The Novels and Tales of D. H. Lawrence* (1963) Moynihan speaks of *The Woman Who Rode Away* as a "heartless tale" which "contains one of the most depressing images in all Lawrence." Revolting indeed in his view is the sight of a "blonde woman crawling on hands and knees along a narrow mountain ledge" observed by "two Indian captors" who are "indifferent to her discomfort and danger" as she inches her way toward an "abyss of senseless blood sacrifice." Misleading as is this version of these events, compared with Anthony West's account Moynihan's is unexceptionable. Perhaps because West appears to be aiming fire both at Lawrence himself and at Lawrence's partisans in England, F. R. Leavis and Graham Hough, in *D. H. Lawrence* (1966) he condemns the writer for fraud. "Pure Lawrence," Leavis had said (*D. H. Lawrence: Novelist*, 1955) the novella "stands alone": "there is nothing else like it in the tales." An "astonishing feat of imagination," its authenticity "derives from the intensity and profound seriousness of Lawrence's interest in human life." And Hough, in echo or approbation of Leavis's vagrant remarks, had agreed (*The Dark Sun*, 1956) that this fiction represents its author's "completest artistic achievement" and "profoundest comment on the world of his time." Nonsense, West said in effect. The story is purest swindle in that its religion, counterfeit Aztec, goes against the drift of Lawrence's career as a whole.[5]

During more than fifty years, therefore, *The Woman Who Rode Away*, a work which seems unable either to hold its focus or stand its ground, has been plagued by a loggerhead of taste and a legerdemain of judgment. For if it's to be taken, according to Eugene Goodheart's contention in *The Utopian Vision of D. H. Lawrence* (1963), as "Lawrence's own contribution to classic American literature,"[6] then surely it cannot legitimately be removed from the American scene, in Leavis's fashion, or divorced from the modernist tradition in the manner of James C. Cowan, a cryptographer who promises to resolve "critical confusion" by examining and deciphering "the myths, rituals and ideas that Lawrence fuses into a single religious metaphor." Immersing himself in an immense archive which runs from James Frazer and Robert Graves to Joseph Campbell and Aldous Huxley, from I Corinthians 13:12 to Kartha Upanishad 3:14; discerning ties between Lawrence's theme and "Chrétien de Troyes's account of Lancelot crossing the sword-bridge to rescue Guinevere from the Castle of Death"; associating the setting of Lawrence's story with festivals that honor a "Dying and Reviving God, the world over" and arriving at last in "a symbolic Gethsemane,"

Cowan links the Woman first to Jesus Himself and then by way of "her blondness" and her "color, blue, the color of fidelity and of the heavens," to His mother.[7]

This is monomythomania, ecstasy not criticism. Skipping diverse vagaries of allusion Cowan finds ways also to accommodate, in a moment I shall skip to two last misreaders, Frank Kermode in righteous wrath against Lawrence's politics and F. J. Hoffman in a muddle about details of plot. No new evidence is needed, however, to augment this recital of complaints against readers who habitually strip Lawrence's thought down to maxims which supposedly report his ideas but in fact thoroughly contort his books. Their favorite text, *The Woman Who Rode Away*, is problematic only when it is used to illustrate a critic's bias rather than to demonstrate exactly which ambitions, which modes of art captivated Lawrence's imagination during his final years of life and work in America and Europe. In the essays, stories, novels written immediately before and after his transfer to America he was certain he'd been granted the key to the creative principle itself, the key principle of organic form in literature and culture. On arriving here and sitting down to write his American books he instantly scrapped the stuff which had ideologized the major work of his English career, the ideology which Birkin in *Women in Love* (1917) had strained to conceive, labored to say. "What I want is a strange conjunction with you," Birkin had told Ursula. Not a "meeting and a mingling" but an "equilibrium, a pure balance of two single beings—as the stars balance each other"—balance which will preserve the life of sex and the life of earth from chaos. Six years later in New Mexico ideas on balance and equilibrium were replaced by the principle of "polarized flow." A law of nature which had been closed to him he suddenly perceived in the "strange current of interchange that flows between men and men, and men and women, and men and things" in the United States. And now instead of a pure stable equilibrium of sex and power Lawrence postulated an alternative state of affairs, that "polarized circuit" O'Neill too was so much drawn to, a "circuit of unstable equilibrium." Though he had in 1921 and 1922 touched on ideas which hinted at instability, ideas included within *Psychoanalysis of the Unconscious* and *Fantasia of the Unconscious*, it was the American "circuit of vitalism" which electrified him. "Everything vital, or natural, is unstable, thank God," he wrote in *Studies in Classic American Literature* (1923), convincing himself that the time had come for him to transport himself to a place where people and things existed in a "state of unstable vital equilibrium."[8] There his art and his life might acquire new force, renewed momentum.

The experience of America did indeed intoxicate his last years, did outlast his few years of residence in the New World. Similarly, an American woman of the most flamboyant kind, one who had removed herself from a famed Florentine villa to a noted Greenwich Village salon and then finally to New Mexico—Mabel Dodge Luhan in this way set the style of his heroine's transformation and fixed the pattern of his own conversion. But before he ventured either to Europeanize the vitalist idea, as in *Lady Chatterley's Lover* (1928), or to Christianize his religious experience, as in *The Man Who Died* (1928), he set out to learn whether or not the condition of dynamic equilibrium could be restored to that monstrous disintegrating American technological state in which self-energized charlatans held power. Really of course he was so captivated by the Indian presence, apparition of primitive myth cloaked in ancient costume, that he hadn't a minute's doubt the world would be saved by what he described as diverse appearances of Pan in America. "Vehemently of Schopenhauer's opinion," we're told in Jessie Chamber's *D. H. Lawrence* (1935), that a "white skin is not natural to a man," not until he put himself in actual touch with New World Indians, whose "brown skin is the only beautiful one," did he finally invent social and literary forms which harmonized pigment and politics.[9] What he could not have foreseen, however, was confirmation of his schoolboy ethnology in the work of Arnold van Gennep and Victor Turner, of Lévi-Strauss and his English disciples Edmund R. Leach and Mary Douglas, work which is the more arresting for light cast on judgments Lawrence drew from early field trips to redskin lands. Like most trips, his turned him into a true believer. And he ended his career certain that it was within the savage mind, nowhere else, men would sooner or later discover the code with which to decipher fundamental structures binding all peoples to one another and uniting mankind to nature in small and at large.

Twenty years ago, in defending Lawrence against the charge that "he had no operative sense of form," Mark Spilka sought to justify the shapes of Lawrence's fiction by tracing a pattern of "ritualistic movement" forward and back from "organic being," both personal and communal.[10] But neither Spilka nor anyone else, so far as I know—even those who treat *The Woman Who Rode Away* as an extravaganza of ritual form—has ascertained why it is precisely on this score that the work vindicates itself. In executing this trial run of restorative art Lawrence wanted a seamless story, template of its subject, about a healing ceremony in which the white protagonist, surrogate of paleface sensibility in general, is purged, freed from the control of witches and fakirs. For only if modern man is prepared to sacrifice the world he's made in favor of the world he's lost—prepared, that is, to forsake those powers of mind which spark the age of industry—can society dispel the inertia of progress and release that flow of energy which will restore the peoples of this continent to their original state, a primal condition of unstable vital equilibrium consistent with the rule of organic not mechanical order in social and cosmic affairs. In this parable of self-renunciation and self-repossession, therefore, a supercivilized modernist writer composed a mythic fiction which fulfills shamanistic function.

Inspired by, written in imitation of and in tribute to his literary hero Fenimore Cooper, *The Woman Who Rode Away* presents a line of action so pure, drops a plumb line of motive so deep, that his tale, like Cooper's epic, concentrates the whole evolution of culture and fixes the entire destiny of race inside the fate of a single and singular life. And although Lawrence's politics, the politics of primitivism, are indeed totalitarian not egalitarian, he's about as far from being Kermode's kind of simpleton, preacher of what Kermode calls "naked doctrine, racial mastery," as he is from being Hoffman's straightforward chap with an untidy end or two. "This simple but powerful story," Hoffman says, "describes the journey of a white woman, away from the tedium and living death of her accustomed life, toward a savage, primitive simplicity of religious and natural practice. When she arrives in the mountain community, the Indian tribe puts her to death as a sacrificial tribute to their gods. She is put under sedation, and the entire ceremony of her death is a graphic illustration of the horrors of relinquishing what Lawrence had often called the 'white autonomous ego,' and submitting to the full implications of the 'unconscious dark realm of the blood.'"[11]

Adding Hoffman and Kermode to a considerable but by no means unrepresentative company, we arrive at the end of a list of those responsible for turning this flawed artifact into a shard of Anglo-American letters. That Hoffman, a scholar respected for exhaustiveness and scruple in assemblage, the collection of fact, in this instance got nearly all the main details wrong is itself worth noting. Sacrifice yes, but horror no and sedation absolutely not: these are effects in reverse of those sought by Lawrence's Indians in administering drugs to a woman who herself elects to follow their barbarous ways of redemption. For according to Chilchui myth in Aztec religion, so Lawrence prepares his ground, "when a white woman sacrifices herself to our gods, then our gods will begin the world again, and the white man's gods will fall to pieces." It's therefore not a numbing of the senses her role requires, not an immersion in or subversion by the blood which enables her to serve as their savior. Rather it's an intensification, an expansion, an elevation of consciousness with which Lawrence rewards the woman who chooses to assume this office, a "dazzling Californian girl from Berkeley" who at age thirty-three is in a state of moral, emotional, and sexual stalemate.

In a struggle to quicken her life once more, she relinquishes two children and husband to whom she is bound in superficial connection only.

Her husband, a "little dynamo of energy" originally from Holland where he'd been a "scrap of a wastrel," is now "more or less rich, owning silver-mines in the wilds of the Sierra Madre." Silver, the shiny substance which provides Lawrence with his figure of speech, his conceit for commerce and industry, is doubtless the most ominous image Lawrence could have chosen to signify an absence of animation in his heroine's spirit and in the spirit of her age and place. A metal found near the surface of earth not deep in, its particular features are malleability and colorless brightness. Vulgar matter, coin of the realm, stuff of trinkets and utensils, it is not acquired by way of any special daring of will or talent of mind or mastery of skill beyond a crude and uncomplicated machinery of shaft and extracting plant. Unlike gold—hard to find and tough to mine, changeless—silver has no history, no resonance. It is in search of gold, then, that our heroine rides out of her husband's realm. Exchanging shallows for depths and summits, she renounces metal for myth in the "secret haunts of those timeless, mysterious, marvelous Indians of the mountains," descendants of Montezuma who "still kept up the ancient religion and offered human sacrifices." Had she not gone, had she accepted her fate as a creature of a bleak world "dominated by men and machines," had she remained with a husband to whom "marriage was the last and most intimate bit of his own works," she would have become as lifeless as her lamentable mate and his fellows, inertia incarnate. "Silver was at a standstill," Lawrence says, underscoring this point. "The great war came and went. Silver was a dead market."

Strikingly, coincidentally, very few years earlier it had been a standstill of silver which had led Adams to indulge in his usual occupation, to formulate a law explaining the life and death of markets. Observing Lawrence's association of silver and stasis, recalling Adams's conjunction of industry and inertia, we must take a moment to appreciate the fitness of Lawrence's figure for this inquiry into the wellspring of American energy. Indeed, it's a circumstance worth noting that Adams's interest in silver and gold, like Lawrence's, rose from metallurgy and climbed toward metaphor. Himself a casualty of markets, caught in the panic of 1893, Adams had been induced to speculate about the merits—for the stimulus and stability of capital in America—of a silver or a gold standard. Undecided whether to switch support from one to the other, uncertain whether gold or silver would advance or impede the pursuits of commerce, he did in fact desert silver for gold but contended that the choice was moot. Either way, by means of silver (which he took to represent limited and dispersed industrial force) or by means of gold (which he took to represent "capitalistic, centralizing, mechanical power")—neither the adoption nor the abandonment of gold or silver would resolve the haunting question of progress in

America. Spectral indeed, the question raised problems which, as John Carlos Rowe observes in *Henry Adams and Henry James* (1976), implicates "mere money, coinage and labor" as well as an "eschatalogical economy of energy."[12] Rowe's grandiose phrase, intended to characterize Adams's devotion to universal law, inflates the subject a little. For the problem that vexed Adams, manifest later that same year at the Chicago Exposition, he put as plainly as language could say: at Chicago society could be observed asking itself "whether the American people knew where they were driving."[13] Eighteen ninety-three, therefore, which began with the threat of bankruptcy and ended with the promise of economic power beyond skills of measurement, was the year in which gold and silver introduced Adams to the property of chaos in the works and wealth of nations.

Surviving the panic and touring the fair, Adams ascertained that there was no hope of resolving the grave question of progress until laws of history were brought into line with laws of science. Believing that a single system joined science and history, history and progress, progress and economy, economy and disorder, he derived a common set of principles by isolating the operation of a single force, inertia, in "the feminine mind." Another aspect of the Woman Question, this was of course the arena to which he returned no matter how far he wandered—to Tahiti where he contemplated the old Queen Arii Taimai, as well as to Chartres where he confronted the Queen of Heaven. Traveling everywhere, he reconfirmed his judgment that the proper study of mankind is woman. Predictably, then, Adams maintained that history would surrender its mysteries only when "the movement of sex" is taken into account. Because "the problem of inertia summed up the difficulties" of sex, of race, of civilization as a whole, it was an unequivocal fact that American women required the closest attention of those who would tease meaning out of motion. And because the fate of civilization in America was prefigured in the waste of women and the disorders of love, there was no question at all in Adams's mind that "the task of accelerating or deflecting the movement of American women"—a task foredoomed to fail, so the *Education* implies—"had interest infinitely greater than that of any race whatever, Russian or Chinese, Asiatic or African."[14]

Lawrence did not of course require the benefit either of Adams's example or judgment for sanction of his own deepest and oldest convictions. Nor did he need the certification of Adams's dynamic theory of history in order to assign himself the task of discovering a new force which could not fail to affect inertia and increase momentum within the mind of a woman deflected from her American fate. Whether or not Lawrence wanted or needed Adams, however, there Adams was. Unavoidable predecessor in this bizarre

American place, he had formulated the proposition which best characterized the aim though not the method of Lawrence's art. "He was studying the laws of motion, and had struck two large questions of vital importance to America—inertia of race and inertia of sex."[15] Committed to resolve at a single stroke exactly this pair of large vital American questions, a writer who yielded to no one his place of priority as a student of the feminine mind, Lawrence removes his dazzling but motionless female from a silver to a gold standard. Inert, a woman whose deepest vein had never been penetrated, she goes relentlessly higher into mountains where a legendary people of epic bloodiness maintain a vigil, await her arrival. In fidelity to ancient doctrine they await the white woman who will unflinchingly offer up her life in self-sacrifice to their gods and thereby provide the energy of sex necessary to overcome inertia of race, red and white and brown and olive, on this great globe of earth.

Wittily evoking the legend of Quetzalcoatl, reversing that Aztec myth in which the expectation of a white-skinned redeemer prepared the way for Cortez's conquest of Montezuma, Lawrence locates the geography of resurrection in the rare air of highlands even as he places the psychology of regeneration in the thickest plasma of passion. But it is on another count that Lawrence deserves special tribute. In inventing a ritual action in which a renewal of motion within the female mind releases and augments the movement of celestial bodies, he devised a process identical to that described in a work of anthropology scarcely known in its own day but today held in especial favor, Arnold van Gennep's *Les Rites de Passage* (1908). Although it's unlikely that Lawrence knew van Gennep's thesis either at first or second hand—indeed, it's today considered a scandal of social science that no trace of van Gennep's thought appears in European or American sociology until 1925—nevertheless a fiction not published until 1928 might well have been enriched with detail drawn from seminal work in print twenty years earlier. For van Gennep's innovative science and Lawrence's visionary art together offer a single program of ceremony intended to establish and reinforce ties linking dissociated spheres of being, however defined or divined.

Maintaining that regeneration is an absolute law of life, van Gennep conceived a scheme of social and religious practice which is today so widely known and so little startling as to be taken for self-evident truth. But seventy years ago his conjectures on the ties uniting individuals and groups, personality and culture, earth and heavens, were nearly unprecedented. According to his scheme, rites of passage, ubiquitous among primitive peoples, are universally associated with pregnancy and birth, puberty and marriage, maturity and death. Accompanying individual cycles in staged procession, safeguarding the group from crises in the lives of separate persons, collective ritual and ceremony guarantee continuity and order. Crises are negotiated by means of rites which align human and social and celestial periods in a rhythm and tempo taken from the cycles of nature: consistency and change, depletion and renewal, death and rebirth of separate beings and entire systems. The rites certify that a person's "passage from one situation to another or from one cosmic or social world to another" occurs in time with this rhythm. Threefold in character and triple in sequence, the process of ceremony includes "*rites of separation, transition rites* and *rites of incorporation*." Those that coincide with the process of "separation from a previous world" van Gennep called "*preliminal*." Followed by "*liminal* (or threshold) rites," this step involves "purification" ceremonies of washing and cleansing and anointing which end with the climactic ritual, "incorporation into a new world" (van Gennep's emphasis).[16]

Van Gennep's italics, which underscore the specific shape of a blurry process, also stress the particular patterns of Lawrence's plot. For the remarkable thing is that the ethnographer's plan not the novelist's whim underlies the tripartite action into which Lawrence thrusts his heroine. Fleeing our modern mechanical white society in favor of an organic brown one, an archaic people biding its time of eclipse, first she applies for admission into tribal lands, next she submits herself to Indian customs of purification, finally she qualifies for service as a mythic figure of redemption—matrix of a polarized flow of energy, sacred and profane, force of regneration in a static and sterile world.

As she ascends the highlands during the initial day of flight she meets three Indians, tells them that she wishes to visit their people. The words she says are straightforward enough—she wants "to see their houses and know their gods"—but they hear meanings, echoes, to which as yet her sensibility is shut. They agree, offer to guide her, and she delivers herself to their charge. Instantly she "knew she was dead." Setting aside Lawrence's melodrama, preserving instead just the intuition itself he wished to convey, we retain her inchoate perception of the process on which she is irretrievably launched. Reinforced by the look of dauntless power in their eyes, her instinct alerts her to their view of her, a view which reflects back the figure of a person whose whiteness and womanhood are appreciable but whose person is not on any other score distinguished. Because their eyes neglect or forbear to register an appreciation of social class, the eminence of a Mrs. Silvery Somebody, Mrs. Somebody is dead.[17] She's dead for another reason too, however, connoted by Lawrence's key word, *dauntless*, code word for an untamed male principle of dominion, that "grim Yankee dauntlessness," as he wrote to Mrs. Luhan, which "has *not* got its bottom swathed in a napkin."[18] It is to this principle she submits with "a thrill of exultation" during that first night on the trail, a "long, long night, icy and eternal." And by morning, having experienced for the first time the excitement and allure of male menace, she's purged of her white female astringency of sex. "The passionate anger of the spoilt white woman" is spent. Dead to the world she's put behind her, now put out of her mind, the degraded land of commerce with its domesticated and daunted men, stunted women, she's ready to go the distance of the adventure on which she is embarked. That next day, therefore, approaching the Indians' village she negotiates "the territorial passage," in van Gennep's parlance, a preliminal rite which enables her to pass from her etiolated realm into a place whose dominant hues are "red and orange and yellow and black," colors of body and earth, life and death.

Climbing higher, they arrive at a "great slant of living rock," the "glossy breast of some earth-beast" which she must cross. "In torment, on hands and knees" she crawls at hazard "from crack to crevice, along the slanting face of this pure rock mountain," an Indian in front and an Indian behind, those conductors and guardians who outraged Moynihan. It's tempting indeed to spell out nuance in the words *living* and *pure* which, applied to rock, sanctify her entrance into tribal lands and ceremony; tempting, too, to assume that Lawrence, in authenticating this action, coached himself in initiation rites. But wherever he found the ethnography he wanted, from sources internal or exterior, he contrived to represent the woman as venturing on no ordinary peril of maneuver up and over a slippery rock face in high mountains. Propelling her on a journey which takes her through barriers that supersede geography or geology, his account of her progress coincides with protocol required for admission into tribal territory, precincts which are always bounded by a "sacred rock, tree, river or lake," as van Gennep observes. And these "cannot be crossed or passed without risk of supernatural sanctions."

In associating this fact of spatial movement with the act of spiritual pilgrimage, therefore, Lawrence sets his own stage and simultaneously prepares the way for van Gennep's second and third steps of ritual, purification and transfiguration. On arriving at the village, borne by litter to the presence of elders, old men whose color is brilliant not bleached, solar not lunar, she is asked the portentous Aztec question: Do you bring your heart to the God of the Chilchui? Naive, not keen enough to take in the bite of their double-edged inquiry, she answers yes. They ask her to undress. But willful still, brimful with sex-laden white suspiciousness, she refuses to bare herself before them. Stripped, seeing in their faces no trace of lust—just an enthusiasm she can't comprehend—she suspends shame, forgoes resistance and permits them to conclude the "preliminal" step of ritual. Moving on to threshold rites, she undergoes those "liminal" procedures which must occur, van Gennep insists, whenever an alien person arrives for entry into a sacred realm. Anointed, isolated, fed a special diet, the stranger "must wait, go through a transitional period, enter, be incorporated" according to a regimen which is designed to protect residents from danger of infection.[19]

What van Gennep decrees Lawrence obeys. Guarding the sanctity of this tribe, shielding it from the blasphemy of American social practice, he causes the Chilchui—who both solicit and loathe her presence—to take precautions of classic kind. Bathed by attendants; garlanded in flowers; dressed in native robes of blue, black, white, scarlet, and green; installed in a dwelling reserved for her at the verge of the village, she is offered a liquor which causes her first to vomit and then to feel the balm of languor. Lying languid she experiences that postnausea transport of consciousness cherished by cultists of peyote. In this state of heightened mind, so vividly does she see the evening star that "she felt as if all her senses were diffused on air, that she could distinguish the sounds of evening flowers unfolding, and the actual crystal sounds of the heavens, as the vast belts of world-atmosphere slide past one another, and as if moisture ascending and the moisture descending in the air resounded like some harp in the cosmos."

Attaining levels of acuteness within the scope of blessed Indian substances but beyond the reach of any gringo drug, she is hardly victimized by those few "moments of terror and horror" Hoffman noticed. For Lawrence in fact underplays the short-lived anxiety associated with this rite of transition in favor of weeks of repose during which she hears the quietest imaginable sounds and detects the play of single smells in a vast concert of odors. Why Hoffman mistook Lawrence's intent, why he confused inspiration with sedation of the senses I am at a loss to comprehend. No less perplexing, equally hard to decipher are clues to muddled judgment in the minds of critics who have tended to understand this woman, as well as Lawrence himself, far too hastily. If indeed there's no good reason to mistake polymorphic expansion of the senses for erasure of mind, there's substantially worse reason, the worst possible reason Lawrence could invoke, to condemn this young woman for embracing an idea of progress that negates or refutes those modernist ideas of Progress—sexual, economic, political—which blemish our lives. Only when she is purged of Progress can her life proceed toward self-realization, can the process continue which will carry her along toward those dual fates, that of a savior and that of a victim, Lawrence causes to converge in the end. Having fled her hearth and home, having survived the dangers of a fearful journey into a feral land, having dared to participate in the liturgy conducted to confirm her breach of connection to the world of her fathers, having shared in exotic customs of purification to qualify for entrance into this sacred realm, now she's ready for those postliminal and climactic rites which will admit her into the historical and religious life of this people.

Identifying her moment of incorporation with her instant of incorporeity, her dematerialization, her death, Lawrence discloses the drift implicit in primitive rites in general and thereby, as van Gennep's final words say—words that anticipate the movement of this story from start to finish—leads us to the bedrock of myth. For it's not just questions of social propriety to which rites of passage are addressed. Rather it's "the celestial passages, the revolution of the planets and the phases of the moon" which, in a "sort of pre-scientific divination," are served by a ceremony that relates "the stages of human existence to those of plant and animal life" and joins all forms of earthly life to "the great rhythms of the universe."[20] Slowly then Lawrence's heroine, under the influence of that mind-dilating liquor, achieves a "heightened, mystic acuteness" so intense, a sensuality so serene that she hears her little dog conceive, knows when its womb goes "complex with young." Sentimental or not, this is incontrovertibly Lawrence's notion. How baffling it is therefore to discover Millett seizing on this detail as a gratuitous insult of the animal, "a little female dog," Lawrence's Woman shares her "prison" with.[21] Strange indeed Millett's notion of insult. For Lawrence introduced the dog in order to punctuate his admiration of a woman who is brave and wise enough to recover kinship with all forms of life. Major accomplishment it is, progress it indisputably is, this recovery of prescientific, prerational connection with being as a whole, and all the more marvelous in that a hypercivilized woman, now Delphic in estrus, acquires sexual bounty which surpasses the physiological limits of rut. Epitomizing the human form of fecundity itself, gaining virtue suited to her need, she attains power enough to perform her legendary role in the sacred drama of that Chilchui myth which describes women as preserving the luminousness of the moon and men as possessing the energy of the sun. "Then when a man gets a woman, the sun goes into the cave of the moon, and that is how everything in the world starts."

And will start again. Committed to the restoration of cosmic rhythm in daily affairs, Lawrence's art and life are crystallized in van Gennep's thesis even as that thesis is documented in a story which exploits the novelist's peculiar brand of pre- and postscientific mania. For in this age of silver, shaped by white male American charlatans who "don't know what they do with the moon"—twin principles of generation out of their orbit—Indians have grown weak. Adopting this conceit, Lawrence reminds us that these weakened guardians of primordial truth are descended from a genius race of horologists, astronomers whose powers of calculation provide one of the grander astonishments in history. Attuned to solar period, they time her moment of ripeness, her readiness for death, to coincide with the winter solstice, as if the survival of these ancient skills of computation justifies the transfer of power, white to red, which her sacrifice is supposed to seal. When under their guidance she is brought to the point of sacrifice, prepared to yield, to cede herself to them, not only is her own inertia deflected and the disorder of the world reversed but also decadent ideas on chaos are dispelled forever. Presiding over a metamorphic process which transforms the usual sort of modern woman into a symbol of femaleness itself, emblem of an impaired Creation; reclaiming men and women from a technology which has dispersed and diminished the self, Lawrence's Indians illustrate the postulate offered forty years later by Arthur Koestler in *The Ghost in the Machine* (1967). "That implacable Second Law" does not apply to "open systems." Which is to say, Entropy Law is not only denied sovereignty over "living matter" but is in fact "*reversed*" in those "open hierarchical systems" which are "capable of maintaining themselves indefinitely in a state of dynamic equilibrium" (Koestler's emphasis).[22]

As she delivers them from silvery servitude so in their turn do they restore earth to the state of golden felicity, a deliverance and restoration which document Lawrence's use of material Norman O. Brown describes as a species of "astrological theology invented by the earliest civilizations." Even the economist Keynes, Brown remarks in *Life Against Death* (1959), recognized that the "special attraction of gold and silver is due not to any of the rationalistic considerations generally offered in explanation but to their symbolic identification with Sun and Moon."[23] However remarkable it was to discover van Gennep's pattern inside Lawrence's plan of redemption, it is even more startling now to detect Lawrence endowing his heroine with silvery and golden traits in tandem. Possessing powers preternaturally right for her astrological role, a special radiance emitted by paired theologies and economies she cannot help straddling, she is charged with the duty of returning Moon and Sun to custodians who are best fitted to maintain a dynamic equilibrium of energy, psychic and sociologic and cosmogonic. She must therefore be white enough to merit her death and woman enough to transcend her flesh. That is, she cannot perform her mythic function unless she retains a trace of her original character, that of a denatured white woman at home in a moribund machine state. Although in the course of her initiation into this tribe she's been cleansed of debasement enough to join in the Chilchui's bid to the "unseen moon to cease to be angry," nevertheless she remains damaged enough, retrograde enough to denote the radical cause of its anger. Sustained by the solidest of Lawrence's dogmas, the doctrine of polarized flow, this anomalous woman is at once willful and pliant, selfless and self-absorbed, demonic and saintly. And because she is a Berkeley girl with a cosmic vocation, a white woman who places her person at the disposal of their god, the Sun, her ambivalence must be preserved until the moment when grace and reprobation, revenge and reward coalesce. Awaiting that final rite of her passage, she remains to the last a defiler of culture and nature, silver reliquary of that white diabolism of will which desecrates and overpowers and undermines the world. And when, finally, she exhibits that saintliness of assent to universal law, that compliancy before death which all mortal beings must struggle to attain, she is unmistakably branded—by Lawrence, by the Chilchuis—a holy sinner to be revered not despised.

These lower depths of ambivalence are not sounded, however, until we bring to bear on Lawrence's mythopoetics an idea central to the thesis presented in Mary Douglas's study of the "Sacred and the Unclean," a chapter in *Purity and Danger*. Unlike Lévi-Strauss who detaches "myth criticism from literary criticism," Douglas proposes a structuralist analysis of linguistic, sociological, and theological themes inherent in dietary laws set down in the Old Testament, the Book of Leviticus.[24] Israelites' rules on dirt and cleanliness Douglas treats as regulations intended less to guard Jews from diseases than to protect Hebrew culture from peril. Always hard-pressed within and without, Jews devised laws annexing health to virtue, sin to illness, integrity of the physical body to the welfare and unity of their group as a whole. Were dirt to pierce any orifice of the well-girded body, Douglas contends, their community itself would be under threat of invasion and danger of collapse, would be endangered by death. "To be holy is to be whole, to be one; holiness is unity, integrity, perfection of the individual and the kind." Properly understood, therefore, Leviticus is a document in which "the integrity, unity and purity of the physical body" mirrors a Jewish determination to codify principles guarding "the threatened boundaries of the body politic" against not just dirt itself, a "pollution symbol," but ultimately against the threat of decomposition as well.

Ancient Jews notwithstanding, Douglas says as she takes up the theme which returns us to Lawrence, it is common practice among primitive peoples to sacralize symbols of pollution so that the "very things which would have been rejected with abhorrence" (dirt, often represented by black) "normally destructive [are] sometimes creative."[25] Why am I the only one to wear blue? Lawrence's heroine asks her attendants as December comes round and her time grows near. "It is the colour of the dead," she is told. "The white woman got to die and go like the wind to the sun, tell him the Indians will open the gate to him." Come back, Indians will then say to the moon, *"the wicked white woman can't harm you any more"* (Lawrence's emphasis). That her informant personally liked her she was certain, "but impersonally he hated her with a mystic hatred"—hatred, let it be said, appropriate to the symbolic threat she poses. For the literal pollution is gone. Her uncleanness, her wickedness their rites of purgation and initiation have made tolerable, have transposed from the realm of matter to the realm of metaphor. Standing surrogate for her race, however, perceived not as "a personal woman" but as "some mystic object," she possesses incalculable worth as a vessel, a relic lustral but unclean. Prepared for sacrifice by Indians who are colored their sacred hue, "golden-red," whose faces glisten "with the transparent red paint" and "bars of yellow," she is stood nude for her last bath before a "great weird device on the wall, coloured blue and white and black," a device colored for foulness and sterility and death. In these final phases of prophylaxis preceding her last rite, her moment of incorporation, "she lay and was rubbed into a misty glow by their uncanny dark hands" until her flesh, "her very bones at last seemed to be diffusing into a roseate sort of mist in which her consciousness hovered like some sort of sunbeam." Her foulness idolatrized, she knew that all this elaborate work upon her was the work of victimizing her, but she didn't care. "She wanted it."

Far better to be their victim than her husband's hostage. Incontrovertibly better to bestow herself on their altar, a benefactor who mediates between this people and its divinities so that the dirt and danger of her machine age—"deadness within deadness," Lawrence had described the town near their silver mine—would cease to threaten the health and holiness of an ancient intact organic eyrie of a place. As in ritual murder among the Dinkas, Douglas says, whose "community can live as a rational order because of the unafraid self-sacrifice" of their ancient spearmasters, so do Lawrence's Aztecs require fearless, knowing self-disposition too. And they have prepared her as well indeed as the old Dinka who "asks for the death to be prepared for him," his "own willing death, ritually framed by the grave itself." Considered to be a communal victory for all his people, his act of "confronting death and grasping it firmly" is understood to express to his society a comprehensive utterance about "the nature of life." Among the Dinkas as among the Chilchuis, therefore, within Douglas's real tribe and Lawrence's imaginary one, when a victim "embraces freely the symbols of death, or death itself," then a "great release of power should be expected to follow."[26]

I labor the idea and worry the point a little. But the point is to anchor in a solid anthropology an action, a story, a plot, a theme, an idea, a character hitherto disembodied, formerly awash in Lawrence's fancy. Douglas's data do indeed have unmistakable bearing on the final scenes of a tale in which Lawrence's Indians, anticipating an immense release and return of power, lovingly take the woman's hateful body, fumigated but still septic, for removal by litter to still higher altitudes where a cave, shaped like a womb, is hidden behind a curtain of ice. Her tomb, this cave, frames a death she is disposed to welcome. "She knew that this was the shortest day of the year, and the last day of her life." Naked, entombed in ice "beyond and above the dark-faced people" who share her vigil, in a state of perfect alertness she and the priests await the exact moment on a cold planet when the sun "would shine full through the shaft of ice deep into the hollow of the cave to the innermost." In perfect passivity "on a large flat stone" held by four men posted at her "outstretched arms and legs," she observed the path of the sun and watched the glint in her executioners' black eyes.

As she waits Lawrence's story ends, ends before the knife falls. Had Lawrence been more resolute, her fate would have been decided once and for all, hers and ours. But now, held permanently supine on the stone, she and her attendants simulate the figures on Keats's frieze, that Grecian urn which remains the most durable symbol in literature for immobility amid motion. The parallel is not exact. But Lawrence's novella, terminating before it reaches term, is Keatsian in that it stimulates and frustrates our hope of issue.[27] There's of course nothing special about someone who goes native on a lark and runs off in search of wilderness thrills. But a heroine who willingly continues on a pilgrimage even though it's borne in on her that she's been chosen to undergo a "status reversal," as Victor W. Turner describes analogous events in *The Ritual Process* (1969), which will conduct her from this world to the next one, a ritual of incorporation which (as she says) will remove her from "the dead I am to the dead I shall be"—such a one has yet to appear on earth. The woman whose passion rises from eros but is light years beyond orgasm has not yet come.

There's still another hindrance to sacrifice. Were a proper climax to occur it would necessarily have the effect that Turner, following van Gennep, ascribes to tribal "liminality" in its full sequence of steps and stages, the effect of bringing "social structure and communitas in right relation once more." In Lawrence's scheme, however, a recovery of right relation implies the defeat of man's deadliest enemy which in his view, Frieda Lawrence says, "had become God." And he was not cheerful enough about victory to dispatch the woman whose epic death would herald the destruction of that apparatus, the megamachine, which in the years since Lawrence's own death—as Mumford perpetually reminds us—has expanded its presence and increased its power. Unlike *The Man Who Died*, therefore, a parable in which our real world is entailed to placeless space and eternal time, *The Woman Who Rode Away* summons culture from mind and conjures history out of art. A palpable being whose American energy is no longer a mere dazzle of will and nil but a radiance of flesh diffused into the circumambient air, in dying she would negate nullity and cancel chaos. That is why, as Douglas concludes *Purity and Danger*, "we find corruption enshrined in sacred places and times." And that is why, too, as this story ends, nullity and chaos await cancellation.

In treating this story as if it were written in response to Adams, in searching out texts of anthropology which may or may not have shaped Lawrence's mind but which unfailingly enlarge or ornament his thought, I've invented a set of circumstances Lawrence himself was perhaps unaware of. But it is not an enterprise he would discredit or disallow. The man who in 1923 confessed that "this wild and noble America is a thing I have pined for most since I read Fenimore Cooper, as a boy," the Englishman who chose an American destiny, Lawrence hoped to lead a van of writers who would oppose self-energized fakirs like Henry Adams. And although Adams, who confessed to a lopsidedness so warped, an instinct "so blighted from babyhood" that he possessed "but half a nature"—though Adams was himself a flagrantly Lawrentian character, he remained fixed on null. Unfortunately, it is Adams's vein not Lawrence's that most influential writers cultivate today, Adams's aversions rather than Lawrence's enthusiasms they are tempted to imitate or advertise. Maybe he is inimitable after all. Dying of consumption, ending the time in Taos, struggling to recover for high art those shamanistic powers inherent in the ritual process, Lawrence took the phoenix as his talisman, symbol of the force of renewal not the principle of ruin in history.

"More obscene than anything is inertia," Henry Miller said in 1934. "I love everything that flows."[28] If it is in part due to Miller's energy that Lawrence was kept alive in America, nevertheless it's been largely through Adams's eyes that modernist writers, with a major exception or two, have viewed the deliquescence of society. Seeing "horrors," Tony Tanner observed in a study of "The American Novelist as Entropologist" (1971), a "chaos of waste and human mutilation," they resort to Adams's laws, theories, proofs of doom and in this way prepare audiences for the "coming victory of entropy." Adams aside, Tanner thinks that it is a signal trait of American sensibility, a chosen people that has never known a stable state, to identify the condition of social disorder with the larger mystery of human dissolution.[29] Although it may well be that pessimism is one of our original sins and bemusing vices as a nation, Tanner's analysis takes no account of homely truth, the plain truth of a clairvoyant collapse of trust in the industrial age. There's no mystery, then, in understanding why those writers who don't flock to Black Mesa prefer to compose what Gore Vidal, in a recent tour of American fiction written with entropy in mind, called the literature of dreck.

By writing fictions into which obsolescence has been built, parodying machine art, writers such as Barthelme and Barth—leading exponents of experiment in the so-called literature of exhaustion—compose texts in which dreck figures not as the detritus of our culture but as its substance. Clinching the point that Lawrence refused to concede they wallow in the befoulments they deplore.[30] And if furthermore a goodly number in their group do invoke the authority of Adams so too it is apparent that others bear another burden of influence, that of our "Henry Ford of culture," as Randall Jarrell said long years ago, Ezra Pound. A propagandist for applying "American industrial methods to literature," Pound insisted that American inventiveness in the artifices of poetry was analogous to American invention in the devices of machinery. Because the "artist just like the discoverer must go on discovering," William Carlos Williams believed, like Pound he's obliged to make it new year in and year out.[31] What endangers vanguard writers in the United States, obviously, is the national habit of confounding "new" and "good," a distinctively native confusion of categories which does indeed "contain the seeds" of ruin "as surely as the built-in obsolescence of machinery."[32]

"Against the sky stands Capitalism without a rag to cover it, naked in its terror," Christopher Caudwell wrote in the mid-thirties as if with Lawrence's tale specifically in mind. Writing his Marxist critique of Lawrence as a failed reformer and miscast prophet, writing in the shadow of his own death, aged twenty-nine in Spain in 1937, Caudwell damned Lawrence for being "to the end a man incapable of that subordination of self to others, of co-operation, of solidarity" which befit a writer of his class and kind. Instead Lawrence remained "the individualist, the bourgeois revolutionary angrily working out his own salvation," a solipsist believing himself "alone in the possession of grace." Although Caudwell's essay is both cloudy and compelling, its politics, like Millett's, once again alert us to the long history of inattention to the mystery memorialized in the final moment of *The Woman Who Rode Away*. Ranting in outrage against a dying culture, a society in which "social relations" had decayed into what Caudwell called an attachment between "*man and dirt*" (his emphasis), Lawrence was implacable to coordinate cosmogonic and communitarian ends. It's therefore not the lusterlessness of his brief against capitalism that's in question but the luster of his heroine's selflessness, her immersion in a communal as well as a cosmic enterprise, that's finally unquestionable.

Although Lawrence sought to adjure both colleagues and Common Reader to exorcise the devilish spell of engines, in England no one listened. And in the United States as an adoptive rather than a birthright American man of letters he lacked standing enough to counter Pound's authority or mute Williams's pronouncements—to which I refer two chapters hence—equating the art of literary composition with the invention of machine technology. Despite his failure to liberate "the genuine America" from the tyranny of Progress, however, he did manage to reinstate a genuinely New Woman to an office Adams had persistently denied her, an office reserved for her in classic American literature where traditionally women celebrated the energies of eros. It's neither a despoliation nor a beatification of self, of individual womanhood, that Lawrence commemorates in the final scene of his story but a syzygy of Woman and globe and orb. Not an immolation without point or purpose but a transfiguration. Unlike the monument Adams commissioned for his wife's grave at Rock Creek Cemetery in Washington, that ensorcelled shrouded female figure designed to fix Entropy Law and the Woman Question in bleak gray stone, in contrast Lawrence imagined a sacrifice of sublimest kind, a reorientation of woman and earth and sun within a dynamic system, open not closed, not hooded in marble but circumscribed by sky.

VII

The Sursymamericubealism of Gertrude Stein

It is about Nature that I am going to write. I shall allow my thoughts to flow from my pen without changing the order in which my ideas come to me; and these thoughts will then represent all the more accurately the movements and process of my mind.
Diderot, *Pensées sur l'interpretation de la nature*, 1754

So for Baudelaire "Americanization" signified the culmination of a process far advanced in Europe in which all other values were superseded by those of "Progress." . . . America was that part of the world where the European materialist revolution raced forward without hindrance.
Stephen Spender, *Love-Hate Relations*, 1974

LAWRENCE'S MASTER PLAN of reinstatement was preceded and in the course of time preempted by the adrogynous figure of William James's prized pupil, Gertrude Stein, whose Delphic voice we must attend now. Fortified by that most impudent agenda for literature and the plastic arts, surrealism, Stein stationed herself at the very hub, the axial center of all those programs for twentieth-century art conveyed by my monstrous word *sursymamericubealism*. Invented to connote that set of movements which enamated from 27 rue de Fleurus, this barbarism of tongue is supposed to review and release the main residue of Stein's influence as well as reproduce the concord and discord of factions with which she was periodically allied. Unlike the surrealists whom she held in disdain her life was itself a performance so indisputably dada that it escapes the tightest-woven mesh of thought. And so ingeniously does Stein's composition mime surrealist catechism that not only is one often mistaken for the other but both are in addition often taken for modernism *tout simple*. Even as dada, the term reserved for the twin principles of negation and creation, is echoed in Nabokov's novel *Ada*, so too recoiling on itself does this indefinable word light on Stein's pet name for her own mistress of love and midwife of fame, Alice B. Toklas: "Ada."

Although surrealists touched a nerve, Stein and Toklas, Cox and Box of modernism, embodied and publicized key vanguard motifs of art long before Tzara in 1918 and Breton in 1924 issued those manifestoes which scholars today declare are germinal in the history of ideas. Despite a ceaseless flow of declaration, despite Herculean effort to codify, to trammel in time and consciousness a movement given over to untrammeling a timeless unconscious, it's by no means an unruly willfulness of self, irrationalism, which distinguished the surrealist enterprise from other ways of imagination in this epoch. Nor indeed is it a ceremony of the Word, of language unmediated by conscious controls, a "high voltage of words," says Anna Balakian, which alone serves as "the key to surrealist poetry." Nor is etymology, though once it was thought to be, a device fit to unsnarl the swirl and swivel of speech. A resort to etymology, both in the making and unmaking of a work, cannot sustain surrealist zeal to leaven the world with the yeast of liberty. Liberty? Well, yes and no. For if liberation is the key, then Breton's first source of inspiration, Freud, is surely barred. Was not Freud at bottom a high priest of reason, of rationality? And does not his religion theologize repression into a dogma of culture, for good or ill? Well, perhaps it's Freud and Marx in constellation, liberty and law in tandem, together these harmonize contrasting wills. Or conceivably it's chance that captures the essence of things. From Giacometti to John Cage it's the fortuitous encounter which under surrealist management combines events occurring in an internal sphere, the unconscious life, with those occurring in an external sphere, the world itself—combines interior and exterior landscape in an image, verbal or visual, a found object that verifies the total experience, validates and consecrates surrealism as the high art of synthesis.[1] "One must conclude, therefore, says Scholar R of Scholar G's disdain of chance (Breton's very crux) that "in spite of his voluminous reading in his subject," G hasn't really "understood what surrealism is about."

Poor G, *mon frère, mon semblable*. For I too know beforehand that I must in the end fail to say convincingly now what I have on occasion tried to convey theatrically, that what surrealism is about is indistinguishable from what modern art is all about. And what modern art is preoccupied with Gertrude Stein long ago tried to exhibit by way of her own practice and to monumentalize in her person. I think I know that what Gertrude Stein is about involves a formula for the pursuits of genius which impelled her to commemorate cubism but to discredit surrealism, a credo that addresses our attention to the mainstream of modernism in which surrealism is not Amazonian but tributary. Which is to say that surrealism early on seized and stressed certain traits common to the play and purpose of imagination in our era, seized these, sought to sanction where it could be found, reached out to clutch any writer or painter who exhibited first traces of faith in what has become the governing doctrine of art from Picasso to Pollock, from Joyce to Mann, Breton to Brecht. For indeed the capital truth about modernist movements is less their distinctness one from another than their interpenetration. And in that third decade of modernism, when Breton's first edict—post-dada, ante-Marx, preparanoia—celebrated spontaneity as the exemplary instrument of human genius, this resourceful man and his irrepressible friends codified in slightly new fashion a practice which Apollinaire in *The Cubist Painters* (1913) had called "Orphic cubism" and discovered in the painting of Picasso, Picabia, Léger, and Duchamp. A "pure art," so Apollinaire thought, its elements were not borrowed from what he described as the "visual sphere" but were "created entirely by the artist himself." Orphism was nearly identical to an allied sort of cubism he called "instinctive," a style whose elements are not drawn from a real world but are "suggested to artists by instinct and intuition." This movement, Apollinaire observed, "has spread all over Europe."

It is cubism of both Orphic and instinctive kind which, I'm sure Gertrude Stein must have believed, had spread over Europe. Not surrealism, as Breton's manifesto proclaimed. But the effect of that first manifesto was to transform Paris, seat of marvels, into the European city most hospitable to modernism at the very moment when hosts of exiles arrived from native lands where fragmentation, discontent, disorientation in the life of the mind were epidemic. From Zürich, Dublin, Petersburg, Rome, London, New York they arrived thinking that they entered a last preserve of imagination, homeland of genius. And they found a brilliant French scheme which justified their unequivocal loyalty to the creative life, the creative faculty of mind. What Paris offered, Valéry remarked, was a "perfect disorder" entirely "characteristic of a *modern* age" and manifest in the "free coexistence in all cultivated minds of the most different ideas, of the most contradictory principles of life and knowledge." Take up the usual kind of current book, he says, and you find nearly identical influences, traits, infatuations: "the influence of the Russian ballets . . . impressions of the Goncourt sort—something of Nietzsche—something of Rimbaud" as well as certain things due to the "frequentation" of painters' ateliers, "sometimes the tone of scientific publications," much else. There's no reason, either, to search out any one book. "It would be a repetition of what I have said about modernism and it would involve the whole mental history of Europe."[2]

Symbolism, cubism, primitivism, expressionism—not every group or movement in Europe or America embraced Breton's surrealist program or adopted his strategy of access to the well of instinct, source of genius. But in the Stieglitz coterie on Fifth Avenue, within the De Stijl circle in The Hague, among the Blue Rider and Bauhaus groups in Germany, all modernist movements held in common some exalted and systematic notions about the creative process itself, reservoir of energy necessary for the ceaseless renewal of life and art, personal and communal. For if we take Breton at his word, his endorsement of a position stated first in 1924 and repeated in 1936, that "surrealism is at the crossroads of several thought movements" which propose "epoch-making" solutions to classic problems of character and civilization, of art and utopia, solutions derived from a "discovery of the relations between the conscious and the unconscious," then surely it's no surprise to discover Gertrude Stein astride those crossroads.

There at the matrix of Old World and New, squat at the point where all streams of modernism coalesce, she discharged her high voltage of words in patterns which exhibit still another "key to the surrealist approach to all forms of art." And this J. H. Matthews discerns in the relationship "between subject and object—between what is perceived and the person who perceives it." Good words these, which exactly fix the coordinates of Stein's position. How she arrived there, cubist by vocation but surrealist by default, this process I must recreate now. And it's a heavy chore which in the end may not render her the less tiresome, for all her collage of theory, or ideology and art. Tiresome or not, she's an amazing figure, this woman who spent a lifetime in France but drew her certitudes from American sources which rose from such immense depths that she could patronize Picabia, dismiss Pound, and despise Breton who, she said, likes "anything to which he can sign his name." And you know as well as I do, she told Picasso, that "a hundred years hence nobody will remember" either his name or that of a movement, the *surréaliste*, which takes the "manner for the matter as is the way of vulgarizers." Oh well, Picasso answered, "they say he can write." "Don't be an ass," she said.[3]

A most confounding woman, Gertrude Stein. Gifted she surely is, but in what measure and to what effect? Is she really formidable on her own page? Her current réclame on TV, Broadway, and in *The New York Review*, in the literature of memoir, of biography—is this just a show-biz, fitful thing of nostalgia, of advertisement, of luck?[4] It was indeed good fortune of birth which superimposed an American origin and income over European breeding and set free this eccentric and quick young person in the great capitals of the Old World at that historic moment when innovation, novelty and anomaly of style in the arts bore first fruits of conquest. Can it be, then, that her current reputation is a result of our rage for anomaly of person and of art—anomalous chic? Or is it surer said by Freud's word, anaclitic? Is she prized for the company she kept, for her fellowship with Picasso, say, or Virgil Thomson, whose own celebrity today increases both by force of age and of music? Or is she a genius of the salon, distinguished, like Swann in Proust's novel, for her choice of friends and her taste in pictures, for her flair? Or is it at last in truth at bottom the devastating thing itself, genius not flair, genius plain and pure?

In her own time, as we know, her claims to preeminence weren't debated, just ridiculed and discarded. Had she submitted herself to Pound's influence and discipline she might have enlarged her sphere outside the circle of expatriates that peopled her salon, beyond the few friends, pupils, advocates who sponsored and circulated her work. But she surrendered to no one. In Paris Gertrude Stein was a potentate who entertained ministers of modernism from New York, London, Berlin, Vienna—writers, editors, publishers who realized that she was formidable but had no idea whether she was a sibyl or a freak. But then the brute fact was inescapable: wherever one turned, in opera, ballet, theater, painting, literary theory and practice, there she was. And today she's a far more vivid and considerable presence than Ezra Pound. If circumambience is a reliable gauge of power, then all those extravaganzas of art in which Gertrude Stein shared from 1900 to the second world war place her first among equals.

A period marked by grand and vainglorious designs, it is also marred as a time of petty bicker for place. Gertrude contending with Hemingway, Hemingway with Fitzgerald and everyone else, William Carlos Williams with Eliot, the New York *Dial* vying with the London *Criterion* or the Chicago *Little Review*, the collectors Leo Stein, John Quinn, Albert Barnes—in that boom time of masters, of pretenders and vulgarizers of mastery, no one was certain who really commanded and who shammed the possession of prodigious powers and energies, who was phony and what was genuine. Nevertheless, despite contentiousness, there was one signal and unimpeachable article of faith beyond dispute: Art was the cardinal work of the human mind and the unparalleled act of human genius. This was unarguable. For it confirmed another, related proposition, the belief that men had arrived at a point in history when long generations of stir and experiment would bear fruit at last. Everyone agreed that modern civilization must assume shapes determined by the most spectacularly endowed minds in all realms of imagination, agreed too that if the European imagination, homeland of collective genius—as Freud insisted in his studies of the horde—if Europe was ever to be fruitful again, its politics must turn out red or black, secular and soviet or sacerdotal and fascist. In contrast, the United States held pride of place among those who treasured the untrammeled energies of progress rather than hierarchic and mechanical engines of order. And because Gertrude Stein, Miss Stein proclaimed, best incarnated the life and myth of vitalism, this modernist myth though international in scope possessed one true homeland: America.

Considered as a Stein or a surrealist era, therefore, plainly its hallmark is a last flare of faith in nineteenth-century nostrums of genius, faith in what Stephen Spender calls "The Voltairean I," trust in the writer-prophet whose "superior social or cultural intelligence" would help to direct the world "from evil into better courses," would show men how to advance through turmoil into an unimagined but imaginable new exuberance of being. The great theme of nineteenth- and early twentieth-century writing, this large matter is taken up by Irving Howe in an essay called "The Culture of Modernism" and set down in the way devised by E. H. Gombrich. Although nearly anyone would do, Howe values Gombrich for stressing the idea of progress.[5] And the best publicist of progress, the figure chosen to embody the tumultuousness of life in the early years of our century was not Carlyle's Promethean hero or Emerson's representative man but the avant-garde artist whose epic will and princely power would raise aloft and propel mankind forward into an eternity of modern times. "The principal characteristic of Delacroix's genius," Baudelaire said in 1861, "is precisely the fact that he knows not decadence; he only displays progress."

In America, where the sociology of progress and the politics of genius modified these ideas a little, it was a central creed of modernism that a writer-prophet fulfilled his calling only when the intensity of his work roused the energy of his people. Then alone did a state of dynamic tension harness him to the audience he was supposed to inspire. In this equation *energy*, the key term, is virtually interchangeable with *intensity*, a highly charged word which has a history all its own. Rising in England among eighteenth-century theorists of the sublime, cresting in the jargon of nineteenth-century aestheticians, it floods literary talk in America during the twenties. But before it assumed its American guise in the period of Resurgence the ideology of genius turned around the sort of claim made by Harriet Monroe in a piece called "Our Birthday" (October, 1915) written for the fifth anniversary of her magazine, *Poetry*. Innocent of any grand program of equilibrium governing the relations between social thought and literary imagination in America, she said that "great art, the highest art, comes only when the profound energy of creation meets the profound energy of sympathy." A leader must have his army behind him, she continued in peroration, "the *vates* hear an outcry of passion and understanding from all the world." A work of high genius, in a word, must bring the energies of high art and high culture into organic connection, however unorthodox. That's the American equation.

That equation was in Pound's view high nonsense. And for many years in fury and in pique he tried to convince a series of editors beginning with Harriet Monroe and ending with Marianne Moore that a writer needed only words and could manage without publics. In 1914 protesting Miss Monroe's choice of a motto for *Poetry* (to have great poets there must be great audiences too), he insisted that a writer scarcely needs an audience but a society can barely survive without its writers. "The governor or legislator cannot act effectively or frame his laws without words, and the solidity and validity of these words is in the care of the damned and despised 'literati.' When their work goes rotten," the whole "machinery of social and individual thought goes to pot."[6] Pound at that time was virtually alone in trumpeting these views. Today, evoking Pound's scorn of any talk about an artist's responsibility toward a public, Howe endorses Pound's rant about self-sufficiency: "necessary irresponsibility" is the modernist poet's credo.

As there's no gainsaying Gombrich's idea of progress, so too there's little use in debating Howe. But in fact any inquiry into the modernist imagination which overlooks what I've called the American equation, the will to justify progress by correlating the idea of genius and the idea of energy, is just not canny or thorough enough.[7] And no account of modernism in America and Europe can dispense with that other disputatious power broker of fame, Gertrude Stein, who at her worst possessed a will to dominion which was at once more overwhelming than Breton's and less crude than Pound's. But at her best she was, as she always said, simply wise. She knew that writers may need just words but that it is the function of art to match new words with deep and archaic needs of great and inchoate publics. And she believed that her own poetic system succeeded in registering the whole machinery of social thought inside the solidest words. Beyond question therefore her methods would sooner or later establish the absolute suzerainty of Gertrude Stein and the final authority of American—not English or German and above all not French—writing in the twentieth century. In search of sanction for her belief, she turned (it is one of the most publicized turnings in the history of ideas) to the grand master, Picasso, to whom she'd been led by her brother Leo, her first ally, a man who spent a good portion of his life trying to detach her from the titles she conferred on herself. The chief difference between Gertrude and me, Leo said, is that she's basically stupid and I'm basically intelligent.[8]

In truth brother and sister were a matched pair, shrewd, vain, desperate for fame. Unlike Leo, who was steadfast in self-adoration, Gertrude was steadfast in the work of self-exhilaration. Unlike Leo, too, who had only splendid taste as a collector, Gertrude possessed a powerful gift of connoisseurship. In addition to paintings she collected geniuses, and she chose for her private collection a heterodox group which included Henry Adams, his colleague and her teacher William James, her friend Apollinaire and his mentor Mallarmé. She had the perspicuity to abstract from all the very heart of a doctrine which only she perceived each shared with the rest. In public, however, she declared herself sole heiress of the great American tradition of disembodiedness in art, of abstraction—a tradition which certified Gertrude Stein as the mother of us all, fecundating source of energy in modern writing, consort in art with Picasso. Spain and America, Picasso the artist-hero who embodied abstraction in its Spanish style, Stein the writer-prophet who incarnated modernism in its American mode, in a cubism of letters which liberates the inherent energies of words and thereby restores vitality to language and culture—recovers civilization from the "complete disorder" of which both Adams and Valéry spoke.

"Emerson Hawthorne Walt Whitman Mark Twain and myself," she said in "Poetry and Grammar" (1935): each expressed the genius of place because each detached English words from the British tongue and discovered the peculiar intensity of speech fit for discourse on this new continent, this first nation of the new age. Her own moment of discovery, her personal invention of a unique language proper to this newfound land, had been first made available in 1914. Although she never disclosed the origins of her theory, it surely stems from Emerson's essay on "The Poet," itself appreciable on a variety of grounds but most remarkably prescient in anticipation of Gertrude Stein's use of speech. "Beyond the energies of [man's] possessed and conscious intellect," Emerson said, he is capable of new energies which derive from his "abandonment to the nature of things." Emerson's vision she made her own in a wholly personal act of conquest, the book called *Tender Buttons* (1914), in which "something happened and I began to discover the names of things, that is not discover the names but discover the things the things to see the things to look at and in so doing I had of course to name them not to give them new names but to see that I could find out how to know that they were there by their names or by replacing their names. And how was I to do so. They had their names and naturally I called them by their names with passion and that made poetry. I did not mean to make poetry but it did, it made Tender Buttons, and the Tender Buttons was very good poetry it made a lot more poetry."[9]

Although I do not propose to translate Stein's poetry or to paraphrase her prose I do intend to justify her method and confirm her claims. Literature in the end may discard her poetry but it must preserve her thought intact—a thought which was first identified, I am delighted to read in James Mellow's *The Charmed Circle* (1974), during the period 1912 to 1914 by Hutchins Hapgood, a journalist writing for the *New York Globe*. "Once equating her work with that of Anton Johannsen, a labor leader indicted in a dynamiting conspiracy," Hapgood remarked of Johannsen that his determination to "express with vitality the turbulent reaching out and reaching up for a new life of submerged masses of men"—this effort inspired a special brand of "fragmentary, vital talk" which "has something esthetically and emotionally similar" to Stein's strain of experimental prose. Whether or not Johannsen's talk or Stein's words emanate from a common fount of inspiration, Hapgood's remark itself reinforces Stein's most persistent claim: the genius of civilization in the United States is indistinguishable from Gertrude Stein's genius as a poet. Poetry, considered as a means of access to the roots of language, takes soundings of the deep inner life of the speaker and resounds with the echoing life of the listener—from French and American models, from American and European myths, she derived and justified a modernist poetry fit to be inscribed in a world inhabited by Picasso.

"It is something strictly American," she said in a lecture called "The Gradual Making of The Making of Americans," to "conceive a space that is always filled with moving, a space of time that is filled with moving and my first real effort to express this thing which is an American thing began in writing The Making of Americans."[10] The key word is *moving*. And it would not catch us up if it didn't belong to a family of terms linked by resemblances of a special kind, terms which report the persistence of an American mystique of *intensity, motion, energy* in the life of imagination. *Motion*, it is widely known, obsessed Henry Adams—to whose work Stein doesn't give the least flick of awareness. If it is barely possible to conceive the mind of William James's distinguished pupil barren of Adams, it is hardly conceivable to think of the Steins, both Leo and Gertrude—whose acquaintance with Bernard Berenson had drawn them to Cézanne and inspired their historic first great act of acquisition—as ignorant of Adams's ideas. For it was exactly at this moment, the period of a Stein–Berenson association, that Berenson and Adams were in close touch.[11] Indeed, by 1909 Berenson in Europe had already read his own copy of the *Education*—unlike Justice Holmes, virtually Adams's neighbor in Washington, who "had to bully [Adams] a little to get a copy," just then made available for private distribution among friends. When later Gertrude was to say that "moving is existing" and describe this as an American thing, it is scarcely credible to think that she didn't share a peculiarly American impulse to system-building which a recent study of Adams's *Education* and Poe's *Eureka* locates at the very heart of those works in particular and of American sensibility in general. Both Poe and Adams, says A. D. Van Nostrand, share a taste for a "cosmology" which "relates the human being to the physical universe in terms of motion: the motion of thought and the motion of natural energy."[12]

Although Stein is not usually characterized as a cosmologist of motion, this is the field in which she scores points against Adams. It is not, incidentally, the field reserved for her by James M. Cox, the only critic so far as I know who correlates Stein's aims and Adams's ends. Trouble is that Cox's very good essay presents Stein as a direct descendant of Adams, whereas I'm convinced that she chose a lineage which set her in opposition to this line of ancestry and descent. According to Cox it was her detachment from science, her absorption in an art where words are "everything and the life nothing," her recognition of America as the oldest country of the new epoch of progress (old because "it was the first to enter the modern world of steam and electricity," Cox says, forcing his point), her determination to invent an "absolute present" in which language is disconnected from any real place—in *The Autobiography of Alice B. Toklas* Cox thinks he recognizes Stein as "the woman whom Adams had tried to imagine emerging from the American scene."[13]

But Stein cannot be contained within the set of roles Cox chooses for her. Her bulges show. For her whole oeuvre has the effect of setting right all Adams's miscalculations of history, his whole cosmology. His study of the laws of motion, the synoptic theme of his autobiography, had returned his mind to the century 1150–1250, "the unit from which he might measure motion down to his own time"—down to Stein's own time indeed, 1927, the year when his calculations forecast that "force, space and time should meet" in a clear display of entropy, the Second Law seen in high relief. That momentous approximation of chaos in history rested on two principles which Adams claimed "any schoolboy could see." First, "man as a force must be measured by motion, from a fixed point." Second, "the laws of inertia" are to be sought "in the feminine mind." Marvelous! Imagine Gertrude Stein in 1925 writing *The Making of Americans* in order to prove that American energies beget movements so intense, so subtle, that only the life of a special kind of genius, a woman with a male sensibility, was qualified to deny Adams's libel of America. "Pablo and Matisse have a maleness that belongs to genius," she observed. "*Moi aussi*, perhaps," our very own Tiresias.[14]

If we assume that her head start on Adams's *Education* dates from 1909, we're the better informed about the reasons why Gertrude in the twenties saw herself as the solitary figure of force fit to dispute Adams's authority over the American avant-garde. "For the intellectuals of the twenties, the *Education* was an epic work after their own hearts. *Epic* is no idly used word," Louis Kronenberger said in 1939, recalling that Adams's autobiography had gained an untold number of followers among young writers who found prophetic and chilling his account of alienation and decay. Adams's account of the failure of his own "exceptional personality to mesh with a prodigious civilization," his choice of impotence instead of mutilation—in the decade following his death in 1918, Adams's work acquired an authority which there's "small likelihood that it will ever have again." Studying his career, reading Spengler and agreeing that the "barbarous materialism" of modern American industrial life represented a "declining phase of Western civilization," the twenties young felt that the *Education* "ennobled their dilemma," gave "dignity to their frustration," and justified their flight to Europe. In describing the process whereby he had got "waylaid and misplaced, had been passed up and slurred over and left to go unsung," Adams gave to "the 1920's not the signal to fight but the leave to withdraw."[15]

In contrast, Gertrude's art gave the signal to fight and flourish. And if she'd done the uncharacteristic thing, if she had identified Adams as a predecessor of theory whose baneful influence she intended to neutralize, whose laws of motion she'd found wanting, surely she'd have set herself up for less belated applause. For if she is to be regarded as a figure of major force, her attainment must be considered from the precise point of view Adams adopted in writing *Mont-Saint-Michel and Chartres*: "I wanted to show the intensity of a vital energy of a given time"—in contrast, naturally, to the dissipation of energy which blights modern times.[16] And Stein, contradicting Adams, demonstrated in a single famed line of poetry, "A rose is a rose is a rose is a rose," her law of motion, a law which proved that the course of history need not be measured against any fixed point at all, not 1200, not 1900. On the contrary, when a literary generation is lively enough, "its intensity of movement is so great" that this movement "has not to be seen against something else to be known."[17] When "the actual movement within a thing is alive enough," she explained, denying Adams's views on chaos, entropy, inertia, when movement is truly lively, its intensity palpitates visibly, objectively, in a word. "Civilization began with a rose," is the line which precedes her famed utterance, her *logos*, her logo. Began with *arose*, the word. In the beginning it arose: was a rose. Both verb and noun. "A rose is a rose is a rose is a rose." Arose (verb) is. Civilization arose and was objectified simultanously and instantly in a noun: rose. A rose is. From the beginning, then, language and civilization pulsate with the eternal beat and exfoliation of life: arose, is; arose, is; arose, is; arose.

In this syntax her trademark, repetition, is not a "literary habit or a trick, but a way to handle life," says her friend Bernard Fay. Gertrude's custom was to take into her confidence selected literary friends who were also admirers and to whom, like a head of state, she leaked news. Repetition in language, Fay reports, was intended to function "like the beating of a heart."[18] Limitless motion of words, inexhaustible energy of being—a rose is a rose is a rose is a rose—in the nature of things *movement*, endless dynamism, is measured against no point of fixity at all, no zenith, no nadir. And because the most vivid and compelling thing in life is "the intensity of anybody's existence," the critical thing in art is to "find out what is moving inside them that makes them, and [to] find out how I by the thing moving excitedly inside in me can make a portrait of them." Stein's equation, therefore, unites energy and genius in an American law of motion. Passion in the poet's act of naming things, of making portraits, she took to be the analogue of energy in the object named, the figure drawn. "That is, if you like, being a genius."[19]

"Where is the *vis nova*," Adams had asked ironically, rhetorically, "that could hold its own" before the force of entropy incarnate in the American woman? First to last, from *Three Lives* to the *Autobiography* and beyond, Stein's career exhibits and justifies the *vis nova* of her hermaphroditic genius in twentieth-century art. For in her far-fetched and far-reaching way, she realized in Paris what Adams in 1907 said all Boston knew: exuberance of force is "a birthmark of genius." Suffused by William James's pragmatism, as we shall now discover, by Picasso's cubism and Mallarmé's symbolism, Stein's art blossomed out of a will to nullify Adams's fatuities on the triumph of entropy in America and in the world. "Also there is why is it that in this epoch the only real literary thinking has been done by a woman."

In any account of the varieties of literary experience accommodated by Gertrude's style, of prime interest is this matter of symbolism. First taken up by Edmund Wilson in *Axel's Castle* (1931), later disputed by Brinnin in his standard work, *The Third Rose* (1960), these French influences are today treated as matters of antiquarian not live value. Wilson thought that Mallarmé and the symbolists were imitated but outdistanced by Stein, whose decision to use words for the purpose of pure suggestion he resisted the temptation to admire. And Brinnin, intending to derogate Wilson, argued that symbolism, an imperviously French affair, was wholly alien in spirit to the work of a writer who saw herself in the way of becoming an American not a European classic. "On intellectual as well as temperamental terms," therefore, Stein couldn't have entertained a serious attachment to these purposes in art. It's a foolish argument. And fortunately Brinnin's book is cleverer in its totality than you'd suspect from this one sequence of ideas. Although he places rigid barriers between the methods of symbolism and cubism, nonetheless he does identify Mallarmé as a predecessor of cubism and does cite a portentous remark. "At last I have begun my Hérodiade," Mallarmé said in 1864, a major work based on a "very new poetic conception, which I can define in a few words: to describe not the thing itself but the effect it produces."[20]

Now, this is extraordinary. Mallarmé's quick reference to the pulse of concept in this new French poetry is hardly distinguishable from the line taken by pragmatism in the United States. *Pragmatism* is a term Charles S. Peirce introduced in 1878, William James said, with an article called "How to Make Our Ideas Clear." Its contribution to philosophy, in Peirce's judgment, was its insistence that the meaning of a thought is determined by the sort of action it is fitted to produce. "To attain perfect clearness of our thoughts of an object," James said, "we need only consider what conceivable effects of a practical kind the object may involve—what sensations we are to expect from it, and what reactions we must prepare." That is to say, James and Mallarmé, pragmatism and symbolism, rest on one central proposition: what matters most in the life of the mind and the life of poetry is the effect, the sensation produced by an object, by a word exactly used. "It isn't with ideas but with words that one makes a poem," Mallarmé told Degas.[21] In the sphere of language, James observed, a pragmatist must not hanker after the kind of unlawful magic men have traditionally ascribed to words. For men have always sought to unriddle enigmas by means of "some illuminating or power-bringing word or name. That word names the universe's *principle*, and to possess it is after a fashion to possess the universe itself. . . . But if you follow the pragmatic method, you cannot look on any such word as closing your quest," James says, pressing hard his strongest opinions, views which his favored pupil was to fashion anew in her own words—method and opinion which were to drench her work. "You must bring out of each word its practical cash-value, set it at work within the stream of your experience. It appears less as a solution, then, than as a program for more work, and more particularly as an indication of the ways in which existing realities may be *changed*." Mallarmé, whose poetry is intended to re-create the effect produced by things; James, whose pragmatism was calculated to attain perfect clarity of mind by studying the effects of actions which words were supposed to induce, who provided Stein with "the really lasting impression" of her Radcliffe life—Mallarmé whose follower Apollinaire was painted by Picasso as the "Pope of Cubism"—James and Mallarmé converge in Stein's linguistics, her experiments in presenting, without benefit of a formal symbol, the insides of things.[22]

This convergence of masters and movements occurred in that year, 1907, already notable for the appearance of Adams's *Education*. It was in that year too that "What Pragmatism Means" was published. It was, coincidentally, the year Gertrude and Alice B. Toklas began their life together. But 1907 is above all auspicious for being the year in which Picasso completed his legendary work of cubism, *Les Demoiselles d'Avignon*. Working his way round space, flattening his nude figures within their two dimensions, he created the object which is generally understood as the starting point in modern visual art. Because in 1905 and 1906 Gertrude sat to Picasso for her famed portrait, sittings which she considered a collaboration, she imagined herself set down in the swirling center, the point of confluence in poetics, philosophy, psychology, and painting, the point of origin in the germination of a style.

If Adams's effect on her imagination, James's influence and Mallarmé's are hard to calculate, Picasso's sway on Stein is incalculable. "If you do not solve your painting problem in painting human beings you do not solve it at all," Stein said in a work which is itself a triumph of cubistic design, the *Autobiography*. When Picasso saw one eye "the other one did not exist for him." And he was right: "one sees what one sees." Picasso's cubism as she described it, then, is joined to James's pragmatism as she could not have avoided knowing it. Cubism, "an effort to make a picture of visible things," was not a solution but a program for bringing out of every object its value in producing sensations, in displaying how reality can be changed. During long years of immersion in the ambience of thought at Harvard and Johns Hopkins, in psychology and medicine, she had been absorbed by the study of "the insides of things, of people, their character and what went on inside them." But after 1905, once Picasso had shown her how to address herself to the unadorned human figure, she had discovered how to denude human speech of adornment. And by 1914 she had united Picasso with James, reconciled Mallarmé to Picasso, object and symbol: "hitherto she had been concerned with seriousness and the inside of things, but in *Tender Buttons* she began to describe the inside as seen from the outside." That work marks the "beginning, as Gertrude Stein would say, of mixing the outside with the inside."

Possessed by an "intellectual passion for exactitude in the description of inner and outer reality," she devised ways of attaining perfect clarity of thought by treating words as sensation-provoking objects. Adapting Picasso's methods of disposing figure, paint, perspective, she made still lifes and portraits in a language which on its surface seemed to be void, nil, to be all outsides. But a careful study of her words has disclosed tight links of etymology. Words superficially dissimilar are intrinsically alike, as in the literary still life, the object called "A Carafe, that is a Blind Glass." Usually taken as a paradigm of Gertrude Stein's cute ways of orchestrating untranslatable signs, this work seems on its face to proceed according to Edmund Wilson's principle of pure suggestion. Her careful disposition of the outsides of words, however, masks a primitivism of speech comparable to that primitivism of design in the disposition of figures which Picasso at about the same time borrowed from Africa. Primitivism in language is a preserve of etymology. And it is in this realm that Allegra Stewart's *Gertrude Stein and the Present* (1967) performs feats of clarification undreamt of hitherto.

Miss Stewart contends that Stein's language is marked not by a disdain of meaning but by scruple of nearly ineffable kind. Her passion for the root-meanings of words is inseparable from her passion to root out the deepest source of her own interior and creative life: the life of genius made manifest in a passion to objectify roots. In a dazzling exercise of philology Miss Stewart unravels linguistic patterns which associate the Indo-European root GHAR with carafe, with light and color, with vision and the Emersonian eyeball, with the mythic origins of speech and even with Jung's mandala. Jung aside, what remains is substantial. A relentless worker, Virgil Thomson described his old friend. And "inveterate analyst both of human nature" and of "paragraphs and sentences, of grammar and parts of speech,"[23] she could well have sought to accomplish exactly what Miss Stewart believes the poetry of *Tender Buttons*—when "read at the appropriate depth of etymology"—is designed to do: summon up the "lightning flash of subliminal intuition" concerning the "secret force of life" itself. For if *Tender Buttons* "tells us little enough about the personality and experience of Gertrude Stein, and almost nothing about [her] ostensible subject matter," nevertheless it is remarkably telling in its exploration of the insides of linguistic sound.

In that Joyce and Proust demand whole lifetimes of learning and attention, it's not preposterous for Stein to require access to the *OED*. And if the payoff is smaller, then of course the investment is less dear. How little preposterous are Stein's requirements is apparent in the phrase "Rub her coke," from *Tender Buttons*. Coke, itself chiefly carbon, is the interior solid material left over when coal is converted to heat by means of the process called "destructive distillation." If we read this phrase properly, we must treat it as an emblem of a process of distillation which converts language into the solidest stuff it can be reduced to. In a first step of conversion, we transpose *coke* into Middle English, *pith* or *core*: *rub her core*. A measurable quantity of human and linguistic energy has been given off but a considerable supply remains: *rubber core* in fact remains. And within *rubber core* there's still harder pith—indeed, when other parts are burnt off *rubber cock* is left. And this, which releases *rub her cock*, returns us to *rub her coke*—Stein's erotic talk serving, from start to finish, as both combustion chamber and distillate, product and proof of Emerson's belief in "The Poet": language is indeed "fossil poetry." The pyrotechnics of Breton's ignited finger are paled by Stein's inflamed cock!

In this witty and cunning way *Tender Buttons*, exhibiting a natural American aptitude for linguistic transformation, provides access to matters of language rather near Chomsky's deep structures of speech, to what Allegra Stewart calls "the interior energies of words." From the "tender buttons of the title to the magnificent asparagus, the living fountain at the end," from budding breasts to ejaculating phallus, Stein's experiment was directed toward the seminal force which governs the laws of speech. Along with fabled others of her modernist generation, she insisted that language discloses the mind's power to savor its own powers of regeneration. But in a way consistent with her reproof of Breton as a vulgarizer who takes matter for manner and calls cubism by an improper name, she reserved for herself alone the power to release radical and organic energies within words whose impotent outsides enfeebled the mind's pursuit of "perfect clearness of [its] thoughts of an object."

For all this inventiveness and daring, *Tender Buttons* is nonetheless a less vivid work of self-realization than *The Autobiography of Alice B. Toklas*. Usually underpraised when praised at all, it is so notoriously self-indulgent as history and so shamelessly self-aggrandizing as memoir that it demands greater kindnesses of judgment than we're accustomed to extend to truly authentic masterpieces. The *Autobiography* at its moment of publication appalled those near and far, Leo Stein, Matisse, who found themselves victimized by her gossip. Today the reach of her malice is short. Today, too, we have better sources of information than Stein's reminiscence on the School of Paris in its formative years. A rather more profitable reason for reading the *Autobiography* is to validate the ground of Stein's fancy, her self-portrait as the first figure of literature in our time. A book written with her left hand, it divulges her aims and ends far more brilliantly than do those overweening texts *Doctor Faustus Lights the Lights*, *The Making of Americans* which she expected would immortalize her. For the *Autobiography* is graced by at least one absolute quality of high art, the power to make visible what is transparent—to convert the diaphanous into an opaque object.

Exploiting in her language the idea of pragmatism, the method of cubism, roots of symbolism, and the key to surrealism, she cast herself, her perceiving self, as an object of perception. In this way she managed to re-create in a single stroke both the object itself and the effect it produces, Gertrude Stein and Alice B. Toklas. Allowing Alice to speak in her own voice what Gertrude thought, wrote, said, ate, but presenting herself, Gertrude, as the subject of her friend's book and the object of her friend's sensibility, Stein transforms herself into an object, a figure in perpetual motion, a figure whose motion is perceived according to two perspectives, Gertrude's and Alice's, and represented in two dimensions, a figure of ceaseless motion in space: a permanent presence in a permanent present.[24] On this ground, too, it was in her view hardly an impertinence to rank herself alongside Proust. Insolence was all on the other side, the side of those who failed to recognize that he, in staking everything on involuntary memory, pursued nearly identical ends with wholly traditional means.

And in truth there are compelling reasons to support her view. The genesis of Proust's motive in art, which Roger Shattuck contends is a conquest of sight based on an optics of vision, was grounded in an aesthetics of perception scarcely different from her poetics of motion. As her quantum leap of art derived from Picasso, so Proust's either stemmed from Einstein—as he intimated—or was confirmed by relativity theory, as Shattuck believes (*Proust's Binoculars*, 1963). "Relativity tells us that no object by itself has either definable location or measurable velocity." Like a memory, like any experience of any kind at all, "an object can be described as located somewhere and in a certain motion only in reference to what is about it. . . . Physiologically and psychologically and metaphysically, *to see* means to see with or against or beside something." Adams, as we know, elevated these principles of motion into a law of civilization and decay. But Proust, says Shattuck, turned these diverse principles into a unitary principle of memory. Knowing that "to see anything in temporal depth, we need at least two impressions of it," he achieved his great triumph of composition when he found a way for our memories, like our eyes, to see double. For then he was free to invent the fiction which caused his dual images "to converge in our minds into a single heightened reality."

The urgency of Proust's novel can be gauged, Shattuck concludes, by the "massive steadiness" with which the *Remembrance* asks "on what level, in what rhythm, and with what intensity are we alive?" Stein's work and life, too, are steadied by this question. Although it is discomfiting to speak of Stein and Proust in nearly the same breath, both were in truth endowed with a noblesse of genius peculiar to that moment of modernism when neither the European idea of order nor the American idea of progress provided men with much solace against a planetary consciousness of chaos. In the early thirties, composing her *Autobiography*, Stein decided that her exercise in double vision, her vision of simultaneity, the intensity of her own peerless life—measured neither against nothing nor against Adams's fixed point—was best exhibited by way of Alice. Selecting the most vital field of energy available to her, Gertrude (who often said that the essence of being a genius was the ability to talk and listen at the same time) presented two separate portraits of two distinct lives in symbiosis so tight that the motion of the one could not conceivably be disjoined from the movement of the other. In this sursymamericubealistic self-portrait drawn by a woman endowed with a male genius, a woman whose idiosyncratic speech exposed her insides as seen from the outside, in Gertrude Stein's will to unite speaker and listener, savior and witness, genius and public, we recognize nothing less than dynamic art and culture in the state of vital equilibrium.[25]

Although her œuvre in its entirety manifests a personal amalgam of ideas culled from the towering figures of modernism, her voice and instrumentation were her own. And even if her repetitions do not approximate a heartbeat, do not liberate the intensest energy of a human life, nevertheless Stein is a phenomenal figure in any history of modernist thought. A thaumaturge of wondrous invention, she concentrated on, immersed herself in, and served as midwife to that exuberant force enclosed inside the private parts of speech. Grafting Emerson and James to Picasso and Apollinaire, she sought to integrate old movements in American civilization with the new bearing of American words. The method worked only for her. And only fitfully in her work did it take her any distance along the new paths she preceded nearly everyone else in exploring. It is the act of creation itself she took charge of, took into her charge, the act of transforming the work of composition, by means of the self of the composer, into the subject of the work composed. Under her auspices, this paramount idea of art in our society—the idea of literature as a sublime calling—was substantiated anew, legitimized in the most elegant way available in letters, the radical ways of words. If art was to assist in the making of America, Gertrude Stein believed, an artist's duty is to induce the observer to participate in an action which links self and other, reader and writer, maker and seer in a collaboration whose final aim, a shared connection within a kinetic pattern, rises from and is sealed by and is solidified in the made object itself.

Even though in her own lifetime few followed her multifarious leads, one major poet, Williams, did indeed find her to be not all an alien but a kindred spirit. Unlike an almost endless list of others who, beginning in the late thirties, seemed to fluctuate between states of fire and ice, high frenzy and deep freeze, Williams joined Stein in reaffirming, rehearsing, renewing, rephrasing a passion to preserve human connection to the end of time. Like her, too, he conceived connection as holding until the end of a verse line that would forever remain open not closed, final and fluid at one and the same time. Because it is Williams's career which exemplifies the high art of progress in America, valedictory art of the age of energy, I save Williams for last. At this juncture it's F. Scott Fitzgerald who presents himself. For it is his career which unavoidably serves as a prototype of the writer in America during that interval of transition, energy to entropy, in the mythology of this nation. He it was who, intuiting the approach of a new epoch and registering the force of its new myth, the power of the Second Law, came forward to serve as its culture hero. Rising to this grim occasion, Fitzgerald assumed his antic role.

VIII

The Goad of Guilt

Adams, Scott and Zelda

As Tocqueville had risen to eminence on both sides of the Atlantic by virtue of his celebration of American political progress, so now would he suffer decline . . . from this self-same celebration. If the cause of decline was the same on both sides of the Atlantic the nature of the process was different. . . . Here, with the rarest of exceptions, the spirit of progress remained ascendant at least down through World War I. In no other country was the idea of progress so deeply, religiously held. There were few then who doubted American destiny. . . . By the 1940's *[however] it was not the progress of democracy and of equalitarianism that was most resplendent either in Tocqueville's book or in the American intellectual mind, but, rather, what might be called the inversion of progress. We found ourselves beginning to suffer doubts concerning the very values of modernity we had for so long revered: the voice of the people, secularism, technology. . . .*

Robert Nisbet, "Many Tocquevilles,"
American Scholar, Winter, 1976–1977

Speed, moreover, has come to be a metaphor for progress, and in the centuries since the Renaissance few Westerners have doubted the worth of progress—at least not until recent years. The first mail coach in England in 1784 *averaged a mere* 10 *miles an hour, the first locomotive in* 1825, *only* 13 *miles an hour. Then there were* 100-*mile-per-hour trains by the turn of the century, air speeds of* 400 *miles an hour by World War II, post-war rocket planes . . . moonbound Apollos. . . . The American decision to abandon [the Supersonic Transport therefore] represents a historic break in the tradition of Yankee ingenuity and the Western idea of progress.*

John Noble Wilford, *New York Times,*
February 8, 1976

"FOR A LONG TIME I THOUGHT I was afflicted by a peculiar curse," Henry Roth said in an interview for the *Partisan Review* (1969), trying to recover some of the reasons why after *Call It Sleep* he'd been unable to carry on. "But I have come to believe that there was something deeper and less personal in my misfortune. That what had happened to me was common to a whole generation of writers in the thirties." Roth mentions Edward Dahlberg, Daniel Fuchs and James T. Farrell, Hart Crane, Nathanael West—writers of special moment to his own sense of personal alliance within the patterns of literary generation in America. He does not mention Scott Fitzgerald, although 1934 brought not only his own novel but too Fitzgerald's laboriously written and long-delayed work, *Tender Is the Night*, at last to print. Fitzgerald was not, indeed, by nature or nurture a man of the thirties, but he is surely the writer par excellence whose own misfortunes constitute a case history of definitive American kind, the kind which associates the private character of ruin with a national drift toward debacle. "How does one explain this peculiarity?" Roth wondered, determined to link private sensibility and national culture. World War II, he thinks, may provide one clue: already in the making by 1934, the war was to be a "dividing line between an era which was coming to an end, namely ours, and another which was coming into being. I think we sensed a sharp turn in historic development. How do writers sense these things? We sense it in our prolonged malaise, and in our art—in the fact that, having been fruitful writers, we suddenly grow sterile. The causes are personal, but they are also bigger than any of us."

What is compelling in Roth's remarks is not his eagerness to discover some general laws governing the crack-up of writers in the United States. It is rather his view of history, of vocation, his belief in a conjunction of fates, a connection linking the personal genius of a writer with the genius of a civilization. It is indeed a peculiarly American mystique he adopts, the notion which assumes the tightest possible fusion between the lifeblood of American culture and the life of imagination. "I will reveal America to itself by revealing myself to myself," Clifford Odets said, vulgarizing the ideology which enabled him to move from the Left market on Broadway in the thirties to the West Coast dream market in the forties and fifties.[1] Fitzgerald, who embodies Roth's mystique and Odets's ideology, did not make it in Hollywood because he was himself the very emblem of a disaster which he never learned how to package. Victim of that long dark night of the soul, as he said, when it's always three o'clock in the morning, Fitzgerald was the first of our writers—after Henry Adams—to insist that his private failure to survive his own apocalypse registered intimations of an

American disaster. Ah yes, Norman Mailer said on his way to a long night in a Southern jail, bless Fitzgerald for his immersion in the abyss of a self whose "dark night may have come from that fine winnowing sense in the very fine hair of his nose that the two halves of America were not coming together, and when they failed to touch, all of history might be lost in the divide." Thomas Wolfe dead too early, Hemingway a suicide—"how much guilt," Mailer asks, "lay on the back of a good writer?"

Guilt is a strange word for this ideology to turn on, but shame and depletion run deep. It is known that a touch of guilt can intensify art. It is uncontestable, too, that remorse thrives on trespass and relishes a redundancy of crime. And it is cliché that our writers, accustomed to assume the cost of crime and the burden of salvation for society as a whole, have been more often immobilized than enlivened by grief. What a mystifying but telling belief this is, therefore, Mailer's exaltation of a colleagueship in torment among artists in America, debauchees of conscience, whose decomposition is a sign of guilt, whose guilt is a proof of grace, grace a goad to genius, and genius a burden too weighty to bear. Unfrocked shaman, blasted redeemer, spoiled priest, this avatar of the American writer occupies a niche of history its very own. Despite Lawrence's savageries and certitudes, despite Stein's ingenuities (in giving body, bulk, and tongue to energy exuberant enough to banish rest and guarantee motion forever), from Melville and Crane to Randall Jarrell and John Berryman, our catacombs have filled with the bones of drunk, insomniac, psychotic and suicidal bearers of bad tidings who didn't make it past 3:00 A.M. In F. Scott Fitzgerald, the doleful shade that first founded and still presides over an American ossuary of letters, Henry Adams acquired his most prominent disciple.

Why is it, said Hemingway in a set piece of literary talk on safari in *The Green Hills of Africa* (1935), that we have no great writers, that "something happens to our good writers at a certain age"? Among numberless victims of countless safaris in Hemingway's wake the instance of Ralph Ellison warrants more than a word or two because he, along with Malcolm Lowry, ranks uppermost among major one-book men in contemporary fiction. Unlike Lowry, however, whose triumph and ruin were entirely private, Ellison is a public man, an ideologue who believes that a writer in America by definition contributes not only to the "growth of literature but to the shaping of the culture. . . . The American novel is in this sense a conquest of the frontier; as it describes our experience, it creates it."[2] Defining himself by way of this obligation, this suffocating and remorseless habit of staking his personal salvation as a writer on the salvation of America, Ellison has been overwhelmed. A similar fate awaited Mailer if he got much freakier. And the impulse to avoid an identical fate may explain why James Baldwin again and again chooses to exile himself from this poisoned banquet, as he described life in the United States in the seventies. For he has been long obsessed by one question alone: "How is an American to become a man? And this is the same thing as asking: How is America to become a nation?"[3] Both questions implicate Baldwin's deepest inner life, too, his fervor, the fever to transform the menace and lure of male sexuality into a millennarian vision which includes the transformation of history, of race. In Ellison's silence and Baldwin's quest we observe the effects of that strange state of mind which Elizabeth Hardwick, quoting someone's remark, offers in explanation of impasse. The American ideal in literature is to take up your cross and relax.

Not every writer in America, goaded by guilt, is compelled to take up his cross, but surely it is legitimate to reserve the phrase *American writer* for those who are. Whoever chooses to explore the farthest reaches of his interior life in order to discover there the genesis of creation, the wellspring of character, and the frontiers of culture, whoever imagines himself to model in minuscule the Big Deal, America itself, that man shares a tradition which emanated from Fenimore Cooper's five Leatherstocking stories, rose to zenith in Walt Whitman, hit bottom in Scott Fitzgerald. Cooper, casting himself in the role of a shaman-seer, improvised a ceremony by way of epic tales which summoned New World civilization from the soul of his people, stripped bare, both soiled and unsullied. Correlating the grand design of national history with central episodes in the life of his hero, Cooper plumbed primal motives of mind itself in search of sanction for an American commonwealth. In the ontogeny of his art he recapitulated the phylogeny of a nation whose unstable embryonic culture was planted at a point of intersection between the laws of nature and the rule of law, between crime and punishment, conquest and surrender. And until about fifty years ago the American writer clasped Cooper to himself and rang variations on these tribal legends.

Indeed, one measure of distance separating modernist writers from Cooper or Whitman or even Melville is not at all a matter of intervening years. Listen to the tone of Baldwin's voice ("I am the history of America") in words addressed to Margaret Mead, and you overhear not just an outrage of negritude, but a recognition of the inefficacy of art or myth to preserve us from a fanatic and national will to damnation despite our zeal for redemption in the United States. Indeed, you overhear Adams's voice. For nearly three-fourths of a century Henry Adams has reminded American men of letters that the life of the species is crystallized in the lives of its poets. A man who by inheritance was inclined to imagine that the cutting edge of history did indeed fall on him, who equated private dispossession with the decomposition of society, who connected personal disorder both domestic and dynastic, marital and familial, with social disarray—Adams it was who revived and reformulated the literary myth of personal and national equivalence. Preparing the way for endless ages of hard times in America and in the world, undertaking to propitiate his ancestors, presidents and coadjutors of presidents—to placate them and simultaneously settle his score with a chaotic culture—he broke the news to his countrymen that their fatuous and vulgar taste in heroes, their admiration of predatory men of business and unprincipled men of government, their betrayal of the American Idea, in sum, was due to a radical fault of nature.[4]

Adrift in a society which once had signified a rebirth of the world but by the late twenties came to symbolize the end of everything, a new generation of writers found its most frenzied member, Fitzgerald, its most flawed and most gifted novelist, eager to present himself as an exemplary witness, by way of his own dissolution, of the death throes of his tribe. And it is this distraught man whose personal "deterioration has the classic elements of a morality play," who most extravagantly embodies this A to Z of paradigm, this idea of entropology, of decay in life and letters—this scapegoat and scapegrace we attend now.[5] It is the tale of a tiger we must recount.

Unlike writers of the sixties and seventies Fitzgerald was no student of entropy, merely its first incarnation in the history of writing in the United States. When and how F. Scott Fitzgerald, no student at all, perhaps the worst-educated major writer who ever lived, homed in on Adams's autobiography, caught and sought to exploit its gist, is uncertain. What is almost beyond disproof, however, are the effects on his imagination of Adams's scholarly fusion of his own fate with the general condition of mankind as well as Adams's denunciation of progress, Adams's dogma of degradation—dramatized by womankind and womanhood in America. Although there's the scantiest trace of evidence to go on, there is of course the actual shape of Zelda to reflect on, both the real Miss Sayre and the made-up versions. In person and personae she too was indistinguishable from all those women, the best people of echt-America, Adams foresaw would personify his prophecies, whose vivacity and cheerlessness confirmed his presentiments of ruin in national history. Like Valéry infatutated by the "perfect disorder" of our "*modern* age" (Valéry's emphasis), Adams alone among countless theorists of decay had the inspired notion of arguing that America was singular among nations in that its culture stood for modernism in all its manifestations—social, political, economic—even as modernism itself registered more persuasively than earlier movements an increase in the forces of chaos within the physical universe.

Fitzgerald, who undoubtedly knew that Adams's theory of the dissipation of energy was manifest in the American Woman—a being he was in any event predisposed to portray as the aptest and most magical image of desire and doom, most enchanting emblem of blight—Fitzgerald popularized Adams's trope by metamorphosing Venus into a Prom Queen. Simultaneously, during decades in which these States came more and more openly to signify a rush toward debacle, in his novels a decline from high civilization at its apogee of glamor, of moral splendor, was presented as a deterioration of tone in revelry, descent from *La Bonne Fête* to the Wild Party. Whatever bizarre personal motives drove Fitzgerald, therefore, whatever psychology explains debauch cannot be severed from the savor of cosmic disaster which Adams—who ended his life's work demonstrating how "the laws that govern animated beings" are not different from the laws that "rule inanimate matter"—made fashionable. And Fitzgerald, ever a man of instinct for fashion, gloried in the vices that aligned him with a view of history which everyone, as Edmund Wilson said in 1932, associated with Adams and T. S. Eliot, a view which assumes that modern society in relation to societies in the past "represents some sort of absolute deterioration."

What Adams foresaw through a thermodynamics of political thought was apparent by way of the politics of sex too. Maintaining that the laws of racial inertia were most clearly visible in women, Adams did not just lament the mildew of lust and erosion of passion. What he deplored beyond a waste and apathy of sex was the prospect of emptiness on the widest possible scale. The gorgeous American woman, generally admired as a coruscating image of peerless brilliance, free to have whatever she willed without restraint or limit, had no idea what to do with her freedom. Since 1840, "volatilized like Clerk Maxwell's perfect gas; almost brought to the point of explosion, like steam"—Dames of this and Daughters of that, buttressed by vast corps of working girls, American women dispelled the energies of sex and became merely mechanical brides. Deciding that the New American Woman failed to represent a new spirit on which mankind could depend to overcome race inertia, Adams believed that he had uncovered exquisitely subtle proof of oblivion. If an American woman couldn't hold her own, no one could. Applying physics to sex and sex to history, devising formulas which he regarded as having historical weight and mathematical exactness, forecasting the end of nations and the death of race, Adams furnished Fitzgerald with the rationale which justified disgrace of sex, of love, of marriage—of self.

In writing *This Side of Paradise* (1919), the book which rang up the curtain on the jazz age, Fitzgerald set himself a characteristically grandiose task. His novel would join Adams and Joyce in conflation. That is to say, he would respond to *The Education of Henry Adams* by means of *A Portrait of the Artist as a Young Man*, both books finally made available and recently read. "Thornton Hancock is Henry Adams," Fitzgerald told his editor Maxwell Perkins in 1919. "I didn't do him thoroughly, of course—but I knew him as a boy." The implication of those flat words no one in the copious company of biographers has undertaken to unravel in print. But the bald fact seems to be, as Matthew J. Bruccoli reports, that Fitzgerald at age sixteen was introduced to Adams by Father Cyril Sigourney Webster Fay. Fay, who later served as headmaster of Newman School, at the time of their meeting lived in Washington. There Scott visited him and there on one occasion was introduced to Adams who turned up twice in the novel Fitzgerald dedicated to Father Fay, *This Side of Paradise*, itself originally called *The Education of a Personage* in presumed echo of Adams's book.[6] Described as the most decadent kind of intellectual, one who no longer struggles to "guide and control life," Adams-Hancock is presented as a cautionary figure in matters bearing on Fitzgerald's home ground, the Church. "Thornton Hancock, respected by half the intellectual world as an authority on life, a man who had verified and believed the code he lived by, an educator of educators, an advisor to Presidents"—like Father Fay, an Episcopalian turned Papist, Adams-Hancock sought consolation in the Roman religion. And this quest Amory Blaine, a birthright Catholic, can't abide. Instead he adopts an idea of duty closer to that of another recreant to the Faith, Stephen Dedalus, another personage to whom Amory is designedly kin. For Fitzgerald's Blaine is surely the first portrait in literature drawn in Dedalus's image.[7] Having made his way to "the entrance of the labyrinth," having overcome "loneliness and disillusion," he is prepared to "help in building up the living consciousness of the race."

Rephrasing Stephen's last words ("to forge in the smithy of my soul the uncreated conscience of my race") Fitzgerald tries to free Amory from prisons of the sort Dedalus too was locked in. Many years later, writing *The Crack-Up* (1945), he said that a lot of people thought *This Side of Paradise* was a fake, "and perhaps it was," but "a lot of others thought it was a lie, which it was not." What it fakes is Adams's medievalism and Joyce's ending. What it represents truly is Fitzgerald's allegiance to the idea of service, the idea of truth, the idea of progress—the American idea of manliness. What it struggles manfully against, what it evokes and evades, is Adams's association of the idea of failure with the idea of love, Adams's scheme synthesizing the failure of love and the failure of civilization.

"There has never been an American tragedy," Fitzgerald was later to observe, explaining why "the story of Aaron Burr—let alone that of Jefferson Davis—opens up things" that we "hardly dare think about."

Not only did he himself dare to think openly about the fearful thing, his addiction to catastrophe, but too he issued an open invitation which I am unable to think of anyone's having refused. Because it is the weight of Adams's heavy hand on Fitzgerald's art we are trying to gauge, we need not try to sort out those facts of biography which are often treated as curios or clues of motive—a mother whose Midwestern family had made money but not got cachet, a father, diminished figure of Southern gentility, who wore a cutaway coat and carried a cane but had neither the power of making money nor of resisting drink. It is axiomatic that correlation is not cause and that contagion is hard to prove. Nor is cause well served by the custom of recalling Fitzgerald's manners on the playing fields of the St. Paul Academy or elsewhere. "Once, in a relay race, he insisted on being anchor man to reap the utmost glory. When his opponent overtook him at the last moment, rather than lose the race outright, Fitzgerald intentionally slipped and fell. Afterwards he explained what he had done . . . as if it were perfectly natural." Later, at Princeton, when it seemed that he would flunk at midyear, "using his sickness as a pretext he withdrew from college in December."[8] The Fitzgerald store of anecdote on these subjects is usually studied for some general principle of psychic stress which might explain why, as H. Dan Piper remarks, "although Fitzgerald himself was determined to be a success, his imagination responded more sympathetically to a tale of failure." Remarks, said Gertrude Stein to Hemingway, are not literature.

We cannot unravel Fitzgerald's crosslacing of character by returning to Summit Avenue, St. Paul, or to Princeton. Books are brothers, he said, and I'm an only child—and thereby gave us as much sanction as we've got to invade childhood. He should have added, however, that wives are counterparts and I'm an irrevocably married man, married in the very way Mailer once willed himself to be married, a way which requires a dilation of the principle of wedlock to include both a real wife and a wifeliness of culture, the belief that society can best be engaged, inhabited, by means of the body and history of a woman. "If one disclosed what one knew of a subject by the cutting edge of the style employed, so one appropriated a culture with a wife, at least so far as one loved a wife." In this way Mailer appropriates Fitzgerald too, the writer whose eminence rests on an act of arrogation, now legendary, of Zelda Sayre, distraught Southern belle and dazzling mirror image whose very being both affirmed and denied America. Associating himself with Fitzgerald, "Mailer finally came to decide that his love for his wife while not at all equal or congruent to his love for America was damnably parallel."

Whether or not we accept Mailer's geometry we must agree that Scott and Zelda are famed for a synchronization of lives, marital and literary, in which parallels are graphic beyond measure. Indeed, it is only when the Fitzgeralds are taken together—as in the thirties their psychiatrists insisted that they must be taken if relief was ever to be found for Zelda's psychosis and Scott's alcoholism—only then can we speak intelligibly about their unique merger of riches and insolvency, of impoverishment and wealth in life and literature. Given the final catastrophe, given the later attainment, given, too, cascading volumes of gossip and speculation treating the derangements of a writer absorbed in transports of prodigality riotous even for that age of conspicuous waste, in search of motive we begin with Adams and end with Zelda.

Zelda, who is a shadowy figure in *This Side of Paradise*, moves to the foreground of the first novel Scott wrote after their marriage, *The Beautiful and Damned* (1922). Interconnected in theme, the two novels provide in double exposure a transparent display of Adams's laws applied to Fitzgerald's nature and art. Indeed, the particular merit of *This Side of Paradise* and *The Beautiful and Damned* is found, in the matter of women, in the law of inertia. Modern love is represented as a form of still life, *nature morte*, which duplicates that state of being Adams described as a "new equilibrium" of fearful kind, the equilibrium of stasis: the Nirvana-principle, Freud said. Of corresponding merit is Fitzgerald's effort to counteract the female "energy of inertia," to reverse the failures of love by revitalizing classic visions of male American virtue and glory. When Amory Blaine returns to the "towers and spires" of Princeton intent to discredit that "disillusioned old critic," Thornton Hancock, he disavows religion, disdains love, and takes up that "endless dream" which had brought him to the University in the first place, that nineteenth-century dream of learning, duty, destiny which Adams had, in fact, located in Quincy and discerned in his great-grandfather and grandfather, second and sixth presidents. What Blaine does not realize—and Fitzgerald is not yet prepared to accept—is that the American dream of progress, like everything else under the sun, is ruled by entropy. Causing Blaine to argue that modern life is a "damn muddle" which "changes no longer century by century, but year by year, ten times faster than it ever has before," Fitzgerald proposes to replace Adams's second law with Blaine's higher law. The greater the momentum, Adams had explained, adapting the paradox of thermodynamics to the ironies of civilization, the greater the unity and momentum, "the worse became the complexity and friction." Well, says Amory Blaine in baby-talk paraphrase of Adams on America and Russia, on sex and race, with "populations doubling, civilizations unified more closely with other civilizations, economic interdependence, racial questions," there's no time to dawdle. "'My idea is that we've got to go much faster.' He slightly emphasized the last word and the chauffeur unconsciously increased the speed of the car."

And there we've got it, the cipher to unravel Fitzgerald's code. Momentum and friction, these are the twin forces ruling Scott's life with Zelda, Fitzgerald's life in art. A writer whose work originates in an ineradicable faith in the idea of progress, he equated progress with momentum, momentum with speed, speed with cars—energy in its characteristic American forms, "dynamos or automobiles," Adams had said. And although his first two novels recognize no drag on momentum, no contradiction in the very notion of progress, in 1925, composing *The Great Gatsby* he consciously paired and precisely calculated the ratio of momentum to friction governing Gatsby's motion. "Child of incalculable coal power, chemical power, electric power and radiating energy," Gatsby enters a "field of attraction so violent," experiences an increase of friction so abrasive, that his energy, his momentum, his progress, his very life must be in the end dissipated altogether, like that of a meteoroid in the earth's atmosphere. I rely on Adams's exact language in order to indicate how schematically *The Great Gatsby* unites the paradox of entropy—which doubtless Fitzgerald could not have explained—with the discontents of American civilization in an instinct of wisdom which there's no explaining or explaining away.

For it was in this incomparable novel, joining Blaine's folly to Gatsby's fantasy in portrayal of our fanatic American faith in the doctrine of going faster, Fitzgerald first fully exploited that particular tic of his genius which was to distinguish his art henceforth, ambidexterity of mind. "Fitzgerald: The Double Man," Malcolm Cowley called him. Fitzgerald the faker who took a dive in a relay race, knew himself given to cunning but thought himself incapable of perfidy. Admitting that he had hoped to be a universal man with a peculiarly opulent American touch, a sort of combination of J. P. Morgan and St. Francis of Assisi, so certain was he of his own versatility and complexity of mind that in 1932 he is said to have raged at his forlorn and desperate Zelda for not having acquired similar skills, for now knowing the difference between authentication and betrayal.

Even Zelda's partisans today agree that in writing *Save Me the Waltz* (1932), an autobiographical novel done following her second breakdown, she had preempted and squandered much of the same material Scott had been long hoarding for *Tender Is the Night*. Drawn from their wild European years, her work was intended, so he felt, both to undermine the man and rob the writer. Why else would she have chosen, in an early manuscript, to name Scott's stand-in Amory Blaine and present him as a vain and waffling man, a mediocre artist? In contrast, his own habit of mining her letters and diaries did not demean her, his wife, but did confer on his glossy portraits of women the texture of flesh. In their quarrels, their contest of bad manners, Nancy Milford, Zelda's biographer, considers him to have been the more superficially hurt. But to Fitzgerald's eye, the first draft of *Save Me the Waltz*—which used "his writing, his life, his material" in order to discredit him and gain personal advantage—exposed his wife's incapacity to distinguish between counterfeit and proof.

For identical reasons Gatsby is ruined too. Unlike Fitzgerald himself, who staked his life on his gift for making discriminations of this kind, Gatsby lost his life in an ecstasy of faith in Daisy Buchanan. "Just tell him the truth—that you never loved him—and it's all wiped out forever." "Oh, you want too much! I did love him once—but I loved you too." "You loved me *too?*" Gatsby's mind, compelled to hold two opposed ideas, cannot function. Prepared to settle for a fake Virgin, he is now in panic before the prospect of a counterfeit Venus. And this is the kind of settlement, of panic, fit for a grand illusionist of love, an autodidact of fraud, a man whose faith in the chimera of progress led him to concentrate his whole will on the "green light" at the end of Daisy's dock on Long Island Sound, on Daisy herself who inspired in him an absolute fidelity to a future which "year by year recedes before us" but which surely won't elude us if only "we run faster, stretch out our arms farther." The irony is Adamsesque. Amory and Gatsby know only one thing, acceleration. But unlike Nick, Fitzgerald's spokesman, unlike Fitzgerald himself by 1925, they have no understanding of its laws. Scott, who shared Gatsby's ecstasy and sympathized with his folly, in inventing that prodigious scene, the most famous single moment in American writing, where Daisy, driving Gatsby's car, the "death car," kills her husband's mistress in a hit-and-run accident for which Gatsby accepts guilt and invites perfidy—at a stroke, Fitzgerald recorded his discovery of the meaning of Adams's law of acceleration and decay. Going faster is equivalent to being brought at last to dead halt. Entropy and progress collide in the end.

"The second my hand reached the wheel I felt the shock," Gatsby says. And immediately "Daisy stepped on it." Innocent, resonant, momentous words whose proper reference is both to an ashy road on Long Island, 1925, and to unpaved carriage paths in France, 1904 and 1924. Nineteen hundred and four was the year that Adams traveled those paths by automobile in search of Our Lady, of monuments built to honor the Virgin "not as a sentiment but as a motive power," monuments "widely scattered and not easily reached." Although the motorcar was "the form of force" Adams "most abominated," it possessed the "one *vitesse*" totally new eighty years ago and impossible to duplicate. It enabled him, "chauffeured from cathedral to cathedral," both to imagine himself going from century to century without break and to entertain the fancy of speeding along "one century a minute." That fantasy ended suddenly at the church in Troyes where he read, stuck in a window, a notice of assassination in Russia. "Chaos of time, place, morals, forces and motive" gave him vertigo. "Was assassination forever to be the last word of Progress?" I tried to make her stop but she couldn't, Gatsby says, "so I pulled on the emergency brake." Daisy then fell over in his lap, and he drove back to the estate where soon he is to be assassinated by the dead woman's husband, a garage mechanic to whom Tom Buchanan had lied about his wife's guilt and Gatsby's innocence. Instead of possessing even this inert, sexless, collapsed icon—a "speed" in the slang of their day—Daisy Buchanan, motive power of progress in Gatsby's mind, he dies "watching over nothing." Adams's brilliance in conceiving images of disintegration which accord with the discourse of science and the drift of history—Adams is well matched in Scott Fitzgerald, who reduced both cosmos and culture to jazz-age style, choreography of chaos in the metier of Princeton.

Unlike Gatsby's Daisy, Scott's Zelda generated passions and motives of unparalleled utility for her husband's work, his life studies in the energy of failure. Theirs was a life's work of collaboration in which each sacrificed the other to their common need. For it was Zelda herself who took over Scott's education and offered him a language of gesture which incorporated vertigo, derangement, assassination—a language fit to portray the central motif of his highest art: betrayal. One anecdote recapitulates nearly all that has been established until now and, too, anticipates directions yet to be taken. In the South of France, in 1924, during the very summer of Fitzgerald's most concentrated labor on *The Great Gatsby*, Gilbert Seldes—who saw in Scott and Zelda a "double apparition" of beauty, a heavenly pair—was appalled to discover that his host and hostess were inhabited by visible demons too. This twice double apparition made an appearance daily at the very point where the carriage path, on which Fitzgerald drove from villa to beach, "dangerously narrowed and curved. Every time, just at this point, Zelda would turn to Scott"—succubus to incubus—and say "'Give me a cigarette, Goofo.'" In the moments of terrified silence that followed, "Scott always managed to give Zelda her cigarette and to straighten out the Renault." What Seldes never understood was why Zelda made her request "repeatedly at just that hazardous point in the road."[9] Today, it is no great stroke of wit to observe the Fitzgeralds, on the road or at the beach, performing preappointed roles. In marrying Zelda, as Mailer said, Fitzgerald embraced his destiny.

For all the metonymy of their lives, despite their suffusion of love and loss, loss and gain, their kind of affinity is not at all uncommon in another kind of literature, the case study of pathology in marriage. According to Robert Seidenberg's psychoanalytic account of *Marriage in Life and Literature* (1970), the alcoholic will to achieve mutuality of ruin in marriage, as banal a form of horror as men have contrived, exhibits a deep and desperate kind of integrity. Victims of the "Dionysian dilemma," Scott and Zelda duplicated the behavior of Frank and Mary—"two against the world," as Seidenberg describes his patients, who honored each other with a "devotion and unity" seldom found in marriages ungoverned by drink. Less worldly than the Fitzgeralds, given to homelier orgy, Mary and Frank followed each other "through each room of the house, performing a different play for each scene. They romped in the cellar, played hide-and-go-seek in the bins," and so on. Because "both lived in a state of high anxiety when they were sober," Seidenberg remarks, as if recollecting tales about Scott and Zelda in the Plaza fountain, they acted out the tragedy of their lives in the form of slapstick comedy. Faked ecstasy, alcoholism is said to be itself a symptom of mutual distrust which unites a narcissistic pair in dramas that rehearse the funeral rites of love.

Mary and Frank and Scott and Zelda, then, confirm what "every experienced clinician knows," that the "alternatives to drinking may be complete disintegration (psychosis) and suicide." Alcoholism, as Karl Menninger said years ago in *Man Against Himself* (1938), is not a disease in itself, but a "*suicidal flight* from disease, a disastrous attempt" at self-cure. And virtually the other day, reconsidering this frightful matter for its bearing on that hard-drinking mob, American writers in general, in a psychiatric study of "The Alcoholism of F. Scott Fitzgerald," Donald W. Goodwin confessed that he could not penetrate this fog. The origins of Fitzgerald's malaise are as "inscrutable as the mystery of his writing talent." Invoking Baudelaire's view of Poe as a man who drank "barbarously, with a speed and dispatch altogether American, as if he were performing a homicidal function, as if he had to kill something inside himself, a worm that would not die," recalling Baudelaire Goodwin wonders what it was Fitzgerald tried to kill. What was Fitzgerald's worm? "Nothing written by Fitzgerald or about him tells us."[10]

Leaving intact the mystery of his genius, I'm certain that every word betrays him. Far below those miseries which are relieved by the euphoria of drink there are relics, shards, an Olduvai Gorge of anguish beyond anyone's powers of restoration because alcoholics, in Menninger's view, are uniformly and unalterably convinced that they have been betrayed by their parents, by the world, by life itself. Menninger makes both much and little of this stunning fact, quite as Fitzgerald himself made both little and much of the twin principles of betrayal and guilt. An obsession with treachery, an unyielding condemnation of the traitor's guilt combined with an unalterable devotion, beyond pathology, to the betrayer—this mad integrity of motive and mood characterizes Zelda's attachment to her parents and husband as well as Scott's relations both to his parents and to his wife. "I'm so bad," he said during the last days of Hollywood, "such a lousy son-of-a-bitch, that I've got to do something good—so good in my work—that it counterbalances the bad."[11] When I was your age, Scott wrote to his daughter at school in 1938, a letter blaming her for having acquired her mother's vices of idleness, frivolity, and conceit, a letter loaded with the kind of self-pity he austerely refused to grant a whole race of men made in his own image, Blaine and Gatsby, Dick Diver and Monroe Stahr—at your age, "I lived with a great dream. The dream grew and I learned how to speak of it and make people listen. Then the dream divided one day when I decided to marry your mother, even though I knew she was spoiled and meant no good to me. I was sorry immediately I had married her but, being patient in those days, made the best of it and got to love her in another way. . . . But I was a man divided—she wanted me to work too much for *her* and not enough for my dream."

Even when we set aside leaps of memory, a drunk's taste for sanctimony, a lust for self-justification, we retain a bill of particulars which tells much about Scott and little about Zelda. And although there is more in the way of accusation directed against Zelda's mother, the main thing is not a measureless quantity of blame, but its play in counterpoint with a force vital to art, remorse. Taken straight, his complaint is a lie. Hearing these accusations, Sara Mayfield, a younger acquaintance of Zelda's in Montgomery, writing *Exiles from Paradise* (1971) chiefly in defense of her friend, was outraged by Scott's misrepresentation of fact. What she overlooks Goodwin stresses: vanity was the warp and shame was the woof of Scott's personality. Contemplating the fiasco of money, the truncation of work, the disaster of health, the extinction of love, Fitzgerald confessed, "I am what I am because of my wife." But although he never properly estimated the exact cost of his debt to Zelda, he did surely recognize that together they had discovered the motive power of chaos which undermined a whole generation of writers, those given to Marx, the god that failed, those given to silence, and those given to drink.

Before the Fitzgeralds succumbed to their *folie à deux*, they engaged in a show of sexual and literary politics undreamt of either by experienced clinicians or vanguard liberationists of love. Nor indeed is there comparable resonance or portentousness, psychic and social, in follies superficially similar—Malcolm and Margerie Lowry's for example, whose marriage, at once symbiotic and poisonous, Lowry's biographer Douglas Day considers stupefying strange. What is not at all strange, in Day's view, is the source of Lowry's alcoholism. Tracking the scent of trauma to etiologies of the most prosaic kind, Day tells us that wayward "sons of austere and autocratic" Methodist fathers, fixated rebellious sons "are apt to express their rebellion by drinking. Guilt and fear, of sexual origin, are likely to express themselves in drinking." And when in addition to *oral fixation* and *resentment* and *guilt* Day turns up *insecurity* he's got more than enough evidence to explain why an alcoholic who wants mothering marries a woman who wants martyrdom and ends a drunk whose feint at murder is deflected into suicide. Data that Day cannot measure with a yardstick he considers dumb. Given the fact, however, that old-fashioned damnation is the obsessive theme of *Under the Volcano*, neither Malcolm nor Margerie (who in 1949 collaborated on a filmscript of *Tender Is the Night*), wallowing in defilement, appears to have perceived that both got what they bargained for. And Day is indeed their perfect biographer in that he imagines his book will prove Freud mistaken for believing that neurosis, by definition "wasteful and destructive," cannot generate "creative energy" but "only expends it."[12]

Not Freud of course but both Lowrys as well as Day fail Fitzgerald's test for first-rate neurotic intelligence, a capacity to hold opposed ideas and still function. An aptitude which identifies exemplary traits of American resourcefulness, too, as the history of this crazy society has proved, it was of course an identical facility of mind which led two keen and foolish people, Scott and Zelda, to join forces so as to engage in the enterprise suited to their own temperaments and simultaneously typical of national temper in their time, the economy of waste, the sociology of betrayal. Exhibiting that principle of "pride-in-risk" which Gregory Bateson calls the ruling motive behind an addiction to spirits, Zelda and Scott as well as Malcolm and Marge united "pride and symmetry" in a recipe for disaster unfailingly sure. It's all very well, Bateson says, for someone to "test *once* whether the universe is on your side, but to do so again and again, with increasing stringency of proof, is to set out on a project which can only prove that the universe hates" and must finally deceive you (Bateson's emphasis). In pursuit of proofs, conducting a test which Bateson describes as "ultimately almost suicidal" in overt intent, an alcoholic always "presumes a real or fictitious 'Other'" with whom he is joined in a "symmetrical" rather than complementary bond. Involving "continuous opposition" a symmetrical bond of this kind Bateson characterizes as a "binary relationship" so looped (his reference is not to liquor but to cybernetics) that "more of the given behavior of A stimulates more of it in B and vice versa."[13]

How extraordinary, it must be said, that Bateson's "Theory of Alcohol" (1971) should read as if it had been lifted all but whole from the plot of *Tender Is the Night*. How remarkable that an anthropologist uninformed in literary history and biography should profess ideas which jell around the life of the very sort of American writer known to possess an unrelenting appetite for rivalry with allies, colleagues, counterparts who are either imaginary "or are gross distortions of persons" on whom the victim depends for affection or nurture. And if Bateson is right then Zelda's madness and Scott's mania, the Fitzgeralds' habit of taxing and matching and surpassing each other in tests of devotion, trials of doom, is beyond demur exemplary, paradigmatic. Theirs was less a marrige than a merger whose mandate was to buy dear and sell cheap. Endowed with a demonic gift of caprice, each found in the other an inspired spendthrift of spirit. "How to Waste Material," Scott wrote in *The Bookman* (1926); "Emotional Bankruptcy" he described for hard cash in *The Saturday Evening Post* (1931). "I hate avarice or even caution," Scott told his mother in 1930, refusing her advice because it could indeed sustain "a man who wanted to be a chief clerk at 50" but scarcely fit his own sense of noblesse.[14] "But Sayra [Murphy]," Zelda said in 1924, the time of hazardous drives down carriage paths, of diving from rocks thirty feet into the Mediterranean, "didn't you know, we don't believe in conservation?"[15] Miss Alabama Nobody she called herself in *Save Me the Waltz*, a title which deliberately muffles in cliché her despair, her last fling of will to authenticate a life without quality. "Tell me about myself when I was little," Alabama asks her mother, pleading not for chitchat but for definition. A child betrayed by a mother who is herself described as an emotional anarchist, Alabama "had been filled with no interpretation of herself." A wife who possessed only a name and a legend, "Zelda" like Miss Nobody connoted an absence, empty space.

Imitating but transposing that moment of self-repulsion in *This Side of Paradise*, when Amory says he hates his reflection as mirrored in Eleanor's pose, Zelda (Eleanor's counterpart) causes Alabama (Zelda's persona) to say of David (Scott's counterfeit) that she finds him hateful, still another betrayer, because he embodies a trait she finds despicable in herself—a dissolute, disintegrating unrest. Simultaneously, choosing her words with a most artful solicitude for nuance, Zelda says that Alabama loves David for his power of investing her with ecstasy, an ecstasy of self-authentication so exquisite as to seem a shimmering illusion of spun glass, a rapture of self-confirmation much like that got when she presses her nose against a mirror and gazes into her own eyes. This is enthusiasm indeed. For when her illusion is broken, as in the course of the novel it is irretrievably broken, Alabama is shattered. She is left with less than loss. She is left with the negation of nothing. And in final abandon, convinced that women "become the things they do," Alabama transforms herself into a fanatic of dance. Because dancing is a way of filling empty space with the shapely and controlled motion of a disciplined body—the self in the state of eurhythmy—Zelda plainly hoped that in dancing Alabama's spirit would put on flesh.

For all the pathos of Zelda's will to separate herself from Scott, to make her own way as a dancer and writer, for all their wretchedness in the grueling times of breakdown and crack-up, for all their talk of apostasy in marriage and art, divorce was only once seriously entertained. And infidelity, hers with the extravagantly martial flier Jozan, his with the film actress Lois Moran, on these single occasions alone became a cause of crisis in their lives. By 1935, indeed, divorce was no longer at issue. For Zelda had become "his invalid," according to Laura Hearne, a friend who acted as Fitzgerald's secretary. Haunted by shame and guilt, "he made a fetish of their love and called it the mating of the age," a love and mating and epoch he monumentalized in the novel with which he made a last lunge at glory, *Tender Is the Night*. Tracing the transmission of worldly power from civilized and humane men to technocrats of barbarism, from Dick Diver to Tommy Barban, Fitzgerald associates this action with Nicole Diver's movement away from her husband toward her lover, Barban, and thereby treats the disintegration of the Divers's marriage as a manifestation of rot in society as a whole at the dawn of a new era. Against a background of war talk, pogroms, purge trials, he deposed Diver and installed Barban as the master spirit of modern times. And then, determined to connect malaise to malice, infection to violation, violation to madness, madness to barbarism, barbarism to tyranny, Fitzgerald invented an equation which tipped the balance toward a politics of betrayal and dehumanization.

Of all the men "who have recently taken their degrees," we learn, Diver is most brilliant. Having spent 1914 as a Rhodes scholar from Yale, having taken a medical degree at Johns Hopkins, having managed in 1916 to get to Vienna for study with Freud, Diver has been, all during this time of public catastrophe, serene at his studies because he believes himself untouched by war. Despite his promise and his luck, we know that he is doomed, that 1919 is no year to arrive at maturity equipped by training, tradition, and taste to deliver men from baseness and to restore among them old-fashioned ways, Princetonian virtues of honor, duty, courtesy, courage, reason. As a diplomate in psychiatry who is also an heir of all the ages, who believes in the illusions of a nation about mankind's essential goodness, Diver is endowed with a code which is valueless as a means to cope with a race so feral that the savageries of soldiers at war are genial in contrast.

Uncorrupted at first he undertakes to perform his professional and historic duty, to instruct certain vile exemplars of the age—the Warren family, Señor Pardo y Ciudad Real—in rudiments of charity and decency. Asking for Diver's help in his daughter's case, Nicole Warren's father confesses that people used to say "what a wonderful father and daughter we were . . . just like lovers—and all at once we were lovers." Pardo consulting Diver says of his son's homosexuality that everything in the way of cure has been tried, an "injection of cantharides" and a trip to a "reputable bordello." Finally "I made Francisco strip to the waist and lashed him with a whip." These persons shape the quality of love and character of power, force, and energy in the life of the age, the Age of Barban. In their world Diver is obviously an improper mentor or therapist—or even husband. For in marrying Nicole he had hoped to harmonize both his gift and her need, hoped to collaborate with her in the magnificent work of restoring the ruins of love so that together they could create a miniature model of the most splendidly civilized *polis* imaginable in any state.

"My business is to kill people," Barban says. And whenever assassination palls, when he finds himself "in a rut I come to see the Divers because I know that in a few weeks I'll want to go to war." By the time Diver realizes that his experiment in civilization has failed he has himself become a philanderer and an alcoholic, no longer a serious man, says his colleague Gregorovius. But in fact he had stopped being a serious man when he had decided to abandon a major career in the great world of Barban's creation. "I've brutalized many men into shape," Barban says, presenting his credentials for power in the thirties. And Diver, who would not support a brutalizing father, will not ally himself with Barban. In a world in which victims of betrayal, the sick, can recover health only if they learn to adore infamy, in such a world, therapy is unspeakable work. If these are the uses of psychiatry—if that indeed is what he was trained for, as Nicole's sister observes—he must renounce his calling.

For Diver is by definition a man whose work undermined every effort to force masses of people to adopt contours conceived by traitors and tyrants. On the contrary, as a genius at the art of drawing people out his duty was to support the resolve of individual persons to discover their own best form of stability, of proportion. Because this contrast is the quintessential issue of the novel as a whole, it informs the rebirth of Nicole out of the state of madness into the condition of sanity. Diver the specialist in restoration has reintegrated his wife into a world which he declares himself unfit to inhabit but for which she is exquisitely made. "The Marguerite of the future could alone decide," Adams said of American women in general, whether "she would rather be victim to a man" or "a machine." Victim

Nicole is destined to be, her father's or her lover's. Choosing Barban, a murderous machine, she proves her worth by fighting her husband-doctor with all the technique she can muster. Using her "unscrupulousness against his moralities" she finds strength in psychosis. "I think Nicole is less sick than anyone thinks," Frau Gregorovius says. Cherishing "her illness as an instrument of power" she generates Diver's disintegration. Because she was "the drought in the marrow of his bones," Fitzgerald said of Nicole and Diver, he could not "watch her disintegrations without participating in them." In his dissolution is her "transference" dissolved. Only so, overcoming the pathology which bound her to this surrogate father, can she qualify as Tommy Barban's villainous mate in our era. In this way, by means of that imposture of remedy which passes for cure, she acquires the simulacrum of health in the time of chaos, of totalitarian tyranny and treachery, of betrayal.

Diver disappears somewhere between Buffalo and Hornell, Fitzgerald's own territory from 1898 to 1908, the decade in which his father tried to make it with Procter and Gamble in upstate New York. Even as Diver's disappearance registers the eclipse of Fitzgerald's own fame in American letters, so too does that eclipse underscore the last crucial fact of biography and art, the fact that Scott's art dried up when Zelda's fate was sealed.[16] For the final truth about that matchless union is given in the final novel, *The Last Tycoon* (1941): Monroe Stahr says that he was so much "in love with Minna and death together" that he wanted to go with her, his wife, into extinction. *The Last Tycoon* is of course a permanent and unfinished tribute to Fitzgerald's unparalleled talent as it responded to new opportunities of love and death in Hollywood, to his affection for and debt to Sheila Graham, her sobriety and generosity during his Garden of Allah years.[17] Neither sobriety nor talent sustained him long. Only by way of debauch could he put himself in touch with the "race consciousness."

"We have no doubt of the loyalty of your affection," Sara Murphy told him in 1929, but you "don't even know what Zelda and Scottie are like—in spite of your love for them."[18] What he did know, as he explained to that "pretty young married Southern woman" whom he engaged in a serious affair during the mid-thirties, is that Zelda had "all the youth and freshness that was in me. And it's a sort of investment that is as tangible as my talent, my child, my money." Had he added my disease, my death, he'd have said it all. But we can say it for him by replacing Stahr's rapture, Minna and death, with Fitzgerald's own devotion to Zelda and gin. He was at his very worst as a man when bedeviled by drink he released Zelda's demons, her zest for doom. But it was then, around that zest, his powers crystallized. Zelda alone could not fecundate his art. And he knew that gin alone despoiled his work. Gin and Zelda, Zelda and scotch—there was a movable feast more lavish, more enviable than even Hemingway's.[19] And although Fitzgerald tended to invite Hemingway's consolation, he knew he was united to Zelda in a synergy of self-realization and ruin. Until his death in 1940, Fitzgerald—who had exploited Zelda's temper and expropriated her culture—though unwived knew himself to be irretrievably wed. To the bitter end when Zelda was in an asylum contained by keepers and Scott was in Hollywood attended by Sheila Graham, he continued to husband the wife he had abandoned.[20]

Fitzgerald, then, was a demoniac uxor and dotard of love. Appraising the phenomenal weight of marriage in the career and work of this eternal only child, we discover the source both of his vitality as a writer and his invalidation as a man. Before he married, Fitzgerald was a bogus hero. In the act of storming battlements he would put on a burlesque show of strength, win a skirmish, lose the fight, mimic a victory, and move on to new conquest—a pattern of behavior, it may not be incidental to note, biographers have found in Woodrow Wilson too. Originating in that man's presidency at Princeton, recurring in his governorship of New Jersey—a period which coincides with Fitzgerald's heyday at his university—it reappeared with disastrous effect in the tour on behalf of the League of Nations, a tour undertaken to turn his failure with Congress into a conquest over the Nation. At the exact moment when Fitzgerald was preparing to take up his cross, Zelda, American civilization incarnate, the President arrived at Calvary. In this interplay of lives there is a coalescence of character worth marking: "I lost everything I wanted in the boom." That line from "Babylon Revisited" is unsurpassed as a key to American experience from Wilson's time to Kennedy's, Johnson's, Nixon's, from Versailles to Saigon and Tehran. And as the epitaph to Fitzgerald's own life, as the epigraph to his career, it is surpassed by one other remark in the same story. Reflecting on the whole circumstance of marriage and art, of Zelda herself, without whose fragile substance Scott could not survive as a man or thrive as a writer, "he suddenly realized the meaning of the word 'dissipate'—to dissipate into thin air; to make nothing out of something." Only in waste could he pay tribute to his genius, itself construed as capital to be spent not hoarded so that he could fulfill his priestly function, teach all men the value of nothing in the age of annihilation.

The act and art of making nothing of something characterizes the last words and pages, the final meaning of *The Education of Henry Adams*. Determined to account for the fall of the house of Adams by connecting its decline with the decay of American civilization, Adams arrives at the last gasp of autobiography. Condemned and vindicated by the Second Law, he offered himself as its symbol. For Entropy Law provided him with undeniable truth: the more inventive, productive, industrious, indomitable, the more energetic ordinary citizens aspire to be, the more tempestuous will their leaders grow and the more unstable must their civilization be. The faster the speed of progress, the more disorderly their state. The end of his *Education*, designed to foreshadow the very end of his life, simultaneously signifies the end of an age and anticipates the end of time. Having got there by means of his "dynamic" theory, his application of the laws of motion to history, "there the duty stopped. There, too, life stopped." Remarking on the death of his friends, King and Hay, he says that it is time for him too to go. "Nature has educated herself to a singular sympathy for death" and like Nature, like Monroe Stahr, like Scott Fitzgerald, Adams's sympathies were similarly concentrated. His book in its final words accumulates all the momentum, discloses all the unity of the preceding five hundred pages and the antecedent seventy years. Contending that the great force of nature is toward equilibrium, that American social, intellectual, and literary history tends toward a "lingering death," *The Education of Henry Adams*, too, makes nothing of something. To make nothing of Adams, nothing of civilization, that's the Americanization of entropy. The battle we win is lost in advance, Adams said, adapting an epigram which reports our contribution to the literature of modernism.

Elevating perversity to heights of inspiration which only Fitzgerald contrived to mime, Adams presented himself as a fool of fortune held hostage by the politics of deceit, the debauch of order, the degradation of matter. Dismissing his own lifelong attainment of learning and labor, a show of genius unequaled by any American literary intellectual before or since his time, Adams discredited his personal, unbridled vitality of intelligence, displayed it as a minatory case, Exhibit A of paradox in the American way of inertia pandemic among those "whose lives were to fall in the generation between 1865 and 1900." Entropy had not in the least exempted Henry Adams from its operation and had indeed throttled his mind. Contending that his whole raveled life proved this irrefutable point, he maintained that the more ingenuity of reason he brought to bear on the Second Law, the keener and quicker and wilier his wit, the more speedily did his intellect achieve its final and proper state: torpor.

To insist that Adams gave grimmest imaginable life to contradiction, to will and nil in twentieth-century American letters, is not to say that modern ideas in general, the arts elsewhere, are unclouded by the umbra of Armageddon. On the contrary. But what is inexplicable, unexpected, is his absence of reputation or following in Europe, particularly among those to whom Freud is a paragon of influence. For Freud too, responding to the menace and magnetism of oblivion, near the end of *Civilization and Its Discontents* (1930) posed "the fateful question of the human species." Can men master their derangements, public and private, and deflect or circumvent or subdue a titanic, perhaps genetic bias toward self-betrayal, self-defilement, self-extermination? Postulating fundamental laws of instinct, eros and thanatos, the pleasure principle and a death drive, Freud's metapsychology added its ploy, its touch of dialectic, to an Adamesque drift into destitution and decay. Perhaps because Freud's question was more portentous than his answer, in the United States this idea of civilization and its discontents has seemed too pat, too crude to accommodate the etiolation of Adams's mind, the despoliation of Zelda Sayre's life, the sedition of Scott Fitzgerald's career, not to speak of the self-crucifixion of two generations of American writers or the deliquescence of one whole century of American history.

Edna St. Vincent Millay, who disguised a distaste for Fitzgerald's character behind an asperity of literary judgment, said that Scott reminded her of a stupid old woman to whom someone has given a diamond of which she is extremely proud. Everyone she shows it to is amazed that "such an ignorant old woman should possess so valuable a jewel."[21] Edmund Wilson reports the anecdote but rejects the parallel. Although he was unable to account for his friend's talent, he was certain that a figure of speech which represents Fitzgerald as a lucky imbecile was to misrepresent his nature absolutely. More stirringly than that of any other figure of American modernism, indeed, Fitzgerald's life, as Milton Stern remarks at the end of *The Golden Moment* (1970) is the absolute wonder of the age. And "the wonder is that depleted as he was, he kept going as long, as persistently, and as brilliantly as he did." Vanity and discipline drove him, Stern says, dissipation impeded him. "What I don't understand, all this ruin and ruinousness considered, is how he ever got that way."

It is the abiding question. Fitzgerald's life, so vulnerable and so durable, defeats the most obdurate will. Like Adams, a man whose deranged life was spent in learning to "talk with the authority of failure," goaded by guilt, Fitzgerald too thrived on thwart. Embodying the entropy of genius in the United States, this apostate-priest of progress is the American laureate of loss. And if we could discover at last why, goaded by guilt, he connected genius and love, love and Zelda, Zelda and narcissism, narcissism and art, art and catastrophe; if truly we could measure this vortex and dialectic of energies, this chaos of energy and power, we would surely explain at last why an acceleration of the impulse to create and to destroy kindles our culture, our nation, our century.

IX

The Healing Image

William Carlos Williams

And how would you [Robert Creeley] evaluate this concept, "energy," as it keeps appearing in any discussion of American art?

Charles Tomlinson, *Kulcher*, IV, 1964–1965

Allen Ginsberg, Paterson born and bred, returns tomorrow to the city on the Passaic River as the honored guest performer at the second annual William Carlos Williams Poetry Festival . . . in the newly restored Rogers Locomotive Erecting Shop, in the heart of the only industrial district in the country that has been designated a historical landmark. . . .

Thomas Lask, *New York Times*, May 4, 1979

Besides [at the Whitney Museum of American Art] they've always seen a dichotomy between Americanism and modernism that is unnecessary. Their position would have been clearer if they'd taken modernism as the major role for all 20th century art.

Robert Motherwell, *New York Times*, January 9, 1980

DURING LONG YEARS SPENT IN preparing and composing this work, I've presented segments in the customary ways of essay or article and in less accustomed ways, as a speaker at meetings held in museums. Not in the least startling as autobiography, the point is of course not to call attention to myself, to an indulgence in professional prattle of the usual sort. Rather, my aim is to stress a motif of social history inherent in those festive and grand occasions. In each instance conferees were convened to appraise and presumably to applaud a modernist legacy of affiliation between literature and allied arts—painting, drawing, sculpture, photography—the visual field in its full spectrum of image and text. Coordinated with a museum display memorializing one or another tendency in the traditions of the new, this legacy is now permanently preserved in proceedings, pamphlets, catalogues raisonées. Often splendid books of the highest merit, this appreciable new literature of art history, these convocations have in recent years taken on a life and authority of their own. And in a stroke of very good luck, William Carlos Williams was not long ago commemorated in this precise way. Himself perhaps the last as well as highest-ranked exponent of the Idea of Progress as a synthesis of values stemming from deepest veins of imagination in American poetry and painting, this writer, these values, those motifs, that new kind of document converge in, coalesce around a celebration I propose to treat as a model of very particular kind.

Although it is Williams in the middle of his journey to whom we're drawn, the time at which his life and his career transect and transcend the course of events, let us start with, settle on 1959. For then it was that Daniel Catton Rich, director of the Worcester Art Museum in Massachusetts, mounted an exhibition, "*The Dial* and the Dial Collection," which casts a lengthening shadow back toward Williams and forward toward almost countless others installed the wide world round. Recalling the weight and amplitude and verve of that magazine in its day, Rich honored not just a select company of contributors, dramatis personae of the visual arts in *The Dial* 1920–1929, but also the standard under which they had joined forces. Inheriting the shreds of a project left in disarray on the sudden death of his predecessor Francis Henry Taylor (himself returned to Worcester, an earlier post in his career, from the directorship of the Metropolitan), Rich inaugurated his period of tenure in Worcester with the program Taylor had intended to preside over as a sort of climax of directorial life. Monumentalizing this unprecedented journal, this reliquary of the modernist imagination at its first peak of fame and authority—a paper at once inseparable from and independent of the biographies of its founding editor Scofield Thayer and its publisher James Sibley Watson Jr.—the Taylor–Rich–Worcester event displayed eighty-nine items of painting, print, drawing, sculpture reproduced in the magazine or purchased by its proprietors during nine and a half years of monthly publication.

Two decades later, now associated with Williams's life in art, more or less the same principle surfaced at the Whitney Museum of American Art, sponsor of a major exhibit "William Carlos Williams and the American Scene, 1920–1940," much attended during the winter 1978–1979 and mainly admired. Having participated in colloquia held at both museums,

1959 and 1979, though unsettled to have arrived overnight at the age of retrospection, I'm nonetheless roused to sort out reflections first elicited by still another ceremony, homage to the founders of surrealism, that cross-cultural rite to which I referred in the chapter on Stein. One of many assemblies generated by the fiftieth anniversary of André Breton's first manifesto, this brought home a peculiarly sharp view of the museum show-cum-symposium as an event somehow unique in the sociology of taste. No matter which personages or movements are honored so, there's a virgin lode of lore and learning not yet assayed in these mid- and late-twentieth-century revels. For if the experience of nostalgia itself does in truth add another digit to the sum of surmise on progress as a lost cause in the creative life of our era then it's to the art museum we must go, the museum fete we must attend. There the arts retain a hectic fever of utopianism despite a collapse of trust both in old-fashioned and new-fangled machinery of redemption.

Perhaps the first and surely the least arguable sign of confluence occurred in June, 1920. For it was in this issue of *The Dial* that Williams, registering by far the best-documented and most resonant shock of discovery recorded in American literary history, "quite by chance" came on John Dewey's essay "Americanism and Localism." Carrying forward ideas offered in the same magazine five months earlier—a paper in which James Oppenheim (a founder and editor of *The Seven Arts*, recently extinct) had maintained that poetry was the only "genuine living art" in America—Dewey issued the proclamation Williams was thereafter to consider gospel truth. "Locality is the only universal." Venturing to paraphrase Oppenheim "in the February *DIAL*" Dewey foresaw large consequences for national life in a proper understanding of the idea of locality in art. Once artists and writers learn to distinguish between the local and the provincial, once that "secret" is known, the secret on which "all art builds," once the secret core of universality has pentrated to the very depths of consciousness, the very marrow of sensibility in the United States, then "the novelist and the dramatist" along with the poet "will discover the localities of America as they are and no one need worry about the future of American art."[1] On this rock Williams built his church.

Remarkable, that union of wills—the editor's, the contributors', the poet's. And hard as it is today to recapture their state of mind in 1920, that bane of exile from the centers of culture which afflicted American intellectuals, nevertheless it is precisely their torment Oppenheim and Dewey and Scofield Thayer, the editor, undertook to ease in *The Dial*. And Williams, composing a lavishly ornamented version of Dewey's theme, in 1925 published *In the American Grain* so as to share Dewey's secret with colleagues and countrymen and thereby secure a future for genuine living art on this continent. Although he failed to muster cohorts in any number, his book did indeed make one major conquest—D. H. Lawrence, whose review was among "the most generous notices" he ever wrote, Mike Weaver reports. Indeed, "two years later the book was one of the very few he was recommending."[2] What charmed this fretful Englishman, torn between European inclination and primitivist leaning, this adoptive American perfervid on the subject of "spirit of place" in our wilderness nation, what Lawrence cheered in Williams's book was its insistence on "Poe's distinction between 'nationality in letters' and the *local* in literature." Because of the "peculiar dynamic energy," the "strange yearning and passion and uncanny explosive quality in men" on these shores, here the "local"—*pace* Henry James—stood at the "very opposite of the parochial." What Dewey invoked and Williams invented Lawrence applauded. "Seek out *this* American element, O Americans, is the poet's charge." Then "touch America as she is, dare to touch her." That is the "really great adventure in the New World. Mr. Williams's book contains this adventure; and therefore, for me has a fascination" unmatched by those mistaken "modernist hundred percenters of America" who hanker after Joyce in order to "Europize," if "you can allow the word," to Proustify the spirit of place on this continent.[3]

Thayer, whose journal did undoubtedly "Europize" the American adventure, nevertheless in 1923 collected thirty works of painting, print, and sculpture for reproduction in a portfolio called "Living Art." Assembling masterworks of modernism—work which included items by the very American painters whom Williams most fiercely favored—choosing examples that were at once vernacular and lofty in style, regional in source but global in address, with this grand gesture Thayer focused attention on the thesis advanced by Dewey's slogan and later elaborated in Williams's charge. And however blurred in Lawrence's view Thayer's vision may have been, his sight was concentrated on artists whose devotion to locale in Germany and France and the United States was a matter of bond not of border, of sympathies not bounded by boundary hence fit to create art of the most transcendent kind, even when judged according to the sternest standard of transatlantic taste. Only when Americans could maintain the pace set by peers elsewhere would an "elite, international avant-garde art held in fructifying relationship with a strongly-felt sense of place"—Eric Homberger's account of Alfred Stieglitz's creed as a witness, host, creator, and avatar of the plastic arts—at last emerge from the energies of imagination in America, itself at that time "on the verge of an international role."[4]

Moved by what Spender calls a final American "refusal to be provincial," *The Dial*, its editor, and one of its most esteemed poets were determined to master Dewey's secret. Recalling that *The Dial* portfolio featured Charles Demuth's "The Tower" (after Sir Christopher Wren), an oil painting usually given pride of place over the hearth at *The Dial*'s office, contained too a drawing by Charles Sheeler and a watercolor by John Marin, we realize that Thayer did in fact select pieces by foremost members of Stieglitz's stable of artists and Williams's circle of friends. It's therefore not in the last far-fetched to observe that from 1923 to 1979, from "*The Dial* and the Dial Collection" to "William Carlos Williams and the American Scene," an ineluctable and unquenchable passion for "living art" presides over a major mode of modernism in the United States. No matter how many alternative styles of imagination are adduced to disclose central traits of sensibility in our time these two convocations together provide faultless clues documenting why "modernism remains a radical movement" only in America today. Not that the catch phrase *living art* alone supports this claim. Rather its gist clarifies a main cause of the urgency with which certain of our writers and artists long continued to pursue ends, as Hormberger is at hand to testify, that were "little less than utopian." And as Dickran Tashjian's Whitney Museum monograph contends and only James Dickey tends to disagree,[5] it's William Carlos Williams on whom attention must fix whenever thought turns to the most celebrated and influential advocates of an idea of culture which equates the dynamism of American culture with the energy of American art—as if the fate of civilization in the United States were in the hands of those painters and poets who shape, mold, make literary and plastic objects inspired by what Hugh Kenner in the *New York Times Book Review* (March 4, 1979) called a love of "their materials and their people."

That these movements, this urgency, this utopianism, this love signify main elements of a Williams epoch no one, I suppose, is prepared to dispute. That it is the remains of utopia, spent spirit of progress, once the most radiant and radical of all ideas motoring the industrial and artistic life of Western civilization, which custodians of high culture—suddenly keen on what might be called the surplus value of nostalgia in the art and museum market of our post-modern age—today disinter for inquest, I am prepared to prove. So many modernist shows have there been the world over during recent years, whole Smithsonians of collection, it's necessary to sniff out a hidden agenda, a conspiracy of curators who foment plots so secret and delicate no word must leak. Not that every show is suspect. On the contrary, there's obvious and choice pedagogical value in *tendenz* exhibits of the Whitney–Williams sort as well as others that recall to public interest those byways of twentieth-century experiment—Gail Levin's study of synchronism, for example—in part disused and discarded, in part assimilated and absorbed. But have there been as many Bauhaus shows and Weimar and Vienna books as I imagine? And Stieglitz: aren't there on record at least as many recapitulations of the career of that heroic man as I imagine we've been provisioned with? Are there to be very many more sister-city shows, Paris and Moscow, imitating those that ran concurrently in 1979? How many more of these must be mounted before the School of Paris squares accounts? For that matter, what account of any profitable kind was settled that year in England by the Goethe Institute extravaganza of theater, books, dance, lecture, poetry, film, music, seminar, and so on; "London–Berlin: The Seventies Meets the Twenties"? Can anyone say what all this installing, mounting, borrowing, monumentalizing, enshrining come to? Art history and museology at a peak of curiosity and ingenuity and scholarship brought to bear on a period whose splendors are inexhaustible? Or does all this bustle of disentombment betray some compulsion or tic, a return of the repressed that won't down, wants out, needs resolution?

Perhaps only an epidemiology of art connoisseurship, nothing less, will enable us to comprehend this invasion of clones within major and minor museums in all capitals and most provincial cities throughout Europe and the United States during the past twenty years. Or perhaps, assuming that there's a trace of truth both in the mood of nostalgia and the notion of need, the peculiar merit of "William Carlos Williams and the American Scene" is an incandescence of light cast on exhibits of similar kind all round. Having presented Williams as the poet whose standing in America today is baronial, the Whitney advertised the fame of a man of letters whose life and art register more vividly than any other's an obstinate though sometimes wavering trust in the transforming, redemptive, curative power of creative imagination. Intransigent, Williams even survived the trauma of Eliot's triumph, also in *The Dial*, as a spokesman for countervailing force, the chill of negation, of nihilism, of chaos, "The Waste Land." For in choosing Williams as the heroic figure of utopianism in the arts Tashjian set right a wrong the poet himself all too obsessively dated from autumn, 1922. Eliot's triumph set me back twenty years, Williams never stopped saying, never ceased to believe. Unquestionably the tritest and most tiresome lament in American literary history, its pain was purified of self-pity, he believed, because his personal rout was at bottom America's loss. Having got himself almost at the "point of escape to matters much closer to the essence of a new art form itself—rooted in the locality which should give it fruit," Williams "knew at once that in certain ways I was the most defeated" of American writers because "Eliot had turned his back on the possibility of reviving my world." Only now, he wrote nearly thirty years later, "have we begun to catch hold again and restarted to make the line over."[6] And though another thirty years were to pass while critics and historians unfailingly re-enacted Williams's trauma, a "repetition compulsion" of loss and presumed defeat, there's no question today that the writer who battled as it were behind enemy lines may well have lost the day but did decisively win the decade, the age.

Generating a radical movement avowedly utopian, a modernist out of phase with Eliot's temper and style, he set about to retrieve the era, to revive the world, with the force of his will to reinvent for himself "a new form of poetic composition, a form for the future." For friends and followers and accomplices and sympathizers in other spheres, furthermore, he sought to extend the poetics of a verse line beyond principles of form and composition in poetry alone. Precisely because Williams did indeed believe that the idea of a line subsumed principles of form in dance and sculpture and paint, he thought of himself as plugged into the creative principle itself and in this fashion aligned with an international culture of art, with the culture of nations. Scaffolding all his flights of speculation on the nature of prosody this unique doctrine, demarcation, therefore supported a network of ideas that joins the optics of his Objectivist phase to the mechanics of Precisionism and the physics, the metrics of indeterminacy involved in his "variable foot." In addition it drew Dewey into alliance with William James and eventually into conflict with writers, intellectuals, philosophers of sterile spirit and distempered mind—especially, inevitably, predictably with Adams.

Although there's little more than a trace of evidence establishing an Adams connection early on, it was in fact Adams's method of linking sex and society, art and natural law that Williams's poetics purported to rebut. Fancying himself an American Antaeus planted in a terra firma fecund with literary and moral and social and historical energy, tethered to this umbilical line, Williams upheld the uses of delineation as a means of circumscribing that portion of fruitful earth inhabited by his countrymen. Deploring the case for dissociation, deriding the merits of deracination, he cut the knot of fellowship with brother poets like Pound who, severed "from the supplying female," dried up their sources. And because he actually seems to have believed that works of art, "dynamized by imagination" and ruled by physical law, did literally become "new forms as additions to nature," Williams throughout his life trumpeted the glory of progress in the social order as a cardinal truth of Creation taken whole: "from disorder (a chaos) order grows—grows fruitful."[7] Lines set down in an early poem, "Descent," these anticipate remarks later addressed at wastelanders throughout the world. When "poets through their energy, receive such a stamp from the age upon their work, that they are marked as having lived well in their time," *In the American Grain* proclaims, then they are eternally blessed for having given dignity and shape to a formless age.

What Eliot's poem obliterated, then, was not just Williams's beloved line but too a particular passion and ardor of love for the world's body itself and in consequence any immediate hope of consummation, of vitalization in art and society. No wonder he was stunned. And how wonderful it is surely that "William Carlos Williams and the American Scene" enabled us to recall the intensity with which Williams sought, during two chaotic decades, to rouse his peers—painters, poets, critics, editors, publishers—in support of his effort to recover lost ground; that is, to dispense the restorative and fructifying and erotic arts of imagination. "I realized the responsibility I must accept," he said, shunning Eliot.[8] So too his heirs—those for whom modernism in the arts remains a radical movement because they too hold that "the work of imagination," as Williams said in *Spring and All* (1923), is "not 'like' anything but is transfused with the same forces that transfuse the earth"—are bequeathed a similar obligation.

Not at all coincidentally, let it be said, do we come round to some fresh and I believe convincing reasons why nostalgia now bedevils the museological mind. In accord with Williams's precept and example, the Whitney Museum invited us all to treasure anew those objects which glorified "the great god Progress," as Wyndham Lewis wrote twenty-five years ago.[9] A "very jealous god" whose absence today banishes us to the especially sorry state Spender described, an "America [that] has the inertia of its energy and the energy of its inertia," the great god's reappearance in Manhattan so puzzled Hilton Kramer that he was at a loss trying to sort out motives for mounting so elaborate "an exhibition based on the career of a writer." What he couldn't get straight was the impulse behind efforts to establish Williams's "creative links to the visual arts of his time," to those arts and artists that shared the poet's interest in the "specific use of American materials and American experience" as well as his appetite for "avant-garde ideas derived from the modern movement in Europe."[10] Not in the least interested in just nailing more than a hundred items to the wall, people at the Whitney did in fact design a celebration in praise of the vanished god. Determined to provide the setting for a portrayal of visual and literary ambitions far vaster in scope than Kramer saw, Tashjian and his colleagues drew us back behind "The Waste Land" to 1907, that fateful year. Not only is 1907 the year of Matisse's "Blue Nude" (which opened their show) but too, as we know, it was the year in which radically opposed views of our prospects as a civilization were first debated by Adams and James.

Torn between an affirmation and a renunciation of progress, "the whole dispute," Adams said in repudiation of James, pivots on the question of whether or not order or disorder "exists as an ultimate law of nature."[11] Their dispute continues more or less unabated. And because the culture of modernism has utterly failed to bestow on mankind a compelling belief in the energy of human genius, in high art as proof of progress, it's their debates we must recall one last time to specify which disagreements Williams's art was supposed to resolve. Returned to 1907, we are indeed set down amid images and texts which do in truth display an "extraordinary compound of the futuristic and the nihilistic, the revolutionary and the conservative, the naturalistic and the symbolic," an enshrining of the age of technology and a savaging of machine culture. And it is James and Adams in tandem who bestow a pure American style on that "bifurcation of the impulse to be modern" of which Malcolm Bradbury and James McFarlane speak in their Pelican Guide, *Modernism* (1976). For whatever contours "bifurcation" took elsewhere, in the United States its pattern was given by the two code words, *energy* and *entropy*, which animated the entire James–Adams dispute. So airtight was Adams's case for the depletion, dissipation, and exhaustion of energy in all its guises, that Eliot, a man of Adams's own stamp, in 1919 remarked that wherever Henry Adams stepped "the ground did not simply give way, it flew into particles."[12]

In direct challenge to James's authority as a tactician of technology, a theologian of order and industry, a psychologist of progress, Adams stressed the irreversibility of physical law within the psychic scheme of things. No matter how many heroic feats of industry and imagination and intellect are accomplished in the name of progress both in the short run of individual lives and in the longest possible run, the history of life on earth, a final count must reckon all the manifold ways in which the mind of man degrades what it dignifies. James couldn't have been more tenaciously opposed. And during the climactic ordeal of terminal illness in 1910, on reading Adams's *Letter to American Teachers of History*, James summoned up health and will enough to rebuke his younger colleague for imagining that he, Adams, could "save himself from the consequences of his [personal] life" by means of sheer brilliance of wit and learning addressed to "a tragic subject. No, sir, you can't do it, can't impress God that way." Besides, James insisted in virtually his last blast of judgment on the entire fateful matter, the Second Law of Thermodynamics, entropy, is "wholly irrelevant to 'history'—save that it sets a terminus," a finite term to epochs and sources of energy on earth.[13] Finite or not, James said, vitalist even in his final breath, it's the charge and discharge, a dialectic of energy, not an increase of entropy which fuels the exercise of genius. It is in short "an energy-exchange" which makes history.

Chanting his old refrain ("Chaos was the law of nature; order was the dream of man"), Adams denounced vitalism as a fraud. For as he was perhaps too chivalrous to remind his dying friend, his position was supported by principles of neurology widely approved in their day, the "somatic style" of medical and social psychology, which held that vital reserves of mind were in fact already spent. Accompanying a turn-of-century "prestige of physics and chemistry," Nathan Hale observes, "important general developments in medicine" led scholars to conclude that nerve cells might well serve as a main source of power, a storage cell of energy for the brain. Like "other unseen natural forces whose properties were known, such as gravity, light, heat, motion, and, above all, electricity," the cell's force also deferred to universal law. Given the fact of a fixed supply of neurological as well as sexual energy with which humanity was endowed, the argument ran, thrift not extravagance of action was deemed wise. In contrast to James's insistence on the inexhaustibility and renewability of our vital reserves, Adams had available to him a neurophysiology which warned that "one could overdraw one's account by excessive expenditure" and thus "become a nervous bankrupt," much in the fashion of Marion Hooper, Adams's wife, a suicide in 1885.[14]

Brain theory in the somatic style therefore enabled Adams to dash any lingering hope either of limitless regeneration of mind or of progress as a controlling idea, remedy for the ills of civilization at last. And though he conceded to James a professional need to "find out what your friend Ostwald" thinks (William Ostwald, Nobel laureate in physical chemistry for 1909), by the time of James's death next year Adams's system of ideas, foreshadowed in *Mont-Saint-Michel and Chartres*, advertised covertly in *The Education* but broadcast loud in his *Letter* to American teachers and in "The Rule of Phase Applied to History" (1909), furnished an irresistible alternative to James's dynamism. Even though by 1909, the time of Freud's visit to the United States, "this coherent social-psychological-physiological system" was under very heavy pressure of attack, Adams stood firm. "As I measure it," in 1914 he wrote to Charles Milnes Gaskell, "our reserves of mental energy are already exhausted." Because "the human mind" was simply a "group of electric ions" governed by the Second Law, human society was doomed to a lingering death, most probably by suicide. And because, finally, the main tendency of democracy in America was an inclination toward chaos, the ultimate end of human inquiry must be to triangulate the vectors of industrial, social, and psychic development so as to compute the time when the whole system would wind down. History is "approaching a speechless end," John Berryman wrote long years before he jumped off that bridge in Minneapolis: "Adams was right."[15]

Right or wrong these notions continue today to provoke the most serious debate among specialists in all the sciences—biological, physical, social. For despite Ilya Prigogine's 1977 Nobel Prize in chemistry for having somehow managed to exclude biologic process from thermodynamic law, the riddle is not yet conclusively cracked. And leading theorists of economics, of whom Nicholas Georgescu-Roegen is by far the most embattled, as well as noted reformists, among whom Barry Commoner is indeed the most impassioned, are certain that "what confronts us is not a series of separate crises but a single basic defect, a fault that lies deep in the design" of societies generally, Commoner says, and in the structure of this wasteful society to uncommon degree. Like Georgescu, whose influential book *The Entropy Law and the Economic Process* (1971) purported to demonstrate why it is that entropy constitutes "the basis of the economy of life at all levels," Commoner traces "stagnation and paralysis" in the United States, a "confusion and gloom that beset the country" now, to our impulse to evade rather than to heed and act on this "most powerful scientific insight into how nature works." Because everything in the universe is "fundamentally connected with energy" the Second Law provides a double lesson: an incitement to "mobilize this energy" for effective use in all the "activities of civilized life" and at the same time a duty to recognize that a "qualitative degeneration" of the power to mobilize energy is continuous and irrevocable, Georgescu adds, not curable only mitigable. And because in America the governing impulse is not to settle for what Commoner calls local islands of order despite cosmic drift—that is, not to obey but to flout the Second Law—it may become our fate as a civilization to dramatize the maleficence of power rather than the magnificence of Law.[16]

As a society, therefore, we remain impaled on the horns of a dilemma posed by Adams and James nearly three-fourths of a century ago. "Like most Americans," Santayana said of William James, his colleague and friend, only more "lyrically" than others of their generation, James felt the call of the future and the assurance that it could be made "far better, totally other, than the past."[17] However hard it is to "pinpoint the precise beginnings" of the conversion of a "uniquely American confidence" into a "uniquely American doubt," there is wide agreement that the "brain that hatched the fullest expression" of a "shattering sense of loss" was in "the head" of Henry Adams. These are Rod MacLeish's reflections on the subject of "National Spirit" written for a popular magazine in its bicentennial number, meditations on a malady so virulent during recent decades that infection has often seemed to be pandemic. Long a cause of nightmare among writers of a sepulchral cast of mind—tombstone humorists such as Joseph Heller and Stanley Elkin and of course Thomas Pynchon—the ghost of Henry Adams may well have convened the "symposium held last week"

(November 6, 1979) at the College of Engineering in Ann Arbor. During a week in which the nation learned that "there was 'no guarantee' against serious nuclear accidents," that the political price for "an arms-limitation agreement seemed to be more money for arms," that farms in Michigan "were still contaminated with an insidious chemical known as PVB"—even as "industrial emissions were causing rain to become more acidic" and "oil was spilling in the Gulf of Mexico and a jetliner was crashing"—crises everywhere that week underscored the subject under study in Ann Arbor, "Technology and Pessimism." That there are in fact and in fancy unbreachable ties between 1907 and 1979 is therefore apparent in the "dark suspicion" Adams was first to articulate, that America not only "never really had an ordained destiny" but perhaps "contains within itself a dreadful canker of destruction."[18]

What was presented in full dress at the Whitney Museum of American Art on December 12, 1978, was nothing other than a final and formal farewell to the era of technology and optimism. What is therefore manifest in modernist exhibits the great globe around—beginning for our purposes in "*The Dial* and the Dial Collection"—what these minister to is a longing to recall and revisit the Age of Progress before anyone knew of acidic rain. And what was re-created and memorialized in "William Carlos Williams and the American Scene" is the record of that man's unexampled response to William James's lyric call. Nearly alone at the start, Williams undertook to reunite particles scattered by Adams and in this way reclaim the future from the nihilists and apocalyptists of the Second Law. That winter 1978–1979, surrounded by those objects of sculpture and painting and photography and printmaking which were supposed to reconstitute, on Madison Avenue, the land- and cityscape of Williams's shattered and reassembled world, a visitor would have been senseless not to feel the velocity of this writer's motion, hear the tone and timbre of his voice, see a distinctive shimmer of light and line. No doubt of it. This was his scene, simulacrum of that actual place, that region of the mind which Williams did once inhabit. No question either that the extravagant force of Williams's career as a man of letters can accurately be gauged by studying this ledger of confiscations, importations, domestications, authentications of those modes of experiment in poems and plays, essays, and fictions with which he hoped not just to develop a new "grammar of American culture," as Denis Donoghue says, but especially to devise an ordering principle drawn from the energies of dynamic imagination in the New World.

On assuming this task Williams engaged in an act of faith and love and courage unparalleled among modern American writers—Gertrude Stein excepted, perhaps—of comparable gift. "What faith then is left to humanity anyway [other] than faith in art?" he brooded either in deliberate or unconscious echo of Henry James. Not long before his own death in 1916, honoring his brother William's memory and attempting to cheer Adams, all the gloomier in that insupportable time of trench warfare in Europe, James had confessed that he found in art (I am "that queer monster, the artist, an obstinate finality, an inexhaustible sensibility") consolation enough come what may. Indeed, the cultivation of consciousness itself was an "act of life" sufficiently glorious to withstand "challenge or quarrel" and should be comforting enough even for you, dear Henry, said James, signing himself Adams's "all-faithful" friend.[19]

Ten years later, however, James's kind of True Believer was a vanishing breed. William Carlos Williams is a poet I have tried my best to admire, Edmund Wilson said in 1926, but I "have never been able to believe in."[20] A startling statement, it is credible chiefly as it reports a state of disquiet, of disbelief, of disillusion common among intellectuals who a half-century ago were unable to fathom why anyone would prefer Williams and optimists associated with the Stieglitz circle rather than catastrophists enrolled in the School of Eliot. To "believe in" Williams was after all to decide whose call, William James's or Henry Adams's, to hear, to heed. And in order to respond to the former's summons, it was necessary to honor a view of history which after mid-decade was held in ever lower esteem. Although others did indeed continue to believe that the "dynamic character of technology," as Charles Beard was constantly prepared to proclaim, would henceforth engage human energies in a manner surpassing the lure of war, a suspicion grew that somehow history was more obedient to Adams's will, Adams's prophecies, than to James's. And in place of Beard's faith in technology as the supremely powerful tool of progress there was a growing expectation of far more complex and less cheerful side effects of our devotion to machines, to modes of production whose every success took its toll and whose ultimate triumph might devastate the earth utterly.[21]

By the mid-twenties, as Hemingway testified, Adams seemed to bestride this continent like a colossus. And though people conducting the ordinary daily life of this society were insulated from a morbid concern with the heat death of the cosmos, increasing numbers of literary intellectuals found frightful proof of entropy in the turmoil of a technocracy carrying on hellbent without hindrance, as Spender observed. What they found especially gripping was the utility of bankruptcy law, of the somatic style in neurological theory, in accounting for the stalemate of sex and the depradation of women in America. Which is to say it was this major event in the history of society, The Woman Question, conceived as an entropic movement in the energies of love, that seemed to confirm a widespread horror of personal decay, of personal disarray beyond any hope of reversal or relief. "I have been reading *The Education of Henry Adams*," Sherwood Anderson had written to Van Wyck Brooks in 1918, and I "feel tremendously its importance as a piece of American writing."[22] What in fact does explain "the prodigious success of *The Education of Henry Adams*," Brooks himself marveled a quarter-century later. Diverting the train of Anderson's thought Brooks fancied that it was Adam's "ingrained New England tone" which verified a national mood.[23] Anderson, however, on second thought had been unable to decide whether or not Adams's analysis—which after all derived from a region so "completely and racially tired," so drained as New England was—referred less to the decline of an entire species than to the depletion of enterprise and energy along Massachusetts Bay. But he wasn't sure. Just suppose that "the giving of itself by an entire generation to mechanical things were really making men impotent." After all, wasn't "the desire all modern peoples had for a greater navy, a greater army, taller public buildings" still another "sign of growing impotence?" His beloved "comrade" Paul Rosenfeld thought so. And he himself sitting in a café in France, watching for and interpreting symbols of all kinds, a man who had "rubbed affectionately the legs of a few race horses," drew a cross-cultural lesson from the fact that American teamsters chose to "unman stallions" while French drovers "did not make geldings" of their drays. Didn't this reveal traits justifying Adams's view of sex and sentiment in the United States? Didn't the castration of horses confirm, alas, views also advanced by Brooks and Waldo Frank? And if they were right in contending that "industrialism was a natural outgrowth of Puritanism," effluent of a society run by Puritans in modern guise who had "renounced life for themselves" and were "determined to kill life in others"—"Was I now a goner?" And "were modern women," Anderson now rounds off these anxious musings on Adams's theme, "going more and more toward man's life and man's attitude toward life because they were becoming all the time less and less able to be women?"[24]

Between Adams's prophecy and Anderson's terror of ruin stood the formidable figure of just one appreciable poet, as Louis Zukofsky wrote a few years later, William Carlos Williams. Planted in the American earth and grounded in the certitude that "always the earth discovered and explored was female,"[25] the poet's passion to convert equivalent energies and powers—potency of flesh and potency in art and potency of place—was unmistakable in an exhilarating prose-poem, "A Matisse." Written in adoration of the master's painting "Blue Nude," published in *Contact* a year before "The Waste Land" appeared in *The Dial*, "A Matisse" presents a French girl "in the french sun, on the french grass, in a room in Fifth

Avenue." Contemplating the painter's image of a girl lying and smiling "at the sun without seeing us," Williams conveys that afterglow of hue and heat and light which engorged his viewer's eye and engendered his poet's art then and thereafter. What Matisse had drawn from local French resources of sun and earth, universal energy, Williams got from the work itself and recast in words arranged for comparable effect. In obedience to natural law, therefore, the French painter and the American poet channel the flow and measure the force of currents uniting the rhythmic, periodic life of earth with the creative life of man. Because "there's force in this cold sun" of March and April, he said to identical effect in *Kora in Hell* (1921), force indistinguishable from the tropical energy that had "entered Matisse's head in the color of sprays and flaming palm leaves," the poet's task was to invest words and lines of words with radiant energy stored in fecund matter found below the crust of one local, modest, circumscribed plot of mother earth.[26]

With Dewey's benediction in mind and Matisse's painting in view, with the sacred legend of Persephone to attest to endless supplies of subsurface heat, Williams engaged to perform his mythic duty: "to bring back Eurydice—this time." And from *Kora in Hell* (in 1921 decorated with an image of Williams's own design, the penetrable, ripe, gravid ovum of a frontispiece) to the latest volume of posthumous cull, from the early twenties to the present day (when Matisse's painting, borrowed from Baltimore, hung as a vademecum to the entire Whitney show), Williams's œuvre consummates in the blessed form of womankind that conversion of dynamic force Adams had placed forever beyond reach at the cathedral in Chartres. Reinforcing his faith in the redemptive power of art, the ancient Orphic myth thus enabled him to devise a proposition he would never forswear. Progress as an idea can sustain and invigorate the life of imagination in America precisely because the whole enterprise derives its energy from and receives the blessing of Woman.

From Adams to Anderson and Fitzgerald and O'Neill, from Stein to Williams and eventually to Robert Lowell and beyond, writers in America have sought to clinch debate on the merits or demerits of the machine age by putting the problem of progress, most theatrically, as a version of the question of Woman. And though I know of no instance in which women themselves directly opposed Adams's lucubrations or Anderson's night thoughts on male impotence and the erection of tall towers, avant-garde women everywhere did surely correlate the value of emancipation with the value of progress. Not that all women were flattered to find themselves put to the test of one or another theory about the future of race in America, in the world. But women in general, drawn into the maelstrom of argument on birth control and the Life Force, for example, or sex education and the

Eternal Feminine, like Williams found turmoil not in the least ruinous, discovered the experience of disorder to be fruitful not sterile. As a result they tended to validate two of Williams's favorite maxims: machine age or no machine age, "Sex is at the bottom of all art." And "without progress there is nothing." Even if blight did abound, a cure will be found—a cure which, furthermore, feminists were certain would provide the key to unravel riddles of femaleness ancient in origin but current and crucial in nature. "How far must [women] be static instruments of the Life Force" in the grip of predestined design, and "how far may they be dynamic," separate, independent persons, autonomously at work on private rather than country matters? These were recurring and pressing questions, said a respected actress and journalist of the twenties, Beatrice Forbes-Robertson Hale. And whatever solution is found, it must hinge on entrée into modern "intense, objective, industrial civilization." For not until women have adjusted themselves to their new environment can they in harmony with men reach a new state in which the experience of love, that most "difficult and laborious art," will be transformed into a truly ennobling force in culture.[27]

Insisting on an end to the begrimements of passion, deriding the honorifics of power but reaffirming the force of biology in revitalizing race, far more cheerfully than most men, particularly men of letters, feminists took disorder in stride.* Imposing on machines the duty to complete nearly all unfinished business of social reform, including the liberation of eros, vanguard women found a natural ally in the one vanguard poet whose vision of salvation rested on a common denominator of energy in the life of sex, the life of art, and the life of technology. Because of his "mother's influence all through this time of writing"—the elder Mrs. Williams being a woman bewildered by "life in a small town in New Jersey after her years in Paris" as an art student—"her interest in art became my interest in art." Under these auspices "poetry and the female sex were allied in my mind" and "the beauty of girls seemed the same to me as the beauty of a poem." Indeed, because poetry itself was a labor of love "personifying" his own actual mother ("an heroic figure," he reminisced in 1958, "my poetic ideal") he

*The habit, once ingrained, is visibly harder to preserve today. "Disorder, alas, is the natural order of things in the universe," K. C. Cole writes in a column addressed to women ("Hers," *New York Times*, March, 18, 1982, C2). "The most profound exception to entropy is the creation of life" but "the catch is that it takes a lot of energy to produce a baby. It also takes energy to make a tree. The road to disorder is all downhill but the road to creation takes work. Though combating entropy is possible, it also has its price. That's why it seems so hard to get ourselves together, so easy to let ourselves fall apart," and so terrifying to consider "the ultimate entropy of nuclear war."

conceived of Kora's return to light of day in America as fulfilling an idea of duty at once filial and fiduciary, both private and mythopoeic.[28] Fusing the genius of language with the genius of gender, using "the tip of my tongue" to "wedge you open," to "inflame you," the poet made "a wife of his writings."[29] Thus eroticized a poem becomes a "small (or large) machine made of words" in which "the great completer" Woman, unmoved mover of movement that's "intrinsic, undulent," of a "physical more than a literary character"[30]—Woman is permanently installed, forever domiciled. An American writer in tune with the new age ("a lover" Williams called himself in *A Voyage to Pagany* [1928], "come of machines"), in his imagination "the precision of the machine [has] become instinct." Zukofsky again. Citing Williams against Adams, juxtaposing the *Voyage* against *Mont-Saint-Michel*, 1929 against 1904, contrasting Adams's submission to the prospect of stasis with Williams's fierce will "to move on to the Beginnings," Zukofsky championed a friend in whose work a sense of the history and destiny of "These States" would be quickened by the energies of eros.[31]

Entered into these lists, Williams in 1928 at last took the time to read his antagonist's *Education*. Deciding that the end of study, "the embodiment of knowledge," was after all to foster an "escape of man from domination by his own machines" not an entrapment in webs of the sort spun by Adams, Williams deplored such "solutions." Although Adams's account of "the acceleration of life" is fashionable today, truth is found elsewhere than in "pseudo-knowledge" characteristic of those "fetishists" of abstract ideas, Adams-minded types who impoverish us all by ignoring "the most patent thing in the world." True knowledge occurs on "the ultraviolet side of the spectrum of intelligence," the side where art is. There knowledge is "pure" because its light is "stripped to penetrate," he wrote in 1929–1930. Reflections finally published under his title essay, *The Embodiment of Knowledge* (1974), in this compilation Williams worked his own way toward that ultraviolet vision which beheld the question of progress in the light of James's not Adams's view. For "the most valuable point of criticism of our time" was not our worship of machines but our "waste and use" of energy in an age when men "live to progress" instead of making "progress merely [i.e., properly] to live." Machinery yes without question. "But as a subsidiary to a deeper reality lost to science completely. *The American Thing*"[32] (my emphasis).

O Dewey! (John)
O James! (William)
O Whitehead!
teach well!

—above and beyond
your teaching stands
the Pink Church:
the nipples of
a woman who never
bore a
child. . . .[33]

In any spectrum of modernist ideas Williams, unalterably his mother's son, is most vividly seen when set alongside that brave band of activist women and feminist intellectuals with whose creeds he made common cause beginning in the 1920s. Like them a devotee of industrial society, like them a chiliast of sex, both he and they engaged to release energies repressed by current philosophy and science and art, the natural and dynamic passions of love. There is "no more necessary step to preserve and promote race progress," wrote the eminent economist and pioneer collectivist Charlotte Perkins Gilman, "than the recognition of the right power of sex and its full use."[34] "I make love greater than life," Williams said at about the same moment, "greater than knowledge." For it goes beyond life "where no knowledge goes and is the most daring of all the mysteries and the most wonderful" and is consequently "sufficient pretext" for the presence on earth of man.[35]

In that Adams was to become ever more powerful as an adversary of every pretext to justify man's presence on earth, neither Gilman's credo nor Williams's "Choral" withstood the force exerted during the next three decades by our reigning authority on eros and entropy. For it was precisely this position that Adams, himself a lifelong captor and captive of the most dazzling and gallant women in his world, had reversed, turned the other way round so as to favor his own predictions, his denial of progress on the score of sex or love or industry in the United States. By far the fastest way to document Williams's triumph as a technician who found in the American "language itself, the means" to convey the character of "our modern consciousness"—the quickest route to "William Carlos Williams and the American Scene, 1920–1940" is by means of Robert Lowell, whose own ambivalence on the subject of Williams is instructive in several priceless ways.

It was in fact at midcentury, the period in which according to Adams's prophecy signs of degradation in American democracy would be unassailable, that Lowell in *Life Studies* (1959) disclosed the innermost secret of blight. A book in which Adams's presence and rule are unmistakable, marvelous work of reminiscence, of lyric poetry and narrative prose, *Life*

Studies systematically charts the power exerted by advanced industrial order, the technology of our military-industrial state, over the history and fate of the poet's ancestral line, the poet's parentage, the poet's parents, the poet's mother. Herself qualified to join Adams's unenviable collection of "nieces" (a pantheon of martyrs), "Mother hated the navy, naval society, naval pay," her son said in mourning her waste, her sacrifice to the American machine. Counterpart of all those forceful, unexampled women who "failed not only to create a new society," Adams had written in the *Education*, but even to hold their own in "the old society of Church and State," like those predecessors who had been left "with no place but the theatre or streets to decorate" and no one but a member of "her own sex who knew enough to be worth dazzling," Mrs. Lowell insisted that her husband resign his commission and buy a house on Revere Street. There the Lowells were to re-create a former style, echt-Boston in its prime. But in that gentle, considerate man she'd acquired no sublime Siegfried of girlish fantasy, her son wrote, locating the specter within a naval machine, merely a twentieth-century "commander interested in steam, radio, and 'the fellows.'" Doomed to dissipate her "subconsciously hoarded energies" in a marriage sterilized by steam, she died a widow in Italy. "Wrapped like *panetone* in tinfoil," goes one of Lowell's painfullest lines, "Mother traveled first class in the hold," returned to Boston a shipment of female wrapped against rot.[36]

Palpably exploiting one of Adams's most prominent ideas—that the sumptuousness and doom of women in the United States heralds the decline of echt-America—Lowell unremittingly presents a catalogue of casualties drawn from the very women and men whose personal cases, whose personal histories portend a collapse of nation and of race. Because the long grim history of Robert Lowell's own collapses implicate mother ("the only time I've ever been in a padded cell," his publisher Robert Giroux wrote in 1980, "was when Lowell's mother asked me to visit him at Baldpate, after he refused to see her") and wives and daughter to exceptional degree and in uncommonly public fashion, his private life study too, astonishingly, follows configurations conceived in Adams's fantastical mind.[37] For when Lowell removed the Virgin and dynamo from Adams's setting in order to insert this epic pair of images into the domestic economy of Revere Street, then Beacon Hill became the site of that inclination toward maximum entropy which both Adams and Lowell—who once told G. S. Fraser that "one of his favourite books is *The Education of Henry Adams*"—portrayed as a wreckage of dynasty and ravage of social class.[38]

Representing the death throes of a famous family as a drama of thermodynamics, Lowell therefore completed a cycle of work first begun "under the rooftree of Allen Tate" and the tuition of John Crowe Ransom. "When I first began to publish" they were preferred mentors, Lowell said shortly before his death in 1977. But "later I was drawn to William Carlos Williams and Elizabeth Bishop," poets with whom he differed so much "in temperament and technical training (particularly Williams)" that nothing he wrote "could easily be confused" with Williams's poems.[39] Nearly twenty years earlier, in 1958, Lowell had written privately to Williams congratulating him on his autobiography, saying that rushed as it was in places "it blazed fire elsewhere." You and Fitzgerald "catch the moment of the 20's better than anybody, except Lawrence." Reed Whittemore, who quotes the letter, muddles its meaning by implying that Lowell had acquired a taste for bohemia, for bootleg whiskey and bathtub gin.[40] But it was rather to dynamism as an American vein in art, the energies of disorder as a positive force in poetry, that Lowell referred.

Publicly transferring fealty to Williams, who "enters me [though] I cannot enter him," Lowell confessed that the "difficulties I found in Williams twenty-five years ago are still difficulties for me." But when "I say that I cannot enter him," he wrote in confession for *The Hudson Review* (1961), "I am almost saying that I cannot enter America. This troubles me" and "I am not satisfied to let it be." So dissatisfied was he indeed that entrance to Williams blocked or not, unready to declare himself either fully reconciled to or estranged from his native land, Lowell decided it was time to renounce old condescensions toward a poet whom he'd hitherto set aside as "fresh, secondary and minor" worth at most a "byline" in the "revolution that had renewed poetry." Recognizing that "times have changed," that Williams like Whitman was "part of the great breath of our literature," he prepared then and there to resign his high post in the Kenyon School of Letters. Exhilarated by the special blend of "exasperation and terror and a kind of love" with which Williams regarded "the dirt and power of industrial society"; braced by the "speed and genius" of poems representing that "drastic experimental art [which] is now expected and demanded," Lowell embraced "Dr. Williams [as] a model and liberator" in "the American style formerly disdained by all those writers" (among whom he included himself) whose "culture seems to have passed them by."[41]

Originally a Back Bay apologist and Brahmin of the Tribal No, with one quick stroke Lowell added his name to cliques of writers previously alien. Like Robert Creeley, for example, who also had come to feel that "Ransom and Tate, as practising poets, had little to teach the younger generation, as distinct from far more neglected poets like William Carlos Williams"—poets who "give you a particular sense of how to deal with your contemporary reality"—Lowell found in Williams's example a means of entrée into mass society.[42] Not to say that this stroke was to stand for a final federation or a last sundering. On the contrary. Annotation of Lowell's apostasies and orthodoxies, deviations and defections and derelictions and devotions of politics and religion and art, a full commentary on Lowell's heresies of love and fame is the work of scientific theologians and specialist scholars. In order to return home, however, he was prepared to track writers not only like that upstart Creeley who denounced Lowell's teachers but also one so alien as Allen Ginsberg—a poet who selected Whitman as his sire and as beldame Gertrude Stein. Placing himself in a totally eccentric line of descent running from Stein ("Gertrude Stein studying with William James at Harvard when James was investigating consciousness": imagine it!) and James to Williams and Pound to Charles Olson, Ginsberg acquired a history which was preserved in the very "measure of the art work" itself.[43] It was therefore the history of vitalism in American consciousness that Lowell and Ginsberg were to learn how to share quite as it was Williams's admonition (poets must write as they talk, in the idiom heard in their ears all day long) both men were to find separate ways to obey.

In these unorthodox and belated ways of influence, centered on measure in verse, Williams's idiom entered the mainstreams of American discourse. Although his example and his dogma were old—in a radio interview given in 1935 he'd said that the English, who always "complained of our corrupt speech," failed to notice that the "words we often used as they used them applied" not to English but to American "objects," hence were no longer British words at all—their effect was sweeping.[44] And by the mid-sixties a campaign launched forty-five years earlier in Dewey's *Dial* essay (to "Americanize" a tongue "strangely known as English") was ended and won, as Donald Davie attests and Spender and Tomlinson confirm. For the British, finally busier studying Williams than complaining of him, were impatient to decide a question of the most importunate kind, Davie said, a question which it was the burden of Williams's career to illumine. How does a poet "stand in relation to the national society that he speaks for, speaks out against?" By then Lowell too, in triumph of timing both in the history of Williams's reputation and the development of his own career, had joined the front rank of writers who expressed "the dissident conscience of their nation" in the sixties.[45] Composing that trilogy of plays which was to provide a model for acts of conscience truly more drastic, even more theatrical than *The Old Glory*, performed in 1964–1965, he confronted the density and dirt of our industrial society in its last imperial war. Imitating the one modernist American poet who had rooted around "deep inside the American spoken language" in search of an "American basic unit of composition" to "discover and liberate"[46]—drawing on the great breath of liberation in verse and drama, Lowell transformed Melville's *Benito Cereno* into a "cultural-poetic masterpiece," Robert Brustein said in review, which tapped "the source of our innermost being" as a nation. In this experimental art of terror and love Robert Lowell at last succeeded in capturing the energy of a culture he could not afford to let pass by.

Wherever one turned in the late sixties both in the United States and the United Kingdom, whatever modernist movement or writer pressed forward for notice, there was Williams pronouncing benediction, holding out his lustrum, a laser of purifying light, sheerest incandescence of art offered in the name of the people. And Lowell, the poet whose own surge added an afterglow of luster—on exorcising Adams, Robert Lowell incarnated the causes of celebration at the Whitney. Commemorating Williams's return to the American scene by way of all those writers and artists whom his spirit pierced and who somehow in their turn penetrated him, the Museum restored Williams to the daily life of what McFarlane and Bradbury describe as our "apocalyptic and modern times." For even if that show failed to revive a passion for progress, the ideology to which Williams's imagination and fame—his immortality, indeed—are inextricably linked, it did manage to retrieve him from the grasp of literary theorists who during the preceding decade carried him off for duty in their cause. Installed in that prison house of language about which it's necessary now to say just a word, untimely ripped from his sole source of creative energy, the motherland to which he'd clung for nurture, at the Whitney Williams found sanctuary from post-modernist critics such as Hillis Miller, for example, or Hugh Kenner, who isolated him from companions-at-arms with whom he had longstanding ties.

As a central text illustrating what in *The Pound Era* (1972) Kenner calls a major discovery of poets, consider the lines of Williams's "Poem":

> As the cat
> climbed over
> the top of the jamcloset
> first the right forefoot
> carefully
> then the hind
> stepped down
> into the pit of
> the empty
> flowerpot

Merely a "syntactic undertaking, purely in a verbal field" the poem is no imitation of real life in a real world but is in Kenner's view simply a "governed system of energies, not the world's but its own." "As a picture realizes potentialities of design purely within the flat picture plane" so too

"Poem" occupies a "place with its own laws," the laws of language, of syntax.[47] Instead of asking what the poem is about, he concludes, we might more sensibly ask what the exploring cat is about and decide that it's about the poem, a node of pure linguistic energy.

Recalling Williams's progress toward his "Pink Church," a journey to love that advanced not through linguistic spin alone but through psychologic twist and historic swirl, we know that all Williams's words obey laws sovereign both in the poem and its world, laws which the poet is alone empowered to make binding. If unavoidably a reader founders wondering what the poem and the poet are about, what the flowerpot stands for and what the flowerpoet is up to, Williams's answer dispatches distraction. In poetry and in paint the artist is simply "nature—in action"! Like the cat's life in "Poem," a human life too is an object, a "thing" as concrete and "absolute and perfect as a tree or a stone." And the sooner a man "regards it as objectively" as he can and with "composure and assurance (not with blind conceit) the sooner he will be of use to himself and his world"—both at once indissolubly forever.[48] Like Kenner, Hillis Miller is to my mind misled in insisting that it is "the independence of the fact from the word that forces the word to be a fact in its own right." On the contrary, it's the very fact of interdependence, thing and word and poet and world, which is in Williams's art, in Williams's sentence, dynamized with meaning.

"It is to the inventive imagination we look for deliverance," Williams wrote at the start of his career, to "the field of art." There imagination attends its own compass, follows no trod path. There too, in the arts, human invention achieves its "richest discoveries." Then in an ostensibly casual but uncommonly self-revealing phrase—prodigious because it encapsulates the full compass of his own genius for divining an American grain within the cornucopia of forms and objects nature bestows, art constructs and mind construes—he crystallized his sense of a calling. On balance, he decided, the process of discovery in the field of art as well as the principle of invention in the sphere of "material progress" would never endanger but would permanently enrich us all once mankind learned how to draw "a discriminating line between true and false values."[49]

With this portentous phrase, to draw a discriminating line, Williams united the world of imagination and the workaday world within a single system. Synthesizing his views on craft and conduct, on a union of the life of imagination and the moral life, on poetry and technology, on progress and energy, on energy and creation, the power to draw discriminating lines in the realm of material values is equivalent to the power of composing, inscribing, and incising lines in the literary and visual arts. Beginning with *Al Que Quiere* (1917) and continuing unabated until *Journey to Love* (1955), from "Metric Figure" to the theory of a "variable foot" Williams sought to complete a single, unique, composite, Herculean labor: to "break down

> the line
> the sentence
> To get at the unit of unit of measure in order to build."[50]

Any suspicion that this famous quatrain is not, despite its elusiveness, an overt allusion to the life of civilization Williams dispels with the confession offered as an epigraph to his work as a whole. "All I have written is one writing," an "attempt, an experiment, a failing experiment, towards assertion with broken means but an assertation, always, of a new and total culture."[51]

In principle and in practice Williams equated constituent units of ordered language with structural units of ordered society, literary structure with social order. Quite as each of Gertrude Stein's words was disinfected, "washed clean," made "straight, sharp" like a new-forged nail "to hold together the joints of the new architecture," so too all Williams's lines were supposed to do double duty of technique and technology. In analogy with words, referring to the ways in which societies "according to their local genius" build forms responsive to every variety of need from the ground up, he maintained that the general composition and character of an age and a nation are manifest in "the whole structure of the line." For the very reasons Zukofsky was to stress, furthermore, Williams placed plenary value on the actual act of setting lines in motion ("I am a beginner, I am an American. A United Stateser.") and therefore on words that open out avenues along which invention and discovery and development—progress, in a word—ineluctably stream. "Without progress then there is nothing," *The Great American Novel* (1923) begins. But "if there is progress then there is a novel." And because force of invention within the social order is indissolubly, organically linked to the energies of words and measured by the motion of lines, the whole powerhouse of culture ("the great dynamo," he observed in 1923 as if anticipating O'Neill's play staged six years later) must necessarily run on raw material natural both to men and to machines. Like his friend Sheeler, who in Constance Rourke's biography is "said to have discovered, or uncovered, the industrial subject for American art"—like Sheeler, Williams possessed a "strongly rooted feeling for dynamic" form, mechanical, architectural, linguistic. "I am progress. I make a word. Listen! UMMMMMMMMMMMMM—"[52]

In Williams's mantra we hear properly at last the poetics of progress during the Pound Era. And in Williams's view of Sheeler's art, his acclaim of Sheeler's "eye for the thing," Sheeler's use of a geometry that "could hold the truth of the thing and could make a statement about the particularity of the American object," an interviewer not long ago observed to Mary and George Oppen: in Sheeler's fusion of treatment and technic didn't Williams discover a capital truth of method and morals in American art? Wasn't there among members of their group, Precisionists, a general assent to Sheeler's doctrine, that it's in the "shape of the thing that the essence lies?" Williams himself of course was entranced by Sheeler's "bewildering directness of vision, without blur," manifest in images of machine-made culture linearly fixed and geometrically confined. The Oppens, however, demurred. Neither he nor Mary saw eye to eye with Bill on Sheeler, Oppen recalled. Williams's talk about "precision in form" they took to be a sort of "populism" in a very personal sort of American grain. And despite their own immersion in the apparatus of industrial society, Sheeler's treatment of this subject they flatly dismissed. In contrast to Constance Rourke's judgment ("If as Henry Adams believed the dynamo has become a twentieth century Virgin, then Sheeler is its Fra Angelico.") the Oppens contended that there is "no third dimension in his drawing," no drama, no emotion "back of those bricks."[53]

It was, however, Oppens aside, Sheeler's vision of a "modern Arcadia" that led Williams during the twenties and thirties to experiment with verses in which a "careful, hard-edged perception of an object generates an infinite line of force." In what may be the most widely reprinted text of this period, "The Rose," his verse line does indeed encode the entire parataxis of being—nature encountered geomorphically, cosmogonically, ethnocentrically—in a coordination of seed and semen, of steel and star.

> From the petal's edge a line starts
> that being of steel
> infinitely fine, infinitely
> rigid penetrates
> the Milky Way

—thus does this fragment of a celebrated poem cleave to its trope with that constancy of devotion which was henceforth to become the singular mark of Williams's art. For he never ceased to believe, as he remarked in the series of conversations paraphrased for *The Williams-Siegel Documentary* (1970), that the "mystery" of creation would be resolved "in terms of the *line*" (Williams's emphasis). Like that "doting-mad camera man" Alfred Stieglitz, photographer-prophet of what Edward Dahlberg called a "kind of biblical USA geography in Art," our "place-crazy poet" sought to draw flawless blueprints of arrangement (words on a line, lines on a page, objects in two-dimensional space), certain that only an immaculate art of disposition could represent a natural probity of configuration, man-made things in an American landscape.[54]

The point is now all but finally made. But because in concentrating on calligraphy we encompass radical motifs of utopianism in modernist American letters and art, we're bound to persist until the last nuance of meaning yields its ultimate jot. In tabulating instances of linear theory, of Precisionism as high policy in the arts, the question to decide is not, say, whether Bram Dijkstra is right in arguing that Williams's designs were derived from Stieglitz's "Equivalents," photographs in which the "direct vision of an object is determined by means of lines of needle-thin, absolute sharpness." It's more decisively a question of collating all those occasions on which intimations of order were supposedly verified by these visionary lines. For surely there's no problem in conceding influence, no question in granting that Williams's poem "Classic Scene" (1937) looks like an "Equivalent" in verse of Sheeler's *Classic Landscape* (1931). Precisionist to perfection, in this painting not only is chiaroscuro treated as a sheer function of line but too billowing smoke is molded in masses as distinct from sky as slag is heaped in shapes disjoined from earth. In "Classic Scene" then, which takes its measure from *Classic Landscape*, Sheeler's "building of a picture" is reassembled as

> A power-house
> in the shape of
> a red brick chair
> 90 feet high[55]

Through the thirteen unfinished, unbroken, and utterly syntactic lines that follow, containing but not concluding Williams's poem, American energies do openly drive. "Classic Scene" in fact is nothing other than a grid incorporating the "live line" of Arthur Dove, the "force lines" Sheeler used "to anchor and solidify his compositions" and inevitably those sharp edges of light with which Stieglitz demonstrated that a vast geodesy of real lines on earth has "all the precision" of the "etched line" favored by Georgia O'Keeffe.[56]

What is upheld, extended beyond either Objectivist or Precisionist theory, what this grid registers is an esthetics of energy put to the service of high culture and American community. Based on reserves of power found in Williams's unity of measure, its rationale does indeed dispel any serious confusion about the authenticity of the Whitney show. For no matter how much else was missing, it surely did display what Kramer insisted was absent, a demonstration of the "esthetic and cultural issues that demand to be illuminated in this conjunction of the poet's career and the artist's work."[57] What was in truth exhibited there, as Rourke's book on Sheeler can be read to clarify, the issue chosen for illumination was nothing less than the American dream of Arcady: the effort to find in art sure guidelines to conduct moral life in a world run by machines. That dream was indeed fortified, Rourke reassured Williams, by Sheeler's sacrifice of color. Confessing that he liked to see "paint more imaginatively used—as paint," Williams told her that it was not an addiction to edges but the moral position implied in Sheeler's starkness of line that vexed him. A geometric art signifies "too much withdrawal from life. I want more of a comment, a cry of some sort—a criticism of life from Charles." And because comment and criticism require heat, in painting a cry wants color. Repeating John Marin's objection to a Demuth show ("How can a painter follow a line, or allow his paint to be controlled by it") he approved Marin's judgment: "The painter should follow *paint*" (Williams's emphasis).[58] Not so, Rourke later responded officially in her book on Sheeler. Observe the subtleties of effect found in the sparest forms of American folk art, New England doorways, wood paneling in New England farmhouses, Shaker things. Exquisitely simple, decorous, none are diminished by an absence of ornament. How therefore can it possibly be inauthentic or illegitimate for a contemporary American artist, drawing on the folk traditions of his culture, to focus on line as a "dominant concern, or form in space as with Sheeler?" So "unobtrusively has color been made to serve the large end," so lucent its values, "that the complex and very beautiful play of tones" is unmistakably sensuous even in Sheeler's most "geometrical drawings."[59]

Perhaps the most striking thing about this exchange of opinions in private and in print is its later reappearance barely altered in what I am certain must be read as Williams's quintessential position on the subject of true and false values in the history of discovery and invention in American art and culture. All but monomaniacal on the subject of technique best suited to capture "the peculiarity of the American object" in painting and poetry, convinced that true value in being as a whole is that "peculiarity which gives an object a character by itself," in an essay for *Art News* ("Painting in the American Grain," 1954) published less than ten years before his death, Williams returned to Rourke's theme. Envisioning the life of society in its earliest period, contemplating folk sensibility in the New World, confronting early portraits, he was astounded to discover how an "intensity of vision" coupled with "isolation in the wilderness" had led native primitive painters to place "on the canvas veritable capsules, surrounded by a line of color, to hold them off from a world which was most about them. They were eminently objective, their paintings remained always things." For despite their terror of what Wallace Stevens called "the slovenly wilderness" those painters depicted a "beginning world, a re-beginning world, and a hopeful one. The men and women and children who made it up were ignorant of the forces that governed it and what they had to face." But in seeing and painting themselves "against the surrounding wilderness of which they themselves were the only recognizable aspect," they discovered an elemental truth about imagination. Once a made object acquires standing, society becomes less slovenly and less wild.

Vindication is ever welcome. And it's surely the more cheering when unsought and unsolicited it arrives from an improbable but thoroughly plausible source. In this instance Williams's belief in an almost magical omnipotence of line among American primitives is supported by Lévi-Strauss's explanations of similar but more ancient attitudes and practices among jungle tribes in Brazil. For it was in the year following publication of Williams's essay, in 1955, that Lévi-Strauss observed that Indian "facial paintings confer human dignity on the individual" in the form of lines drawn as arabesques denoting social rank and social class, distinguishing mankind itself from a wilderness world. How really remarkable! Condemned to a common state of being, motivated by an innate will perhaps, both South American face painters and North American portrait painters "draw the line," Williams said, knowing that the "more clearly the line was drawn, the more vividly, the better."[60] In this classic way American wilderness artists on two continents stylized a transition from "animal to civilized man" and thereby, according to Lévi-Straussian opinion, ensured crossing "the frontier from Nature to culture."[61] In this unanticipated way, finally, this oblique rather than frontal way of speculating on the work of his friend Charles Sheeler, Williams may well have provided us with truly convincing clues to a structuralism of the visual and the verse line. Principled order in morals and art and history, like organic progress in civilization, this most myth-minded of modernist American poets conceptualized as a line of poetry written, a line of color drawn with the most exacting discrimination conceivable in our world.

Where in the world does one turn, Kramer asked in a full stop of rhetoric, where does one go to find reasons for that idiosyncratic Whitney show? For all its wanton heterogeneity of image, however, neither should the eye blink nor the mind boggle at its collocation of objects. Beholding pictures in which nature is seen according to Sheeler's prescription, "from the eye inward," reading poems made in conformity with the double rhythm of Williams's invention—"from outside inward and from inside out"—we follow a single circumambient line, infinitely fine and infinitely strong, safely through Daedelian ways within the unmapped labyrinth of modernist art. "With all his newly acquired proficiencies of technique,"

Williams wrote in 1951 (as much in autobiographic disclosure as in biographical comment on his friend, his portraitist), Emilio Romano is "furiously at work, working night and day," struggling to get down on canvas the "healing images which he alone sees reflected" in his mind. For Romano "knows that only if he can get them out," we're told in a paper unpublished until 1966, others "may be blessed," everyone "may be healed."[62]

To invade the mind in pursuit of a blessed healing image—from *Kora in Hell* to *Paterson* it is this enterprise that kept Williams going from start to finish, this endeavor that joins the poet's career and the artist's work. "The imagination will not down," he had said in 1923 at the start. Because the play of "creative energy" is what "imagination requires for satisfaction" and because "flamboyance" of invention is the most powerful available human means to express "faith in that energy," let us join together, let's publish still another little magazine, *Midas*, in which native-born artists and refugee-artists will join in a "hatred of the terror, the negative." Let's search out some common "alchemy of the mind" which will enable us to achieve a great release of energy, an explosion that will come as an antidote to "deformity" because it has "nothing to do with the Death." Make no mistake, Williams said in reiteration of William James's judgments on war and its equivalent, "war released energy" without question. But energy delivered so serves as a "dispersing agent" merely. Nothing is created, all is lost. "There are no arts of war. Everything is stolen there—except the energy released which is not its own." And unless artists mobilize their energies for defense and counterattack at once, "the offspring of this energy, released by war, will all be bastards."

In short, Williams concluded this recapitulation of James's classic attack on war and its infamies, on energy and its profligacies, in sum it's a blessed act of proper fatherhood which is betokened in an artist's readiness to "legitimize the products of that power released by death" and "induct them into the service of life."[63] And because it is the performance of that service to which the "arts are addressed," a grave task of theory, as Charles Olson declared years later, an ultimate dilemma of imagination is to achieve that transfer of energy "from where the poet got it" all the way over to the reader. How does the poet capture, contain, and convey—so Olson enlarged on Williams's extrusion of James's theme—"at least some equivalent of the energy which propelled him in the first place," energy which the audience can take away.[64] How does the poet transmit his healing image?

By way of the line, was Williams's answer, by way of the sentence. "I've been writing a sentence with all the art I can muster," he said in a fateful and pivotal essay, "Against the Weather," published in Dorothy Norman's *Twice a Year* at the moment that the thirties ended, 1939. And "here it is: a work of art is important only as evidence, in its structure, of a new world which it has been created to affirm." Infusing standard American speech with new words for progress, Williams locks us in a "fraternal embrace, the classic caress of author and reader. We are one." That's his line, all right, best recognized in those verses where "a dangling clause," as Tomlinson notes, "pulls the main clause toward completion and asymmetry."[65] That's what he believed creation to be at bottom anyway, a "moving process" in which the verb dominates: "You are to make."[66] In this benediction we are charged with the historic burden of making Williams's clauses and our national causes inextricably unite.

X

The Tribal No

Kenneth Burke

Gênet's origin is a blunder . . . *then* a rejection . . . *then a* failure. *Blunder, rejection, failure: these add up to a* No. *Since the child's objective essence was the No, Gênet gave himself a personality by giving himself the subjectivity of the No; he is the absolute opponent, for he opposes Being and all integration.*

Jean-Paul Sartre, *Saint Gênet, Actor and Martyr*, 1963

AS IF INTENT ON REISSUING Williams's summons, on inviting contemporary artists and audiences to stand against foul weather today even as William Carlos Williams, in the waste land between two wars, withstood a worse climate, the Whitney Museum that winter 1978–1979 reopened lines of transmission long gone dead. Whatever residual national impulse this may disclose, nevertheless the gesture itself was short-lived. The poet's work, however, the poet's place in American literary history, the poet's influence are of course commanding. And in conceiving of creation as a "moving process" dominated by the verb *to make*, Williams's poems do embody an affirmation of our will to become, as Karl Popper says, the "makers of our fate." This is consolation enough, to my mind, for members of a generation and a society forced to accept loss of energy, its replacement by entropy, in the American dream of progress. In order to conclude this book, however, it's not Williams's consolations I must refer to. It's his admonitions. And, astonishingly, it's the least strident of these which is perhaps the most prophetic, his Jamesian warning to resist "the negative" lest a dispersed and deformed energy create a general condition of bastardy, of alienation, in culture and art. Premonitory to really striking degree, the remark foreshadows prodigious work by his friend Kenneth Burke, whose studies in the Negative, whose theory of language, whose passion of mind and equanimity of temper in treating subjects of gravest implication for the history of ideas, for the history of society, have guided this inquiry from its start.

That it is Burke who brings us full circle is in itself a cause of wonder. For Kenneth Burke, during more than sixty years of literary enterprise, staked out ground which scarcely anyone hitherto has sought either to cultivate or contest. On his own page long found to be rebarbative enough to repel both poachers and colonists, his influence was pretty well confined to a coterie whose first leader, Stanley Edgar Hyman—himself thirty years ago a Pied Piper beyond the pale—attracted a following but barely a crowd. Given this record it is pleasing to find in Burke a force, a power which, as Robert Coles says of Williams, is less a matter of poetics than of temperament rare among writers in the United States: a knack of survival. For all that Coles intends his phrase to isolate and delimit the American grain of Williams's life in art, its bearing on Burke's career is indisputable. And although the secret of survival is in Coles's small book undivulged, its central feature is shared by writers, somehow set apart, who stand outside literary generation because they possess a genius too foxy for trapping, too fleet. Forever inimitable, at once out of fashion and always in touch, out of reach though always at hand, copious in invention, they dazzle not because there's stardom in store but because their glow is a glory of genes. They have a knack of being what they do.

"My own early encounters with Burke," Wayne Booth said in talk and in print some years ago, "led me to a quick and easy dismissal. I heard him say, with his own lips, that 'bombs' and 'poems' are the same word; I heard him demonstrate that Conrad put himself into *Heart of Darkness*, the proof being that the sound involved in Conrad–Kurtz and the sounds involved in *Heart of Darkness* are equivalent if you'll allow . . ." and so on. I skip details of Booth's confession and of Burke's proof. Neither the one nor the other is any longer needed to clinch any case whatever, either for Burke's "outlandishness" or for Booth's straitness of mind. What this testimony offers, recollection of the "young student of Ronald Crane" that Booth was at the time, is a memory both identical and antithetical to my own. On hearing Burke's words, Booth decided that he "had heard enough: if criticism was to be the effort to *know* something, Burke was not a critic. It took me nearly twenty years to discover how wrong I was."[1]

Burke's a long way round from Ronald Crane. I'm a long way removed from Booth. But Wayne Booth does indeed capture a trace of memory not unlike my own dating back about thirty years when, as a student of Lionel Trilling's and Jacques Barzun's I wasn't in truth urged to apply my mind to Burke himself but was indeed instructed to appreciate the virtue of pursuits associated with his name. No literary critic drawn, by way of the mentors I chose and through them to *philosophes* of history and psychology, to the sociology of literature and of knowledge—no question in my mind that whatever it was I hoped to get from these not yet celebrated men ("Read Merton," Trilling said. "Talk to young Hofstadter. Go see Wright Mills.") implicated the system of criticism Burke was trying to invent. Though very little sense of sequence, of chronology, is left in my mind, I recall subscribing to a series of lectures on theology and literature given one season at the Jewish Theological Seminary, just north on Broadway. In part because I hoped to see the fabled Louis Finkelstein—stories about whom along with selected tales of Tillich and invocations of Niebuhr encircled the Upper West Side in the late forties—but mainly in order to get from spoken words what was impenetrable in print, I piously and purposefully went.

Of scheduled speakers I recall two, Burke and Delmore Schwartz, both irregulars of the lectern in that Uptown trove of academe, the one ablaze with talk and the other uncharacteristically damp. Unlike Booth, who was put off by bizarre Burkings of text (Keats's famous last line should really be read 'body is turd, turd body'"), I was bewitched. As a result I remember little of how Burke looked, very vividly some fragments of what he said. "Those who have heard him speak," as Kermit Lansner was later to write in a review of *A Rhetoric of Motives*—a review which placed Burke within the camp of evangelical utopians "driven by a great enthusiasm for social reform," by a belief that "man in some way can find salvation on this earth"—Burke at lecture was irresistible, as Lansner said. Observing him sweep "together art and life, pouring forth a stream of commentary," the mind is "amazed at the wonder of it all."[2] In my instance, wonder was the more intense because Schwartz not Burke was by reputation a spellbinder. In fact I remember nothing of what Delmore said, only how sodden he looked, how bewildered by that audience, mixed bag of seminarians and their teachers, of culture addicts off the street, of graduate students, all bloodshot. Many years later he would become a colleague and when the wind was right, a friend. But that day he was a stammerer whose fits and starts came out strangled, a glue of condensations and condescensions.

On the other day, however, there was Burke at full blast on those ways of language he himself described as "Version-, Con-, Per-, and In-." And from that day until now indeed, whenever I land on the words "Once you turn things round," it's his voice I hear turning Yeats round to get Devil-torn, God-tormented from dolphin-torn, gong-tormented sea. In contrast to Booth's boggle at Burke's presumed foreclosure of sense in equations of this kind, I was instantly sure of and grateful for "joycings" that got me turned round, headed right. It's obviously not a superior prescience I claim, just a fiercer desperation of need which led me to find in Burke a deliverer then and there. For all that Booth confesses to a delay of twenty years in discovering "how wrong" he was, unquestionably he's traveled farther than Burkophobes both younger and older than he, gone deeper in and farther out than Burkophiles like me. Nevertheless, it is with a dangle of filament in hand, with Minotaur in mind and Burke's "logology" in view, that I've sought to distinguish snare from kink, pleach from pinion within this maze of history and culture and language in which, during many years, I have been entangled.

It was therefore not at all accidental when, a decade or so beyond that day at the Seminary, I found myself in touch with my deliverer, corresponding about one thing and another in connection with *The Dial*. Chiefly in courtesy and devotion to James Sibley Watson, Jr. (W. C. Blum in the pseudononymous role Watson adopted as a critic for the magazine he published), to whom both *A Rhetoric of Motives* and *Language as Symbolic Action* are dedicated, Kenneth Burke—unacknowledged mentor—became an indispensable "source." Having already written as it were under auspices of Burke in his Freudian aspect, determined to try my hand at the uses of synechdoche for the study of intellectual history, I undertook to turn that magazine right side out by way of selected figures whose character and attainment seemed to disclose previously unidentified traits of modernism—particularly, during *The Dial*'s final phase, by way of Burke. Those activities and pursuits which could not be accommodated in this program were set aside. But what was set aside in the early sixties would not subside. And in reviewing the subject of progress, I've been eager to make provision for, concerned to release the pressure of two words which flare up in Burke's prose and fiction and verse. The "negative" is one, "victimize" is the other. And "logology," the instrument toward which both conduce, I first sought to apply tentatively, intermittently, then more or less schematically and now comprehensively. It all dates from 1958 when, in a letter of December 23, Burke spoke of the uses of logology in the study of behavior and history, art and morals.

> I was delighted to receive the copy of your article (in Winter no. of The Yale Review). It moves along most convincingly, at least to this reader! Incidentally, it reënforces a consideration of this sort which I have been tending more and more to tinker with: Just what is the ultimate difference btw. actual

> matricide (or any other form of the kill) and its sheerly *symbolic* form, as an artistic *imitation*? I incline more and more to feel that the symbolic form (the sheer imitation) should be treated primarily as a species of *negative* (which I take to be a purely linguistic construct). A further bepuzzlement arises from the fact that imagery of physical violence can often be a surrogate for a sheerly sexual motive (though here again, there should be a qualitative difference between positive sexual conduct, as with actual incest, and its sheerly symbolic analogues, as with ideas along the slope of "communion," "community," and "communication"). If you have a chance, and feel so inclined, I'd be most happy if, before you came here, you took a glance at some articles I did in The Quarterly Journal of Speech (Oct., Dec., 52; Feb., Apr., 53). They indicate somewhat the ubiquity of the role I think might be ascribed to the negative in language (though its negativity is generally concealed by quasi-positives, as when an act of rejection is symbolized in terms of the kill, which is a quasi-positive symbolization, as with the symbolizing of penance). Maybe I'm slapping this down too haphazardly, but I'm trying merely to indicate the drift, and we could discuss the point at greater length when we meet. (Cf. on Negativity in Hegel's Phenomenology of Mind, then translate his remarks from statements about metaphysics to statements about language.)[3]

As I write these words, he was to say in an essay called "The Thinking of the Body" (1963), an essay reflecting on "the genius of the negative," on ties binding purgation to negation—writing these words, "I am living on a Florida key, where I love to walk among the whole and broken shells (skeletons and parts of skeletons) that waves toss up on the beach. Never for a moment do I cease to think of these things as the detritus of *death*, aspects of life's *offal*. I live with the thought that digestion and fertilization involve the life-giving properties of *corruption*, that life grows out of *rot*."[4] Particularly vivid in modernist fiction and verse (a "sprout-out-of rot" literature, according to Denis Donoghue), No may well be "the marvel of language."[5] For it is the negative that might possibly explain why today we speak of fighting "our dirty wars with 'clean' bombs," why "in the name of power and progress" we pollute our waters with detergents and our food with chemicals—or even why, in the name of God, as he wrote in *The Rhetoric of Religion* (1961), we derive an "Iron Law of History / that welds Order and Sacrifice."

> Order leads to Guilt
> (for who can keep commandments!)
> Guilt needs Redemption
> (for who would not be cleansed!)
> Redemption needs Redeemer
> (which is to say, a Victim!)

Order
Through Guilt
to Victimage
(hence: Cult of the Kill). . . .[6]

Hence too interdiction of the classic American cult of the child. And by these means, by relying on Burke's analysis of the "ritualistic use of the 'scapegoat'" and the "'curative' role of victimage," we are led to confront a problem—the craft, crime, and cost of child abuse—which dramatizes, in the most current and authentic though distressing ways conceivable, the accuracy and authority of Burke's linguistics of negation. A plenary subject and odious problem in the popular and professional literature as well as in the domestic life of our time and place, "victimage" of this sort not only occurs along a slope of "'communion,' 'community,' and 'communication,'" but too locates the precise point at which theological meditation and physiological function, psychological intent and poetic motive and political purpose, order and sacrifice, intersect. Lest this seem too clever or parochial an exercise, consider the degree to which Burke's cult of the kill squares with analysis and appraisal offered today by nonliterary intellectuals. Pioneers in a social science of No, they argue that this is an era of delirium in the United States, unsurpassed as a period in which, Philip Slater remarks in *The Pursuit of Loneliness* (1976), Americans of every "age group, social class or educational level" seem to be "most entertained by watching people get killed, bludgeoned, or mutilated." Perhaps the widest read in a rush of books treating what Burke would call the genius of the negative and Slater calls "American culture at the breaking point"—work by Herbert Hendin, Christopher Lasch, William L. O'Neill, and many others—*The Pursuit of Loneliness* equates "life-destroying technology" with primitive power exercised by the fiercest of patriarchs. As if engaged to prove the irreversibility of Burke's iron law, Slater argues that people in the sixties and seventies have taken a certain joy in oppressing others with whatever tools and devices of oppression they are themselves subdued by. As a result the young, chief victims of an almost feral appetite for devastation, are "poisoned, bombed, gassed, burned"—in a word, nullified, scrapped by guardians who seem to adore the impersonal democratic vengefulness of machines far more than they love life itself.[7]

Although the neglect or pollution or murder of a dependent child is now a scandal of American society, the remarkable thing about abuse is not its nationality or its promiscuity or even its antiquity. Whatever features of technological distemper stylize the act of "victimage" in our era, the extraordinary thing is its conformity to theories of language with which Burke, roused by a chapter called "The Idea of Nothing" in Bergson's

Creative Evolution, nearly three decades ago hoped to fuse the life of imagination and the life of society. A "big eye-opener," that chapter. Having realized "that the negative is a peculiarly linguistic marvel," that "there are no negatives in nature, every natural condition being positively what it is,"[8] thereupon Burke was free to design a synoptic system in which language and power, ritual and culture are concentrated, encapsulated, within *The World Within the Word* (1979). William Gass's entrance into Burke's realm, as felicitous and welcome an arrival as can be imagined, had been prefigured in an earlier book which burked "blue," even as Burke joyced "mater, matter, matrix, matrimony, matricide, pater, patronage, patriotism, patrimony, patricide. Oof, wadda woild!"[9] Adding grace to genius Gass reaps a harvest logologically sown. So too do we, in retracing the pattern of ideas which trail Burke's effort to locate within a sweep of negation the tightest possible fit "between human body, world's body and body politic"—even so do we, assigning No to rites and ceremonies not usually associated with speech, fashion a framework for an American cult of the kill.

Signifying the moment of origins, start and stem of Burke's most original, inspired, and sustained work, we recall that it was Bergson whose recognition of the "paradox of the negative" provided Burke with a vision of the incandescence of No. Realizing that nature discloses no nays only ayes, Bergson initiated a "major movement in the history of language." Perhaps the momentous thing about this movement, Burke maintained, supplementing Bergson's authority with Spinoza's and Hegel's, was its efficacy in diagnosing both the health of language ("to use words properly we must spontaneously have a feeling for the *principle of the negative*") and the ills of culture (which "by its nature necessarily culminates in the Negative"). During the fifties, therefore, at the outset what engaged his mind was the work of differentiating his own interest in a rhetoric of No from the existentialism of reigning philosophers, Heidegger, Sartre, whose attention centered on the operation of "Nothing." Instead of Nothing he preferred Not and No, "The hortatory negative (thou shalt not)" rather than "the propositional negative (it is not)" of European thought. For as he told Daniel Fogarty in 1957, it is within the hortatory world of No and Not "that we find the deepest root of language as specifically and essentially human in its symbol using function."[10]

In the process of arriving at this famed definition, unflaggingly held —man is the "symbol-using animal" who passes the "ultimate test of symbolicity" because of "an intuitive feeling for the negative"—Burke precipitated and retrieved No from *Nichts*. And though he was willing to grant that Heidegger's "kind of Weltanschauung" doubtless was "inescapably operating in all of us," he was himself not cheerless enough by nature to retain *Angst* as the ground of being. Conceding that an individual's thoughts might not take any one of us "to the end of the line," nonetheless he agreed that thought itself might "well imply this end if we were minded to follow" its drift.[11] For if it is true that No identifies what he called the "one great motivational principle that man, in his role as the language-using animal, has added to nature"; and if it is in truth due to speech that human awareness is objectified, that the human animal achieves self-consciousness; and if, as Freud himself contended, comity on earth is derived from the principle of prohibition—then it must surely follow that a Burkean logologist must attend language and its operations as carefully as a "Freudian psychologist watches the nonsense of a patient's dream."[12]

Despite Kenneth Burke's absorption in language and literature, therefore, his bent is incurably toward studies in the hazards and costs of compulsion, dangers which manifest that "vast system of Nays" which govern our real and imagined worlds and symbolize an "Annihilating Nothing" not subject to repeal. When we speak of child abuse as an unspeakable act, therefore, it is Burke who enables us to appreciate what's at stake in what we say. What is at stake, "victimage," he sought to illustrate in the most dramatic (and "dramatistic") as well as the most discursive ways possible.

CREATION MYTH

In the beginning there was universal Nothing.
Then Nothing said No to itself and thereby begat Something,
Which called itself Yes.

Then No and Yes, cohabiting, begat Maybe.
Next all three, in a menage a trois, begat Guilt.

And Guilt was of many names:
Mine, Thine, Yours, Ours, His, Hers, Its, Theirs—and Order.

In time things so came to pass
That two of its names, Guilt and Order,
Honoring their great progenitors, Yes, No, and Maybe,
Begat History.

Finally, History fell a-dreaming
And dreamed about Language—
(And that brings us to critics-who-write-critiques-of-critical-criticism.)[13]

In dreaming up an American dialectic and history of negation, Burke has repeatedly invoked the voice and figure of a progenitor, a myth-maker no less authentically tribal than Ralph Waldo Emerson. Start with the ordering spirit of the Ten Commandments, Burke proposes in an essay on Emerson's "I, Eye, Ay," begin with those "shalt-nots of the Decalogue" which supposedly rule our civilization. Then reflect on the theme of Emerson's historic chapter, "Discipline," in the fabled essay "Nature," and you discover Emerson growing "edified" at the notion "that all things, for man, are permeated with the spirit of the 'Thou shalt not.'" Begin, that is to say, with "Compleat Negation and every material thing encountered" along the way cannot but be negatively infused." And because No though omnipresent is "not picturable," can be "properly shown by a *sign* only"—a minus sign, the mark for zero, a handshake—the negative is especially pronounced in any act of "victimage" with which people attempt to "unburden guilt within by transference to chosen vessels without."[14] In this dream of negation, this "Dialectic of the Scapegoat," he wrote in *A Grammar of Motives* (1945), human offspring are seen as "substantially one" with parents who "would ritualistically cleanse themselves by loading the burden of their iniquities" on proxies of the same flesh. "That which was once a 'part of' the parent has become 'apart from' the parent" but may "still be considered consubstantial with its ancestral source" and therefore ripe for the role of deputy victim and savior. According to this logology of signs, then, a victimized child in the United States today serves as a choice vessel of guilt and "vicarious atonement" among those members of society who enact rituals rooted in, inspired by what Burke calls the Tribal No.[15]

Whether or not he's right about dialectic and speech, about consciousness and culture, right or wrong, in correlating negation and "victimage" he contrived to spot an eerily national motif within those constellations of thought around which literary theory drifts today. At the moment, of course, its drift is from France. Seat of our age of semiology, structuralist and deconstructionist, of ideas radiating from the Ecole pratique des Hautes Études and the Collège de France, the Parisian schools, despite the industry of a local branch in New Haven, are not concerned with the history of ideas or sensibility in the United States. More's the pity. For the pity is that American dilemmas do indeed add measurable pith to some postmodernist twaddle. So too does this ghastly matter of child abuse, sad to say, appear to anchor in concrete circumstance, in history, in case study, certain of Burke's more fanciful concoctions of pure reason. The critic who has long written critiques of critical criticism, who long ago arrived at the degree zero of motive, language itself, who now finds allies among structuralists convinced that "social life and culture in general [are] a series of sign systems which which the linguistic model may clarify in revolutionary ways"[16]—Burke and the semiologists together compose an international circle of literary intellectuals whose researches into the innermost nuance of tongue turn up evidence, perhaps proof, that "violence is the father and king of everything."

Within any code that men can imagine, René Girard argues in *Violence and the Sacred* (1977), code of law or of language or of religion, provision is always made for ritual murder. Seizing a creature that can be struck down "without fear of reprisal since he lacks a champion," men have killed in order to localize and discharge, purge the will to disorder in society. Traditionally, this figure, the scapegoat, the pharmakos, is selected from a short list of candidates that includes "prisoners of war, slaves, the handicapped and those too young to have undergone initiatory rites, precondition of status within the community at large." It is Girard's view, then, that those best suited for sacrifice have usually been utterly powerless people whose very circumstance—as foreigners or enemies or captives or children—is itself a denial of standing within, hence a perturbation of the life of society. Not at all an aberrant act however abhorrent, the brutalization of children is instead a pervasive and purposive and portentous event in the history of crimes committed in the name of law and order.

Although Girard does not refer to American tribal customs, his recipe clearly strikes home. Indeed the exclusion of data drawn from the United States is the more noticeable in that it is the custom of this country to elevate far beyond the reach of every child the powers and privileges, before the law, of natural parents no matter how unfit. Speculating why it is that their rights take precedence over nearly all other civil rights and civic duties, one wonders: Can it be that in America child abuse is an accursed act somehow blessed by laws or conventions which confer on natural parents a covert but unquestioned authority to dispatch a sacrificial victim as if in performance of some unacknowledged service to the state? Service of this kind is often, we know, overtly associated with father-daughter incest within families which would otherwise disintegrate. So too do societies everywhere, as Girard concludes a book saturated with evidence taken from anthropological, psychoanalytic, mythical, linguistic, and literary sources the whole world round—so it is that societies attempt to withstand collapse. If Girard's thesis is true, if as he says not only do "all religious rituals spring from the surrogate victim" but too all great institutions of civilization (government, science, medicine, law, art, learning itself) "spring from ritual," then it follows that stability among the nations of earth rests on a need to propitiate a killing passion, a phylogenetic passion, invariably and unavoidably directed against those powerless and dependent ones who stand nearest at hand.[17]

Tendentious, circular, both far-fetched and far-reaching, Girard's book has unquestionably caught a glimpse or two of one or another principle of ambiguity in the social life of this language animal manUNkind, as the poet Cummings said. Not only does Girard review the antiquity of dogma sustaining the political uses of cruelty but too *Violence and the Sacred* enables us to locate a likely source of American resistance to reform, to radical change. For even if Girard fails to prove his case for the sanctity of violence, there's no end of proof that a connoisseur's taste in victims, drawn from nearly all categories of scapegoat and entrenched both in families and in government, underlies those characteristic American attitudes which William Ryan describes in *Blaming the Victim* (1971). Defect in the social order, Ryan says, referring to the Moynihan Report and matter of like kind, is habitually mistaken for stigma of person wherever social policy conforms to the sort of opinion exhibited by Cyril Burt's infamous work on IQ, on race and intelligence.

Ryan's theme, the sociology of blame and its devastations, recurs in a book of entirely different kind and purpose: Michel Foucault's *Discipline and Punish* (1977). Technically an account of "the birth of prisons," this book—which transposes parts of the body almost literally into parts of speech—is in fact a "history of the body" stretched on a wheel that runs from political assassination to parental murder during three centuries of more or less modern times. *Discipline and Punish* therefore subsumes the abuse of children within a very long history of codes devised by nations to justify butchering the flesh of condemned persons. "Whatever systems of punishment" the world has developed, it is always the human "body that is at issue—the body and its forces, their utility and their docility, their distribution and their submission." The control of convicts or the rule of parents, Foucault says, no matter: "in our societies" the history of punishments is inescapably a "history of bodies" selected, appointed to project in public the inner self of a nation. Bounded by a "network of relations" which "go right down into the depth of society," a network that links "colonized" workers in an underdeveloped economy to union members "stuck at a machine" in our computerized and overdeveloped West, it is the supervised, trained, contained, corrected, and coerced human body which stylizes the spirit of an era. And it is by studying the constraints and cruelties and tortures visited today on madmen, on working classes, "on children at home and at school" that we acquire unimpeachable means to comprehend "the history of the present."[18]

Adventitious it may well be but it is not in the least factitious to attach Burke's linguistics of negation, "that essence of motive," to prototypical themes in this history of imagination and culture in the United States. Studying the dialectic of the scapegoat from Burke's angle of vision, locating an offal of persons at the eye of a vortex toward which all lines of self-inquiry, of national identity and self-definition most suitably tend, speculating on the root causes of an American cult of the kill, we are led back to one of Burke's most coherent, comprehensive, and least appreciated books, *The Rhetoric of Religion*. In a fanciful coda called "Epilogue: Prologue in Heaven," Satan asks God whether He agrees that the creation of "these new Word-Using Animals, the Earth-People," free to "disobey your all-powerful authority," must perforce rest on a "nagging contradiction." Responding with an utterance Burke transforms into a reprise at once ludic and linguistic, the Lord answers, "It is more complicated than that," far more complicated, we learn, because Earth-speech is an instrument intended for use at an opposite pole of utility from heavenly talk. In contrast to the Lord's "eternal, Unitive Word," which distinguishes "between *is* and *is not*," Earth-men, drawing distinctions of a different sort, are equipped by speech merely to differentiate between "*shall* and *shall not*." As a result, the Lord continues, they "can in principle carry the negative a step further to say no to any thou-shalt-not. Thus the negative, in giving them the power to be moral, by the same token gives them the power to be immoral." Elevating this parable of linguistics to the highest imaginable plane of analogy in metaphysics and morals, isolating the curative from the contaminative effects of "victimage," Burke in effect exempts a carnage of children from that law of history which welds order and sacrifice.[19]

Effectively burked, therefore, considered logologically, abuse is one of those serpentine strokes of tongue in which Satan excels. Confounding "shall not" and "is not," inviting disasters both of discourse and civility, sacrifice is ruinous in that it subverts the perfection of No. Or said in a way that fuses logology and sociology: to the degree that a dismemberment of the very young in America today, like the dispatch of the very old, represents a conspiracy of assent to cloistered vice, to that degree do we as a people exercise a demented will to say No to Thou-Shalt-Not. To the degree, furthermore, that a wantonness of crime and atonement rules the domestic habits of people in our time, in that exact measure does the neglect or pollution or murder of a dependent child touch a nadir of iniquity in a suicidal American vein. Not for nothing, therefore, are we a people of paradox. For even as our bicentennial year produced a bumper crop of bastards (nearly one-third of births in New York City that year were illegitimate) so too was it accompanied by a burst of books and movies about "children sired by machines and possessed by devils." Prodigious killers, "emissaries of death and destruction," they attain their power not just from new technologies but as well from forces native to this continent and by no means foreign to its first immigrants: "witchcraft, ancestral curses, demonic possession."[20]

It's therefore not American Gothic but a flair for Satanism that's dreadful. And for all our rationalizing, our Freudianizing of evil, a Puritan substratum it is that provides a kind of American bedrock. Indeed the current rate of popflicks and quickiebooks must bespeak a scifi recapitulation of what the Puritans and their successors knew as Original Sin. "Thou embryo-angel, or thou infant-fiend," are you one or the other or both, in perplexity the Reverend Samuel Davies addressed his newborn child a century earlier. Writing his poem, "On the Birth of John Rogers Davies, the Author's Third Son," Davies raised the inevitable "issue of infant depravity and damnation"—unavoidable issue surely, given the "strength of the negative side of parental perceptions of infancy" which so beset that third of a nation, "moderates," in Philip Greven's usage, which was unable to decide whether children were monsters or seraphs. It's of course well known that moderates of theology in the eighteenth century inherited their dilemma from those whom Greven in *The Protestant Temperament* (1978) calls "evangelicals," guardians of a fanatic and obdurate zeal to "abase, to deny, and to annihilate" the "corrupted and sinful self," adult's or child's, out of conviction that abasement conformed to "the sovereign will of God." What has until now not been appreciated is the degree to which in this post-Freudian age we revive a kind of cultural memory of post-Puritan ancestral times, times in which parents whose "sense of love and affection for their infant children" is negated by a "sense of distrust and fear as well."[21] For it is by no means uncommon today, experts say, both in and out of psychiatric practice to hear parents insist that their infant's instinctual demands are deliberately intended to "suck the life out of them" and to drive them crazy. How easily, how naturally, how aptly do children serve as "targets for our sadism and convenient receptacles for our fantasies."[22]

"Perversion," says Kenneth Burke, is a "major aspect of No," both "sexual deviation from the biologic norm" and nays of another kind as well, typical of a people who habitually "get things upside down, inside out and backwards"[23]—typical, surely, of that small tribe of provincials responsible for applying a theology of negation, Puritan theology and religious observance, to one of the most sterile and perverse systems of "victimage" known to Christendom. Terrified of the very children over whom as parents they possessed power derived from the Lord, authority confirmed by the State, absolute literalists of dogma, to immoderate degree they devoted themselves to the work of carrying out God's will by breaking the child's will. In this way alone could so "filthy" a being attain a right relation, submission to parents and Deity. From that time forward, it's only a touch melodramatic to say, an ancestral curse has been affixed to our history as a nation, fixed by that perverse band of settlers who first got things turned round on this continent. Whether or not negation is our sole legacy as a people is not at all the point. What is unalterably to the point is the fact that a Tribal No antedates, reverberates within, and periodically swamps subsequent Rousseauized utterances of Yes.

Unlike Europe indeed, where the discovery of childhood occurred later, it was not an exorcism of demons but a reliance on the regimen of education as the right route to a "good and holy life"—pedagogy justified those punishments Foucault spoke of and Philip Ariès, in *Centuries of Childhood* (1962), describes as usually reserved for convicts of the lowest order. An "obsessive love," he says, utterly unlike "the old indifference," underlay that severity which French parents visited on babes imprisoned at home and in school.[24] Which is to say that the remarkable thing about victimization of children in the United States, whole epochs before a pathology of parental power was called abuse, is its eccentricity, its ferocity, its fixity in the sexual, spiritual, secular, imaginative, and fantasy lives of people on this continent from the early seventeenth until the late twentieth centuries. Despite "the ancestral nature of the scapegoat" as a "vessel of vicarious atonement," Burke says, whenever a "ritual transference of guilt" is frustrated, then do "motives of self-destruction" come irretrievably, inexorably "to the fore."[25]

For some time now, Kermit Lansner concluded his *Kenyon* essay, "certain critics have been in mourning" for a loss of "political sense" among colleagues. "As I understand it, they feel that no one with a simplistic view of human nature or a Utopian view of human destiny can say anything relevant about that activity they call political. Well, Mr. Burke does."[26] Twenty-seven years later still another critic, Fredric Jameson, mourned the absence of good political sense in Burke's judgment. Encumbered by what Jameson called "the baggage of thirties Marxism," Burke advances claims for the "free creativity of human language" and thus commits a blunder of precedence. By ignoring the prior role of "transindividual historical forces" in determining and defining radical connection "between sign systems and modes of production," Jameson argues, Burke bumbles theory. Because in any dialogue between "Marxism and semiotics" production must precede language, Burke's œuvre, a "rewriting" of "cultural artifacts and works of art as symbolic acts," constitutes at best itself a text which may well be useful to "any properly Marxist analysis of culture" and at worst a "sandbox affair which threatens no one."[27]

Maybe so. But Burke's logology, which insists that all inquiry "must *begin, start with, start from*" the question "What is it to be the typical symbol-using animal?," simply dispenses with the iron law of class struggle. In its main tenet logology therefore leads us to "study 'the human condition' from a theory of terminology in general" rather than Jameson's way round. In Burke's behalf, moreover, a historian of American ideas can point to two hundred fifty pre- and post-Marxian, pre- and post-Freudian years during which this symbol-using people, his countrymen, have portrayed their disillusion with theology, their bewilderment by democracy, their distrust of technology, of progress as a dogma, and of the American political and economic process as an ideology, in literary texts that register a violence of oscillation between the perversion and the perfection of No.

Adopting the body of a debased and defiled child as an archetype of all those earmarked for slaughter, victims of historical process in the United States—those sentenced, as Foucault says, "to carry out ceremonies, to emit signs" we become more and more adept at decoding—we trace manifestations of a Tribal No to the womb of a teenage whore, a battered wife, a sexually used infant. When we add to this doomed company the charred remains of an incinerated mate and the inert remains of an abandoned parent—not to mention the trashed countryside in which litter is landscape, just another feature of growth—we are in fact compiling lists which coordinate the dreck of progress with a presumption of entropy in our post-industrial age. Add to this reckoning the membership lists of Parents Anonymous. For if we agree that the stigmata borne by an abused child radiates a system of signs we begin to know how to interpret, we must also assume that the Anonymous Parent—panicked by hazards of self-government, bewitched by the spell of self-revulsion, benumbed by the habit of acquiescence to atrocity—does not indulge in a secret act, wanton and witless, but emits signals, pulsations linking each of us in a network of disordered impulses that come from depths and distances far and near, time present and time past. "Logology's only contribution to the cause," Burke comments in his latest and perhaps last word on the entire subject (1979), "is the reminder that, to our knowledge, the Law," sacred and secular, "is the flowering of that humanly, humanely, humanistically and brutally inhumanely ingenious addition to wordless nature, the *negative*," without which neither heaven nor hell would be possible.[28]

Recoiling back near the end of these reflections on No to Philip Slater once more, to Slater's thoughts on the origins of species in the United States, we find him preoccupied with pedigree. Searching out the beast that lurks "at the very root of American character," he suspects that a "kind of natural selection," not yet fully comprehended, governs the modern history of a civilization which "was disproportionately settled by a certain kind of person," one quite opposite in temperament from those founders in whom traditionally we've taken especial pride. If truly there are ties linking a gain of rapacity in this machine age to a surge of intensity in our assault on offspring, these ties are certified by institutions which reinforce a "negative side" we inherit from our original settlers. However many of the "energetic and daring" arrived on these shores, Slater says, this largely untenanted land "also gained a lion's share of the rootless, the unscrupulous," a pioneer line of Americans that long ago mistook piety for love and self-aggrandizement for loyalty.

Consider, finally, the refusal by representatives of Kent State University to accept in November, 1978, George Segal's statue honoring the memory of protestors killed in Ohio. PRINCETON TO GET SCULPTURE REJECTED BY KENT STATE, the headline goes. People around here, a member of the art faculty said, are very conservative and "many of them believe that the kids who were shot got what they deserved." Many Ohioans felt that it was decidedly inappropriate, somebody in administration agreed, to "observe the killing of four students and the wounding of nine others with a sculpture that indicates someone committing violence on someone else. We are afraid that people will see only the violence." That George Segal's treatment of Abraham and Isaac should at Princeton be deemed an apt expression of "our culture and our society" but in Ohio be regarded as a capitulation to "radicalism" in politics and art—this is authentication indeed for Foucault's analysis of signs treating the body of the condemned, for Girard's proposals on violence and the sacred, for Slater's thesis connecting patriarchs and predators. For Burke's calligraphy of No.

What sort of people have we become in this century, a logological American critic and historian is forced to ask? What is it that leads officials at Kent State, speaking for many compatriots, to say "no" to thou shalt not and refuse a gift of sculpture which Segal himself describes as intended not to vilify anyone but to portray "the moral underpinnings of everyone's belief"? As "Abraham moves to do violence with his right hand, his compassion and love for his son are expressed in a gesture made" by the fingers of his left hand, fingers which dig into his thigh in "an agony of doubt."[29] Who can it be, after all, Stanley Elkin mused as he turned page after page in the Johnson Smith mail-order catalogue of jokes, tricks, and "practical gadgets" which since 1914 has been distributed from the Midwest everywhere in the United States? What manner and kind of being is it that searches the whole globe over to compile this volume of dippy games, this zany store of novelties? Who is this mountebank? What rack of nature, what inversion of wit stocks this warehouse with "electrical and scientific kits, fortune telling, magic," practical jokes for every occasion? An American he must unquestionably be, Elkin believes: "*A*merican, like some ingrained quality of the privative." That is, there's an American grain in that prefix *A* which is the grammatical sign of absence, of the state of being deprived—as in "*a*moral or *a*political" or "*a*ssimilation"—of being beggared, dispossessed.

Artfully and cleverly arguing a humorlessly held point, Elkin finds a clue to character and sensibility in the United States in nomenclature in which denial, the Negative, precedes the very assertion to which it adheres. As confirmed by a catalogue which fails to distinguish between more and less, ours is a society hard put to differentiate between taking from and adding to, between promotion and privation, between confidence man and honest broker, between ravishment and ravagement. Contemplating a culture which for generations has sped "joy buzzers and whoopee cushions to the world," fusing history and literature, grammar and art, Elkin concludes that the American spirit beats time to the "rhythm in chaos."[30] In all of which finally, ending where we began, with language and prophecy, we construe signs of semiotic, lexical, oral, and national equivalence: A-merica as in a-buse. To use wrongly. To use up. Held in the grip of a dialectic which alters its terms and shifts its ground from generation to generation, America—its literature, its people, its history—embodies a confirmation of Yes and a malediction of No.

Notes

Index

Notes

I. STRANGENESS OF PROPORTION IN AMERICA

1. Bernard Bailyn, *The Ideological Origins of the American Revolution* (Cambridge, Mass.: Harvard Univ. Pr., 1967), p. 57.

2. George Steiner, *New York Times Book Review*, Nov. 26, 1972, pp. 12, 16–17.

3. Hugh Kenner, *The Pound Era* (Berkeley and Los Angeles: Univ. of California Pr., 1971), p. 98.

4. Quoted by A. Alvarez, *Under Pressure* (London: Penguin, 1965), p. 132.

5. I repeat here two paragraphs used in my introduction to *The Genius of American Fiction* (Boston: Allyn and Bacon, 1970), v, xiii.

6. Alexis de Tocqueville, *Democracy in America*, ed. Henry Steele Commager (New York and London: Oxford Univ. Pr., 1947), pp. 292–94.

7. Wasserstrom, *American Fiction*, xiv–*xv.*

8. Richard Chase, *The American Novel and Its Tradition* (Garden City, N.Y.: Doubleday, 1957), pp. 6–7.

9. David Borrows, "Style in Culture," *Journal of Interdisciplinary History*, IV (Summer, 1973), pp. 1–23 passim.

10. E. A. Burtt, *The Metaphysical Foundations of Modern Science* (Garden City, N.Y.: Doubleday, 1954), p. 297. See also I. Bernard Cohen, *Franklin and Newton* (Philadelphia: American Philosophical Society, 1956).

11. Wylie Sypher, *Four Stages of Renaissance Style* (Garden City, N.Y.: Doubleday, 1954), p. 256. For thoroughly keen comment on Sypher's standing in this field, see Morse Peckham, *Man's Rage for Chaos* (Philadelphia and New York: Chilton, 1965), pp. 15, 306–7.

12. Sigurd Burkhardt. *Shakespearean Meanings* (Princeton: Princeton Univ. Pr., 1968), pp. 145–46, 165, 183.

13. Steiner, *Times Book Review*, p. 20.

14. Quoted by John Bayley, *The Uses of Division* (New York: Viking, 1977), pp. 157–58.

15. Gordon S. Wood, *The Creation of the American Republic* (Chapel Hill: Univ. of North Carolina Pr., 1969), pp. 10, 14.

16. *New York Times*, Oct. 4, 1968, p. 20.

17. Ralph Ketcham, *From Colony to Country* (New York and London: Macmillan, 1974), p. 63.

18. Quoted by Alvarez, *Under Pressure*, p. 132.

19. Henry Adams, *History of the United States of America During the Administrations of Jefferson and Madison*, ed. Ernest Samuels (Chicago and London: Univ. of Chicago Pr., 1967), pp. 116–19.

20. Quoted by Irving Dilliard, *The Building of the Constitution* (St. Louis, 1937), pp. 8, 28.

21. Ernest H. Hutton, "Symmetry in Physics and Information Theory," *Diogenes*, 72 (Winter, 1970), pp. 1–21 passim.

22. Claude Lévi-Strauss, *Tristes Tropiques* (New York: Atheneum, 1964), pp. 187–88.

23. Adrienne Koch, *Madison's "Advice to my Country"* (Princeton: Princeton Univ. Pr., 1966), p. 64. In contrast to Madison's advice, Hamilton insisted that "the true principle of government is this": create a "system complete in its structure, give a perfect proportion and balance to its parts, and the powers you give it will never affect your security" *Alexander Hamilton and the Founding of the Nation*, ed. Richard N. Morris (New York: Dial, 1957), p. 238.

II. THE ABORIGINAL DEMON: IRVING, COOPER, HAWTHORNE

1. Michael Kammen, *People of Paradox* (New York: Knopf, 1972), pp. 89–90.

2. Leo Marx, *The Machine in the Garden* (New York and London: Oxford Univ. Pr., 1964), p. 226.

3. Howard Mumford Jones, *O Strange New World* (New York: Viking, 1964), p. 275.

4. D. H. Lawrence, *Studies in Classic American Literature* (New York: Viking, 1962), p. 54.

5. *Collected Letters of D. H. Lawrence*, ed. Harry T. Moore (2 vols. New York: Viking, 1962), vol. II, p. 896.

6. Philip Young, "Fallen from Time: The Mythic Rip Van Winkle," *Kenyon Review*, XXII (Autumn, 1960), pp. 553–56, 567–72 passim. A reading dissimilar to Young's and unlike mine in disapproving of Rip was long ago proposed in an essay which founders on a misconstruction of Irving's skittishness in favor of Rip. Maintaining that Irving gave no credence to "contemporary primitivism," it came down on the side of colonial "common sense and hard-headed vitality"—as if a hard head alone was standard equipment for the "founding of a new republic." Terence Martin, "Rip, Ichabod and the American Imagination," *American Literature* 31 (May, 1959), pp. 142–45.

7. J. Huizinga, *Homo Ludens* (Boston: Beacon, 1955), pp. 3–7passim.

8. Ibid., p. 10.

9. Henry Bamford Parkes, "Metamorphosis of Leatherstocking," in *Literature in America*, ed. Philip Rahv (New York: Meridian, 1957), p. 434.

10. James Fenimore Cooper, *The Prairie: A Tale* (New York: Rinehart, 1950), pp. 4–5, 98–100, 162–63, 418–19, 424–25.

11. In recent years a modest increase of respect for Freud's speculation is apparent among anthropologists who, in returning to *Totem and Taboo*, discover that "what Freud actually said is substantially different from what a number of his anthropological critics have thought that he said!" See *The Structural Study of Myth and Totemism*, ed. Edmund Leach (London: Tavistock, 1967), xiv. Presumably Leach referred to Alfred L. Kroeber's condemnation, first in 1920 and again more circumspectly in 1939, and echoed many years later by a disciple, Lillian B. McCall, who regretted seeing Freud's "fairy tale" taken seriously by students of culture. "Freud and Scientific Truth," *Commentary*, VII (Apr., 1948), p. 348. Leach's comment, however, refers to an essay in reassessment by Robin Fox, who filters Freud's

argument and finds in it residue worth preserving, especially material that bears on the origins and evolution of social systems marked by "deep feelings about mothers, sisters, sex, and power." Because Freud's "origin myth" is directly "concerned with the breakthrough from nature to culture," Fox finds that main tenets of *Totem and Taboo*, recast into "the language of evolutionary anthropology instead of the language of myth," do indeed offer remarkably useful thought on ties connecting human emotion and human motive with social structure. "'Totem and Taboo' Reconsidered," in *Structural Study of Myth*, pp. 175, 168.

12. Sigmund Freud, *Moses and Monotheism* (New York: Knopf, 1939), pp. 102–4.

13. Erich Fromm, *Sigmund Freud's Mission* (New York: Harper, 1959).

14. Quoted by Theodore Roszak, *The Making of a Counter Culture* (Garden City, N.Y.: Doubleday, 1969), p. 227). See also Aileen Ward, "The Forging of Orc: Blake and the Idea of Revolution," *TriQuarterly* 23/24 (Winter/Spring, 1972), pp. 244–45; Martin Price, "The Study of Energy," in *Romanticism and Consciousness*, ed. Harold Bloom (New York: Norton, 1970), p. 266.

15. Quoted by Herbert L. Sussman, *Victorians and the Machine* (Cambridge, Mass.: Harvard Univ. Pr., 1968), pp. 26–27.

16. Raymond Williams, *Culture and Society 1780–1950* (Garden City, N.Y.: Doubleday, 1960), pp. 84–88 passim. In England, furthermore, the expansion of the capital city manifests the "true condition" of the "country as a whole," a country which in the 19th century concentrated the power of industry and commerce and government within a single metropolis. See Raymond Williams, *The Country and the City* (New York and London: Oxford Univ. Pr., 1973), pp. 146–47.

17. Fruitlands, Bronson Alcott's and Charles Lane's community near Worcester, Massachusetts, is typical in that its actual life span was short but its reputation and legend are unending. Restored during 1914 by Clara Endicott Sears it survives today as a monument to its seven months of failed utopia, 1833–1834, seven months given over not to "recreation," Miss Sears said, but to "inspiration." Drawing on a vast literature of American utopias John Reedy wrote a splendid short journalistic account for the *New York Times*, Aug. 12, 1973, XX, pp. 3, 23.

18. Henry Adams, *History of the United States During the Administrations of Jefferson and Madison*, ed. Ernest Samuels (Chicago and London: Univ. of Chicago Pr., 1967), pp. 52–55 passim.

19. Elting Morison, *From Know-How to Nowhere* (New York: Mentor, 1977), p. 45. Countering these fervid years of engineering, leading men of letters and of art identified "the health, the very personality of America, with Nature, and therefore set it in opposition to the concepts of the city, the railroad, the steamboat." Perry Miller, *Nature's Nation* (Cambridge, Mass.: Harvard Univ. Pr., 1967), p. 199. (Emerson of course led the way and in "The American Scholar" [1837] looked toward a time "when the sluggard intellect of this continent" will come to "something better than the exertions of mechanical skill.") Larzer Ziff, *Puritanism in America* (New York: Viking, 1973), pp. 126–27. "Elsewhere, divinity in nature was in the spiritual eye of the beholder." American Puritans proclaimed their "sainthood" by "identifying" the "Literal-spiritual contours of the land." Sacvan Bercovitch, *The American Puritan Imagination* (New York: Cambridge Univ. Pr., 1974), p. 14.

20. Gertrude Himmelfarb, *Victorian Minds* (New York: Knopf, 1968), pp. 289–90.

21. Millicent Bell, *Hawthorne's View of the Artist* (New York: New York Univ. Pr., 1962), p. 68. See Richard J. Jacobson, *Hawthorne's Conception of the Creative Process* (Cambridge, Mass.: Harvard Univ. Pr., 1965), p. 27, in which Warland is described as a man embarked on a "single-minded quest for intense aesthetic experience." See also P. K. Gupta, "Hawthorne's Theory of Art," *American Literature*, 40 (Nov., 1968), pp. 309–24. Even F. O.

Matthiessen somehow got Warland wrong, referred to him as a "sensitive carver" who "won his way to equilibrium" within "this sketch," itself one of Hawthorne's "barest statements of a profound theme." *American Renaissance* (New York: Oxford Univ. Pr., 1941), pp. 223, 224. Hawthorne's sole reference to carving occurs very early on in the story and is meant to distinguish Owen from other "schoolboy artisans" who possessed a knack of the "pen-knife." Having recently happened on two pages of commentary in which Owen's powers are given their due, I am pleased to discover an account which overlaps and reinforces my own. In Charles Sanders's "Note on Metamorphosis in Hawthorne's 'Artist of the Beautiful,'" it is the four encounters with Danforth, Annie, and Peter Hovenden which are said roughly to "correspond to the stages of a butterfly's metamorphosis from embryo to adult." In my view a misreading, the case is in any event undeveloped—noted not argued. The particular merit of Sanders's proposal, however, is to help confirm my rather more portentous efforts to justify Warland's passage from a fussy morbid little man to a heroic figure endowed with commanding and prophetic "strength of inspiration." *Studies in Short Fiction*, 4 (Fall, 1966), pp. 82–83.

22. N. Hawthorne, *Mosses from an Old Manse* (New York: Hurst, n.d.), pp. 313–16 passim.

23. Lewis Mumford, *Technics and Civilization* (New York: Harcourt, 1934), pp. 14–15. "There's a vast literature on the subject today," Jacques Le Goff remarked nearly thirty years after Mumford's early work, a literature that confirms the case argued in *Technics*. That is, merchants and craftsmen of the Middle Ages in alliance with moralists and theologians did indeed enhance the prestige of commerce by resolving the "conflict and contradiction between business and religious time." See Le Goff's essay "Temps de l'Eglise et temps du marchand," *Annales*, 3 (May–June, 1960), pp. 417–33.

24; *Of Men and Machines*, ed. Arthur O. Lewis, Jr. (New York: Dutton, 1963), pp. 58–64. Sacvan Bercovitch, *The American Jeremiad* (Madison: Univ. of Wisconsin Pr., 1978), pp. 29–30. By the 1840s, furthermore, "American were manufacturing on the assembly line, not only clocks and guns, but their own machines." Carolyn Porter, *Seeing and Being* (Middletown: Wesleyan Univ. Pr., 1981), p. 64.

25. George M. Beard, "Causes of American Nervousness," in *Popular Culture and Industrialism 1865–1890*, ed. Henry Nash Smith (New York: New York Univ. Pr., 1970), pp. 61, 62. See also Henry G. Fairbanks, "Hawthorne and the Machine Age," *American Literature*, 28 (May, 1956), pp. 155, 156, 161.

26. Laura Makarius, "The Blacksmith's Taboos," *Diogenes*, 8 (Summer, 1968), p. 48.

27. Quentin Anderson, *The Imperial Self* (New York: Knopf, 1971), pp. 14–17.

28. V. Nabokov, *Nikolai Gogol* (Norfolk, Conn.: New Directions, 1944), p. 56. "Pigmentary and structural" rather, one learns from a current and comprehensive inquiry into the Lepidoptera, though it is apparently true that "some of the most striking colors are due not to chemical pigments but to small structural features of the scales." Diffracting or scattering light, "iridescent scales also bear a pigment, usually a dark melanin, that absorbs much of the transmitted light and causes the reflected component to appear particularly brilliant," H. Frederik Nijhout, "The Color Patterns of Butterflies and Moths," *Scientific American*, 245 (Nov. 1981), p. 140.

29. Alfred Appel, Jr., "Nabokov's Puppet Show II," *New Republic*, Jan. 21, 1967, p. 26. See Thoreau's journal entry for March 3, 1839: the Poet is "another Nature, Nature's brother. . . . Each publishes the other's truth." Quoted by Miller, *Nature's Nation*, p. 177. See also Nabokov's university lecture, the posthumous essay on Dostoyevsky, in which art is described as a "divine game." A man who participates in this "enchanting game" becomes a

true creator in his own right and in this way "comes nearest to God." *New York Times Magazine*, Aug. 23, 1981, p. 63.

30. Millicent Bell, *Edith Wharton and Henry James: The Story of Their Friendship* (London: Peter Owen, 1966), p. 189.

31. Daniel J. Boorstin, *The Genius of American Politics* (Chicago: Univ. of Chicago Pr., 1953), pp. 21–22.

32. Harry A. Bent, *The Second Law* (New York: Oxford Univ. Pr., 1965), p. 28.

33. Lawrence, *Studies in Classic American Literature*, pp. 88, 83.

III. ABANDONED IN PROVIDENCE: HARRIET BEECHER STOWE, HOWELLS, HENRY JAMES

1. Tony Tanner, *The Reign of Wonder* (New York and London: Cambridge Univ. Pr., 1965), pp. 8, 12, 142.

2. Michael Kammen, *People of Paradox* (New York: Knopf, 1972), pp. 34, 47.

3. Writing about "the most influential architect in history," Palladio, Ada Louise Huxtable contends that Palladio's "pure geometry of architectural form" is more "pertinent today than ever," not by reason of a classical revival but of a "skilled irony" which is especially appealing to those past-modern designers who now hold sway over the profession in America. *New York Times Magazine*, July 17, 1977, pp. 22–25 passim. Beyond irony, aspiring to show that it's "possible to make comfort and beauty out of ugliness and ordinariness"—taunting chaos," vanguard architects incorporate and repudiate dogmas of order, of form, of environment. See also the *Times*, May 17, 1979, C6.

4. Thad W. Tate, "From Survival to Prosperity," *The Key Reporter*, XLIV (Autumn, 1978), p. 2.

5. Henry Adams, *Mont-Saint-Michel and Chartres* (Boston and New York: Houghton, 1905), p. 377.

6. *The Times Literary Supplement*, Sept. 17, 1954, xliv.

7. Earl Rovit, "The American Concept of Home," *American Scholar*, 29 (Autumn, 1960), pp. 523–27 passim. I discovered Rovit's excellent short essay long after I'd worked through the materials and argument of this chapter. He concludes, incidentally, that our style of "institutionalized chaos" doesn't undermine but in truth strengthens the American "house of government."

8. Edward Dahlberg, *Alms for Oblivion* (Minneapolis: Univ. of Minnesota Pr., 1964), p. 27.

9. George F. Whicher, "Literature and Conflict," in *Literary History of the United States*, ed. Robert Spiller et al. (3 vols. New York: Macmillan, 1948), vol. I, pp. 581–86 passim.

10. Although Stowe did not parcel out guilt in equal shares, she was careful "to contrive her story in such a way that the Southern states and New England shall be shown as involved in equal degree in the kidnapping into slavery of the Negroes and the subsequent maltreatment of them." Edmund Wilson, *Patriotic Gore* (New York and London: Oxford Univ. Pr., 1962). p. 6.

11. Edwin H. Cady, *The Road to Realism* (Syracuse: Syracuse Univ. Pr., 1956), pp. 235, 237.

12. Paul Goldberger, *New York Times*, Aug. 6, 1976, c 19.

13. William Wasserstrom, "William Dean Howells: The Indelible Stain," *New England Quarterly*, XXXII (Dec. 1959), pp. 486–95.

14. Quoted by Dennis Farney, *Wall Street Journal*, Jan. 4, 1974, p. 20.

15. Quoted by Paul Goldberger, *New York Times*, June 27, 1977, p. 20. See Robert Venturi, Denis Scott Brown, Steven Izenour, *Learning from Las Vegas* (Cambridge, Mass.: M.I.T. Pr., 1972); Charles Jencks, *The Language of Post-Modern Architecture* (New York: Rizzoli, 1977). As if staged to dramatize the authority of post-modern theory in American taste, the Pruitt-Igoe public housing project in St. Louis was reduced to rubble on April 21, 1971, fourteen years after its completion. Inspired by Le Corbusier's *Vers Une Architecture* (1928), a celebrated essay in praise of a machine ethic of social order, Yamasaki, its designer, aspired to achieve what Le Corbusier called "a bridge to progress." See Wolf von Eckhardt, *New Republic*, Aug. 6 and 13, 1977, pp. 31–33.

16. R. W. B. Lewis, *Edith Wharton* (New York: Harper, 1975), pp. 120–21.

17. Claude Bragdon, *More Lives Than One* (New York: Knopf, 1938), p. 164.

18. Walter Blair, *Mark Twain & Huck Finn* (Berkeley and Los Angeles: Univ. of California Pr., 1960), p. 314.

19. Leslie A. Fiedler, *Love and Death in the American Novel* (New York: Criterion, 1960), p. 29.

20. Harriet Beecher Stowe, *Uncle Tom's Cabin* (New York: Washington Square Pr., 1962), pp. 12, 220–21, 224–25, 248, 275, 450, 458.

21. William James, "What Psychical Research Has Accomplished," *The Will to Believe and Other Essays in Popular Philosophy* (New York: Dover, 1956), pp. 311, 303, 301.

22. Henry James, *The American Scene,* ed. Leon Edel (Bloomington and London: Indiana Univ. Pr., 1968), pp. 102–5.

23. The matter of smell is crucial and needs extended comment. In a far-reaching inquiry into James's sources Oscar Cargill turned up at least one discovery, "parallels between *The Turn of the Screw* and 'The Case of Miss Lucy R.'" in the Breuer–Freud *Studies in Hysteria* (1895). In a case whose implications Cargill himself didn't quite exhaust there are indeed large quantities of evidence, chiefly circumstantial, supporting Cargill's belief that Freud's patient Lucy R. (an English governess in Vienna, charged with the care of two Austrian children and stirred sexually by their father) served James's turn. For it was specifically in search of relief from a "chronic purulent rhinitis" that Lucy R. came to Freud; that is, relief from neurosis concentrated in "the subjective sense of smell," the smell of burn. Whether or not James was taken by Freud's analysis of these difficulties, Cargill says, James's governess also "has a peculiarly keen organ" and is remarkably sensitive to the "fragrance and purity of the children." Convinced too that James's story included the experience of Alice James, Henry's beloved sister, Cargill labors to prove that the Governess, though "befuddled," was heroic. As a result he lost his hold on "The Case of Miss Lucy R." and also lost sight of James's arabesque of reasons for choosing the term *fragrance* to describe the odor of children befouled by the air of evil whose "reek," not unlike the poisonous vapors of "Rappacini's Daughter," saturates the story. By no means is it inconceivable, therefore, that it was Lucy R.'s rhinitis to which James alludes in the final scene when the Governess's senses are assaulted by an "overwhelming presence" which fills the room like the "taste of poison." Watching Miles for a sign that he too has caught Quint's spoor, she observes the boy, in shaking his head, "make the movement of a baffled dog on a scent" then give a "frantic little shake for air and light" just before he dies a split second before that "hot breath from the Pit" tinctures his last gasp. See Oscar Cargill, "*The Turn of the Screw* and Alice James," PMLA, LXXXVIII (June, 1963), pp. 238–48.

24. *The James Family*, ed. F. O. Matthiessen (New York: Knopf, 1947), p. 197.

25. Sigmund Freud, "The Uncanny," *Collected Papers*, ed. Joan Riviere (London: Hogarth, 1953), vol. IV, pp. 37, 405. See also a more recent account of the word *canny* as

referring in Scottish usage to houses "free from commotion, disturbance, noise." Maria M. Tatar, "The Houses of Fiction: Toward a Definition of the Uncanny," *Comparative Literature*, 33 (Spring, 1981), p. 1.

26. For anyone "fortunate enough to be born into the old ruling class in Britain, those first terms at a public school were the only time one learnt what life is like for the weak and vulnerable; what it is to suffer permanent fear and hunger; what it is like to experience savage injustice without any real chance of restitution; what it is like to be dependent on the arbitrary whims, fancies and prejudices of the powerful; what it is like to be subjected to humiliation and persecution by the forces of law and order, or at least with their connivance." Peregrine Worsthorne, "Boy Made Man," in *The World of the Public School*, ed. George MacDonald Fraser (London: Weidenfeld & Nicholson, 1977), p. 95. See also Nigel Nicolson, *Portrait of a Marriage* (New York: Bantam, 1974), p. 92.

27. The concept "of the child's nature has changed radically during the past 100 years, from the view of 'infant depravity' of the nineteenth century, through the turn of the century view of the child as a 'bundle of impulses' needing control, to the current emphasis on children as 'reservoirs of rich potential.'" Colleen L. Johnson and Frank A. Johnson, "Attitudes toward Parenting in Dual-Career Families," *American Journal of Psychiatry*, 134 (Apr., 1977), pp. 391–92.

28. Mary Douglas, *Purity and Danger* (New York: Praeger, 1966), pp. 94–114 passim.

29. James's Flora is a younger and nastier sister of Lewis Carroll's Alice just before the latter's conversion at the end of a book where the "symbolism is franker and more simple." A "grown queen" with the "conventional dignities of her insane world, suddenly she admits their insanity, refuses to be a grown queen and destroys them"—destroys that "self-stultifying machinery of luxury" which in Victorian England took "on a hideous life of its own." See William Empson's remarkable essay, "Alice in Wonderland: The Child as Swain," in *Art and Psychoanalysis*, ed. William Phillips (New York: Criterion, 1957), p. 217.

30. Blackmur, ed., *Art of the Novel*, "Preface to 'The Altar of the Dead,'" pp. 254–56. Both here and in the preface to "The Aspern Papers" (ibid., pp. 170, 175), James uses phrases which have been customarily misread as expressing low esteem for *The Turn of the Screw* and tales of similar kind. In fact these are the very phrases James was accustomed to deploy ("fairy tale side of life," "Ghost-story," "fairy-tale pure and simple," "pure romance") in order to snare the most elusive trait of his most appreciable doctrine of composition. For it was in *The Art of Fiction* he defined "romance"—telltale trace of that side of life to which he was instinctively drawn—as referring to those "things that with all the facilities in the world, all the wealth and all the courage and all the wit and all the adventure, we never *can* directly know; the things that reach us only through the beautiful subterfuge of our thought and our desire" (James's emphasis). A ghost story then is in James's lexicon set within a class of narrative, romance, reserved to represent all those things which, incalculably, we can know only by subterfuge, by indirection. As a genre of fiction, Hawthorne had said, the art of romance treats matters that fall "somewhere between the real world and fairy-land." See Richard Chase, *The American Novel and Its Tradition* (Garden City, N.Y.: Doubleday, 1957), pp. 18, 57.

31. John Lydenberg, "The Governess Turns the Screws," in *A Casebook on The Turn of the Screw*, ed. Gerald Willen (New York: Crowell, 1960), p. 289.

32. Mark Spilka was so far as I know the first to observe that the "tale matters, finally, precisely as it orders and expresses the intense domesticity of Victorian times." He makes the point in order to laud a "maternal young lady, full of domestic affection and attuned to sexual evil," the "sexual bogeys of Victorian childhood." Only one such as she could have enabled James to reveal "the moral and psychic cost of hothouse life." See "*Turning the Freudian Screw:*

How Not to Do It," in *The Turn of the Screw*, ed. Robert Kimbrough (New York: Norton, 1966), pp. 250–53. I am myself more sympathetic to what's been called "the theme of alienation" manifest in a scapegoat child caught in a "confusing and hostile environment." Muriel G. Shine, *The Fictional Children of Henry James* (Chapel Hill: Univ. of North Carolina Pr., 1969), pp. 176–77.

33. Henry James, "Preface to 'What Maisie Knew,'" in *The Art of the Novel*, ed. R. P. Blackmur (New York: Scribner's, 1948), pp. 142–47 passim.

IV. HYDRAULICS AND HEROICS: WILLIAM JAMES, STEPHEN CRANE

1. Henry James, *The Golden Bowl* (New York: Scribner's, 1904), pp. 477–78. See also Carlos Baker, "Emerson, Henry Adams, and the Dance," *New England Quarterly*, LII (Mar., 1979), pp. 27–37.

2. *The James Family*, ed. F. O. Matthiessen (New York: Knopf, 1947), p. 106.

3. *The Letters of Henry James*, ed. Percy Lubbock (2 vols. New York: Scribner's, 1920), vol. II, p. 43. Ruminating on the complex state (and fate) of brotherhood, on "the difficult, emotional and perhaps incestuous relationship that Henry James maintained with his brother William," Richard Hall's "psychocritical" essay takes up *The Golden Bowl* as a capital event of fraternity. Marking a "new inner freedom" in its author, the novel treats "a whole network of altered relationships, all deriving from his new liberation from William." See "An Obscure Hurt: Part II," *New Republic*, May 5, 1979, p. 26.

4. Cynthia Eagle Russett, *The Concept of Equilibrium in American Social Thought* (New Haven and London: Yale, Univ. Pr., 1966), p. 9. Relying mainly on Russett's account Martin Green, in his splendid and strange book on D. H. Lawrence and Max Weber, presents—mistakenly, I think—a Germanic and Weberesque stimulus and setting for the sociology of dynamic equilibrium in America. Green's analysis does accurately associate the creed of homeostasis with a politics of conservatism, a view of order that doesn't welcome destabilizing change. See *The Von Richtofen Sisters* (New York: Basic Books, 1975), pp. 322–23.

5. Ibid, pp. 43–54 passim. In contrast to American dynamism consider that English passion for symmetry which Steven Marcus discovers in Victorian erotic fantasy. The image he especially cherishes, flawless indeed, encompasses sexual, social, moral, economic values within a closed system that can't be improved on for tidiness of equipoise. Describing "a man and woman reversed upon each other, sucking away, 'spending' and swallowing each other's juices," Marcus observes that "this fantasy may be the immemorial one, but it is also peculiarly apposite to the eighteenth and nineteenth centuries" in England. "It imagines nothing less than a perfect, self-enclosed economic and productive system. Intake and output are perfectly balanced; production is plentiful, but nothing is lost, wasted, or spent, since the product is consumed only to produce more of the raw material by which the system is fulfilled. The primitive dream of capitalism is fulfilled in the primitive dream of the body." *The Other Victorians* (New York: Basic Books, 1966), pp. 243–44. The idea persists in less fantastical form, toward more pedestrian function today. Against the drift of sociological opinion, we're informed that middle-class family life in Britain is stronger now than heretofore, no less tightly managed as a "unit of consumption" than it was in remoter times when a family served as a "unit of production." For even as nowadays there are more women who live extracurricular lives, so too there are increasing numbers of home-centered men. As

a result both sexes achieve newly complementary roles in what Michael Young and Peter Wilmot describe as *The Symmetrical Family* (New York: Pantheon, 1973).

6. Walter B. Cannon, *The Wisdom of the Body* (New York: Norton, 1939; 1963), p. 323. "It seems not impossible that the means employed by the more highly evolved animals . . . for preserving homeostasis may present some general principles for the establishment, regulation and control of steady states that would be suggestive . . . even [for] social and industrial" organizations. Ibid., pp. 24–25.

7. Walter Buckley, *Sociology and Modern Systems Theory* (Englewood Cliffs, N.J.: Prentice-Hall, 1967), pp. 10–15 passim. Buckley mentions some additional proponents of theory but refers chiefly to those invoked by Russett and Green; that is, Henderson, Cannon, Talcott Parsons, and more recent others.

8. William James, *On Vital Reserves* (New York: Henry Holt, 1911), pp. 5–6.

9. John Humphrey Noyes, *History of American Socialisms* (New York: Hilary House, 1961), pp. 628–35 passim.

10. Matthiessen, ed. *The James Family, "Socialism and Civilization*," p. 53.

11. James, *On Vital Reserves*, p. 8. What we need, James remarked, anticipating the thesis of his later essay on a moral equivalent for war, is a study of "the different ways in which [human] energy-reserves may be appealed to and set loose." Ibid., p. 39.

12. George Santayana, *Character and Opinion in the United States* (London: Constable, 1924), pp. 82–83.

13. Stephen Crane, *The Red Badge of Courage and Other Writings*, ed. Richard Chase (Boston: Houghton, 1960), xv. I have also relied on Hershel Parker's text, itself a collocation of formerly lost or cut or misplaced manuscript pages, restored by Parker's former student Henry Binder, whose own edition of *The Red Badge* was published in 1982. See the *Norton Anthology of American Literature*, ed. R. W. Gottesman et al. (2 vols. New York: Norton, 1979), vol. II, pp. 802–906.

14. Larzer Ziff, *The American 1890s* (New York: Viking, 1966), p. 198. John Berryman had in fact made the opposite point, that Crane's prose and poetry had the enigmatic, hallucinatory, barbaric character of dreams. See Carol Schloss, "John Berryman and Stephen Crane," *Literature & Psychology*, XXIX (1980), pp. 169–75.

15. Eric Solomon, *Stephen Crane in England* (Columbus: Ohio State Univ. Pr., 1964), p. 3.

16. Corwin K. Linson, *My Stephen Crane* (Syracuse: Syracuse Univ. Pr., 1958), p. 43.

17. Stephen Crane: *Letters*, ed. Robert W. Stallman and Lilliam Gilkes (New York: New York Univ. Pr., 1960), p. 105.

18. Quoted by Edwin H. Cady, *Stephen Crane* (New York: Twayne, 1962), p. 91.

19. F. Scott Fitzgerald, *This Side of Paradise* (New York: Scribner's, 1948), p. 282.

20. Quoted by Nathan F. Hale, Jr., *Freud and the Americans: The Beginnings of Psychoanalysis in the United States, 1876–1917* (New York and London: Oxford Univ. Pr., 1971), p. 110. Despite the archaism of James's diction there is apparently long-lived power in his thought. For it's got enough currency to warrant more than ornamental use by Saul Bellow in *Humboldt's Gift*. To be "a thriving energy system," Citrine (Bellow's persona) says, "was part of my American training." And it's this training and system, adds Von Humboldt Fleisher (Delmore Schwartz's surrogate), which "by a damn peculiar arrangement" are exaggerated in lunatics who "always have energy to burn. And if old William James was right, and happiness is living at the energetic top and we are here to pursue happiness, then madness is pure bliss and also has political sanction." *Humboldt's Gift* (New York: Viking, 1975), pp. 395, 327. See also Henry Bamford Parkes: "The genius of American life lay in its

unprecedented capacity to release for constructive purposes the energies and abilities of common men and women." *The American Experience* (New York: Vintage, 1959), p. 11.

21. "Stephen Crane at Syracuse University," in *Love Letters to Nellie Crouse*, ed. E. H. Cady and L. G. Wells (Syracuse: Syracuse Univ. Pr., 1954), p. 65.

22. "Just like the great classics of literature, *The Red Badge of Courage* speaks of different things to different minds. However, only an oversimplified interpretation could see in Henry's final charge the proof that he has become as he himself thinks, 'a man.'" Jean Cazemajou, *Stephen Crane* (Minneapolis: Univ. of Minnesota Pr., 1969), p. 41.

23. Quoted by Solomon, *Stephen Crane in England*, p. 41.

24. Matthiessen, ed., *The James Family*, "The Moral Equivalent of War," pp. 636–46.

25. Not only was futurist theory "committed totally to the notion of the machine as the material basis of modern industrial life" but, startlingly, futurists in the early 1920s proclaimed themselves given to hope that "man would become like the machine, not the machine like man." Ronny H. Cohen, "Italian Futurist Typography," *The Print Collector's Newsletter*, VIII (Jan.–Feb., 1978), p. 168. See also Arthur A. Cohen, "Marinetti and Futurism, ibid, pp. 170–72.

26. Albert Guerard, "Romanticism and Stoicism in the American Novel: From Melville to Hemingway, and after," *Diogenes*, 23 (Fall, 1958), pp. 95–110.

27. George Monteiro, "The Education of Ernest Hemingway," *Journal of American Studies*, 8 (Apr., 1974), p. 91.

28. Quoted in Morris Ginsberg, *Evolution and Progress* (London: Heinemann, 1961), p. 1.

29. Franklin Henry Giddings, *The Principles of Sociology* (London: Macmillan, 1896)), pp. 358–60.

30. J. B. Bury, *The Idea of Progress*, intro. Charles A. Beard (New York: Dover, 1955), p. 244. Von Hartmann's remark, which refers to progress and evolution, Bury himself does not support but offers in order to provide for "a pessimistic as well as an optimistic interpretation." A day "may well come," he adds, "when a new idea will usurp its place as the directing idea of humanity" even as progress has displaced Providence from "the commanding position" in which it had been formerly enthroned.

V. NOTES ON ELECTRICITY: HENRY ADAMS AND EUGENE O'NEILL

1. Robert Penn Warren, "Bearers of Bad Tidings: Writers and the American Dream," *New York Review of Books*, March 20, 1975, pp. 17–18.

2. Henry Adams, *The Education of Henry Adams* (London: Constable, 1919), pp. 417–18.

3. Werner Heisenberg, "Planck's Discovery and the Philosophical Problems in Nuclear Physics," *Science and Society: Selected Essays*, eds. A. Vavoulis and W. Wayne Culver (San Francisco: Holden-Day, 1966), p. 133.

4. Edward W. Said, *Orientalism* (New York: Vintage, 1979), p. 5.

5. J. B. Bury, *The Idea of Progress*, intro. Charles A. Beard (New York: Dover, 1955), xx–xxi.

6. Quoted by George Jean Nathan, "Eugene O'Neill," in *American Drama and Its Critics*, ed. Alan S. Downer (Chicago and London: Univ. of Chicago Pr., 1965), p. 98.

7. Quoted by Norman Nadel, *A Pictorial History of the Theatre Guild* (New York: Crown, 1969), p. 419.

8. Ezra Pound, *Antheil and the Treatise on Harmony* (Chicago: Pascal Covici, 1927), pp. 53–54. "O'Neill betrays himself in so feverish a personal mood that one achieves much the

same feeling that comes over one when listening to that boiler-works symphony of Antheil." Nathan, "O'Neill," in *American Drama*, ed. Downer, p. 102. Cf. Mel Gussow forty-eight years later: At "The Impossible Ragtime Theater, George Ferencz has taken [*Dynamo*] and recharged [it] with theatrical electricity." *New York Times*, Apr. 4, 1977, p. 30.

9. Henry Adams, *Letters to a Niece* (Boston and New York: Houghton, 1920), pp. 128–30.

10. Lewis Mumford, "Apology to Henry Adams," *Virginia Quarterly Review*, 38 (Spring, 1962), pp. 215–17.

11. Eugene O'Neill, *Dynamo* (New York: Horace Liveright, 1929), pp. 126–27, 132–34, 139.

12. W. H. Auden, *The Dyer's Hand* (New York: Random House, 1962), p. 63. At prayer Reuben is "but making obeisance to the Catholic Devil thus materialistically refurbished." Kenneth Burke, *Philosophy of Literary Form* (Berkeley and Los Angeles: Univ. of California Pr., 1973), pp. 42–43.

13. Quoted by Gelb, *Eugene O'Neill*, p. 675.

14. Quoted by Lee Simonson, *The Stage Is Set (New York: Harcourt,* 1932), pp. 117–19. See also Lawrence Langner, *The Magic Curtain* (New York: Dutton, 1951), pp. 238–41.

15. Stark Young, "Dynamo," *New Republic*, Feb. 27, 1929, pp. 43–44.

16. Walter Lippmann, *A Preface to Morals* (New York: Macmillan, 1929), pp. 233, 235, 239–41.

17. *Collected Letters of D. H. Lawrence*, ed. Harry T. Moore (2 vols. New York: Viking, 1962), vol. I, p. 396.

18. Ibid., II, p. 786.

19. Frieda Lawrence, *Memoirs and Correspondence*, ed. E. W. Tedlock, Jr. (New York: Knopf, 1964), p. 354.

20. Robert Brustein, *The Theatre of Revolt* (London: Methuen, 1965), pp. 343, 359. See Stephen R. Grecco, "High Hopes: Eugene O'Neill and Alcohol," *Yale French Studies*, 50 (1974), pp. 142–49.

21. "Beginning with *The Hairy Ape* and continuing through . . . *Dynamo*, Mr. O'Neill's character studies are interspersed with plays in which the author . . . assumes the role of prophet." Francis Fergusson, "Eugene O'Neill," *Chimaera*, III (Jan.–Mar., 1930), p. 153.

22. "In November [1921] Mabel Dodge Luhan . . . urged him to come to Taos . . . and study the Pueblo Indians there. With Mrs. Luhan's letter went an Indian necklace . . . which supposed to have some magic property that would draw the Lawrences to Taos." Eliot Fay, *Lorenzo in Search of the Sun* (London: Vision, 1955), p. 30

VI. PHOENIX ON TURTLE ISLAND: D. H. LAWRENCE IN HENRY ADAMS'S AMERICA

1. *Collected Letters of D. H. Lawrence*, ed. Harry T. Moore (2 vols. New York: Viking, 1962), vol. I, pp. 421–22, 722, 998.

2. David Cavitch, *D. H. Lawrence and the New World* (New York and London: Oxford Univ. Pr., 1969), p. 100. "I think New Mexico was the greatest experience from the outside world that I ever had. Curious as it may sound, it was New Mexico that liberated me from the present era of civilization, the great era of material and mechanical development." Quoted by Eliot Fay, *Lorenzo in Search of the Sun* (London: Vision, 1955), 107. "Mexico exasperates," he wrote in 1923, a few pages called "Au Revoir, U.S.A.," but "the U.S.A. puts an unbearable tension on one." A "queer continent," taken all in all: "the an-

thropologists may make what prettiness they like out of the myths. But come here and you'll see that the gods bit." *Phoenix: The Posthumous Papers of D. H. Lawrence*, ed. Edward D. McDonald (New York: Viking, 1936), pp. 104–6.

3. Moore, ed. *Collected Letters*, I, p. 499.

4. *New York Times*, Nov. 5, 1971, p. 32.

5. Julian Moynihan, *The Novels and Tales of D. H. Lawrence* (Princeton: Princeton Univ. Pr., 1963), p. 178; Anthony West, *D. H. Lawrence: Novelist* (New York: Simon and Schuster, 1969), p. 273; Graham Hough, *The Dark Sun: A Study of D. H. Lawrence* (New York: Macmillan, 1957), pp. 140–46 passim.

6. Eugene Goodheart, *The Utopian Vision of D. H. Lawrence* (Chicago and London: Chicago, Univ. Pr., 1963), p. 130.

7. James G. Cowan, *D. H. Lawrence's American Journey* (Cleveland and London: Case Western Reserve Univ. Pr., 1970), pp. 70–78 passim. See also Paul Delany, in whose view even *Women in Love* prefigures a "turning away from the English literary tradition toward something more like the American," a turning from fictions in which mankind is "confirmed by social forms" toward "romance." *D. H. Lawrence's Nightmare* (New York: Basic Books, 1978), p. 228.

8. D. H. Lawrence, *Studies in Classic American Literature* (New York: Viking, 1962), pp. 116–17. "Have you seen anything of my *Studies*," he asked B. W. Huebsch. "I wrote them for America, and think a lot of them myself." Moore, ed. *Collected Letters*, I, p. 577. See also Tony Tanner, " D. H. Lawrence in America," in *D. H. Lawrence Novelist, Poet, Prophet*, ed. S. Spender (New York: Harper, 1973), pp. 195, 171.

9. Jessie Chambers, *D. H. Lawrence* (New York: Barnes and Noble, 1965), p. 11.

10. Mark Spilka, "Ritual Form in 'The Blind Man,'" in *D. H. Lawrence: A Collection of Critical Essays*, ed. Mark Spilka (Englewood Cliffs, N.J.: Prentice-Hall, 1963), p. 115.

11. Frank Kermode, *Lawrence* (London: Fontana/Collins, 1973), p. 111; F. J. Hoffman, *The Mortal No: Death and the Modern Imagination* (Princeton: Princeton Univ. Pr., 1964), p. 417. In the matter of Lawrence's politics, Kenneth Rexroth also speaks harsh words. Associating Lawrence with leading modernist writers from Yeats to Unamuno, Rexroth nearly two decades ago called for a revaluation ("book by book and almost sentence by sentence") of writers who were dedicated to express "the fascist unconscious." And he nominated Lawrence as a candidate for "a first chapter" in this comprehensive study. "D. H. Lawrence: Prophet Corrupted by Naivety," *Peace News*, Dec. 18, 1964, p. 6. Granted that there was a virulence of temper, a malice of power in Lawrence, it's fairer to regard the man more or less in the fashion Irving Howe regards *The Woman Who Rode Away*, "at once so impressive and ridiculous." See *The Decline of the New* (New York: Harcourt, 1971), p. 25.

12. John Carlos Rowe, *Henry Adams and Henry James* (Ithaca and London: Cornell Univ. Pr., 1973), pp. 51–52.

13. Henry Adams, *The Education of Henry Adams* (London: Constable, 1919), pp. 343–44.

14. Ibid., pp. 440–42 passim.

15. Arnold van Gennep, *The Rites of Passage* (Chicago and London: Chicago Univ. Pr., 1961), pp. 11–12, 21.

16. "'Oh!' cried Gudrun, 'Then we shan't have names any more . . . I am Mrs. Colliery-Manager Crich,'" D. H. Lawrence, *Women in Love* (New York: Penguin, 1976), p. 95.

17. Moore, ed. *Collected Letters*, II, p. 982.

18. Van Gennep, *Rites of Passage*, pp. 15, 28.

19. Ibid., p. 194.

20. Kate Millett, *Sexual Politics* (New York: Avon, 1971), p. 290.

21. Arthur Koestler, *The Ghost in the Machine* (Chicago: Regenery, 1967), p. 198.

22. Norman O. Brown, *Life Against Death* (Middletown: Wesleyan Univ. Pr., 1959), p. 245.

23. Mary Douglas, "The Meaning of Myth," in *The Structural Study of Myth and Totemism*, ed. Edmund Leach (London: Tavistock, 1967), p. 62.

24. Mary Douglas, *Purity and Danger* (New York: Praeger, 1966), pp. 54, 159.

25. Ibid., p. 178.

26. Add to this Kenneth Burke's side glance at Lawrence in "Symbolic Action in a Poem by Keats." Given a "peculiar inclination to erotic imaginings that accompany [consumptive] fever (as with the writings of D. H. Lawrence) we can glimpse a particular bodily motive expanding and intensifying the lyric state in Keats's case." *A Grammar of Motives* and *A Rhetoric of Motives* (Cleveland and New York: World, 1962), p. 452.

27. "He knew how rotten Europe was, nobody better, but never lost his deep belief in a renewal of its oldness; he was a steppingstone from the old to the new; he chose the Phoenix for his symbol." Frieda Lawrence, *Memoirs and Correspondence*, ed. E. W. Tedlock, Jr. (New York: Knopf, 1964), p. 439.

28. Henry Miller, *Tropic of Cancer* (New York: Grove, 1961), pp. 225, 232.

29. Tony Tanner, "The American Novelist as Entropologist," *London Magazine*, 10 (Oct., 1970), pp. 5–18.

30. "Barthelme is often guilty of opportunism of subject," William H. Gass is reported as saying, "and to be opportune is to succumb to dreck." The idea is to use dreck, Gass says, "not to write about it." Quoted by Richard Locke, *New York Times Book Review*, Dec. 19, 1976, pp. 17–18.

31. "The lesson of machines is precision, valuable to the plastic artist, and to literati." There would indeed be "something weak about art if it couldn't deal with this new conetnt," Pound said, pursuing his hobby horse of the twenties. Let this major chance not be lost on American artists: for "if America has given or is to give anything to general aesthetics it is presumably an aesthetic of machinery," a "desire for order" from which "a beauty, a proportion of painting and architecture" might unfold. *Antheil and the Treatise on Harmony* (Chicago: Pascal Covici, 1927), p. 52.

32. Jerome Mazzaro, "The Legacy of Modernism," *Salmagundi*, 31–32 (Fall, 1975–Winter, 1976, pp. 304, 306.

VII. THE SURSYMAMERICABEALISM OF GERTRUDE STEIN

1. Hans Richter, *DADA Art and Anti-Art* (New York: McGraw-Hill, 1965), p. 57–58.

2. Paul Valéry, "The Intellectual Crisis," in *Paths to the Present*, ed. Eugen Weber (New York: Dodd, Mead, 1960), p. 372.

3. "Surrounded by his disciples," numbering "as many as forty," Breton, "a marvelous talker," was more like an actor or a preacher than a poet." Peggy Guggenheim, *Out of This Century* (New York: Universe, 1979), p. 189.

4. See Rosalyn Regelow, "Was She Mother of Us All?" *New York Times*, Nov. 5, 1967, D5; Clara More de Morinni, "Miss Stein and the Ladies," *New Republic*, Nov. 11, 1967, pp. 17–19; Grace Glueck, "TV: by Gertrude Stein," *New York Times*, July 30, 1970, p. 60: Virgil Thomson, "A Very Difficult Author," *New York Review of Books*, Apr. 8, 1971, pp. 3–7; Richard Eder, "Photography by the Performance Group," *New York Times*, Sept. 22, 1977, p. 21. Concerning revivals of the Thomson–Stein opera, see Raymond Ericson, "Four

Saints Takes a New Trip," *New York Times*, Apr. 26, 1970, D1; Allen Hughes, "The Opera: Some Reminiscent Samplings of Gertrude Stein," *New York Times*, Oct. 7, 1972, D39; Harold Schonberg, "Minimet's Playful 'Four Saints,'" *New York Times*, Feb. 24, 1974, D17. At the Grolier Club, installing "Tribute to Gertrude Stein, 1874–1946," it was apparent that "the younger generation of students had rediscovered her. She's more popular now with undergraduates than she was in her lifetime." *New Yorker*, Mar. 11, 1974, p. 29. And finally Michiko Kakutami, concerned to report on the actress Pat Carroll's one-woman piece "Gertrude Stein Gertrude Stein Gertrude Stein," collected a considerable quantity of new material on the current cults of Stein, *New York Times*, Aug. 1, 1979, C17.

5. Irving Howe, *Decline of the New* (New York: Harcourt, 1971), pp. 6, 8, 15.

6. Ezra Pound, *How to Read* (To, France: Le Beausset, 1932), pp. 14–15.

7. "Genius," Matthew Arnold said in 1876, "is mainly an affair of energy." And poetry like science "is mainly an affair of genius." It followed, therefore, that a nation "whose spirit is characterized by energy may well be eminent" in poetry and science—just so long as "that energy, which is the full life of genius," is assured "the fullest room to expand as it will." Quoted by Morton D. Paley, *Energy and Imagination* (London: Oxford Univ. Pr., 1970), p. 2.

8. Leo Stein, *Journey into the Self*, ed. Edmund Fuller (New York: Crown, 1950), p. 149. "He thought she was silly, she thought he was tiresome. One thing they shared until the end, however, was the Jamesian care for shared space and its necessary arrangements." Pamela Hadas, "Spreading the Difference: One Way to Read Gertrude Stein's *Tender Buttons*," *Twentieth Century Literature*, 24 (Spring, 1978), p. 64.

9. Gertrude Stein, *Lectures in America* (Boston: Beacon, 1957), p. 235.

10. Ibid., p. 160.

11. In 1902 Berenson had come "under the ministrations of Gertrude Stein," a "doctor in spirit if not in fact," on whose treatment ("a raw egg in milk") he thrived. Beginning in 1904 Adams and Berenson developed "an enduring friendship which was to link Berenson closely with the fashionable colony, in Paris, that circled about Adams, [Elizabeth] Cameron and Edith Wharton." Ernest Samuels, *Bernard Berenson: The Making of a Connoisseur* (Cambridge, Mass.: Harvard Univ. Pr., 1979), pp. 382, 429.

12. A. D. Van Nostrand, *Everyman His Own Poet* (New York: McGraw-Hill, 1968), p. 197.

13. James M. Cox, "Autobiography in America," in *Aspects of Narrative*, ed. J. Hillis Miller (New York: Columbia Univ. Pr., 1971), p. 170.

14. Quoted by James R. Mellow, "Gertrude Stein on Picasso," *New York Times Book Review*, Nov. 20, 1970, p. 4. "If the appropriate joke about the women's movement is that it needs a good man to direct it, the attitude of Gertrude Stein was that although the male role was the one worth playing, the only good man was a woman." William H. Gass, *The World Within the Word* (New York: Knopf, 1978), p. 104n.

15. Louis Kronenberger, "The Education of Henry Adams," in *Books that Changed Our Minds*, eds. Malcolm Cowley and Bernard Smith (New York: Kelmscott, 1939), pp. 45–57 passim.

16. Quoted by Ernest Samuels, *Henry Adams the Major Phase* (Cambridge, Mass.: Harvard Univ. Pr., 1964), p. 344.

17. Stein, *Lectures in America*, p. 166.

18. Gertrude Stein, *The Making of Americans*, preface Bernard Fay (New York: Harcourt, 1934), xvi. Fay's good words, sounding promotional as well as critical, both embroider and gloss Stein's text. "I have never seen any other book where the United States could be seen as it is here in this unbroken continuity, in its monotonous variety, in its perpetual invention which never stops and is never satisfied" xx–xxi. It is to my mind unimaginable that Fay in these observations did not impart Stein's own thought.

19. Stein, *Lectures in America*, pp. 180–83 passim.

20. Quoted by John Malcolm Brinnin, *The Third Rose* (London: Weidenfeld & Nicolson, 1960), p. 132.

21. Anna Balakian, *The Symbolist Movement* (New York: Random House, 1967), p. 87.

22. "I was sure that in a kind of a way the enigma of the universe could in this way be solved," Stein wrote in "The Gradual Making of the Making of the Americans." After all "composition is explanation and if I went on and on and on enough I could describe every individual thing that could possibly exist." Not quite in the same breath but unquestionably in the same vein, she added: "When I was working with William James I completely learned one thing, that science is continuously busy with the complete description of something . . . with ultimately the complete description of everything." *Lectures in America*, pp. 142–56.

23. Thomson, "A Very Difficult Author," p. 103.

24. With or without benefit of Stein, William Faulkner also decided that narrative art should organize "impressions of speed and energy in order to build the most intense concentrations of force" words can command. Conceiving of motion as a stream whose power cannot be felt by someone moving with or in it, his idea—as Richard P. Adams proposed—was to cause someone "to stand still against its flow" so that art could disclose a "dramatic and possibly disastrous manifestation of its energy." *Faulkner: Myth and Motion* (Princeton: Princeton Univ. Pr., 1968), pp. 3–5 passim. It is in fact a disposition of art in this century, says a well-regarded Steinian, Donald Sutherland, to "intensify the movement of the quality of a single thing" so that energy, concentrated in this way, is seen moving about even as it stays where it is, "like the water of a fountain." *Gertrude Stein: A Biography of Her Work* (New Haven: Yale Univ. Pr., 1951), pp. 196–97. In somewhat other connection, Wendy Steiner refers to Stein's thoughts on wandering, geography, and national character as an effort to validate her theories of art. "She said that it was seeing the squared-off countryside from a plane that made her know that cubism was in fact an accurate picture of the modern. Furthermore, she claimed that the American countryside was uniquely suited to wandering, the activity of saints and the symbol of the movement of the human mind." *Exact Resemblance to Exact Resemblance* (New Haven and London: Yale Univ. Pr., 1978), p. 193.

25. "One may really indeed say that is the essence of genius, of being most intensely alive, that is being one who is at the same time talking and listening." Stein recalled, too, that when she began "to feel the outside inside and the inside outside," she "wrote *The Autobiography of Alice B. Toklas* and told what happened as it had happened." *Lectures in America*, pp. 170, 205. Given this explanation, this confession—given above all these specifications, this edict—it should be impossible for anyone to burden her with every vagrant idea dreamed up in her name. See Lynn Z. Bloom, "Gertrude Stein's Alice is Everybody: Innovation and Point of View in Gertrude Stein's Autobiographies," *Twentieth Century Literature*, 24 (Spring, 1978), pp. 81–93. See also Robert F. Fleissner, "Stein's Four Roses," *Journal of Modern Literature*, 6 (Apr., 1977), pp. 324–28. I am, incidentally, grateful to have found in this essay a reference I'd missed in Brinnin's *The Third Rose*, to Stein's variant line, "Civilization began with a rose." Fleissner, p. 32.

VIII. THE GOAD OF GUILT: HENRY ADAMS, SCOTT AND ZELDA

1. Quoted by Alden Whitman, *New York Times*, Mar. 8, 1972, C34.

2. *Writers at Work: Second Series*, ed. Van Wyck Brooks (New York: Viking, 1963), pp. 125–26.

3. James Baldwin. "As Much Truth as One Can Bear," *New York Times Book Review*, Jan. 14, 1962, p. 1. See Margaret Mead and James Baldwin, *A Rap on Race* (Philadelphia and New York: Lippincott, 1971); Nikki Giovanni and James Baldwin, *A Dialogue* (Philadelphia and New York: Lippincott, 1973), p. 39.

4. Echoing Auden on this perennial theme, Stephen Spender recalled hearing "Randall Jarrell give a very famous talk at Harvard about the obscurity of the American poet . . . I've thought about it a great deal since, and I think that American poets do regard the position of poetry in America as proof of something wrong with the whole society. So that, in a way, their suicides are to be taken as protests" against those whom they measure themselves against, "self-advertisers, businessmen, politicians, and so on." In contrast, writers in Great Britain share "the strain of values" with the "monarchy, the aristocracy, the one church" and therefore "don't feel that values stand or fall by them in their work and in their lives." The American writer, frustrated, "disappointed in his whole conception of the society in which he lives," finds it intolerable that "his own life and his own work are sort of daily proof of the disappointing nature of society, I think." "A Conversation with Stephen Spender," *American Poetry Review*, Nov./Dec., 1977, p. 18. Refusing to talk cant on alienation, Spender chooses not only to revive Auden but to reproduce Robert Lowell as well. Lowell, ever ambivalent on these themes, in his noted essay on Williams resisted a temptation to join the older man on a "Dantesque journey." Precisely because Williams loved this nation excessively, so Lowell believed, his "exasperation" too was excessive—"as if there were no other hell." Robert Lowell, "William Carlos Williams," *Hudson Review*, XIV (Winter, 1961–62), p. 534.

5. Calvin Tomkins, "Living Well Is the Best Revenge," *New Yorker*, July 28, 1962, p. 64.

6. "Father Fay, of the Catholic University of America," was a constant visitor in Adams's Washington home "from 1912 to the end. Round, jolly, worldly to a degree that only an ordained priest can attain without loss of spirituality," Father Cyril Sigourney Fay was a favored guest among the "many Catholics at Adams's house in the late years." R. P. Blackmur, *Henry Adams*, ed. Veronica A. Makowsky (New York and London: Harcourt, 1980), p. 322. Unidentified further, Adams's guest appears to be the man who served as Scott's mentor. Matthew J. Bruccoli, *Some Sort of Epic Grandeur* (New York: Harcourt, 1981), pp. 36–37. See also George Monteiro, "The Education of Ernest Hemingway," *Journal of American Studies* 8 (Apr., 1974), pp. 91–99.

7. At the time I made this statement I did not know that "the discarded name for Fitzgerald's hero was Stephen Dalius." See Alan Ross, "Rumble Among the Drums," *Horizon* XVIII (Dec., 1948), p. 420.

8. Andrew Turnbull, *F. Scott Fitzgerald* (New York: Scribner's, 1963), p. 65.

9. Nancy Milford, *Zelda* (New York: Harper, 1970), p. 111. The Fitzgeralds' history of near-misses did not present psychiatrists with behavior hitherto unobserved, just intractable. See Karl Menninger, "Purposive Accidents as an Expression of Self-Destructive Tendencies," *International Journal of Psychoanalysis*, 17: 6–16 (1936). Self-mutilation, Menninger noted, in some way or other a ransom, protects the ego against the death penalty. See also C. W. Wahl, "Suicide as a Magical Act," *Bulletin of the Menninger Clinic*, 21: 91–98 (1957); E. S. Schneidman, "The Enemy," *Psychology Today*, 10 (Aug., 1970), pp. 37–41, 62. Whatever one reads indeed, it's apparent that Scott and Zelda engaged in all categories of activity (death-seeking, death-daring, death-experimenting) devised to account for a profligacy of terror. Not until A. Alvarez's recent book on the subject of literary suicide, *The Savage God*, has it been commonly held that "the nihilism and destructiveness of the self—of which psychoanalysis has made us sharply and progressively more aware—turns out to be an accurate reflection of the nihilism of our own violent societies." Quoted by Joyce Carol Oates, *New York Times Book Review*, Apr. 16, 1972, p. 28.

10. Donald W. Goodwin, "The Alcoholism of F. Scott Fitzgerald," *Journal of the American Medical Association*, Apr. 6, 1970, pp. 86–90.

11. Turnbull, *Letters*, pp. 260–61.

12. Douglas Day, *Malcolm Lowry* (New York and London: Oxford Univ. Pr., 1973), pp. 97–98. In *Under the Volcano* "drink is the Consul's mistress, his muse, his God." Dale Edmonds, "Mescallusions or the Drinking Man's *Under the Volcano*," *Journal of Modern Literature*, 6 (Apr., 1977), p. 283. See also William James: "Sobriety diminishes, discriminates and says no; drunkenness expands, unites and says yes. It is, in fact, the great exciter of the Yes function in man. It brings its votary from the chill periphery of things to the radiant core . . . and it is part of the deeper mystery and tragedy of life that whiffs and gleams of something . . . excellent should be . . . so degrading a poison." Quoted by Berton Rueché, *The Neutral Spirit: A Portrait of Alcohol* (Boston and Toronto: Little, Brown, 1960), pp. 72–73.

13. Gregory Bateson, *Steps to an Ecology of Mind* (New York: Ballantine, 1972), pp. 322, 323, 328.

14. Turnbull, *Letters*, p. 496.

15. Quoted in Tomkins, "Living Well," p. 50.

16. "In 1932 and 1933, his book royalties came to a total of only $50." Richard Severo, *New York Times*, Mar. 20, 1974, M42. See also Matthew J. Bruccoli, *The Composition of Tender Is the Night* (Pittsburgh: Univ. of Pittsburgh Pr., 1963).

17. "It seemed to me, as I walked through the Garden of Allah [residence of Hollywood writers] that everybody I knew was a shooting star that had described its brilliant arc in the sky." Budd Schulberg, "The Four Seasons of Success," *Intellectual Digest* (Jan., 1973), p. 59.

18., Quoted in Tomkins, "Living Well," p. 63.

19. Because in this relation with Hemingway Fitzgerald may well have "courted humiliation," it's reasonable to propose that their lifetime rivalry, their duel, may well have symbolized Scott's "struggle with the world." On all counts, however, Fitzgerald posthumously, "unexpectedly emerges the victor." The point is persuasively argued by Ruth Prigozy, "A Matter of Measurement," *Commonweal*, Oct. 29, 1971, pp. 108–9.

20. "Thirty-five years after the church denied him burial with his ancestors in the cemetary of the Roman Catholic Church of St. Mary's," on Nov. 7, 1975, the bodies of Scott and Zelda were reinterred near Scott's parents in a family plot at Rockville, Maryland. Since 1940, because of a diocesan ruling, their coffins had "lain under rain-gullied, grassless earth, their joint headstone listing in neglect," at a nondenominational graveyard about two miles from the church. Ben A. Franklin, *New York Times*, Nov. 8, 1975, M29.

21. Quoted in *F. Scott Fitzgerald: The Man and His Work*, ed. Alfred Kazin (New York: Collier, 1962), p. 78.

IX. WILLIAM CARLOS WILLIAMS: THE HEALING IMAGE

1. John Dewey, "Americanism and Localism" *The Dial*, LXVIII (June, 1920), p. 688.

2. Mike Weaver, *William Carlos Williams: The American Background* (London: Cambridge Univ. Pr., 1971), p. 149.

3. D. H. Lawrence "*In the American Grain*, by William Carlos Williams," *Phoenix*, ed. Edward D. McDonald (New York: Viking, 1968), p. 334.

4. Eric Homberger, "Chicago and New York: Two versions of Modernism," in *Modernism*, eds. Malcolm Bradbury and James McFarlane (Harmondoworth, Eng.: Penguin, 1976), p. 156.

5. "Regrettably, perhaps, I no longer feel it necessary to pay any sort of lip-service to

William Carlos Williams, who is in my opinion a poet of no merit whatsoever. A good doctor, I am sure, a reasonably good observer of some aspects of American Life . . . but as a writer, flat, obvious and uninteresting beyond the telling." James Dickey, "Backward to Byzantium—and Babel," *Antaeus*, 43 (Autumn, 1981), p. 126.

6. Quoted by Rod Townley, *The Early Poetry of William Carlos Williams* (Ithaca and London: Cornell Univ. Pr., 1975), p. 174.

8. William Carlos Williams, *I Wanted to Write a Poem*, ed. Edith Heal (New York: New Directions, 1978), p. 30.

9. Wyndham Lewis, *The Demon of Progress in the Arts* (London: Metheun, 1954), p. 40.

10. Hilton Kramer, *New York Times*, Dec. 15, 1978, C22.

11. Quoted by Max I. Baym, "William James and Henry Adams," *New England Quarterly*, 10 (1937), p. 741.

12. Eliot's review appeared in the *Athenaeum* for May 23, 1919. See Louis Simpson, *Three on a Tower* (New York: Morrow, 1975), p. 119.

13. Quoted by Gay Wilson Allen, *William James* (New York: Viking, 1967), p. 48. See also William Barrett: "For what James, coming from his studies in physiology, saw in the neural impulses was that consciousness is primarily connected with the discharge of energy, with action, and that motivation must therefore be a prime force in human conduct. Happy the thinker who knows his direction so early." *The Illusion of Technique* (Garden City, N.Y.: Doubleday, 1978), p. 165.

14. Nathan G. Hale, Jr., *Freud and the Americans* (New York and London: Oxford Univ. Pr., 1971) pp. 50–51, 56.

15. John Berryman, "The Moon and the Night and the Men," *Poems* (Norfolk, Conn.: New Directions, 1942), pp. 22–23.

16. Barry Commoner, *New Yorker*, Feb. 2, 1976, pp. 38–39. See also Nicholas Georgescu-Roegen, *The Entropy Law and the Economic Process* (Cambridge, Mass.: Harvard Univ. Pr., 1971), pp. 4–6; "Georgescu: A Prophet of Energy Economics." *Business Week*, Mar. 24, 1975, pp. 108–14. Among their number too we discover Robert Heilbroner. Neither a disciple of the Second Law nor a polemicist against growth, nonetheless Heilbroner assents to the "death sentence" of industrial civilization even as he proposes to rally us all to move "beyond doomsday." A "contingent life sentence"—Kafkan in kind—is our probable fate if we're prepared to renounce the "spirit of conquest and aspiration," the "Promethean spirit," in favor of the spirit of Atlas. With endless perseverence of his sort mankind must bear whatever burdens are required to maintain life on this "fragile biosphere." In the name of Atlas not Prometheus, then, Heilbroner summons us to rescue a future from the ashes of post-industrial ages now current and yet to come. See *An Inquiry into the Human Prospect* (New York: Norton, 1974), pp. 142–44, 136.

17. George Santayana, *Character and Opinion in the United States* (London: Constable, 1924), p. 88.

18. Rod MacLeish, "National Spirit: The Pendulum Begins to Swing," *Smithsonian*, VII (July, 1976), pp. 28–30.

19. Henry James, *The Letters of Henry James*, ed. Percy Lubbock (2 vols. New York: Scribner's, 1920), vol. II, p. 261. "Consciousness is an illimitable power," the "most valuable thing we know anything about." Quoted by Tony Tanner, "Henry James and Henry Adams," *TriQuarterly*, II (Winter, 1968), pp. 101–2.

20. In a surprising gaffe of recognition Wilson lumped Williams with Maxwell Bodenheim. *The Shores of Light* (New York: Farrar, Straus, 1952), p. 241.

21. J. B. Bury, *The Idea of Progress*, intro. Charles A. Beard (New York: Dover, 1955), xl. "Belief in man-made progress was the new faith" leading the American judiciary in our time

to feel obliged to "move things along in the right direction." See Alexander M. Bickel, *The Supreme Court and the Idea of Progress* (New York: Harper, 1970), p. 19.

22. *Letters of Sherwood Anderson*, eds. Howard Mumford Jones and Walter B. Rideout (Boston, Little, Brown, 1953), p. 43. See also Helge Normann Nilson, "Waldo Frank and the Idea of America," *American Studies International*, XVII (Spring, 1979), pp. 27–36. Nilson surveys Adams's hold on American intellectuals in this period.

23. Van Wyck Brooks, *Opinions of Oliver Allston* (New York: Dutton, 1941), p. 187.

24. Sherwood Anderson, *A Story Teller's Story* (New York: Huebsch, 1924), pp. 375–81 passim.

25. Reed Whittemore, *William Carlos Williams: Poet from Jersey* (Boston: Houghton, 1975), p. 199.

26. William Carlos Williams, "A Matisse," *Selected Essays* (New York: Random House, 1954), pp. 30–31.

27. Beatrice Forbes Robertson-Hale, "Woman in Transition," in *Sex in Civilization*, eds. V. F. Calverton and S. D. Schmalhausen (New York: Macauley, 1929), pp. 67–81.

28. Heal, ed., *I Wanted to Write a Poem*, pp. 14, 16.

29. Quoted by Joseph N. Riddell, *The Inverted Bell* (Baton Rouge: Louisiana State Univ. Pr., 1974), pp. 80, 26.

30. William Carlos Williams, *Selected Poems*, intro. Randall Jarrell (Norfolk, Conn.: New Directions, 1949), xvi. See also Williams, *Selected Essays*, p. 256.

31. Louis Zukofsky, "Beginning Again with William Carlos Williams," *Hound & Horn*, IV (Jan.–March, 1931), pp. 261–64.

32. William Carlos Williams, *The Embodiment of Knowledge*, ed. Ron Loewinsohn (New York: New Directions, 1974), pp. 63–64, 81, 121, 190, 113.

33. Jarrell, ed., *Selected Poems*, "Choral: The Pink Church," p. 120.

34. Charlotte Perkins Gilman, "Sex and Race Progress," in *Sex and Civilization*, eds. Calverton and Schmalhausen, p. 122.

35. Loewensohn, ed., *Embodiment*, p. 185.

36. Robert Lowell, *Life Studies* (New York: Farrar, Straus, 1959), pp. 17, 78.

37. Quoted by Donald Hall, *New York Times Book Review*, Jan. 6, 1980, p. 22.

38. G. S. Fraser, "'Near the Ocean,'" *Salmagundi*, 37 (Spring, 1977), p. 74.

39. Robert Lowell, "After Enjoying Six or Seven Essays on Me," *Salmagundi*, 37 (Spring, 1977), p. 113.

40. Quoted by Whittemore, *Williams: Poet from Jersey*, p. 186.

41. Robert Lowell, "William Carlos Williams," in *William Carlos Williams*, ed. J. Hillis Miller (Englewood Cliffs, N.J.: Prentice-Hall, 1966), pp. 157–59. Cf. Williams in 1957: "There are younger poets I am interested in. They date back. Robert Lowell, seen for the first time some fifteen years ago, a much younger man than me, appealed to me. . . . The American virus was in his veins. . . . I was intrigued [by his line] and have been eager to follow whatever he writes." Heal, ed., *I Wanted to Write a Poem*, p. 97. In his earliest public comment on Lowell (that is, I know of none earlier), a review of *Mills of the Kavanaughs* for the *New York Times Book Review* (Apr. 22, 1951), Williams ended saying "I prefer a poet with a broader range of feeling." See *Critics on Robert Lowell*, ed. Jonathan Price (London: Allen & Unwin, 1974), p. 54. I'd be remiss not to record a fairly serious misstatement of fact in the history of things said on both sides in this affair. In a well-received and helpful book by William H. Pritchard it is said that two eulogies written on Williams's death are especially telling, Kenneth Burke's and Lowell's. "Always at his best on such eulogistic occasions," Lowell is quoted as saying that Williams "loves America excessively, as if it were *the* truth and *the* subject—his exasperation is also excessive as if there were no other hell." *Lives of the*

Modern Poets (London: Faber, 1980), pp. 293–94. Lowell's remarks, reprinted by Hillis Miller in 1966, were published more than two years before Williams died.

42. Charles Tomlinson, "Don't Bury the Hatchet," *Times Literary Supplement*, March 5, 1964. See also Linda Wagner and Lewis Macadams, Jr., "A Colloquy with Robert Creeley," *Paris Review*, 44 (Fall, 1968),pp. 155–87.

43. "Louis and Allen," *The Daily Orange*, Syracuse University, N.Y., Oct. 30, 1970, p. 6.

44. A. M. Sullivan, "Dr. William Carlos Williams, Poet and Humanist," in *William Carlos Williams*, ed. Charles Angoff (London: Associated University Presses, 1974), pp. 42–43.

45. Donald Davie, "The Poetry of Protest," *New Statesman*, Feb. 11, 1966, pp. 198–99.

46. Stephen Spender, "Uncommon Poetic Language," *Times Literary Supplement*, Oct. 5, 1967, p. 940.

47. Hugh Kenner, *The Pound Era* (Berkeley and Los Angeles: Univ. of California Pr., 1971), p. 400.

48. Letter to Louis Grudin, Jan. 26, 1930, quoted by Weaver, *William Carlos Williams: The American Background*, p. 52.

49. Williams, *Selected Essays*, pp. 10–11.

50. William Carlos Williams, "An Approach to the Poem," *English Institute Essays 1947* (New York: Columbia Univ. Pr., 1948), p. 47.

51. William Carlos Williams, *The Selected Letters of William Carlos Williams*, ed. John C. Thirwell (New York: McDowell Obolensky, 1957), p. 186.

52. Many of Williams's utterances on these themes are assembled by Riddell, *The Inverted Bell*, pp. 53–55. See also James E. Breslin, *William Carlos Williams: An American Artist* (New York and London: Oxford Univ. Pr., 1970), pp. 127–29.

53. Kevin Power, "Conversation with George and Mary Oppen, May 25, 1975," *Texas Quarterly*, XXI (Spring, 1978), pp. 37–39. Strikingly, the subject still provokes debate. At an exhibit called "German Realism of the Twenties" (Minneapolis Institute of the Arts, 1980), the subject of Sheeler, of technology and art and progress, recurs in an essay which contrasts Sheeler with Carl Grossberg. Unlike Sheeler, it's said, whose art lovingly portrayed the industrial landscape to a "society which still has faith in progress," Grossberg and other German New Realists scorned a "blind admiration of progress" as an American trait, reviled an *Americanismus* which "killed Eros in favor of the man-machine." Emilio Bertonati, "Neue Sachlichkeit in a Wider Cultural Context," in *German Realism of the Twenties: The Artist as Social Critic*, ed. Louise Lincoln (Minneapolis: Minneapolis Institute, 1980), pp. 57–59. Cf. Robert Jensen, "Industry": "In canvases by Sheeler and Grossberg the machine is completely disembodied from its function. Smokestacks, oil tanks, and railroad engines are painted strictly for their beauty of form." Ibid., p. 165. That the painting, its subject, its stylization of the Ford plant at River Rouge remain compelling, whatever the reasons may be, is confirmed by its sale at auction "for $1.8 million, the highest price ever paid at auction for a Sheeler or for any 20th-century American painting," held by Sotheby Parke-Bernet on June 2, 1983. See Rita Reif, "Sheeler Work Sets a Record," *New York Times*, June 3, 1983, C 26.

54. Edward Dahlberg, *Alms for Oblivion* (Minneapolis: Univ. of Minnesota Pr., 1964), pp. 14, 24.

55. William Carlos Williams, *The Collected Earlier Poems* (Norfolk, Conn.: New Directions, 1951), p. 122.

56. Bram Dijkstra, *Cubism, Stieglitz and the Early Poetry of William Carlos Williams* (Princeton: Princeton Univ. Pr., 1978), pp. 154–55.

57. Kramer, *New York Times*, Dec. 24, 1978, D23. Addressing this vexed subject, consider the case of Charles Demuth's painting, "I Saw the Figure 5 in Gold." Beginning in 1924 Demuth made a series of poster-portraits, "all dedicated to artists whom he knew well and/or admired . . . including tributes to Georgia O'Keeffe (1924), Arthur Dove (1924), John Marin (1925), Eugene O'Neill (1927), Gertrude Stein (1928), and culminating in 'I Saw the Figure 5 in Gold'" and "Homage to William Carlos Williams" confessedly inspired by Williams's poem "The Great Figure." This painting, "possibly the best in the series has certainly proved the most influential, provoking, in its turn, such works as 'The Large Black Five,' (1960) by Jasper Johns and 'The Demuth American Dream N. 5,' 'The Demuth Five,' 'The Small Demuth Five,' and 'The Figure Five,' all done in 1963 by Robert Indiana. Williams's 'The Great Figure' was published in his *Sour Grapes* in 1920, and it is significant that Demuth," recalling the period of his closest relation with Williams, didn't "attempt simply to recreate the picture presented by the poem; nor does he try to find visual equivalents for the poem's style. Instead, he tries to recreate in terms of his own medium the effect of the poem at the same time that he seeks to define the character of Williams and his work." James E. Breslin, "William Carlos Williams and Charles Demuth: Cross-Fertilization in the Arts," *Journal of Modern Literature*, 6 (Apr., 1977), p. 258.

58. Quoted by Weaver, *William Carlos Williams: The American Background*, p. 62.

59. Constance Rourke, *Charles Sheeler: Artist in the American Tradition* (New York: Harcourt, 1938), pp. 176–79.

60. Williams, *Selected Essays*, pp. 330, 332–36 passim. John Malcolm Brinnin nominates Edward Hopper as the painter with whom Williams shares "the clearest technical and thematic affinities," and rebukes the poet for failing to mention "Hopper in his memoirs." Inexplicably, Brinnin remarks, Williams remained "curiously unaware of a contemporary whose career parallels his own." But because Williams's passion centered on line even as Hopper's focused on light, Brinnin is I think wide of the mark in believing that "their successes are of the same nature." *William Carlos Williams* (Minneapolis: Univ. of Minnesota Pr., 1963), pp. 22, 23.

61. Claude Lévi-Strauss, *Tristes Tropiques* (New York: Atheneum, 1973), p. 195. "The amazing thing was how Williams caught in the very style of his writing something of the style of these American primitives, with an eye indifferent to any but the most elementary perspective and the attention riveted on the details making up the world of these paintings," as if he found in this style of composition, this style of art, a "syntax, attention to eccentric detail, an oblique autobiography." Paul Mariani, *William Carlos Williams: A New World Naked* (New York: McGraw-Hill, 1981), p. 683.

62. William Carlos Williams, "Emanuel Romano," *Form*, Sept. 1, 1966, pp. 22–25 passim.

63. Williams, *Selected Essays*, pp. 245–48 passim.

64. Quoted by Williams, *Autobiography*, p. 330.

65. William Carlos Williams, *Spring and All* (Dijon: Contact, 1923), pp. 3–4.

66. William Carlos Williams, *Selected Poems*, ed. Charles Tomlinson (Harmonsworth, Eng.: Penguin, 1976), p. 13.

X. THE TRIBAL NO: KENNETH BURKE

1. Wayne Booth, "Kenneth Burke's Way of Knowing," *Critical Inquiry*, 1 (Sept., 1974), pp. 2–3.

2. Kermit Lansner, "Burke, Burke, the Lurk," *Critical Responses to Kenneth Burke*, ed. William H. Rueckert (Minneapolis: Univ. of Minnesota Pr., 1969), p. 261.

3. Letter, Kenneth Burke to William Wasserstrom, Dec. 23, 1958; quoted by permission.

4. Kenneth Burke, *Language as Symbolic Action: Essays on Life, Literature and Method* (Berkeley and Los Angeles: Univ. of California Pr., 1966), pp. 341–43.

5. Denis Donoghue, "When in Rome, Do as the Greeks," in *Critical Responses*, ed. Reuchert, p. 488.

6. Kenneth Burke, *The Rhetoric of Religion: Studies in Logology* (Boston: Beacon, 1961), pp. 4–5.

7. Philip Slater, *The Pursuit of Loneliness* (Boston: Beacon, 1976), pp. 59–61.

8. Burke, *Rhetoric of Religion*, p. 19.

9. Letter, Kenneth Burke to William Wasserstrom, Nov. 3, 1958; quoted by permission.

10. Daniel Fogarty, "Kenneth Burke's Theory," in *Critical Responses*, ed. Reuchert, p. 330n.

11. Burke, *Rhetoric of Religion*, pp. 19–23.

Ibid., p. 21.

13. Kenneth Burke, *Collected Poems 1915–1967* (Berkeley and Los Angeles: Univ. of California Pr., 1968), p. 5.

14. Burke, "A Dramatistic View of the Origins of Language," *Language as Symbolic Action*, pp. 430, 469, 478–79.

15. Kenneth Burke, *A Grammar of Motives* and *A Rhetoric of Motives* (Cleveland and New York: World, 1962), pp. 405–8.

16. Jonathan Culler, *Saussure* (Great Britain: Fontana/Collins, 1976), p. 117.

17. René Girard, *Violence and the Sacred* (Baltimore and London: Johns Hopkins Pr., 1977), pp. 148, 12, 13, 306.

18. Michel Foucault, *Discipline and Punish* (New York: Pantheon, 1977), pp. 25, 26, 31.

19. Burke, *Rhetoric of Religion*, pp. 273–315 passim.

20. Peter Kihss, *New York Times*, Sept. 29, 1977, p. 39; James S. Gordon, "Demonic Children," *New York Times Book Review*, Sept. 11, 1973, p. 3.

21. Philip Greven, *The Protestant Temperament: Patterns of Child-Rearing, Religious Experience and the Self in Early America* (New York: Knopf, 1978), pp. 12–13.

22. Gordon, "Demonic Children," p. 53.

23. Burke, "Dramatistic View of Origins of Language," pp. 473–74.

24. Philip Ariès, *Centuries of Childhood* (New York: Knopf, 1962), p. 413.

25. Burke, "Dialectic of the Scapegoat," *Grammar of Motives*, p. 408.

26. Reuchert, ed., *Critical Responses*, p. 270.

27. Fredric R. Jameson, "Ideology and Symbolic Action," *Critical Inquiry*, 5 (Winter, 1978), pp. 418–22.

28. Kenneth Burke, "Theology and Logology," *Kenyon Review*, New Series, 1 (Winter, 1979), p. 171.

29. Grace Glueck, *New York Times*,)Nov. 18, 1978, p. 23.

30. Stanley Elkin, "A la recherche du Whoopee Cushion," *Esquire*, 82 (July, 1974), pp. 126–29.

Index